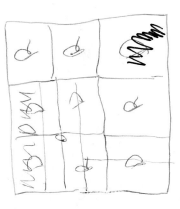

Public Policy

Public Policy
A Contemporary Perspective

Radhakrishan Sapru

*Professor (Retd.), Department of Public Administration,
Panjab University, Chandigarh*

SAGE | **TEXTS**

Los Angeles I London I New Delhi
Singapore I Washington DC I Melbourne

First published in 2017 by

SAGE Publications India Pvt Ltd
B1/I-1 Mohan Cooperative Industrial Area
Mathura Road, New Delhi 110 044, India
www.sagepub.in

SAGE Publications Inc
2455 Teller Road
Thousand Oaks, California 91320, USA

SAGE Publications Ltd
1 Oliver's Yard, 55 City Road
London EC1Y 1SP, United Kingdom

SAGE Publications Asia-Pacific Pte Ltd
3 Church Street
#10-04 Samsung Hub
Singapore 049483

Published by Vivek Mehra for SAGE Publications India Pvt Ltd, typeset in 10.5./12.5 pt Helvetica Neue LT Std by Zaza Eunice, Hosur, Tamil Nadu, India.

Library of Congress Cataloging-in-Publication Data

Name: Sapru, R. K. (Radha Krishan), author.
Title: Public policy : a contemporary perspective / Radhakrishan Sapru.
Description: New Delhi, India : SAGE Publications India Pvt Ltd, 2017. |
   Includes bibliographical references and index.
Identifiers: LCCN 2016048654 | ISBN 9789386062178 (pbk. : alk. paper)
Subjects: LCSH: Political planning.
Classification: LCC JF1525.P6 S27 2017 | DDC 320.6--dc23 LC record available at https://lccn.loc.gov/2016048654

ISBN: 978-93-860-6217-8 (PB)

SAGE Team: Amit Kumar, Indrani Dutta, Sudeshna Nandy and Ritu Chopra

To

*the Sweet Memory of My Mother Shrimati Lakshmi Devi
and Father Shri Dewan Chand*

Thank you for choosing a SAGE product!
If you have any comment, observation or feedback,
I would like to personally hear from you.

Please write to me at **contactceo@sagepub.in**

Vivek Mehra, Managing Director and CEO, SAGE India.

Bulk Sales

SAGE India offers special discounts
for bulk institutional purchases.

*For queries/orders/inspection copy requests,
write to* **textbooksales@sagepub.in**

Publishing

Would you like to publish a textbook with SAGE?
Please send your proposal to **publishtextbook@sagepub.in**

Subscribe to our mailing list

Write to marketing@sagepub.in

BRIEF CONTENTS

DETAILED CONTENTS

सर्वधर्मान्परित्यज्य मामेकं शरणं व्रज ।

अहं त्वा सर्वपापेभ्यो मोक्षयिष्यामि मा शुच: ।।

श्रीमद्भगवद्गीता (१८, ६६)

Abandoning all duties, take refuge in me alone.

I shall absolve you of all sins; grieve not.

Srimad Bhagavadgita (xviii, 66)

PREFACE

'Public policy', as a fascinating field of enquiry and an indispensable product of government for governance, has of late acquired growing importance in both developed and developing nations. And yet the field has received little attention from social scientists and academics in nations which are at a societal transformation stage. The government as a group of people governing the state has a big responsibility to facilitate societal action through adoption of 'good' policies. Its capacity to make policies and to act is the singular obligation for which governance should be judged. But inputs for public policies must come from the masses, the policy community and those engaged in think tanks. The wider purposes of public policy involve the full development of individuals and the society as a whole.

It is a theme which has occupied the research and writings of scholars in the field of policy analysis. Against this background, this present work provides the readers more than just an introduction to major works of leading scholars in the field of public policy and policy analysis.

This textbook has evolved out of some 20 years of teaching and research experience at the Panjab University. However, much of the inputs for this work has been derived from standard books and seminal works, notably by Harold Lasswell, Herbert Simon, Charles Lindblom, Geoffrey Vickers, Y. Dror, Amitai Etzioni, James Anderson, Aaron Wildavsky, Thomas Dye, Robert Lineberry, Peter deLeon, Jeffrey Pressman, Paul Sabatier, Wayne Parsons, Thomas Birkland, Larry Gerston and many more. Their works and ideas have been essential to easing the completion of this project for which I have been in a 'black box' since my superannuation in August 2005 as a professor of public administration at the Panjab University, Chandigarh.

The contributions in forms of articles in national and international journals, documented lessons on public policy for the Indira Gandhi National Open University (New Delhi) and lectures to the students and teachers at leading universities and national institutes have greatly helped me in forming my ideas about the concepts, theories, models and the processes of the policy. The academic interest, enthusiasm and feedback which I gained on the evolving text have been a constant source of motivation to finish this work which just kept on expanding.

Perfection in writing a book on public policy is hard to attain without art, knowledge and experience. Only a writer who is earnest in his actions and has overcome the obstacles in his pathway can succeed in his goal of perfection. Time has, however, revealed that perfection is practically an 'ideal'; it cannot be achieved. Our limitations of knowledge, lack of computational capability and existence of multiple individual and societal values stand in the way of reaching any high degree of optimality and rationality. The view that we cannot optimize or achieve the best by our efforts results in an intense emotional pietism. But the author's effort is directed towards reconciling the desire for the best with the demands of authoritative rich material. To the author, a good publication (like the present one in my decisive opinion) will do even if it is not the best choice.

As a reading strategy to supplement this textbook, the author is of the view that both students and teachers alike familiarize themselves with the core work of some of the founding figures in the field of policy analysis. The reader is also advised to look at the footnotes for a better appreciation of this work. But it cannot be a substitute for the study of leading texts.

In the writing of this voluminous work, my debt remains to the authors of some of the earliest texts in the field. I am happy to record my thanks and appreciation for all those scholars and authors who provided such admirable work for both teachers and students alike.

I owe a great debt to my late mother, Shrimati Lakshmi Devi, and late father, Shri Dewan Chand, for all their labour, love and encouragement. But for the loving forbearance of my wife Sushma and our son Yudhishthira and daughter-in-law Sugandha, this project could have hardly been completed.

My special gratitude goes to our sons-in-law, Pankaj and Alkesh, and daughters, Sugeeta and Ujjawal, for their moral support and advice on health.

To those friends and students whose help I have failed to acknowledge, I thank you all for your support, ideas and encouragement.

Chandigarh

Radhakrishan Sapru

ABOUT THE BOOK

Public Policy: A Contemporary Perspective is both a comprehensive and an enlivening textbook, covering not just the basic topics but also the new realities in policy analysis and management. The textbook provides the readers with more than just an introduction to major works of leading scholars in the field of public policy. Each chapter is complemented by explanation of the key concepts, and footnotes suggesting supplementary readings. The author's effort is directed towards reconciling the desire for the best with the demand for authoritative, rich material for the readers. The textbook has been written to tailor the student's need and is illustrated with figures and charts where required. This text is very much a dynamic learning and thought-provoking book on public policy. It will markedly improve the learning experience and help motivate students of public policy.

ABOUT THE AUTHOR

Radhakrishan Sapru studied at Panjab University, Chandigarh, which awarded him master's degrees in Political Science (1970), Public Administration (1972) and English (1976) and subsequently a doctorate in Public Administration in 1983 and an LLB degree in 1992.

Initially appointed as teaching-cum-research assistant at the Department of Public Administration, Panjab University, Chandigarh, in February 1976, Dr Sapru rose to the position of Professor. He headed the Department of Public Administration at Panjab University from 1 April 1990 to 31 March 1993 and again from 1 April 2002 to 31 March 2005. Dr Sapru retired as Professor in August 2005, after serving nearly three decades at the Panjab University. During his academic career and after superannuation, Dr Sapru published more than 50 articles in national and international journals besides 10 books in the field of public administration.

PUBLIC POLICY
Introduction to the Concept and Process of Policy

INTRODUCTION

This book begins with an introduction by bringing into prominence the nature, scope and significance of 'public policy'. It also deals with questions of why government intervention is necessary and what makes to study public policy. Although 'public policy' as an academic pursuit emerged in the beginning of the 1950s,[1] its analysis dates back to the beginning of civilization. As a social science, it draws on the humanities, and political science in particular, for its development. Theoretically speaking, public policy is formulated in the present, based on the past, with the object of improving the society's future. The purpose of studying public policy is to understand the problems of the people and to provide insights into a range of policy options to deal with matters of public concern. Public policy is an area which had to do with those spheres which are labelled as public.

Historically, political science, to some extent, was preoccupied with the activities of the various political institutions and groups in relation to their success in pursuit of political power. It hardly recognized the role which such organizations played towards the formation of policy as one of its main concerns. Yet the policy is an important element of the political process. Thomas Dye, a leading scholar of policy analysis, says, 'Traditional (political science) studies described the institutions in which public policy was formulated. But unfortunately the linkages between important institutional arrangements and the content of public policy were largely unexplored'.[2] He further observed that today the focus of political science is shifting to public policy—'to the description and explanation of the causes and consequences of government activity'. While the concern of political science about the processes by which public policy was determined has increased, most students of public administration would acknowledge that the public servants themselves are intimately involved in the shaping of the policies. The study of public administration has hitherto tended to concentrate on the machinery for the implementation of given policies. It has addressed issues regarding organization of public authorities, the behaviour of

---

[1] It was only in 1951 that the first book on public policy analysis appeared. But the universities' interest in public policy can be traced to a conference held in 1965 under the auspices of the Social Science Research Council. See Austin Ranney, 'Preface', in *Political Science and Public Policy*, ed. Austin Ranney (Chicago, IL: Markham, 1968), i–xiii. The classic literature that founded policy studies is not very old and began only with Harold Lasswell's call for the development of a distinctive policy science. See Harold Lasswell, 'The Policy Orientation', in *The Policy Sciences*, eds. D. Lerner and H.D. Lasswell (Stanford, CA: Stanford University Press, 1951).

[2] Thomas R. Dye, *Understanding Public Policy*, 10th ed. (New Delhi: Pearson Education, Indian reprint, 2004), 13.

public servants and, increasingly, the methods of resource allocation, administration and review. With such an approach, it is difficult to determine much about the way policy is formulated, although it is generally contended that the experience of policy implementation feeds back into the furtherance of policymaking process.

Thus, the past studies on public policy have been mainly dominated by the scholars of political science who largely concentrated on the structural aspects of the government. But presently, the scholars of policy analysis and public administration have tended to concentrate more on the content of policy and the process of its formulation, implementation and evaluation. The study of public policy has evolved into what is virtually a new branch of the social sciences—the so-called 'policy sciences'.[3] This concept of policy sciences was first formulated by Harold Lasswell in 1951.[4] Today, the policy sciences have gone far beyond new and naïve aspirations for societally relevant knowledge. The credibility of policy sciences in the recent past, and beginning of the 21st century in particular, remains elusive. However, considerable debate remains over whether there is one coherent set of principles that govern the study and understanding of the public policy process.

What Makes Public Policy Public?

Since the 1950s much of scholarship has resulted in a significant accumulation of knowledge regarding public policy and policy analysis. Given the complexity of issues involved in the policy process, it is important for the readers to know the definition of basic concepts of public policy.

The term 'public policy' comprises two words. In the first instance, it is important to understand the concept of 'public'. We often use such terms as 'public interest', 'public sector', 'public opinion', 'public health' and so on. The starting point is that 'public policy' has to do with those spheres which are labelled as 'public' as opposed to spheres involving the idea of 'private'. The concept of public policy presupposes that there is an area or domain of life which is not private or purely individual, but held in common. 'Public' dimension is generally referred to 'public ownership' or control for 'public purpose'. The public comprises that domain of human activity which is regarded as requiring governmental interventions or social action. The question is: Does the sphere of public require a different analysis to that of private? In a representative democracy, it is assumed that power flows from the consent of the governed, that is, the people themselves. The people are therefore sovereign. Thus, when policy advocates seek to induce the government to make policy or when government actively engages in actions these advocates support, we can say that the government does so in the public interest. However, there has always been a conflict between what constitutes public and what private is.

For Baber, there are 10 key differences between public sector and private sector:

(i)   It faces more complex and ambiguous tasks.
(ii) It has more problems in implementing its decisions.
(iii) It employs more people with a wider range of motivations.

---

[3] Y. Dror is one of the foremost advocates for the development of policy sciences. See Y. Dror, *Public Policy-making Re-examined* (San Francisco, CA: Chandler, 1968), 8–9.
[4] Lasswell, 'The Policy Orientation', 3–15.

(iv) It is more concerned with securing opportunities or capacities.
 (v) It is more concerned with compensating for market failure.
(vi) It engages in activities with greater symbolic significance.
(vii) It is held to stricter standards of commitment and legality.
(viii) It has a greater opportunity to respond to issues of fairness.
(ix) It must operate or appear to operate in the public interest.
 (x) It must maintain minimal levels of public support than required in private industry.[5]

Beginning of the first quarter of the 20th century saw the emergence of the state as a means of reconciling public and private interests. Public administration emerged as an instrument of the state for securing public interest rather than private interest, whereas for the political economists, only markets could balance private and public interests. The new liberalism was based upon a belief that public administration was a more rational means of promoting the public interest. For Max Weber, the growth of bureaucracy was due to the process of rationalization in industrial society.[6] The civil servant was the rational functionary whose main task was to carry out the will of those elected by the people. Public bureaucracy was, therefore, different to that which existed in the private sector because it was motivated to serve the public interest. The rational public interest argument started eroding after the Second World War. Invariably the bureaucrats did not function in the public interest and displayed the capacity to have distinct goals of their own. In this connection, a comparative study of bureaucracy by Aberbach observed, 'The last quarter of this century is witnessing the virtual disappearance of the Weberian distinction between the roles of the politician and the bureaucrat, producing what may be labelled as a pure hybrid'.[7] The public and private sectors reveal themselves as overlapping and interacting rather than as well-defined categories.

What Public Policy Is?

The concept of 'policy' cannot be objectively defined. Among other definitions, policy can be denoted as

(i) a declaration of goals for common action,
(ii) a set of rules for guidance and
(iii) a statement by government of what it intends to do.

Although a public policy is made by a government in response to public's problem and demand, it may be implemented by public or private actors or both. Public policy is ultimately made by the government even if the ideas or opinions come from the private actors or through the interaction between government and non-governmental forces. Judicial decisions also do matter in the formation or implementation of a public policy. For example, the Supreme Court (India) on 19 April 2016 pulled up the state governments for their failure to prevent unauthorized construction of shrines on public land. The bench said, 'None of the states are doing anything to comply with the SC's directions. God never

---

[5] Quoted in A. Massey, *Managing the Public Sector* (Aldershot: Edward Elgar, 1993), 15.
[6] Max Weber, *The Theory of Social and Economic Organization*, translated by A.M. Henderson and Talcott Parsons (New York, NY: Free Press of Glencoe, 1947), 337.
[7] J.D. Aberbach et al., *Bureaucrats and Politicians in Western Europe* (Cambridge, MA: Harvard University Press, 1981), 16.

intended to obstruct footpaths and pavements or encroach upon public land. Persons building religious structures on public land and footpaths are insulting god'. The court had on 13 September 2011 said it had undertaken the exercise primarily to ensure that 'henceforth no public land, public park or public street is encroached for constructing religious structures'.[8]

There is thrust to designate policy as the 'outputs' of the political system. David Easton defines public policy as 'the authoritative allocation of values for the whole society'.[9]

The magnitude of the problem can be visualized from other definitions which are offered: Dye, a leading scholar of public policy, observes, 'Public policy is whatever governments choose to do or not to do'.[10] Similarly, Robert Lineberry says that 'it is what governments do and fail to do—to and for their citizens'.[11]

To Schneider and Ingram, 'Policies are revealed through texts, practices, symbols, and discourses that define and deliver values including goods and services as well as regulations, income, status, and other positively or negatively valued attributes'.[12] This definition means that policies are not just contained in laws and regulations, but they continue to be made as the implementers make decisions about who will benefit from policies.

Parsons regards policy as 'an attempt to define and structure a rational basis for action or inaction'.[13]

Anderson describes public policy as 'a relatively stable, purposive course of action followed by an actor or set of actors in dealing with a problem or matter of concern'.[14]

Taken as a whole, a policy may be defined as a purposive course of action taken or adopted by those in power in pursuit of certain goals. Perceptibly, the term public policy includes government activity. 'Public policy consists of political decisions for implementing programs to achieve societal goals'.[15]

At a minimum, Peters observes, 'Stated most simply, public policy is the sum of government activities, whether acting directly or through agents, as it has an influence on the life of citizens'.[16]

Thomas Dye argues that this search for a definition of public policy can degenerate into a word game that, eventually, adds little more understanding. Because of scholars' lack

---

[8] See *The Times of India* (Chandigarh), 'God Never Intended to Encroach on Footpaths: Supreme Court', 20 April 2016, accessed on 15 November 2016, http://timesofindia.indiatimes.com/india/God-never-intended-to-encroach-on-footpaths-Supreme-Court/articleshow/51903339.cms

[9] David Easton, *A Systems Analysis of Political Life* (New York, NY: Wiley, 1965), 212.

[10] Dye, *Understanding Public Policy*, 1.

[11] Robert L. Lineberry, *American Public Policy: What Government Does and What Difference It Makes* (New York, NY: Harper & Row, 1977), 2.

[12] Anne L. Schneider and Helen Ingram, *Policy Design for Democracy* (Lawrence, KS: University Press of Kansas, 1997), 2.

[13] Wayne Parsons, *Public Policy* (Cheltenham: Edward Elgar, 1995), 14.

[14] James E. Anderson, *Public Policy-making*, 3rd ed. (Boston, MA: Houghton Mifflin, 1997), 9.

[15] Charles L. Cochran and Eloise F. Malone, *Public Policy: Perspectives and Choices*, 3rd ed. (New York, NY: McGraw Hill, 2007), 5–6.

[16] B. Guy Peters, *American Public Policy: Promise and Performance* (New York, NY: Chatham House, 1999).

of a consensus definition of public policy, Birkland discerns following key attributes of public policy:

(i)   Policy is made in response to some sort of problem that requires attention.
(ii) Policy is made on the 'public's' behalf.
(iii) Policy is oriented toward a goal or desired state, such as the solution of a problem.
(iv) Policy is ultimately made by governments, even if the ideas come from outside government or through the interaction of government and non-governmental actors.
(v)   Policy is interpreted and implemented by public and private actors who have different interpretations of problems, solutions and their own motivations.
(vi) Policy is what the government choose to do or not to do.[17]

Birkland defines a policy 'as a statement by government—at whatever level—of what it intends to do about a public problem'. Such statements can be found in the constitution, statutes, regulation or court decisions. A statement by the government on a public concern is also a policy.

All the variants of the definition suggest that public policy is concerning the public as it affects a greater variety of people and interests than do private decisions. As the public is the source of political authority, in a democratic country, it is obvious that government is at the centre of efforts to make public policy. It should be added here that public policy focuses on what Dewey once described as 'the public and its problems'. Public policy is about people and their needs, values and preferences. Public policies are the policies adopted and implemented by government bodies and officials. Public policies are purposeful decisions made by authoritative actors in a political system who have the formal responsibility for making binding choices among societal goals.

In a democracy, most public policymakers are elected officials (such as members of Parliament). Legislative bodies and executives (ministers) play a key role in the policy-making process. Judges at the state and national levels who are appointed also interpret what constitutes a public policy. Non-elected bureaucrats or civil servants may also have limited policymaking authority. Whether elected or appointed, however, public policymakers are managers of the public trust and their actions are subject to public scrutiny, which in the cases of elected officials, sometimes, lead to their defeat in the election.

POLICY PROCESS

A fascinating aspect of public policy is to understand how policy is shaped by social, political, economic and other institutional factors. The policy focus is on the analysis of the policy process. It is concerned not only with knowledge in and for the policy process, but also with knowledge about the formation and implementation of public policy. It involves study of constitutions, legislators, interest groups and public administrators.

---

[17] Thomas A. Birkland, *An Introduction to the Policy Process*, 3rd ed. (New Delhi: PHI Learning, Indian reprint, 2011), 8–9.

The process does seem to be showy but worthless to many people. According to *Webster's New Collegiate* dictionary, a 'process' is 'a natural phenomenon marked by gradual changes that lead toward a particular result' or 'a series of actions or operations conducting to an end'. The idea of breaking down the making of public policy into stages or phases, which begin with defining problems and setting agendas and with implementing and evaluating policy, may well be to impose stages on a reality that is interactive. What is important, however, is that we understand and explain this complexity of the policy process which exists within a context of a multiplicity of frameworks.

Public policy is largely the outcome of arguments between government and non-governmental actors. It involves questions whether something is a solvable problem, what the possible solutions are, what the costs of those solutions are, whether the solutions will be meeting the people's demands and so on. Indeed, there are a lot of people who work to promote the potential solutions to a problem. All these aspects relate to the policy process. The process, in main, refers to a series of stages or courses of actions. Policy process is cyclical, and it assumes that there is a relationship between one stage and the other. It suggests that there is some sort of system that translates policy ideas into policy effects—formulation, implementation and evaluation. The participants in the policy process—be they the members of the policy community, interest groups or association leaders—are not all or even primarily neutral participants. As Cochran argues that there are few 'neutral policy analysts' and by description no neutral advocates of particular policy alternatives.[18] The results of scientific policy analysis are often given up when other conventional tools seem to work better. For illustrations, the act of identifying a problem is as much a normative judgement as it is an objective statement of fact. Thus, if the problem is defined normatively, then one cannot say that any subsequent analysis is 'neutral'.

NATURE OF PUBLIC POLICY AND BASIC CONCEPTS

Policy, like many other terms, is a complex concept. It takes different forms. A policy may be general or specific, broad or narrow, simple or complex, public or private, written or unwritten, explicit or implicit, discretionary or detailed and qualitative or quantitative. Here the emphasis is on 'public policy', which is what a government chooses as guidance for action. Public policy is a form of government control usually expressed in a law, a legislation, a regulation or an order. Public policy is the outcome of the struggle between government and powerful groups. But because public is the source of political authority, it is clear that government is at the centre of efforts to make public policy. It typically contains a set of intentions or goals, a mix of instruments of means for achieving the goals. Understanding public policy is an art as well as a craft. It is an art as it requires insights and creativity in identifying societal problems, in devising public policies that might alleviate them and in finding out whether these policies lead to a better quality of life. Public policy is a craft because tasks often require some knowledge of social sciences.

Government activities or decisions for the performance of its functions may be divided into two major categories: those which are based on definite policies and those which

---

[18] Clarke E. Cochran, Lawrence C. Mayer, T. R. Carr and N. Joseph Cayer, *American Public Policy: An Introduction*, 6th ed. (New York: St. Martin's Press, 1999).

are not so based. Ideally, a government should have a set of consistent policies to cover all of its activities. In practice, a government rarely has a set of guidelines for its actions. Furthermore, policies are often too vague (e.g. India's foreign policy with Pakistan) or too general (e.g. National Youth Policy of India, 2014) and are not always consistent with each other. In a turbulent environment, governmental units often have to take immediate action without policy guidance.

A public policy may cover a major portion of its activities which are consistent with the development policy. Socio-economic development, equality or liberty or self-reliance or similar broad principles of guidance for action may be adopted as a developmental policy or national goal. A public policy may also be narrow, covering a specific activity, such as family planning. A public policy may also be applied to all people in a country, or it may be limited to a section of its people, say belonging to the scheduled caste.

Besides, each level of government—central, state and local—may have its specific or general policies. Then there are 'megapolicies'. General guidelines to be followed by all specific policies are termed as 'megapolicy'.[19] According to Dror, 'megapolicies' form a kind of master policy, as distinct from concrete discrete policies, and involve the establishment of overall goals to serve as guidelines for the larger sets of concrete and specific policies. All policies generally contain definite goals or objectives in more implicit or explicit terms.

A public policy is a purposeful decision. It may be either positive or negative in form. In its positive form, it may involve some form of overt government action to deal with a particular problem. It includes actions of government to convert competing private objectives into public commitments. On the other hand, in its negative form, it involves a decision by public servants not to take action on some matter on which a governmental order is sought. Public policy has a legally coercive quality that citizens accept as legitimate; for example, taxes must be paid unless one wants to run the risk of fines or jail sentences. This legally coercive quality of public policies makes public organizations distinct from the private organizations. Public policy is coercive and must constrain the individual in order to promote the general welfare. Moreover, much of the reluctance of public policy-makers to deal with private issues is due to the well-established conventions and values of limited government. The constitution also sets boundaries on what governments can do, leaving considerable freedom for individuals. But on intervention of judiciary, these boundaries are occasionally rearranged or blurred.

The nature of policy as a purposive course of action can be better or more fully understood if it is compared with related concepts and terms.

Decisions, Non-decisions and Policymaking

In public administration, the use of decision and policy is common although these two concepts differ from each other. Policymaking does involve decision-making, but a decision does not necessarily constitute a policy. Decision-making often involves an identification of a problem, a careful analysis of possible alternatives and a selection of one alternative for action. Generally, decisions are taken by the administrators in their day-to-day work

---

[19] This term 'megapolicy' has been introduced by Yehezkel Dror, *Public Policy Making Re-examined*.

within the existing framework of policy. The policy decisions eventually taken thus provide a sense of direction to the courses of administrative action. In this context, Anderson says, 'Policy decisions are decisions made by public officials that authorize or give direction and content to public policy actions'.[20] These may include decisions to issue executive orders, promulgate administrative rules or make important judicial interpretations of laws.

In policymaking, one must be aware that non-decisions are just as important as decisions and policies which initiate some new relationship between government and citizens. To Bachrach and Baratz, non-decisions are also part of the policy.[21] Attention should not focus exclusively on decisions which bring change, but must also be sensitive to those which resist change and are difficult to observe because they are not represented in the policymaking process by legislative measures. Bachrach and Baratz argue that power can be used to prevent decisions and restrict choice as well as to initiate change.

Policies, Goals and Policy Goal

Policies are distinct from goals and can be distinguished from the latter as means from ends. By goals or objectives, one means the ends towards which actions are directed. It is reasonable to expect that a policy indicates the direction towards which action is sought. Policies involve a deliberate choice of actions designed to attain those goals and objectives. The actions can take the form of directives to do certain actions (e.g. register a marriage, birth or death) or refrain from certain actions (e.g. smoking in public places). They may take the form of publicly oriented financial services, such as education, health care or pension to widows. Further, policies create obligations for both the citizen (e.g. not to set up a factory without seeking permission) and the state (to provide information under the Right to Information Act, 2005).

Policies as well as objectives are chosen under the influence of values. Decision-makers often act on the basis of their beliefs or perceptions of the public interest concerning what is a proper or morally correct public policy. Studies of the Supreme Court show that the judges are influenced by policy values in deciding cases.[22] Thus goals and objectives depend on the values of the policymakers. For example, the reduction of poverty may be an objective, but the policies adopted will be determined by views of advocates on the desirability of redistributing wealth. Thus, indeed, public policy comprises political decisions for implementing programmes to achieve societal goals. However, policies and their goals are often vague when they are established. A policy goal is a desired outcome of a policy which may be explicitly stated or implicit in the policy.

Planning, Policymaking and Policy Design

Policymaking must be distinguished from planning. Broadly speaking, a plan is a programme of action for attaining definite goals or objectives. In this sense, a plan is a policy statement, and planning implies policymaking. The objectives tell what can be achieved

---

[20] Anderson, *Public Policy-making*, 10.

[21] P. Bachrach and M.S. Baratz, 'Two Faces of Power', *American Political Science Review* LVI (1962): 947–52.

[22] Rajvir Sharma, 'Judiciary as Change Agent: Some Insights into the Changing Role of Judiciary in India', *Indian Journal of Public Administration* LVIII (2) (2012): 264–86.

with policy and who will be affected by policy. Policy programmes outline the process of the necessary steps to achieve the policy objectives. Often the goals or policies of a plan are not stipulated in the plan documents. They may be stated only in very general or vague terms, or are found to be internally inconsistent or contradictory. A national development plan, broadly speaking, is a collection of targets or individual projects which, when put together, may not constitute an integrated scheme or a plan.

Assigning and allocation of sources for investments and showing of targets in different sectors of the economy are considered to be the core of planning. However, it has been aptly stated that a policy plan needs a policy design. Policy design is a process by which policies are designed, through both technical analysis and the political process, to attain a desired goal. Targets cannot be achieved just because investments are provided for. They have to be drawn within the framework of policies. Successful policies make for successful plans and administration.

Policy Analysis and Policy Advocacy

Social scientists share the conviction that policy studies based on scientific methods are better than those focused merely on values. By the early 20th century, there was a general retreat from any sort of policy advocacy. Policy analysis usually deals with assertions of cause and effect. Henry says, 'Public policy analysis is the study of how governmental policies are made and implemented, and the application of available knowledge to governmental policies for the purpose of improving their formulation and implementation'.[23]

Policy analysis is an applied subfield. Policy analysis is not the same as prescribing what policies governments ought to pursue. Policy advocacy is concerned with what governments ought to do, or bringing about changes in what they do through discussion, persuasion, organization and activism. On the other hand, policy analysis is concerned with the examination of the impact of policy using the tools of systematic inquiry. Policy analysis is nothing more than finding out the impact of policy. It is a technique to measure organizational effectiveness through an examination and evaluation of the effect of a programme. 'Policy analysis is a systematic and data-based alternative to intuitive judgments about the effects of policy or policy options. It is used (i) for problem assessment and monitoring; (ii) as a 'before the fact' decision tool; and (iii) for evaluation'.[24]

The focus in policy analysis is on rational thinking. Thomas Dye labels 'policy analysis' as the 'thinking man's response' to demands. The policy analysis has three basic concerns. First, its primary concern is the 'explanation' of policy rather than the 'prescription' of policy. Second, it involves a rigorous search for the causes and consequences of public policies through the use of the tools of systematic inquiry. Third, it involves an effort to develop and test general propositions about the causes and consequences of public policies. Thus, policy analysis can be both scientific and relevant to the problems of society. The role of policy analysis is not to replace but to supplement political advocacy. As Wildavsky argued, 'The purpose of policy analysis is not to eliminate advocacy

---

[23] Nicholas Henry, *Public Administration and Public Affairs*, 12th ed. (Upper Saddle River, NJ: Pearson Education, 2012), 342.
[24] Ralph C. Chandler and Jack C. Plano, *The Public Administration Dictionary* (New York, NY: John Wiley, 1982), 88.

but to raise the level of argument among contending interests.... The end result, hopefully, would be higher quality debate and perhaps eventually public choice among better known alternatives'.[25] Thus, policy analysis deals with the examination of policy issues.

Policy Analysis and Policy Management

A distinction has to be made between what constitutes policy analysis and what policy management is, though in practice these two related processes overlap to some extent. According to Dror, 'policy analysis' deals with the substantive examination of policy issues and the identification of preferable alternatives, in part with the help of systematic approaches and explicit methods. 'Policy management' deals with the management of policymaking and policy-preparation process, to assure that it produces high-quality policies. The interdependence of policy analysis and policy management can be seen in the necessity of assuring that adequate policy analysis is undertaken as part of crisis management systems to reinforce innovativeness. Policy analysis covers several methods and concepts, some of which are quantitative in character, including methods such as social experimentation, game simulation and contingency planning. Despite such distinctions, both policy analysis and policy management are interrelated aspects of policymaking and cover a major part of the tasks of senior administrators. Therefore, it is essential that these two processes should be treated jointly. Managing public policy, according to Lynn, is typically 'the result of executive effort directed at affecting governmental outcomes by influencing the processes that design and carry out governmental activity'.[26] Thus, this requires a policy design.

Policy Inputs, Policy Outputs and Policy Outcomes

An understanding of terms such as policy inputs, policy outputs and policy outcomes is equally important in the area of policy management. Policy inputs are the demands made on the political system by individuals and groups for action or inaction about some perceived problems. Such demands may include a general insistence that government should do something to a proposal for specific action on the matter. For example, prior to the passing of the Juvenile Justice Act in 2015, some organizations voiced a general desire for enactment of law to deal with teenagers who commit heinous crimes.

In the Eastonian model, outputs are regarded either as effects on the environment or as 'feedback' to the political supports of the system. Easton says that outputs are said to constitute a body of specific inducements for the members of a political system to support it, either by threats of sanctions or by socialization into the political norms of the society.

In other words, policy outputs are the actual decisions of the implementers. They are what a government does, as distinguished from what it says it is going to do. Examples of policy outputs relate to such matters as the education institutions built, taxes collected, compensation paid or curbs on trade eliminated. Outcomes are real results, whether intended or unintended.

The concept of outcomes lays stress on what actually happens to the target groups intended to be impacted by the policy. If the intended changes on target groups do not

---

[25] A. Wildavsky, *The Art and Craft of Policy Analysis* (London: Macmillan, 1980), 15.
[26] L. Lynn, *Managing Public Policy* (Boston, MA: Little, Brown, 1987), 19.

occur, something is wrong. Labour welfare policies in India may be used to illustrate this point. Although one can measure welfare policy outputs—the amount collected by way of taxation, the number of persons helped, the amount of benefits paid and the like—it is difficult to measure the consequences of these actions. In other words, it means assessing whether the policies actually achieve what they are intended to achieve.

Comparative Public Policy

Comparative public policy is a technique of studying public policy by adopting a comparative approach to policy processes and policy outputs and outcomes. The comparative approach tends to use three main methods: single case study of one policy area (say health) in one country, statistical analysis of several case studies and countries or a more focused comparison of a policy area between selected comparable countries (e.g. Asian countries). Current writing and analysis lay emphasis on comparisons between nations and within a nation among states.

Power and Policy Monopoly

Policymaking is partly a manifestation of power. Power is the ability or capacity of an individual to modify the conduct of other individuals or groups. In terms of public policy, the exercise of power means determining the way decisions are made. In policymaking, power is exercised by those who are regarded as elites. Public policies are formulated by what Easton calls the 'authorities' in a political system, namely, 'elders, paramount chiefs, executives, legislators, judges, administrators, councilors, monarchs, and the like'. According to him, these are the persons who 'engage in the daily affairs of a political system', are 'recognized by most members of the system as having responsibility for these matters' and take actions that are 'accepted as binding most of the time by most of the members so long as they act within the limits of their roles'.

Each exercise of power constitutes one of the influences which together make up the policymaking process. The process consists of sequence of related decisions made under the influence of powerful individuals or groups. The sources of power to effect change in other people's behaviour are many. First, power flows from the office which a person holds. This is to say that someone is in authority. Second source of power is the expertise. Administrators and professionals in the service of government are said to enjoy power because of authoritative knowledge which may be based on learning or experience. Third source of power is effective use of sanctions. Policy decisions are taken in the context of overt or latent threats of punishments. Power expresses the notion of a capacity to impose penalties through coercion of a kind usually reserved to the state itself.

'Policy monopoly' is a term coined by Baumgartner and Jones to describe a fairly closed system of the most important actors in a domain, who dominate or monopolize policymaking.[27] In this context, powerful groups attempt to keep policy issues low on the agenda. The point is that powerful groups retain power by working to keep the public and out-groups unaware of underlying problems or alternatives to their resolution.

---

[27] F. Baumgartner and B. Jones, *Agendas and Instability in American Politics* (Chicago, IL: University of Chicago Press, 1993).

SCOPE OF PUBLIC POLICY

The notion that public policy is about the people, their values, needs and problems is to emphasize that the scope of public policy is quite vast. Government action must respond to the people's aspirations. At present, the functions of practically all governments, especially of the developing countries, have significantly increased. They are now concerned with the more complex functions of state building and socio-economic progress. Today, the government is not merely the keeper of peace, the arbiter of disputes and the provider of economic and social services; it has, directly or indirectly, become the principal innovator, the major determiner of social and economic programmes and the main financier as well as the main guarantor of large-scale enterprises.

Today, people expect government to do many things for them. There is great pressure on government to accelerate human development, make use of up-to-date and relevant technological innovations, adopt and facilitate necessary institutional changes, increase national production, make full use of human and other resources and improve the level of living. These trends and developments have, therefore, enhanced both the size and scope of public policy. Michael Teitz describes the outreach of public policy in terms of the citizen's life cycle:

> Modern urban man is born in a publicly financed hospital, receives his education in a publicly supported school and university, spends a good part of his time travelling on publicly built transportation facilities, communicates through the post office or the quasi-public telephone system, drinks his public drinking water, disposes of his garbage through the public removal system, reads his library books, picnics in the public parks, is protected by public police, fire, and health systems, eventually, he dies, again in a hospital, and may even be buried in a public cemetery. Ideological conservatives notwithstanding his everyday life is inextricably bound up with government decisions on these and numerous other public services.[28]

Throughout most of the 20th century and even today, most government activities are carried out by state and local governments. The point is all of us are greatly affected by the myriad public policies in our everyday lives. The range of public policy is vast: from the vital to the trivial. Today, public policies may deal with such substantive areas as defence, environmental protection, medical care and health, education, housing, taxation, inflation, science and technology and so on. The expanding sphere of public policy is reflected in the governmental expenditures. It is largely in these policy areas that organized interests and political parties address problems and advocate policies for the people.

Public policy focuses on the public and its problems. It is the study of, what Heidenheimer said as, 'how, why and to what effect governments pursue a particular course of action or inaction'.[29] Government spending is a common indicator of the scope of public policy.

---

[28] Michael Teitz, 'Towards a theory of Urban Public Facility Location', *Papers of the Regional Science Association* 21 (1968): 36.

[29] A. Heidenheimer et al., *Comparative Public Policy*, 3rd ed. (New York, NY: St. Martin's Press, 1990), 3.

PUBLIC POLICY TYPOLOGY

Public policies have also been categorized on the basis of issues and method of control. These facilitate comparison between issues and policies. Lowi, for example, suggests a classification of policy issues in terms of being (i) distributive, (ii) regulatory, (iii) redistributive and (iv) constituent policy issues.[30]

Distributive Policy Issues

Policies concerned with distribution of new resources are distributive policies. These include grants and subsidies that give protection to certain interests against competition. The recently enacted National Food Security Act, 2013, is an example of the distributive policy. Under this legislation, a legal right has been conferred on beneficiaries to receive entitled quantities of food grains at subsidized prices.

Redistributive Policy Issues

Redistributive policies are concerned with changing the distribution of existing resources. These policies control people by managing the economy as a whole. The techniques of control involve fiscal (tax) and monetary (supply of money) policies. Redistribution of income to reduce inequities falls under this category. Changing the income tax laws from 2013–14 to 2016–17 by the National Democratic Alliance (NDA) government at the centre, for example, significantly reduced the taxes of senior citizens compared to other income groups in society.

Regulatory Policy Issues

Regulatory policy issues are those which are concerned with regulation and control of activities. The most obvious examples of regulation techniques include criminal penalties for certain behaviours. For example, the Criminal Law (Amendment) Act, 2013, provides for life term and even death sentence for rape convicts besides stringent punishment for offences such as acid attacks, stalking and voyeurism. Similarly, environmental regulations (under Environment Protection Act [EPA], 1986) impose significant costs on individual and businesses.

Constituent Policy Issues

Constituent policy issues are those which are concerned with the set-up or reorganization of institutions.

Each of these policy issues forms a different power arena. However, it may be mentioned here that Lowi's view of politics as a function of policies has been criticized as over-simplistic, methodologically suspect and testability. Cobb and Elder, for instance, observe that Lowi's typology has basic limitations. It does not provide a framework for

---

[30] T.J. Lowi, 'Four Systems of Policy Politics and Choice', *Public Administrative Review* 32(4) (1972): 298–310.

understanding change as the types become less clear and more diffuse.[31] Besides, Lowi's typology is based on substantive rather than analytical criteria.

Conflict Policy Issues

Cobb and Elder were concerned with the analysis of agenda process between the social system as a whole and policymaking. They propose an alternative classification of policy issues in terms of conflict rather than content. Their focus is on the way in which conflict is created and managed. To them a conflict may arise between two or more groups over issues relating to the distribution of positions or resources. These may be created by such means and devices as

(i) manufacture by a contending party who perceive unfairness or bias in the distribution of positions or resources;

(ii) manufacture of an issue for personal or group gain; and

(iii) unanticipated human events, natural disasters, international conflict, war and technological changes.

Such issues then constitute the agenda for policy or decision-making. But a link must be made between a trigger and a problem which then transforms the issue into an agenda item.

Bargaining Policy Issues

Hogwood uses the criteria of costs and benefits from the point of view of forms of bargaining and conflict and a range of alternatives.[32] There are redistribution or cuts issues which involve bargaining over who gets what, who gets more and who gets less. For Wilson, criteria of costs and benefits may be concentrated or dispersed. An issue, which may have very concentrated benefits to a small section of society but whose costs are widely dispersed, is of a different kind to one that may be for 'the greatest happiness of the greatest number'.[33]

Cochran categorizes policies into three types: patronage, regulatory and redistributive. (i) Patronage or promotional policies include those government actions that provide incentives for individuals or corporations to undertake activities.[34] He classifies promotional techniques into subsidies, contracts and licences. (ii) Regulatory policies allow the government to exert control over the conduct of certain activities. (iii) Redistributive policies are characterized by actions intended to manipulate the allocation of wealth, property or civil rights among social classes.

Randall Ripley and Grace Franklin classify policy types (derived from Lowi's work) into (i) distributive, (ii) competitive regulatory, (iii) protective regulatory and (iv) redistributive.[35]

---

[31] R.W. Cobb and C.D. Elder, *Participation in American Politics: The Dynamics of Agenda-Building* (Baltimore, MD: Johns Hopkins University Press, 1972), 96.

[32] B.W. Hogwood, *From Crisis to Complacency: Shaping Public Policy in Britain* (London: Oxford University Press, 1987), 31.

[33] J.Q. Wilson, *Political Organization* (New York: Basic Books, 1973).

[34] Cochran and Melone, *Public Policy*, 14–16.

[35] Randall Ripley and Grace Franklin, *Bureaucracy and Policy Implementation* (Homewood, IL: Dorsey Press, 1982), 70–72.

However, in actual practice, the various types of policies are often mixed. Policy typologies in main draw our attention to the identities of direct targets.

INSTITUTIONAL DEVELOPMENT FOR POLICY — Re Read

Public policy as an art and craft is a vast and complex area. It involves in the first instance the state (government as an institution) and the subjects (the citizens as the object of attention). Governments in democratic countries are doing a great many things for the people. Indeed, there is hardly any personal or societal problem for which some citizens will not ask for a government intervention or solution, that is, 'a public policy designed to alleviate personal discomfort or societal unease'. The point is that governments are instruments of and for people to reduce their problems. It is through the policies, governments regulate conflict within society, organize bureaucracies, distribute benefits and extract taxes.

In most developing countries, however, the actual policy outputs have continued to be governed by *ad hoc* and incremental concerns. To some extent, this is inevitable, and more so in the least developed countries which do not have sufficient resources. A larger private sector competing for resources with the public sector causes a high degree of unpredictability regarding policy outputs.[36] In some mixed economies, there are as yet few attempts to involve the private sector in policy development.

While much experience has been gained in planning and policy formulation, the records of their successful implementation are meagre. Planning can be made more operational by strengthening the linkages between the agencies active in the process and by improving the instruments for policy formulation and implementation. The building up of institutions is a major policy concern in developing countries. The lack of an environment of stable political conventions seems to be a major obstacle to institutional development. The predominance of partisan political criteria over the rational one for the evaluation of policies and administrative obstacles also tend to affect the development of institutions for planning and perspective policies adversely. A rational and technical analysis has to be the basis for political decision-makers in order to reach realistic and feasible policy outputs.[37] The effectiveness of this approach, however, would depend upon the availability of qualified and motivated personnel and the establishment of proper linkages.

Attempts have been made to link policymaking, planning and budgeting to constitute a systems approach. In developed countries, such an approach has already gained recognition; in most developing countries, it is still in the process of development. In the wake of the new challenges for development, efforts must be made not only to link planning and budgeting, but also to ensure that both development plans and budgets are consistent with the development policies of the government. Broadly speaking, the structure of public policymaking involves the whole political system. The ultimate authority in policymaking, planning and budgeting rests with those who hold the power to legitimize policies. In view of the technicalities and complexity of various policy questions today, a

---

[36] Jaspal Singh, 'Impact of Globalisation on Society', *Indian Journal of Public Administration*, 49(1) (2003): 66–76.
[37] E.J. Mishan, *Economics for Social Decisions: Elements of Cost-Benefit Analysis* (New York, NY: Praeger, 1972).

President/Prime Minister or a political party alone cannot make public policies. There is, therefore, the necessity for the establishment of 'special central policy units' to carry out the work of policy formulation and policy analysis.

In most developing countries, the executive branch of government has

(i) the policymaking bodies such as the Cabinet and Prime Minister's Office (PMO),
(ii) the National Institution for Transforming India (NITI) Aayog (Government of India [GOI]) and
(iii) a budgeting unit of Finance Ministry.

An important question here is, whether these units work together with an integrated approach that is independent of each other. From the point of view of institutional development, it is important for these units to be organized into an integrated central policy cluster. This cluster should consist of the head of the government, the cabinet ministers and their key political advisers. Under the political advisers in the central policy cluster, there must be economists, statisticians, public administrators, planners, specialists, financial and other experts to analyse the existing policies and to suggest policy alternatives to alleviate personal discomfort or societal unease.

Further, within the central policy cluster, appropriate machinery should also be established for (i) policy and programme management, (ii) reporting and feedback, (iii) reviewing and (iv) the adjustment and revision of policies and plans.

The central policy cluster must ensure that adequate machinery is provided for policy and plan implementation; that the progress of policy and plan implementation shall be reported back to the centre; that the feedback will be enough for the central policy cluster to provide evaluation and control; and that on the basis of such an evaluation, adjustments and revisions will be made on the policies and plans. These four aspects—implementation, reporting, reviewing and readjustment—are interdependent and must be treated as a whole. In brief, it must be emphasized that policymaking, planning and budgeting should be approached as an integrated whole to control government performance.

It may be noted that although programme/performance budgeting rewards efficiency in implementing public policy, or tries to, it cannot enlighten us if those policies are worth having in the first place.

WHY GOVERNMENTS INTERVENE?

While many economists are of the view that markets are the most efficient way to organize economic activity to provide goods and services, there are equally number of economists who argue that market forces do not allocate resources efficiently. The market mechanism holds good as long as an exchange between a buyer and a seller does not affect the third party.[38] But all too often, a third party is affected causing 'market failure'.

In situations of market failure, government intervenes through regulation. Public policy is a form of government intervention and control usually expressed in a legislation, a

---

[38] The process of privatization in India began in 1992.

regulation or an act of order. Government policy is usually (must be) coercive and constrains the individual and business with a view to promoting general welfare. It is important to keep in mind that although markets are a good way to organize many of activities (both social and economic), there are several areas where markets fail to produce and provide goods and services to society's general welfare. In those cases, the government can improve on market outcomes through public policy solutions. However, not all public policy solutions are without flaws.

One reason for calling government's interventions is to break the monopoly power. Where the market does not allocate resources efficiently because of little price competition, government regulation is inevitable (e.g. drinking water monopoly by one person in a tribal area may deprive others who need water).

Second, many believe that market mechanism does not distribute income fairly and guarantee equality. They hold that the market is overly generous to those who are successful and too ruthless in penalizing those who fail in market competition. On the contrary, the goal of public policies is to provide a system that is closer to social equity.

Third, it is believed that markets fail to perform adequately in the provision of what policy analysts call public goods. The benefits of consuming a specific good or service are available only to those who have the purchasing power. If it is shared, more for one must mean less for another. But no one can be excluded from the use of a public good. For example, national defence network provides protection to everyone under its umbrella, whether one has contributed to its purchase or not. The decision to purchase public goods is made collectively in comparison to individual decision for purchase of private goods.

Fourth, the market mechanism violates the sense of equity and security. It is seen as socially unacceptable. Individuals who are poor (belonging to weaker sections of the society), unemployed, aged, disabled or poor women may be unable to earn income and need to be protected from such risks inherent in life in a market economy. Government intervention is sought for income distribution through taxes, social security and poverty alleviation programmes. Moreover, leaving inequalities of wealth solely to market mechanisms would produce the phenomenon of the free rider (those who did not so contribute would be taking a free ride on those who did). Help by the private entrepreneur in government core responsibilities would mean the risk of influencing government's control and accountability.

Although government can improve market outcome through regulations, it is not always that it will. Public policy is the result of a political process. Sometimes policies are designed for political campaigns; at other times, they merely reward elites of the society. Frequently, they are made by politically powerful leaders forced into so many compromises that the resulting policy hears little or no intended objectives. Moreover, government itself emerges from a 'social contract' among people who agree for their mutual benefit to obey laws and support the government in exchange for taking care of their lives and socio-economic development.

SIGNIFICANCE AND WHY STUDY PUBLIC POLICY?

Public policy, as we have analysed, is an important component of democratic government. It is an area which has to do with those spheres which are labelled as public. Government objectives for society's welfare can be largely achieved with the implementation of good policies. Because of resource scarcity, government is forced to adopt public policies. The study of public policy represents a powerful approach for this purpose. Public policy is an important mechanism for moving a social system from the past to the future. It helps to shape the future.

Public policy is made in the present, based on the past, with the objective of improving the society's future. The purpose of studying public problems is to provide insights into a range of policy choices with a view to coping better with the future. We can understand the future by extrapolation of the present trends. People cannot avoid being concerned with the consequences of public policy. As Gibson Winter observes, 'The problem of policy is ultimately how the future is grasped and appraised. The essential meaning of responsibility is accountability in human fulfilment in shaping of the society's future'.[39]

Public policy is conditioned by the past. How the present dimensions of public policy in the developing countries emerged, how they now appear and how the present sustains them are important questions in the study of public policy. In these countries, the scope and size of the public sector have grown enormously in response to the increasing complexity of technology, social organization, industrialization, urbanization and environmental hazards. The increase in public functions has paralleled the growth of public policies. The study of the past is very important as it helps in explaining the present policy system. The past policies perpetuate themselves into present and future polices.

An important goal of the study of public policy is to help us judge when government action is justifiable to promote specific objectives such as social justice, equity or efficacy, and which policies can reasonably be expected to achieve those goals or otherwise.

The study of public policy is of vital importance for the present. It deals with the definition of a policy problem. The definition of a problem may generate more conflict than consensus. In policymaking, political power tends to impose upon the definitions of a problem. In this context, Schattschneider says, 'He who determines what politics is about runs the country, because the definition of alternatives is the choice of conflicts, and the choice of conflicts allocates powers'.[40] Thus, present policymaking can be thought of as problem-solving behaviour, realizing that 'the definition of the alternatives is the supreme instrument of power'.

One is thus led to seek an answer to the question: Why study public policy?

Earlier, most people assumed that once the legislature passed a law and appropriated money for it, the purposes of the law would be achieved. They believed that governments could achieve such goals as the elimination of poverty and the prevention of crime through the adoption of right policies. But now there is a growing uneasiness among social scientists and politicians about the effectiveness of governments. The result has been the sudden awakening of interest in the study of public policy. Public policy can be studied for a good number of reasons.

---

[39] Quoted in Garr D. Brewer, *Politicians, Bureaucrats, and the Consultant: A Critique of Urban Problem Solving* (New York, NY: Basic Books, 1973), 50–51.
[40] E.E. Schattschneider, *The Semi-sovereign People* (New York, NY: Rinehart & Winston, 1960), 69.

For Theoretical and Practical Reasons

First of all, public policy can be studied with a view to gaining greater knowledge and understanding of the causes and consequences of policy decisions. Public policy may be regarded as either a dependent or an independent variable. When it is viewed as a dependent variable, our focus of attention is on environmental factors that help shape the content of policy. For instance, how do environmental protection and industrialization help shape the content of policy? On the other hand, if public policy is viewed as an independent variable, our focus of attention shifts to the impact of policy on the environment. For example, what effect does economic policy have on the labour class? By raising such questions, we can improve our understanding of the linkages between environment and public policy.

Policy study helps us learn about these linkages, which in turn contribute to the development of policy sciences. An understanding of the causes and consequences of public policy also helps us to apply scientific knowledge to the solution of practical social problems. The professionals, if they understand and know something about public policy, are in a position to say something useful concerning how governments or public authorities can act to achieve their policy goals. Such advice can be on either what policies can be pursued for achieving particular goals or what environmental factors are conducive to the development of a given policy. Indeed, factual knowledge is a prerequisite to solve the problems of society. In other words, the study of public policy helps the development of professional advice about how to achieve particular goals.

Cochran and his associates and Anderson argue that one studies public policy so that one can know more about the process, both in pursuit of knowledge for its own sake and to inform practitioners.[41] One might compare the pursuit of knowledge to 'pure science' and the practitioner orientation to 'applied science'. The practical and applied study of public policy takes its cues from theory. Students of public policy derive theory by observing the collective activity of the practitioners of public policy. Think tanks such as NITI Aayog are more concerned with the practical application of knowledge about policy than with scientific theory.

For Political and Administrative Reasons

Related to the practical reasons for studying policy are administrative and political reasons. The study of public policy has much to offer to the development of administration in different sectors of the economy. It will enable the administration to engage in such issues as they are of public importance and are concerned with effective delivery of public services by the meaningful actions of public servants. The social scientists, especially political scientists, manifest concern with what governments should do with appropriate public policy. They contend that political science cannot be 'silent' or 'impotent' on current social and political problems and that political scientists and academics in public administration have a moral obligation to put forward a particular policy on a particular problem. They should advance the level of political knowledge and improve the quality of

---

[41] Clark E. Cochran et al., *American Public Policy: An Introduction*, 6th ed. (New York, NY: St. Martin's Press, 1999); James E. Anderson, *Public Policy-making*, 4th ed. (Boston, MA: Houghton Mifflin, 2000).

public policy in whatever ways they think best, notwithstanding the fact that substantial disagreement exists in society over what constitutes appropriate policies. Therefore, the study of public policy must promote a better understanding of government and its relationship with the society it governs. Also people with political goals study public policy to learn how to promote their preferred policy choices.

For Promoting Policy Education Values

The study of public policy has an important role in education. For Lasswell, public policy as public education was essential if democracy was not to fall prey to the interests and manipulations of powerful elites. The major aim of policymaking, he wrote, was the formation of values which could shape the full development of individuals in the society.[42] The study of public policy has its aim of clarifying the values which inform both the analysis of the policymaking process and the forms of knowledge which are used in this process.

In the decision to study public policy, there is an implicit ethical view that people and their welfare are important. For the researcher, it is important to learn about all forces that affect the well-being of individuals and of society as a whole. The desire to improve the well-being of the society's future is the basis of public policy.

CONCLUDING OBSERVATIONS

The study of public policy, although rooted in the study of political science, is a recent innovation. The purpose of the study of public policy is to understand the problems of the people and to provide insights into a range of policy alternatives to deal with a matter of public concern. To wind up this discussion, it can be noted that the field of public policy has assumed considerable importance in response to the increasing complexity of the society. It is concerned not only with the description and explanation of the causes and consequences of government activity, but also with the development of scientific knowledge about the forces shaping the public policy.[43] The study of public policy helps us understand the social ills of the subject under study. Public policy is an important mechanism for moving a social system from the past to the future.

In the current phase of liberalization, privatization and globalization, the role of the government has changed. The delivery of goods and services is important, but it is not the critical role of government. Kirlin notes, 'Government is the institution of society with singular obligations to facilitate societal choice-making and action'.[44] Its ability lies in making policies and executing them. Public policy involves improving the democratic or political capacities of people, and not simply the efficiency and effectiveness of delivery of goods and services.

---

[42] Harold Lasswell, 'The Emerging Conception of the Policy Sciences', *Policy Sciences* 1 (1970): 3–14.
[43] Dye, *Understanding Public Policy*, 4.
[44] J.J. Kirlin, 'A Political Perspective', in *Public Sector Performance: A Conceptual Turning Point*, ed. T.C. Miller (Baltimore, MD: Johns Hopkins Press, 1984), 164.

Lasswell commented in 1948 that the ultimate goal of policymaking was 'the progressive democratization of mankind'.[45] Parsons also concludes, 'It is the clarification, shaping and sharing of values so as to extend and enhance democratization which still remains the core and vital task of the theory and practice of public policy'.[46] Policies do more than effect change in societal conditions. They also hold people together and maintain an orderly state.

Good policies depend upon good government. And 'good government', according to Henry, 'rests on three pillars: honesty, democracy, and competency'.[47] Good policies and their effective management are essential to each pillar. Public policies in good sense are meant to promote a better understanding of government and its relationship with the society it governs.

Review Questions

(i) Public policy is based on the past, formulated in the present, with an objective of improving the society's future. Discuss the statement with the help of examples.

(ii) How and why is the crux of public policy 'public'?

(iii) A public policy may be general or specific, explicit or implicit, discretionary or detailed and qualitative or quantitative. Illustrate how public policies qualify as all of the above.

(iv) Discuss Lowi's classification of policy issues. Do you think this classification has some limitations? Enumerate with examples.

(v) Explain in brief the role of government intervention in public policymaking and implementation.

---

[45] Harold Lasswell, *Power and Personality* (New York, NY: W.W. Norton, 1948), 221–22.

[46] Parsons, *Public Policy*, 616.

[47] Henry, *Public Administration and Public Affairs*, 5.

CHAPTER 2

POLICY ADVOCACY
Power and Influence of Non-officials

INTRODUCTION

Public agenda[1] for policy consideration is triggered by individuals or organizations with the capability of capturing the attention of public policymakers.[2] These individuals and organizations that place issues of concerns before public policymakers may be called agenda-builders. By calling for action, these agenda-builders often act as advocates because they persuade others to take a course of action. Advocacy is an important part of the public policymaking process. It 'involves research and arguments which are intended to influence the policy agenda inside and/or outside government'.[3] Thus, policymaking begins with the opinion citizens, non-government organizations, civil society organizations or interest groups (referred to as non-officials who do not hold office within the government structure) have about the actions they want the government to take. In other words, individuals or organizations bring influence to bear on those entitled to take decisions on some perceived problems. This interaction between the non-officials (interest groups and other actors) and officials (policymakers in the government structure) involves power, influence and conflict in which both compete to impose decisions on opposing parties.

The study of public policy is regarded as an important aspect of politics. And politics invariably involves power. Thus, policymaking is essentially a manifestation of power. It is, therefore, important to understand exactly how power is exercised in the policymaking process. Power is regarded as an ability of an individual to bring about some changes in the behaviour of other people. In a social context, it is defined as 'the capacity of an individual, or a group of individuals, to modify the conduct of other individuals or groups in the manner which he desires'.[4] In terms of public policy, power may be defined as the capacity of an individual, or groups, or holders of public offices to determine policy decisions. Such decisions may relate to the choice of individuals for political offices and also to the selection of different purposive courses of action. In policymaking, power is exercised by different individuals and groups such as the members of the Council of Ministers, members of Parliament, bureaucrats and leaders of organized interests (e.g. individual citizens). Each set of forces exercises certain influences which, taken together, make up the policymaking process. This is to say that there is a 'process' through which public

---

[1] Public agenda consists of an ever-changing group of issues at various stages of resolution.
[2] For discussion of agenda-building, see John W. Kingdon, *Agendas, Alternatives, and Public Policies*, 2nd ed. (Boston, MA: Little Brown, 1995), 21–70.
[3] Parsons, *Public Policy*, 55.
[4] R.H. Tawney, *Equality* (London: Allen & Unwin, 1931), 229.

policies are made. The process consists of complex interrelationships of the decisions made under the influence of powerful individuals and groups. Systems modellers argue that we can think of a policy as the product of a system.

In this chapter, an attempt is made to explain how individuals and organizations acting as advocates bring influence to bear on those who are vested with the power of taking and enforcing decisions. Such decision-makers comprise those who occupy formal offices within the constitutional system of rules. Altogether, there are five categories of non-officials who are away from the centres of policymaking, but who, in a particular situation, may perform one or more of the specialized roles which according to Lindblom constitute influential behaviour.[5]

CITIZENS AS INDIVIDUALS

The power to influence the public policymaking process lies, in the first instance, with the ordinary citizen. Although it is difficult to imagine that an individual voice would ever be heard, it happens all the time. When Mahatma Gandhi, the Father of the Nation, refused to get down from the train in South Africa, he not only voiced against racial discrimination, but his actions also influenced the oppressed Indians in the Transvaal as well as the African people against colonialism. Cumulatively, these actions of Gandhi helped to change public perceptions and awaken the nation's public policymakers on the question of political and civil rights.

The citizen is the centre of object for public analysis. Harold Lasswell, the father of 'Policy Sciences', enunciated that policy sciences should function so as to facilitate the interaction between the citizens and its problems.[6] The issue is how citizens can make a real and meaningful input to the policy process. An example of this policy input is worth extending.

When 10 former chiefs of the Indian armed forces on 17 August 2015 wrote to PM Narendra Modi demanding immediate implementation of the 'One Rank, One Pension' (OROP) policy, it is assumed that these individual citizens are placing issues of concern before public policymakers. The former chiefs in their letter to the PM stated,

> We stand steadfastly by the side of our colleagues and fully support their just cause. Our silence so far was due to the need to observe propriety... we are dismayed at the inability of the political leadership to clinch the issue of the OROP for the forces.[7]

By calling for action, these citizens act as advocates as they persuade the political masters to take a policy action. According to Pickles, in a democratic form of government, the government has to be not only representative, but also responsive.[8] In a representative democracy, it is assumed that power flows from the people. Representation carries with it the clear implication of delegation from the people to a legislature. Through legislature,

---

[5] Charles E. Lindblom, *The Policy-making Process* (New York, NY: Prentice Hall, 1968), 4.
[6] Lasswell, 'The Policy Orientation'.
[7] See *The Tribune* (Chandigarh), 18 August 2015, accessed 16 November 2016, http://www.tribuneindia.com/news/nation/implement-orop-10-ex-chiefs-to-pm/121147.html
[8] Dorothy Pickles, *Democracy* (London: Faber, 1965), 13.

the representatives of the people frame laws and decide policy by a majority vote. In a democracy, people initiate the process of legislation and policymaking by voting for candidates whose opinions and values they know.

Yet in practice, citizen participation in policymaking is negligible. Many people do not seem to be exercising their franchise or are engaging in party politics. Acting alone, the individual citizen is hardly a significant political force. The public or the people, on the contrary, suggest a unity of will and purpose. In politics, groups rather than individuals affect the way a policy is made. A relatively small group of office-holders may be held responsible for the actions they perform. In recent years, students have served as effective policy advocates, helping to raise a number of issues on national policy agendas.

It can safely be concluded that politics holds attraction for relatively few people. The people are not a particularly satisfactory force for analysing political power. However, it is a fact that no government, however dictatorial, can afford to go against the wishes and customs of the people. As such, 'the lay voice (of the citizen) should be taken seriously and that the enhancement of that voice should be a matter of concern for both policy analysts and policy-makers'.[9] The point here is that individuals, acting alone or with others, can be powerful forces in influencing the content of the public agenda. Thus, the political system is necessarily open to citizens making their case.

COMMUNICATIONS MEDIA

It is the news that appears on the television or in the newspaper creates substantial impact on the people and the policymaking process. In creating stereotypical threats, the mass media can shape the context within which policy responses take place and influence public opinion by setting a public agenda in terms of an incident or event. The media select what is newsworthy. The news media can serve as a 'fourth branch' of government, thereby providing a check on the other three branches. This is known as 'watchdog' function of the media.

People want to see change when they suddenly become aware about a critical issue described in the mass media. For instance, the Parliament enacted the Criminal Law (Amendment) Bill, 2013 brought against the backdrop of national outrage over the gang rape and murder of a 23-year-old physiotherapy student in Delhi in December 2012.[10] Journalists and academics have strengthened the belief that the news media act as a channel of communication between the government and the people. By amplifying what otherwise might not be heard, the mass media force policymakers to focus on issues that they might otherwise avoid. Since the media are acting as channels of communications, it is important to determine whether they are politically biased in their presentation of information. If they are biased in the way they present the decisions and actions of government to the public or public opinion to the government, they may distort the very concept of democracy.

---

[9] Parsons, 542.

[10] The Anti-Rape Bill was passed by the Lok Sabha on 19 March and Rajya Sabha on 21 March and the President of India accorded his assent on 2 April 2013.

The media may serve to manipulate rather than illuminate social problems. It is often said that news media function in the interest of the powerful. To quote from *The Tribune*,

> There is a subtle but well-planned move engineered as a fallout of current corporate democracy in which the media has been sought to serve the corporate interest…. In corporate democracy, the space available for public discourse on issues of social concerns is filled by light, nay, vulgar entertaining soap operas. In pre-globalization democracies, this 'public space' was available independent of both state and business control, which permitted citizens to interact, study and debate on the public issues of the day without fear of immediate reprisal from political and economic powers that be.[11]

On the contrary, it is argued that the media have the capacity to bring issues to the forefront of public attention. Sometimes the news can have national, or even international, implications, such as in August 2014 when PM Narendra Modi asked the Defence Research and Development Organisation (DRDO) to 'visualize, anticipate and eventually set the agenda for global defence community'.[12] He asked the scientists to connect with the ultimate end user of their products—the soldier—who can suggest practical innovations in defence technology.

Some of the thought-provoking information provided by media is found in small communities. News such as homeless families, incidents of rape and dowry and other offences against women and children, polluted water supply, generation of hazardous plastic waste and lack of toilet facilities can jolt a local population into demanding action from public decision/policymakers, especially if there is a potential for harm. When the media can influence opinions in a situation where the government is seen to be responsive and responsible to the public, then they are correspondingly influenced in determining the policy.

Internet for Websites

Internet is another category of mass media institutions which places issues on the public agenda. In today's information technology age, the Internet has become a powerful tool of advocacy and a 'valuable ally of the grassroots politics that characterize so much of our agenda building today'.[13] The use of 'online social networking sites to communicate with family and friends and to meet people has had a significant effect on the ways in which people interact'.[14] By overcoming the traditional barriers of time and space, the Web has internationalized civic life and facilitated coalition building within and across the international community.

---

[11] See *The Tribune* (Chandigarh), 28 September 2008, accessed 16 November 2016, http://www.tribuneindia.com/2008/20080928/edit.htm

[12] See *The Financial Express* (Chandigarh), 21 August 2014, accessed 16 November 2016, http://pib.nic.in/newsite/mbErel.aspx?relid=108896

[13] See 'BO, U R so Gr 8', *The Wall Street Journal*, 26–27 May (2007): A1, A5.

[14] V. Rajeswari, 'The Social and Psychological Impact of Online Social Networking', *South Asian Journal of Socio-Political Studies* 14(1) (2013): 86.

Internet allows people to read news of their choice at any time and even more to the point. Internet news sources allow people to customize their news reading of issues that they find most interesting. According to Birkland,

> the growth of the Internet is important for three reasons: (i) because of its influence on traditional media; (ii) because of the potential for changes in agenda-setting process as a result of narrowing of the news; and (iii) because of the potential for a greater diversity of news sources.[15]

Anyone can become part of the mass media by setting up his/her own social networking site, making this information centre utterly accessible. During the 2014 parliamentary elections in India, some candidates establish their own websites (the World Wide Web) for information dissemination related to elections. Through e-mail and instant messaging, online communities are created where 'a gift economy and reciprocal altruism are encouraged through cooperation'.

However, the Internet as a class of mass media is not without its limitations. People who place information can hide behind anonymity or deceit. In an educational setting, for example, Facebook is seen by many teachers as a frivolous and time-wasting distraction from schoolwork. To avoid this cyberbullying, many schools at the middle and higher secondary levels have blocked access to social networking services such as Facebook, Myspace and Twitter within the school environment. Some critics argue that there are dangers of online social networking and call for increased regulation and accountability of providers of these sites. Similarly, the Union Ministry of Home Affairs has drawn a 'blueprint' to keep tabs on social media websites and applications to counter the growing radicalization of the youth and the threat emerging from the Islamic State.[16] In reply to a question for his remarks, Minister of State (MoS) for External Affairs V.K. Singh said, 'Cyber attackers use masquerading techniques and hidden servers to launch snooping'.

However, there is considerable concern as to the quality of the media in their role of providing the public with information about the government. It is found that ability of the press in particular to deal with political issues is counteracted not so much by the scope and complexity of the government alone but by legal and political rules such as the Official Secrets Act, Parliamentary privilege, ministerial responsibility and the laws of libel. Press coverage of the government is declining in standard, and there seems to be not strong pressure from either the elected persons or the electorate to reverse this trend. Many advocates believe that the institutional biases of the news media can be overcome and controlled by the proliferation of Web 2.0, or social media products such as Facebook and Twitter. These sources are useful as they allow people to read information at any time of the day.

---

[15] Birkland, *An Introduction to the Policy Process*, 151.

[16] See *The Tribune* (Chandigarh), 2 August 2015. In connection with cybercrime, the Chinese police arrested about 15,000 people for crimes that 'jeopardized internet security'; See *The Financial Express* (Chandigarh), 19 August 2015. Also see *The Financial Express*, 11 December 2015, accessed 16 November 2016, http://www.ndtv.com/india-news/blue-print-to-counter-islamic-state-and-radicalisation-soon-home-ministry-1202870

INTEREST GROUPS

Importance and Types of Interest Groups

'Interest groups', also called 'pressure groups', are an important channel of communication between the official and non-official forces for action or non-action on some perceived problems. There is a huge network of non-governmental organizations (NGOs) across the country.[17] They are important means of enhancing the effect of public opinion. They can communicate more effectively than individual citizens with public officials on policy decisions. The exercise of political influence by organized citizens is a predominant feature of the democratic form of government.[18] Group action is considered a more effective method than individual action for the ordinary citizen to influence the public policies. Unless large numbers of citizens are organized for some common purpose or interest, the chances of transmitting their messages and policy issues will become bleak. Public opinion expressed by individual citizens reflects neither the intensity of the view nor does it serve as the basis for a change in policy. Acting alone, the individual citizen is rarely a significant force.

Interest groups are organizations with formal structures whose members share a common interest. They strive to influence the decisions of the government without attempting to occupy political offices. According to Birkland, 'an interest group is a collection of people or organizations that unite to advance their desired political outcomes in government and society'.[19] Interest groups including NGOs consisting of individuals with similar needs and values generally exist for protecting and promoting their interests.

These organizations aid their members and individual citizens in communicating their hopes to public officials by offering personnel and expertise in the substantive matters and the procedures of policymaking. To policymakers, the interest groups offer expertise and political support as well as the intensity of view of large numbers of citizens with some common interest. In return, the interest groups are able to create areas of influence on citizens as well as policymakers. Sometimes they sponsor candidates in elections for testing support for their cause. They are, however, rarely successful.

Further, interest group staffs may be invited or associated either to sit on public boards, councils or committees on account of their expertise, qualifications and proficiencies. They often 'bring valuable technical knowledge to policy formation as well as political information about their group's position on the issues'.[20]

Since the 1970s, interest groups at the local, regional and state levels have grown not only in number, but also in size. Interest groups at the local and state levels (students body, women organizations, sweepers' unions, senior citizens councils, children's rights advocacy groups) attempt to influence local and state public policy and government agendas. Sometimes, interest groups refocus national issues at the local levels of applications.

---

[17] According to Department of Statistics, GOI (2014), there is a huge network of 3.3 million NGOs across the country. In April 2015, the GOI shared a list of over 42,000 NGOs with financial Intelligence Unit.
[18] Rajni Kothari, *Rethinking Democracy* (New Delhi: Orient Longman, 2005).
[19] Birkland, *An Introduction to the Policy Process*, 134.
[20] Dye, *Understanding Public Policy*, 41.

On some occasions, interest groups (also civil society organizations) get into the public policymaking process. On other occasions, representatives of the well-organized interest groups bring issues to the attention of the public policymakers. In some instances, interest groups contribute to the election campaigns of candidates or political parties friendly to their issues.

Regardless of the fruition of their actions, these groups endeavour to raise the consciousness of policymakers. But there are so many associations and civil society organizations in India involved in the effort to lobby policymakers that it is usually hard for any one or two to have much success. The experience suggests that very few of them will have any voice in policymaking.

The Union Ministry of Home Affairs (GOI) in the second quarter of 2016 cancelled the licences of some 11,319 entities including NGOs and interest groups (which included Supreme Court Bar Association, Vikram Sarabhai Foundation, Kabir Greenpeace India, etc.) for their violation of Foreign Contribution Regulation Act.[21]

A distinction between different types of interest groups is desirable since some can expect to be successful in influencing the emergence of public policy.

Sectional Interest Groups

First, there are 'sectional interest groups' such as the Bhartiya Kissan Union, the All India Bank Officers' Confederation, Indian University Teachers' Association, the Federation of Indian Chambers of Commerce and Industry (FICCI), All India Drug Action Network (AIDAN), Confederation of Indian Textile Industry and Punjab Private Sugar Mills Association. The aims of such groups or associations are determined by the needs and interests of their members, whether they are individual members or corporate bodies grouped as confederation. Their leaders are spokespersons and act as delegates of the membership. Their influence over their members originates in their ability to formulate the positions that come to be identified with their members. Sectional interest groups enable their members' economic and social interests to be represented in the process of developing issues of public policy.

Cause–Promotion Groups

Second, there are 'cause–promotional groups' such as Environmental Protection Society Malaysia, People's Union for Civil Liberties (India), the Society for the Prevention of Cruelty to Children (England), Ekal Nari Shakti Sangathan (ENSS—a women's welfare organization in Himachal Pradesh), Social Uplift Through Rural Action (SUTRA) and Association for Democratic Reforms. They seek to promote causes and are consequently engaged in lobbying activities. They exert influence over either the public generally or sectional interest groups, in particular, by appealing to their conscience. The aims of the promotional groups are not determined by the interests and needs of their members since they are usually not spokesmen of any social groups.

---

[21] See *The Tribune* (Chandigarh), 10 June 2015, accessed 16 November 2016, http://www.ndtv.com/india-news/government-cancels-licenses-of-4-470-erring-ngos-entities-barred-from-funding-supreme-court-bar-asso-770210. See also *The Tribune*, 5 November 2016.

For example, the Durbar Mahila Samanwaya Committee (DMSC), a forum for some 1,30,000 sex workers in West Bengal, asked the workers not to entertain Africans for sex in the wake of the Ebola outbreak in West Africa.[22] Similarly, the Society for the Promotion of Area Resource Centers (SPARC, set up in 1984) with the help of National Slum Dwellers Federation (NSDF—representing the interests of slum dwellers in India) successfully reha- bilitated over 15,000 families in Mumbai from 2013 to 2015. Thus, interventions by such organizations and societies have largely influenced the policymakers to come out with the policies that promote economic and social segments of the society.

Expertise-based Organizations

Third, there are organizations which are research based and working on projects for the benefits of the poor sections of the community. Participatory Research in Asia (PRIA), for example, has a network of 3,000 organizations which have worked on social issues with Dalit girls in Haryana, tribal girls in Chhattisgarh and Odisha and Muslim girls in Uttar Pradesh (UP), giving them access to quality personal education by developing their skills and improving their knowledge regarding their health and growth opportunities.[23]

There are many other organizations such as HelpAge India, Sammaan Foundation, Ford Foundation, Sir Dorabji Tata Trust and the Indian Society of Agribusiness Professionals (ISAP). The new initiative of ISAP 'focuses on raising yield using quality seeds with appro- priate spacing and plant population while reducing the use of fertilizers as well as of cost'.[24]

Professional groups, including scientists and academics, are often represented as the creators and proponents of particular bodies of knowledge that play important roles in shaping both social policy and the institutions of everyday life.[25] New policy emerges as professionals bring their ideas to bear on problems which political parties wish to solve. Professionals and expertise-based organizations are repositories of knowledge and can argue from positions of great strength about the political repercussions likely to be faced from the interests most affected. For instance, there are a host of organizations involved in the effort to lobby policymakers for the creation of an All India Education Service. It is a key recommendation of the committee on National Education Policy which submitted its report to the Human Resource Development (HRD) Ministry on 27 May 2016. A the- matic consultation was held by the HRD Ministry, University Grants Commission, All India Council for Technical Education, National Council for Teacher Education, National Council of Educational Research and Training (NCERT) and a host of professional groups.[26]

---

[22] See *The Tribune*, 18 August 2014. Durbar is also imparting training to sex workers to identify the signs of an Ebola-affected person, accessed 16 November 2016, http://www.tribuneindia.com/2014/20140818/nation.htm

[23] See *The Tribune* (Chandigarh), 7 October 2013.

[24] See *The Financial Express* (Chandigarh), 22 August 2014, accessed 16 November 2016, http://www.financialexpress.com/archive/isap-joins-farmers-to-increase-crop-yields/1281405/

[25] E. Freidson, *Professional Powers* (Chicago, IL: University of Chicago Press, 1986), ix.

[26] See *The Tribune* (Chandigarh), 28 May 2016.

Role of Interest Groups in Influencing Policy Process

Interest groups including civil society associations are an important part of democracy and do play an influencing role in the emergence of public policy. Although it is very difficult to predict the circumstances under which a particular pressure group can expect to be successful in influencing the emergence of public policy, it is possible to explain the resources of pressure groups which make the legislation more effective in policy action.

Using Publicity Campaigns

Interest groups use the public opinion campaigns from time to time in attempts to bring influence to bear indirectly on government or legislatures. They are the means of enhancing the effect of public opinion. For the cause, group or association appeals to public opinion are usually the first stage of its campaign, to be followed later perhaps by negotiations with policymakers in government. Greenpeace India, for example, cautions bidders by voicing, 'Out of the 101 (coal) blocks earmarked for auction this year at least 39 are in ecologically critical areas'.[27]

Advisory Functions

Consultations between policymakers (especially the ministers) and the leaders of the interest groups form a continuous process and range from the statutory obligations to consult them to the informal appeals and deputations to ministers. Since organized interests have expertise, experience and proficiencies, they are invited or associated in the policymaking committees, councils or bodies. It may be mentioned here that besides the legislative and executive branches, the judiciary also feels the influence of interest groups. For example, expressing concern over expensive life-saving drugs for major diseases, the Supreme Court asked the central government to consider the objections raised by AIDAN, an NGO, on pricing of essential drugs in the country and also the Drugs (Prices Control) Order, 2013 (DPCO) notification.[28]

Role in Policy Implementation and Monitoring

Third, the government has to rely on the cooperation of interest groups in the implementation of its polices. Many government programmes would remain unimplemented without the cooperation of vested interests. Such interests can gain control in the formulation of policy as a price of its successful implementation. Protection of the human environment is an example. Hence, every policy programme has to be planned with the cooperation of affected groups.

---

[27] See *The Financial Express* (Chandigarh), 8 August 2015, accessed 16 November 2016, http://www.newindianexpress.com/business/2015/aug/07/Greenpeace-Cautions-Bidders-on-39-Coal-Blocks-Ahead-of-Auction-796135.htm

[28] See *The Financial Express* (Chandigarh), 16 July 2015. The directions were given by the Supreme Court after AIDAN asked the government why the new drug pricing policy, which intends to put a cap on prices of 348 essential medicines, had changed the formula for deciding the cap from a cost-based mechanism to a market price-based mechanism. Accordingly, the National Pharmaceutical Pricing Authority (NPPA) has fixed the ceiling prices for 530 essentials medicines, including 47 for cancer and 22 for HIV. See *The Financial Express*, 23 December 2015, accessed 16 November 2016, http://www.financialexpress.com/lifestyle/health/sc-asks-govt-to-revisit-new-drug-pricing-policy/101837/

In Putnam's views, patterns of trust developed within associations provide the basis for 'generalized trust' throughout the society, building a basis for civic engagement, public spiritedness and effective government.[29]

Interest groups also attempt to ensure government accountability by monitoring public policies. Some well-organized associations such as the Federation of Indian Export Organisations (FIEO) and FICCI conduct innovative research and activities in certain policy areas and implementations of development programmes with a view to sharing their results with the government and public. These efforts in monitoring and sharing of results contribute to the effective functioning of the government policy delivery agencies.

Access to Stages of Policymaking

Another aspect of the role of organized interests is related to their access to the different stages of the policymaking process. Powerful associations and interests can exert pressure on ministers and public officials, before the government has decided to legislate. Similarly, a group may petition a minister or appear before an enquiry committee, commission or court in an attempt to involve the government in policy action. The interest groups articulate the interests and demands of society, seek support for these demands among other groups by advocacy and bargaining and strive to transform these demands into public policies. With access to information and support from various political parties, these organized interests foster democracy by limiting the state, providing space for protests groups, generating demands, monitoring excess, confronting powerholders and sustaining a balance of power between the state and society.[30]

Initiating and Influencing Policy Issues

It is observed that government is less likely to have adopted major policy commitments on certain moral issues such as divorce, capital punishment, women's rights and abortion. It is only on the initiatives of organized interests and court's directives that the government takes up the legislation. The chances of successful interest groups influence are greater when the government has no fixed objective in view. For example, women's organizations (All India Women's Conference, Self-Employed Women's Association, ENSS) have influenced the enactment of a number of statutes such as the Anti-Dowry Act, Juvenile Justice Law and the Suppression of Immoral Traffic (among women) Act.

Recently, the Mahila Kalyan Parishad (Kinnaur, Himachal Pradesh), after a long struggle with the National Commission for Women and the National Commission for Scheduled Tribes and finally with the High Court, Himachal, got the court's verdict in its favour entitling the tribal women to ancestral property under the Hindu Succession Act, 1956 and not as per customs and usages.[31]

---

[29] Robert Putnam, 'Bowling Alone: America's Declining Social Capital', *Journal of Democracy*, 6 (1995): 167–75.
[30] Gordon White, 'Civil Society, Democratization and Development', *Democratization* I(3) (1994): 382.
[31] See *The Tribune* (Chandigarh), 26 June 2015. Similarly, passed by the Lok Sabha in May 2014, the Juvenile Justice (Care and Protection of Children) Bill was discussed in the Rajya Sabha and passed on 22 December 2015 against the backdrop of uproar over the release of a juvenile convict in the gang rape

The strength of organizations is an important factor in the policymaking process. The leaders of such groups usually belong to a higher socio-economic status than most of its members and are likely to place a higher priority on the social and political objectives of the groups.

It is further pointed out that most members of a particular service or a labour group join an organization because they have no choice. Physicians, lawyers and teachers must join their professional associations to receive the benefits from them.

Conclusion

Although organized interests or interest groups have many benefits and positive attributes, they are not an absolute blessing for democracy. These organizations, whether formal or informal, can also create problems for the governing institutions. Organized interests may build into the policy process a systematically biased distribution of influence. They also tend to impose an elaborate and obscure process of compromise upon political life, the outcome of which can be policies which remain unimplemented or which no one wanted in the first place.

Moreover, lobbying between the interest groups and elected and appointed officials involves secret dealings, often 'accompanied by the exchange of cash in the form of campaign contributions, or, in less savory transactions, in the form of bribes and graft'.[32] The implication is that there is an exchange taking place that is 'unfair and undemocratic'. It is sometimes argued that we now have a corporate state in which policy decisions are taken on the basis of cooperation between politicians, officials and the leaders of the organized interests. Moreover, in the current political scenario, the elected representatives of the people have been replaced by the leaders of organized interests. Interest groups now form the main channels through which influence is brought to bear on decision-makers. Public opinion is no longer aggregated by political parties; it is now articulated by organized interests pursuing their separate objectives by pressuring the policymaking bodies.

POWER IN POLITICAL PARTIES

Introduction

'Political parties' like the interest groups also exert influence greatly over the policymaking process. They enhance the effect of public opinion which forms the basis of public policy. Like the pressure groups, they serve as intermediaries between citizens as voters and policymakers as legislators. But political parties differ from the interest groups. Interest groups in that their primary concern is to gain public office rather than merely influence those who serve in public office. The power to government office is conferred on the leaders of a political party by virtue of their parliamentary majority in the Lok Sabha.

Party platforms on which elections are fought form a basis for the party leaderships when, as a government, it engages in the making of public policy. Political parties are

---

and murder of 23-year-old Nirbhaya on 16 December 2012. See *The Tribune* (Chandigarh), 23 December 2015.

[32] Birkland, *An Introduction to the Policy Process*, 139.

thus regarded as important agents for establishing popular control over government and public policies. They play an important role in reflecting the issues at stake and in setting value goals for the society. Downs argued that 'parties formulate policies in order to win elections, rather than win elections in order to formulate policies'.[33] On the contrary, Tullock argues that parties use policies to win votes. Invariably, it is observed that political parties shape voter preferences.[34] They play an important role in building the public agenda at the local, state and national levels.

Meaning and Conditions for a Responsible Political Party

Edmund Burke (1729–97) defined 'political party' as 'a body of men united for promoting the national interest on some particular principles on which they are all agreed'. Edwards and Sharkansky lay down following conditions which must be fulfilled by responsible political parties:

(i) Parties must have programme.
(ii) Each party's candidates must be committed to its programme.
(iii) Parties must present their programmes to the public.
(iv) Opposing parties must present alternative programme.
(v) There must be only two major parties.
(vi) People must vote for programme and not individuals.
(vii) The party that receives a majority of the vote must take control of the government.
(viii) The party that wins the election must have the internal cohesion and discipline to carry out its programme.
(ix) The party that wins the election must implement its programme.
(x) The governing party must accept responsibility for the performance of the government.
(xi) The opposition party must be ready to take control of the government.[35]

Edwards and Sharkansky further say, 'A two-party system operating under these conditions would simplify the alternatives presented to voters, allow constituents to effectively express their attitudes towards policy, active public participation in politics, make majority rule effective, and establish popular control over government'. As a body of influence, the political party provides organizational and publicity resources.

Strategy for Shaping Voter's Preferences

Although party organization may not be as powerful in shaping voter's preferences, it still plays a very important role in building political agenda at national, state and local levels. Dunleavy identifies four main strategies for shaping preferences of voters employed by the political parties in power[36]: (i) partisan social engineering, (ii) adjusting social relativities, (iii) context management and (iv) institutional manipulation.

[33] A. Downs, *An Economic Theory of Democracy* (New York, NY: Harper & Row, 1957), 28.
[34] G. Tullock, *The Vote Motive* (London: Institute of Economic Affairs, 1976), 66.
[35] George C. Edwards and Ira Sharkansky, *The Policy Predicament* (San Francisco, CA: W.H. Freeman, 1978), 48–49.
[36] P. Dunleavy, *Democracy, Bureaucracy and Public Choice* (Herts: Harvester Wheatsheaf, 1991), chap. 5.

On the contrary, parties which are out of office have following four choices: (i) to shape voter preferences, (ii) to capitalize on social tension, (iii) joint institutional manipulation and (iv) agenda setting.

Influence of Party Leadership

A political party can have clout. If the party leadership is pressurized that 'your issue' is consistent with its own agenda and that supporting the issue may further its objectives, the local or state political party can be a powerful ally. Leaders may even go to the extent of inserting statements of legislative objectives. In addition, the political party as a body of influence assures organizational and publicity resources as well as its many contacts in government. Party leadership when in power exercises a great deal of influence in taking policy decisions. However, the distribution of power in a political party is primarily a function of cabinet government and the parliamentary system.

In the first place, the power of the leadership, and within that of the leader himself, is of paramount importance. It is found that policy changes are initiated by the party leadership, and the party leaders owe their positions to the rank-and-file selectors. In this way, the latter makes a substantial contribution to the policy choice, even though the general picture which emerges is one of the leadership dominance.[37] The leader of the party exercises the powers of appointment which enable him to control the party organizations. He has also the right to select the members of the Cabinet when in office. It is found that the party leaders themselves keep a firm grip on party offices. They (party leaders) are selected by their parliamentary colleagues and not by the parties at large. In a parliamentary democracy, the party leader is selected by a ballot of the parliamentary party. However, subject to annual re-election, he is rarely opposed and enjoys greater security of tenure. As far as choice of ministers is concerned, when the party musters a majority, this choice usually lies with the leader, as the PM.

Most state-level political parties in India are largely brokerage organizations committed to winning public office rather than to advancing policy proposals with regard to societal conditions. Many studies on political parties in India indicate that they do not approach the conditions for responsible parties.[38] They have different programmes and appeal to different sections of society. They are unable to take a single national position and then enforce it. Further, it becomes difficult for the party leaders to exercise control over the actions of elected officials. Moreover, the fact that the executive branch can remain controlled by a PM, who has to depend on the legislature, weakens the party's position when

---

[37] It was on the initiative of PM Narendra Modi that the Planning Commission was replaced by the NITI Aayog on 1 January 2015. His other initiatives include: commitment to Swachh Bharat, Skill India Mission, Smart Cities Mission, Digital India Mission, Legislations on Undisclosed Foreign Income and Assets (Black Money), Demonetization of Currency Notes, Goods and Services Tax (GST) and so on. Raising the issue of the plight of the youth in Chandigarh, the City Member of Parliament (MP) in the Lok Sabha, Kirron Kher, today demanded that the centre should consider increasing the upper age limit for the jobs available with the Chandigarh Administration. See *The Tribune* (Chandigarh), 11 December 2015, accessed 16 November 2016, http://www.tribuneindia.com/news/chandigarh/community/increase-upper-age-limit-for-jobs-available-with-ut-admn-kirron-kher/169450.html

[38] Ashutosh Pandey, 'Crisis in Indian Democracy: Trends and issues', *South Asian Journal of Socio-Political Studies* XIV(1) (2013):11–17.

it comes to ensuring discipline and cohesion in policymaking. Further, party infl is only effective where the parties represent separate and distinct socio-economic and political ideology. In addition, the choice of policies can also be influenced wh opposition parties in the Parliament are taking a stand on national policy issues.

The mass memberships of the political parties are thus engaged in a largely supporting role. The party's rank and file mainly exists to support and serve their leaders. However, the rank-and-file support may be crucial for the success of a faction on issues of fundamental importance, such as the role of the state in the economy, foreign policy and taxation policy. Factionalism in the political parties creates problems for the party leadership when the party or parties in power is a coalition of different ideological viewpoints.

Conflict is also bound to take place among parties at the time of presentation and the passing of the budget at the central and state levels. The budget is identified as the product of the PM or Chief Minister and carries the label of his party. Often, parties have disagreed on certain aspects of bills (e.g. no-confidence motion against the Manmohan Singh government in the Parliament on the India–US civil nuclear cooperation in August 2008).

CONCLUSION

Considerable disagreement exists today within the political parties over the outcome of policy discussion and disputes.[39] Some observers argue that party candidates are keen on winning elections rather than on advancing policy choices. As such they have more to fear from the electorate than from the constituency organization which selects them as candidates. Others maintain that diminishing voter loyalty for a particular political party and the increasing role of the interest groups have helped to weaken parties as organizing agents of power. Regardless of their influencing powers, political parties still play a very important role in political life and, indeed, in placing policy issues on the public agenda at the local, state and national levels.

Review Questions

(i) Do you think policymaking is essentially a manifestation of power? Support your argument with examples.
(ii) Critically discuss the role of mass media as the 'fourth branch' of government.
(iii) Define pressure groups. Explain with suitable illustrations the role pressure groups may play in the public policymaking process.
(iv) Provide a classification of pressure groups as seen in the public policy space.
(v) Define political parties. How do you think political parties and leadership in India have affected the country's overall policies over the last two decades?

---

[39] For example, the Modi government's attempts to push through the GST Bill in the Rajya Sabha were stalled on 11 August 2015 by the Congress party. Earlier, the Land Acquisition Bill could not be taken up in the session of Parliament amid disruptions from the Congress party. See *The Tribune* (Chandigarh), 12 August 2015.

APTER **3**

CONSTITUTIONAL RULES AND POWER OF STATE ORGANS IN POLICYMAKING

INTRODUCTION

Policymaking is a complex and continuously changing process which is conditioned by a multitude of factors. It involves not only the interplay of numerous political, economic and social forces, but also the structure of power derived from the constitutional rules. Policymaking is a manifestation of power. In terms of public policy, it means the exercise of political power for making policy decisions (policies) relating to the people and their problems and needs. Public policy mainly comprises executive (government) decisions, parliamentary statutes, constitutional laws and judicial orders. Public policy reflects societal goals, and its breach warrants punishment in accordance with procedure established by law (in India) and due process of law (in the USA). Here, in this chapter, an attempt is made to discuss the constitutional rules and structure of power for policymaking in India.

CONSTITUTIONAL ARCHITECTURE FOR POLICYMAKING

The Constitution of India prescribes the rules as well as structure for policymaking at the central, state and local levels. Constitutionally, India has been described as a union of states,[1] but organized on federal lines, with jurisdiction of powers between the centre and the states and an independent judiciary to determine the constitutionality of actions of the legislature and the executive. Thus, rules for policymaking in government at the centre, state and local[2] are found partly in the Constitution and partly in those aspects of the political culture which prescribe how political activity should be carried on. Thus, the Constitution is the principal statute prescribing rules and provisions which specify how those in authority are to be recruited and how they are to use their official positions in making policies.

To appreciate the dynamics of public policymaking in India, we must first understand the constitutional architecture in which public policymaking occurs. Though many of its features have been imitated and adapted, constitutional system reflects four features which stand out most prominently.

---

[1] Predominantly, India is federal comprising 29 states and 7 UTs (2016).
[2] By the 73rd and 74th Constitution Amendments, local governments (panchayats and municipalities) have been given the constitutional status to function as institutions of local self-government.

Democratic and Republican Self-government

The Preamble—though by itself not enforceable but reflect the objects which the Constitution seeks to establish and promote—to the Indian Constitution envisages for the country not only a democratic form of government, but also a sovereign republic infused with the spirit of 'justice, liberty, equality and fraternity'. The Constitution declares India to be a democratic and sovereign republic. This means that all governments, whether central, state or local, derive their powers from the people. The people are sovereign. The sovereignty of the people has come to mean that the final authority which determines the policies for the country lies with the government at different levels. The elected representatives of the people form the government and hold office at the people's will.

The Indian system of government is fundamentally democratic. The requirement for it is that the wishes of the people are reflected in the policy decisions of governments. There are basically two requirements which must be fulfilled for a democratic system of government. Pickles states,

> It must, first, be able to elicit as accurately as possible the opinion of as many people as possible on who shall be their representatives and on how the country ought to be governed. Second, it must provide ways of ensuring that those chosen for the public do in fact do what the electorate wants them to do or that they can be replaced if they do not, even between elections.[3]

In India, the people may be thought to be politically sovereign, transmitting their will and opinion to the government. The people in a democratic set-up initiate the process of legislation and policymaking by voting for candidates whose opinions and intentions they know and understand. In India, the government is dependent on the support of the Parliament or the state legislature for its existence. Through the legislature, the representatives of the people frame laws and decide policy by majority vote. The outstanding feature of policymaking in government is characterized by accommodation and settlement of conflicting interests. Being a multiparty system, certain national policies are modified at times, as a result of discussion in Parliament. In determining policy, and in order to resolve conflicts on policy issues, majoritarianism is adopted because the alternative would be authoritarianism. However, the constitutional provisions and rules prevent any abuse of the powers which derive from a majority position. The courts in India further guard against the tyranny of the majority by providing for an impartial judiciary which will arbitrate free from any bias towards the interests of those in authority.

For instance, the SC on 21 July 2015 dismissed the centre's plea requesting it to review its verdict quashing the latter's decision to include Jats in the central Other Backward Classes (OBCs) list for reservation in jobs and higher education.[4] Similarly the SC struck down the 99th Constitution Amendment Act, 2014 and the National Judicial Appointments Commission (NJAC) Act, 2014 as unconstitutional on 16 October 2015.

---

[3] Pickles, *Democracy* 13.
[4] See *Hindustan Times* (Chandigarh), 22 July 2015.

Parliamentary Executive

Direct democracy being impossible, representative (indirect) democracy is the next alternative, for it entails the free choice of representatives by all adults through fair elections. The Indian system of government purports to be parliamentary type of executive both at the centre and in the states. In this system, the real executive power of the government is to be exercised by the Council of Ministers comprising the leadership of the political party or parties holding a majority in the legislature and collectively responsible to it in its working. The following are the distinctive features of a parliamentary executive:

(i) All ministers are members of one or the other house of Parliament. They hold office at the pleasure of the President.

(ii) The government, both at the centre and in the states, is responsible for its actions to the respective legislature. Responsibility refers to both the collective actions of the government and the acts and omissions of individual ministers and their departments. Governments are answerable to the legislature and must resign if their policies prove unacceptable, or if they lose the confidence of the legislature. Under the concept of individual responsibility, ministers are required to answer for their own acts and the conduct of their departments. That is, if a minister or civil servant makes an error, it is the minister who is answerable to the legislature and should resign from the office if found guilty. The link between representative and responsible government is to be found in the fact that the accountability of the executive to the legislature ensures that the government is both responsive and respectable.[5]

(iii) In a parliamentary form of government, civil servants are required to observe the principles of political neutrality, impartiality and anonymity. Responsible government is designed to prevent democracy from falling prey to an over-dominant bureaucracy. It presupposes that politicians, not civil servants, are to be blamed for executive action.

Federally Organized Polity

The Indian constitutional system has been devised in such a way as to reflect not only unitary but also striking federal features. The federal structure of the polity is divided into states and union territories (UTs).[6] The parliamentary democracy combines broadly a unitary form of government with a dominant central government with many federal features containing a large area of governmental autonomy and even a degree of independence to the states of Indian Union. A conscious effort has been made to define and demarcate clearly the areas of policy formulation between the central government and state governments by listing subjects in the union list (entries increased from 97 to 100), the state list (entries decreased from 66 to 61) and the concurrent list (entries increased from 47 to 52).[7] All residuary powers are vested in the union government. If the Parliament enacts a law on the entry (subject) under the concurrent list, the states are debarred from entering that

---

[5] A. H. Birch, *Representative and Responsible Government* (London: Allen & Unwin, 1964), 21.
[6] The Indian Union consists of 29 states and 7 UTs (2016). The word 'federation' does not figure in the Constitution, although the Supreme Court characterized the Indian polity as federal.
[7] The distribution of legislative power is done under Articles 245 and 246 read with the Seventh Schedule of the Constitution.

field. However, in a situation of dispute between the central and state governments, the matter is decided by the SC.

The framers of the Indian Constitution created a strong national government. Parliament is authorized under Article 249 to enact legislation on any subject in the state list and under Article 312 to create new all-India services, provided the Rajya Sabha by a two-third majority empowers it to do so. Again, Articles 256 and 257 place a state government under an obligation to comply with the union laws and directions issued by the central government. Articles 200 and 201 empower the Governor of a state to reserve a bill passed by the state legislature for the consideration of the President who has the power to veto it without giving any reasons. Under Article 253, Parliament may enact a law to give effect to international treaties even though the subject falls in the state list.

The powers of the central government become far-reaching in situations of emergency. The union can virtually function as a unitary state when

(i) the security of the country is threatened,
(ii) there is a failure of the constitutional machinery in a state or
(iii) there is a threat to the financial stability of any state.

Where the President's rule is imposed in any state under Article 356, the Parliament gets the power to exercise the legislative powers of the state.

Further, under Article 3, the Parliament can also form a new state, increase or diminish its area.[8] Constitutional rules regarding the appointment and certain conditions of services of officers of All India Services, serving the state governments, the judges of the state High Courts and the Comptroller and Auditor General (CAG) of India, auditing the accounts of the state governments, favour the unitary features of the polity.

The central government has enjoyed wide powers for the formulation of policies in the development sectors of the economy. In many cases, the implementation of the programmes and policies involves both the union and the state governments and the two have to jointly share responsibility for results. The central government often subsidizes many schemes (e.g. of the 27 centrally sponsored schemes [CSS], the centre funds fully 10 and provides 60% of the funds for the 17 others) and has used the concurrent list to develop many new administrative institutions in respect of agriculture, social welfare and community development, and many other programmes. Thus, the process of policymaking has to contend with the federal form of the country's polity. In a federal set-up, the intergovernmental relations (IGR) gain wide significance in policymaking (see Figure 3.1).

Socio-economic Philosophy

For the socio-economic philosophy underlying our Constitution, Dr Radhakrishnan once said, 'Poor people who wander about, find no work, no wages and starve, whose lives

---

[8] Thus, Hyderabad and Madhya Bharat were abolished. In the year 2000, three new states were formed, namely, Chhattisgarh, Uttarakhand and Jharkhand. Telangana became the 29th state of India in 2013. The process of territorial change does not require special majority in Parliament or consent of the states.

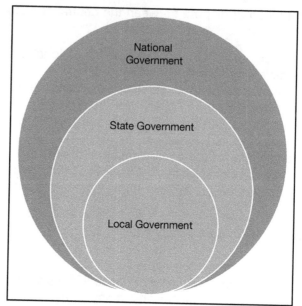

■ Figure 3.1: Structure of Policymaking in IGR Context (India)
Source: Author's own.
Distribution of Legislative Powers
Union Government List = 100 entries
State Government List = 61 entries
Concurrent (Union/States) List = 52 entries
Local Government List = 47 entries
(i) Panchayats = 29 entries
(ii) Municipalities = 18 entries

are a continual round of sore affliction and pinching poverty, cannot be proud of the Constitution or its law'.[9]

The Constitution enunciated the basic principles of the State and its structure and included a detailed description of the political and other institutions to be established. Public policies must conform to the provisions of the Indian Constitution, such as those laid down in the Preamble, the Fundamental Rights and the Directive Principles of the State Policy. The Preamble declared India to be a sovereign, socialist, secular, democratic republic securing to all its citizens justice, equality and liberty.[10] The Directive Principles of State Policy indicates, inter alia, that India must be a welfare state, whose economic, social and welfare aspects should form part of the governance of the state. Among other directives, the State shall direct its policy towards securing 39 '(a) that the citizen, men and women equally, have the right to an adequate means of livelihood; (b) that the ownership and control of the material resources of the community are so distributed as best to subserve the common good; and (c) that the operation of the economic system does not result in the concentration of wealth and means of production to the common detriment; (d) that there is equal

---

[9] Speech of the Vice President at the Seminar on Parliamentary Democracy, 25 February 1956.
[10] Words 'socialist', 'secular' and 'integrity' were inserted by the Constitution (42nd Amendment) Act, 1976 in the Preamble.

pay for equal work for both men and women; (e) that the health and strength of workers and the tender age of children are not abused and that citizens are not forced by economic necessity to enter avocations unsuited to their age or strength; and (f) that childhood and youth are protected against exploitation and against moral and material abandonment'.[11]

Although these directives were described as fundamental in governing the country and it was the duty of the state to apply them in making laws, they were not the source of legislative powers but only their political justification. Fundamental Rights and Duties and Directive Principles have been the subject of public debates and disputes among the political parties regarding their importance and place in the Indian polity. The current judicial thinking is that the Fundamental Rights and the Directive Principles are complementary to each other, since they are mutually reinforcing in nature. Now both levels of government are under an obligation to formulate public policies, taking into account the Directive Principles.

PRINCIPAL ORGANS OF THE STATE POWER

Policymaking cannot be properly understood apart from the environment in which it is conditioned. Demands for policy actions are made on the political system by various constituents of the society—civil society groups, citizens, pressure groups, political parties and so on. At the same time, the environment places constraints upon what can be done by policymakers. Included in the environment are geographical characteristics such as natural resources and topography; demographic factors such as population size, age and sex; and other socio-politico-economic variables. Our discussion here focuses on the government organs of the state that shape policymaking in government. Principal organs of the state—legislature, executive, judiciary—draw their strength and powers from the Constitution. The Constitution itself empowers Parliament to supplement the provisions of the Constitution by legislation. But the Parliament or Executive may exercise power much more than what is suggested in the Constitution. The Indian Judiciary sits over the wisdom of any legislative policy or executive action.

Power in Legislature

The Indian Constitution, as has been explained in this chapter, has adopted the parliamentary form of democracy, also called the Westminster system, which affects a harmonious blending of the legislative and executive organs of the state. People are the sovereign. The sovereignty of the people is exercised through legislature elected on adult franchise with a Council of Ministers both at the centre and in the state, collectively responsible to it in its working. In law and constitutional theory, the Parliament in India[12] or in England and the Congress in the USA are supreme public policymaking bodies. They are at the heart of public policymaking. Indeed, in a parliamentary form of government, the legislature reigns supreme because the PM is dependent on support from a parliamentary majority to

---

[11] Article 39 (f) was substituted by the Constitution (42nd Amendment) Act, 1976. Other changes included insertion of Article 51A with 10 fundamental duties.
[12] The Parliament of India consists of the President and two Houses (the House of the People, *Lok Sabha* and the Council of States, *Rajya Sabha*). See Article 79.

remain in office. Wade and Phillips observe, 'Neither devolution nor delegation of legislative authority infringes the supremacy of (the British) Parliament'.[13]

Government powers are, in theory, shared among three branches of government. The Parliament makes the laws and legitimizes the decisions of the government. It authorizes taxation and expenditure and makes the government accountable for financial decisions. In addition to its legal role, it subjects administrative actions to criticism and scrutiny. It serves as a forum for public debate on issues of public policies, besides a forum for the expression of complaints and grievances. The parliamentary power enhances further as fewer votes are made into votes of confidence, over which a government can fail. When a vote is not a vote of confidence, individual MPs have greater freedom to vote without threatening the continuation of their government. The parliamentary systems in Germany and the UK as well as India work somewhat along these lines. No court in England since the 17th century has struck down an Act of Parliament for violating some fundamental principle.

Law-making power resides in the elected members in the Parliament.[14] Within the powers devolved to them by the Constitution, the Parliament is the final determinant of policy. Thus in law and constitutional theory, the power of the Parliament is unlimited in democratic systems. On the other hand, the Congress in the USA has less power than a Parliament, because it does not participate in the process of choosing the head of the executive branch. Moreover, the Constitution of the USA prohibits legislators from holding positions in the executive. For example, the officials of the President's Cabinet, unlike the Cabinet in the parliamentary system, may not be members of the Congress.

Parliamentary Realities

It is now widely recognized that the power of the Parliament in policymaking is more real in a legalistic sense than in terms of practical policies. In reality it does not reign supreme. The Council of Ministers, including the Cabinet and the Prime Minister, become representatives and leaders of the parliamentary majority. They are assured a legislative majority for the proposals they present. The Prime Minister or other Cabinet members initiate policy proposals and use the resources of government ministries to do so. There is thus the likelihood of Parliament being described merely as a rubber stamp. It is described as a 'forum for influence not direct power, advice not command, criticism not obstruction, scrutiny not initiative, and publicity not secrecy'.[15]

However, in practice, the Indian Parliament or Congress in the USA does not gain apparent ascendancy over the executive. Any control which Parliament might be said to exercise over the executive is apparently indirect, inducing responsibility under the threat of exposure. It does not determine policies except in a legal and constitutional sense. The concept of legislative power has been formulated as a response to the political reality of executive dominance reinforced by the party system.

---

[13] E.C.S. Wade and G.G. Phillips, *Constitutional Law* (London: Longman, 1960). 49.
[14] In India, power of the Parliament (state legislature) is constrained by the judicial review exercised by the Supreme Court (Article 32) and High Courts (Article 226).
[15] United Kingdom, *Study of Parliament Group Memorandum to the Select Committee on Procedure, Fourth Report*, 1964–5 Session H.C. 393 (HMSO, 1965), 139.

As common in parliamentary countries in Europe also, much of the legislation in India and USA is now prepared within the executive branch and introduced by a minister in India or the President in America. But, if the President or a minister proposes, the Parliament/Congress still disposes. Consequently, the role of Parliament in India in policymaking can be more correctly understood if Parliament is considered to be a constitutional procedural device for legitimizing the decisions of the government, rather than as an independent decision or policymaking unit. The passing of the Taxation Laws (Second Amendment) Bill, 2016 by the Parliament in India in the face of stiff nationwide opposition is an example of the executive-controlled status of the elected body, that is, the Parliament, like the Nuclear Act, NJAC Act, 2014 was passed by Parliament with near-unanimity (although this Act was struck down by the SC on 16 October 2015 as unconstitutional). As such, power does not reside in Parliament, but in the group of individuals (executive members) who at a particular time gain ascendancy over its procedures, thereby succeeding in making policy decisions. When Council of Ministers, headed by the Prime Minister, is selected by a parliamentary majority of the same party, automatic approval of the policy decisions or proposals becomes possible. Having been elected, the PM and the Council of Ministers are then able to create majority within the Parliament with varying degrees of support from outside the Parliament.

Again, it must be emphasized that it is not the strength or weakness of the Parliament which is crucial to the policymaking process. What is crucial is the creation of alliances beforehand between different parliamentary groups or committees to influence legislation or policy decisions. The government usually does not depend on the support of the opposition. It has, however, to rely on the backbenchers to provide it with the majority necessary to conduct government business. Hence the government is more afraid of its own backbenchers than the opposition members. It fears that its own backbenchers may form a majority in the opposition division lobby. Then, there is also the need to maintain the support and morale of the majority party. When a government is confronted with the prospect of rebellion from its backbenchers, constant attention is paid to them through whips and party committees. Excessive conflict has to be resolved more by compromise on both sides than by expulsion or the threat of dissolution.[16] However, it has been observed that most MPs would rather see their party in power than the opposition, even when they disagree with the leadership on particular policy decisions. The discipline which gives the parties their cohesion is more often self-imposed than enforced on frightened and reluctant backbenchers by the whips. Whatever its cause, however, the party unity and discipline are usually real enough to reinforce the power of the government. The convention of the majority party government also enables the leaders of the party to assure themselves of a legislative majority for the proposals they present. In many cases, it is observed that Bills on a new policy are not approved by the Parliament because of certain flaws in the Bills and protests from certain sections of the community. Since 1834, some 6,612 central statutes have been enacted. At some point or the other, 3,831 have been repealed. Of the remaining 2,781 central statutes (in October 2014), the Ramanujan Committee (set up

---

[16] For example, when the Dravida Munnetra Kazhagam (DMK) chief M. Karunanidhi threatened to snap ties with the United Progressive Alliance (UPA) (the Manmohan Singh government) over the resolution seeking an international probe into 'genocide' by Sri Lankan troops against Tamils in the last phase of the anti-Liberation Tigers of Tamil Eelam (LTTE) war (2009), the UPA rushed three central senior ministers to pacify the chief. See *The Tribune*, 19 March 2013.

in September 2014) identified 1,741 Central Acts for repeal.[17] The Parliament on 27 April 2016 passed two bills repealing 1,053 old laws which had become redundant legislations.

The power vested in Parliament or Congress must become decentralized if it is to give due weightage to policy proposals. To be able to discuss these genuinely, it needs to develop expertise about the issues involved in proposals. Hence is need of the decentralization of parliamentary power to various committees. The idea for legislative committees actually came from the British parliament, but in England, the committees atrophied with the growth of the cabinet government.[18] Once parliamentary committees have been set up to allow more expert consideration of proposals, the Parliament will show a reasonable degree of deference towards the committees' decisions. Thus the committees are crucial in determining the fate of legislation. In the USA, the power of the Congress is decentralized to the level of the individual member, permitting him to introduce a bill. On the contrary, in countries with a parliamentary form of government, bills are generally introduced by the cabinet ministers. In contrast to the Congress which give genuine consideration to many law proposals, most Parliaments rarely consider proposals that are too new, too vague or have too little political support. In a parliamentary system, ideas, however, must incubate within the executive branch.

Apart from decentralization, to increase the workload would mean giving legislators less time to consider the content of the policy proposals on which they must vote.[19] Most legislators in India do not, however, spend much time doing research and reading about legislation. When they have to decide quickly, they are more likely to take cues from colleagues who sit on the committee in the policy area in which a vote is taking place. Increasing time pressures and loads on legislators make them harried and further increase the power of committee members over bills in their policy areas.

It may also be pointed out that legislators who would be policymakers are bedevilled by the exacting demands of other roles. As representatives they must be responsive to their constituents' requests. If they are interested in re-election, legislators will spend much of their time appearing at countless public functions in their constituencies. Such visits and

---

[17] See The Financial Express (Chandigarh), 22 July 2015. Similarly in March (2015), there were more than 70 Bills pending for 2–15 years before the Indian Parliament. These include 'Communal Violence (Prevention, Control and Rehabilitation of Victims) Bill, 2005'; the Code of Criminal Procedure (CrPC) was proposed to be amended in 2006; a bill to bring about the 103rd Amendment to the Constitution has been pending since December 2004; Pension (Regulations) Bill, 2005; Amendment to the Land Acquisition Act, 2013; Benami Transaction (Prohibition) Act, 1988; and so on. In contrast, the Commercial Courts Bill, the SC/ST Amendment Bill, Atomic Energy Bill and the Arbitration Bill got five minutes a piece before getting passed on 23 December 2015 by the Rajya Sabha (See The Financial Express, 24 December 2015).

[18] Wilfred E. Binkley, President and Congress, 3rd ed. (New York, NY: Vintage Books, 1962), 50.

[19] For example, the Defamation Bill was introduced in the Lok Sabha on 29 August 1988, and the members were given just half an hour to table amendments. It was passed on the same day despite the staging of a walkout by the entire opposition except All India Anna Dravida Munnetra Kazhagam (AIADMK) members in the Lok Sabha. Similarly, the Parliament on 23 December 2008 passed nine vital legislations in a span of 17 minutes without any discussion. Four bills passed in the Lok Sabha were not even listed for the day, forcing a walkout by the Left parties. Enraged by government's 'casual' attitude towards important legislations, the Left later boycotted the closing ceremony, marking its adjournment sine die.

meetings strengthen the connection between policy choices and electoral choices in the minds of voters.

Conclusion

The role of Parliament in policymaking is thus understood as a procedural device for legitimizing decisions. Moreover, in a parliamentary type of executive, a mass of legislation is made under the powers delegated to the ministers by parent statutes for reasons of pressure on parliamentary time, the technical quality of much legislation and the need for sufficient time to develop adequate administrative machinery. Only a small proportion of statutory instruments receive any parliamentary scrutiny at all, although what there is can be relatively effective. In reality, the bulk of delegated legislation in India seems to be treated by most legislators with complacent indifference. Also many policies approved by the Parliament are initiated by the members of Cabinet or Council of Ministers, having been planned within the departments of state after consultation with affected interests. Legislatures everywhere play a little role in the policymaking process. Rather, it is the ability of politicians to create majorities within the legislature which is of significance to the policymaking process.

Power Within the Executive

The Constitution in many of the countries creates powerful executive to carry on the administration of the affairs of the state (excepting legislative and judicial functions and functions which are vested by the Constitution in any other authority). The ambit of the executive power has been thus explained by the SC of India:

> The executive function comprises both the determination of the policy as well as carrying it into execution, the maintenance of order, the promotion of social and economic welfare, the direction of foreign policy, in fact, the carrying on or supervision of the general administration of the State.[20]

The Union Executive consists mainly of (i) the President or the King/Queen (in India, the President/Governor being head of the State exercises his powers on the advice of the Council of Ministers under Article 74 of the Indian Constitution), (ii) the Council of Ministers (comprising the leadership of the political parties holding a majority in the legislature)[21] and (iii) the services (government servants to assist the Council of Ministers in the discharge of its functions). The Council of Ministers shall be collectively responsible to the House of the People.[22]

In government, office-holders, who have the right to make policy decisions and expect them to be obeyed, are the members of the Cabinet. This system, it was believed, would provide competent leadership to the legislature in all matters—legislation, policy

---

[20] Ram Jawaya versus State of Punjab, 1955 (2) SCR 225, pp. 238–9.
[21] With the enactment of the 91st Amendment Act in 2003, the total number of the ministers including the PM shall not exceed 15 per cent of the total number of members of the Lok Sabha.
[22] The principle of collective responsibility is codified in Article 75 (3) of the Constitution.

enunciation, finance and so forth. Thus, executive plays an important role in the policy-making process.

Sources of Executive Power

Before investigating the role of the executive, especially the Cabinet in policymaking, it would be worthwhile to analyse the sources of its power.

Power is partly a function of authority. Authority may be created by a legal office. First source of executive power lies in the support of a legislative majority. Government can in most cases depend on its backbenchers to provide it with the majority required to conduct government business. Support is usually extended (despite the sanction of whips and the threats of the withdrawal of party support), because most members of the legislature prefer to see their party in power than the opposition, even they disagree with the leadership on particular policy issues.[23] The discipline which gives party cohesion, in fact, reinforces the power of the government.

The second source of power is unity among the Council of Ministers. The vast majority of policies approved or sanctioned by the legislature are initiated by the Cabinet members having been planned within the secretariat and department concerned after consultation with affected interests (including the civil society organizations). The process of consultation and planning which takes place within the departments or secretariat when a bill on policy is being drafted and prepared gives government proposals an authority which cannot be matched by backbenchers or opposition criticism and charges. Many amendments which are of a relatively minor and technical nature, of course, are made to government bills by backbenchers working in standing committees. Successful amendments tend to be introduced by the government itself after having been considered by the Cabinet.[24] Thus, even successful amendments which originate with the opposition succeed because these are agreed to by the minister concerned and not because these are forced on an unwilling government.[25] Such concessions are more likely to be made on less partisan policies than on legislation which is based on ideological lines. In the event of concessions being forcefully obtained by party alliances in committee, they need to be similarly supported in the Parliament as a whole.

Third, the Cabinet is able to control and coordinate the work of the executive. The vast majority of policy decisions are made by ministers and secretaries under delegated

---

[23] Leader of the House in the Rajya Sabha Arun Jaitley defended the External Affairs Minister Sushma Swaraj by asking the opposition to 'point out one provision of the laws she had violated in trying to help Lalit Modi'. He sought to turn the tables on the Congress referring to allegations of financial irregularities against its CMs in Himachal Pradesh, Puducherry and Kerala. See *The Tribune* (Chandigarh), 23 July 2015.

[24] The Anti-Rape Bill which was passed by the Lok Sabha on 19 March 2013 and by the Rajya Sabha on 21 March 2013 replaced an ordinance promulgated on 3 February 2013 is now called the Criminal Law (Amendment) Act, 2013.

[25] Consequent upon the Supreme Court's order (10 April 2008) allowing the implementation of Central Educational Institutions Act, 2006 for 27 per cent reservation to OBCs, minus the creamy layer, the Union Cabinet on 3 October 2008 approved 80 per cent raise in the income ceilings from ₹2.5 lakh per year fixed in 2004 to ₹4.5 lakh year (2008). This was seen to pacify Congress allies (LJP, RJD, DMK and PMK) and to expand the voter base ahead of general and assembly elections.

powers. Only a small proportion of statutory instruments receive any parliamentary review and investigation at all, implying that the ministers stand in a powerful position. Each minister has the responsibility to instruct his department for departmental action.

Fourth, the leaders of the majority party who form the government tend to adopt consensus-oriented policies. Consequently, there is a little criticism by the backbenchers. The government, of course, could rely on the support of the opposition. For example, potential coalitions in the Lok Sabha and in the committee were in evidence on the US–India civilian nuclear agreement (2008).[26] Similarly, agreement reached between Japan and India on 12 December 2015 for cooperation in the Peaceful Uses of Nuclear Energy will have to withstand the scrutiny of Diet (Parliament) and parliamentary approval before two countries go ahead with the implementation side of the deal.

Power Within the Cabinet

The influence of what Lindblom calls the 'proximate' policymakers,[27] or those who occupy formal offices prescribed by the political community as authoritative, is of critical importance. In government, the office-holders who are immediate or proximate policymakers are the members of the Cabinet. The Cabinet is a relatively small body consisting only of the Cabinet ministers and the PM.

The broad theoretical framework of cabinet government in India is derived from the British model. The Cabinet in India acts as a collective body where ministers take an integrated decision. Generally speaking, it meets frequently (at least once in a week) and acts as a decision-making body on broad policy outlines as well as specific matters related to it. It is the constitutional task of the executive to decide the policies which are to be submitted to Parliament. The real executive is the Council of Ministers consisting of the PM, Cabinet ministers, MoS and the Deputy ministers. It is well known that the Council itself hardly meets, and all the policy functions are performed by the Cabinet, functioning on the principle of unity. It is the top policymaking body in the government, but only major proposals are taken to it for its decision; other matters of less significance are disposed of by the minister concerned.

For facilitating its work, the business rules provide for the constitution of standing committees of the Cabinet to ensure speedy decisions on issues of national importance and other vital matters.[28] The numbers as well as the tasks for which the Cabinet committees are appointed vary, and occasionally, *ad hoc* committees are appointed for specific purposes. Two Cabinet committees, namely, the Political Affairs Committee and the Economic Affairs Committee, both presided over by the PM, are of great importance.

---

[26] On 11 October 2008, the US–India civilian nuclear agreement was signed between India and USA. See also *The Tribune* (Chandigarh), 13 December 2015.

[27] Lindblom, *The Policy-making Process*, 30.

[28] For example, on 19 March 2013, the Union Cabinet cleared the Food Security Bill (originally introduced in Parliament in December 2011) incorporating 55 Amendments as suggested by the Standing Committee of Parliament on Food (which submitted its report in January 2013). This act of the government was seen as a major plank of the Congress party for the general election in 2014. Other examples include GST (Bill), Land Acquisition Bill and Uniform Civil Code.

The Cabinet is serviced in its policy role by the 'cabinet secretariat' headed by the Cabinet Secretary, who attends all the meetings of the Cabinet and its committees. The Cabinet Secretary often prepares the agenda for cabinet meetings, takes minutes, circulates decisions and follows them up to see that action has been taken in departments. In the policymaking process, the role of the Cabinet Secretary is critically important.

Power of the PM and PMO

Though formally all executive powers are vested in the President (India), he acts as the constitutional head of the Executive such as the British Crown, acting on the advice of the Council of Ministers with the PM at the head (Article 74(1)) responsible to the House of the People (Lok Sabha). Article 75(1) of the Indian Constitution provides that the PM shall be selected by the President and the other ministers shall be appointed and removed by the President on the advice of the PM.

Within the Council of Ministers, in general, and the Cabinet, in particular, the PM enjoys a special attention in the realm of policymaking. The PM is thought to exercise control over the Cabinet decision-making process. In areas of external affairs, defence and economic affairs, he takes a personal interest. But the Cabinet as a whole has to be persuaded of the rightness of most decisions. In other areas of policy, especially domestic, where he rarely takes the initiative, his views in the Cabinet will be of vital significance. It is, there-fore, correct to say that Cabinet decisions are taken by the PM together with the respon-sible ministers. However, this is not always true. While the PM can exert exceptional influence over policy decisions through the assistance of the Cabinet Secretariat, it is now widely accepted that a PM has to obtain the support of his colleagues for his decisions and cannot obstruct a discussion on matters which a minister wishes to bring before the Cabinet. A PM who habitually ignores the Cabinet colleagues can be overruled by them and even driven from the office.

The PM is assisted by his office which was set up in 1947. Since June 1977, PM's Secretariat is known as the PMO and is headed by the Secretary to the PM who is now designated as the Principal Secretary. The PMO consists of the immediate staff of PM as well as multiple levels of support staff. It advises the PM on matters of importance and follow-up issues as necessary. Its responsibilities include dealing with papers that are received in it, preparing notes on various issues, contacting ministers concerned and handling such matters which require the attention of the PM. Although the PMO has been performing most of the important functions, including developing policy alternatives, all Cabinet matters must go through the Cabinet Secretariat. The Cabinet Secretary also briefs the PM personally. The interaction between the PM and his colleagues, the role of the Cabinet Secretariat and the PMO and the usefulness of the Cabinet committees, respectively, depend on the personal style of the PM and the political strength of the ruling party. An instance of the image and style of the functioning of former PM Manmohan Singh can be given. A newspaper editorial states that Singh may have presided over bad policy, '… it may be but Singh's tragedy that he knew auction was a better policy than allocation ensuring higher revenues and forestalling favours but couldn't push it through. Arbitrariness was the hallmark of captive mining allocations. The cost of this arbitrariness became glaring during the economic boom years'. It further adds that the debacle of the

UPA 'at last year's hustings made clear was that arbitrary, opaque policies are now electorally unaffordable in addition to being economically costly'.[29]

In conclusion, it may be briefed that the real business of policy decision in the government takes place in Cabinet committees rather than the full Cabinet and that vast majority of policies sanctioned by the Parliament are initiated by the responsible ministers in consultation with the PM after having been planned within the departments in consultation with the affected interests.

Power of the Judiciary

In India, there is a unified judicial system unlike in the USA where double system of courts exists. In the hierarchy of courts, which administer both central and state laws, there is the SC (Articles 124–147) at the apex, High Courts of the different states and UTs (Articles 214–232), subordinate courts (Articles 233–237) and panchayat courts (set up under the state legislation).

Unlike the British judiciary which is highly politicized by the absence of a clear separation of powers,[30] the Indian and American judiciary shares its supremacy with the legislature of the state. In India and the USA, where the separation of powers is institutionalized to a larger extent than in Britain, the Constitution entitles the SC to exercise judicial review.

The power of judicial review is inherent in Articles 32, 226 and 227 of the Indian Constitution. Judicial review is a necessary concomitant of Fundamental Rights. The judicial review is the power of the judicial courts to determine the constitutionality of actions of the legislature and executive and declare them *null* and *void* if such actions do not conform to the constitutionality of a legislative act.

The judicial courts, generally speaking, do not interfere with the policy matters of the legislature or executive (e.g. centres policy decision on demonetization of high currency notes on 8 November 2016) unless the policy is against the Constitution. But, of late, courts, notably the SC, greatly affected the content of public policy through the exercise of the powers of judicial review of legislation. The judiciary in India plays a constructive role in shaping and influencing public policies in two ways: by its power of judicial review and judicial decisions.

Judicial review has become the most important expression of the country's commitment to constitutional government. The Constitution entitles the SC, and the High Courts at the state levels, to exercise a judicial review of legislation. Through the power of judicial review, the courts determine the constitutionality of legislative and administrative actions. If such actions are found to be in conflict with the constitutional provisions, the courts can declare them *null* and *void*. They are not only specifying the government's limits with regard to certain actions, but also stating what it must do for the public interest.

---

[29] See *The Times of India* (New Delhi), 'Editorial', 12 March 2015.

[30] The British courts accept the sovereignty of Parliament. The country's most senior judge, the Lord Chancellor, is both a member of the Cabinet and Speaker of the Upper House of the Legislature. In India, the Supreme Court in various cases rules that separation of powers is a basic feature of the Constitution.

For example, the SC on 15 July 2015 asked the central government to revisit its new National Pharmaceutical Pricing Policy, 2012 for fixing prices of essential medicines in the country and also the DPCO, notified in May 2013.[31]

In all democratic countries, judiciary by virtue of its constitutional status plays a significant role in the policymaking process. Courts are approached to interpret and decide the meaning of legislative provision that are often vaguely stated and contain conflicting interpretations. In a public interest litigation (PIL) by the National Human Rights Commission (NHRC) for a directive to the centre to submit proper inquiry reports in cases of death of persons at the hands of Army personnel, the SC said, 'We cannot direct the government to do something which is not contained in the statute' (Protection of Human Rights Act, 1993).[32] Similarly, the SC on 7 December 2015 refused to entertain a PIL plea for directing Parliament to enact a Uniform Civil Code.

The power of the judiciary to make policy is inherent in the judicial function in any democratic polity. This is largely due to the following explanations: In the first place, it is contended that there exists in a democratic polity a significant body of judge-made 'common laws' rules that have grown alongside legislative laws and acts. The courts determine rules for what constitutes criminal conduct. The courts also interpret the language of the laws the legislature has passed. They may also lay down the requirements that they may determine to be demanded by a law.[33] They may also decide upon the constitutional limitation. In Indira Gandhi versus Raj Narain (1975), for example, separation of power was treated as a basic structure of the Constitution.

Second, the judicial review is important because it assures that all public policy is justifiable. Here the SC has the power of judicial review for administrative bodies. The decisions of administrative tribunals, whether in adjudication, individual cases of rule-making decisions of general applicability, may be appealed against them to the High Court or SC in India.[34] The decision of the court can have significant impacts on the future decisions of administrative bodies. By contrast, as Walter Bagehot once wrote, 'There is nothing the British parliament cannot do except transform a man into a woman and woman into a man'.[35] In England, judges cannot test the validity of parliamentary enactment against some higher norm in contrast to the US SC justices who 'regularly test the validity of legislation against constitutional standards of which they are the guardians'.[36] But in the USA and India, judicial review of administrative decisions has been an established fact. The courts can strike down the administrative actions, which are not in accordance with authorizing legislation. For example, the SC on 14 October 2008 directed the government

---

[31] See *The Financial Express* (Chandigarh), 16 July 2015.

[32] See *The Tribune* (Chandigarh), 14 May 2015 and 8 December 2015.

[33] For example, in order to protect women against gender discrimination and social exploitation, the High Court in Himachal Pradesh said that women belonging to the tribal areas of the state will inherit property under the Hindu Succession Act, 1956 and not as per customs and usages. See *The Tribune*, 26 June 2015.

[34] Article 136 of the Indian Constitution empowers the Supreme Court to hear an appeal by special leave from any order or determination of tribunal.

[35] Quoted from Henry J. Abraham, *The Judicial Process* (New York, NY: Oxford University Press, 1980), 311.

[36] F.L. Morrison, *Courts and the Political Process in England* (London: SAGE Publications, 1973), 97.

to fill vacant OBC seats by 31 October in Indian Institutes of Technology (IITs), Indian Institutes of Management (IIMs) and other centrally run higher educational institutions with eligible students from the general category.[37] The five-judge Constitution Bench, headed by Chief Justice K.G. Balakrishnan, also observed that the government was trying to benefit the 'cream out of the creamy layer' by raising the income ceiling to ₹4.5 lakh a year for OBC families for availing the 27 per cent quota for OBC students. The court clarified that the cut-off marks for the OBC candidates for admission cannot be beyond 10 per cent less than that of the general category. This is clearly a step towards social justice, and also the SC does not want central educational institutions, including the IITs and IIMs, to dilute the merit.

Third, the courts play a passive role of interpreting the law rather than becoming involved in political matters. They may not take the initiative. Law suits are placed before the courts in specific and particularized form. The demands made by the litigants and the rules of the judicial process determine the manner in which the problem is presented to the court. A person seeking to invoke the power of the courts must show direct legal injury and must have exhausted all administrative remedies before a judge will listen to the case. The judge must take that particular set of facts and make a decision that will resolve the immediate problem. If the decision is accepted by other judges, the judge has made a policy for all jurisdictions in which that view prevails. For instance, the right of the female employees not to be sexually harassed at the workplaces as in the case of Vishaka versus State of Rajasthan (1997) became a court-made policy.[38] In fact, the SC meant the decision to have general application in all public and private organizations. If the judge does not decide, a policy choice cannot be made because it leaves the status quo intact. However, he is constrained not only by precedent, but also by constitutional requirements and legislative action. For example, the SC ruled that dismissal of a government servant for committing bigamy was neither 'shockingly disproportionate nor unconstitutional'.[39]

It is noted that the judiciary in democratic systems has played a major role in the formation of social and economic policies. Much of the law relating to matters such as equal protection of law, property ownership, employer–employee relationships and the position of women in society have been developed and applied by the courts in the shape of common law. Judges pronounce judgements on social and economic areas which have a wider policy implication. In this context, Anderson observes, 'Not only are the courts getting involved but they are playing a more positive role in policy formation, specifying not only what government cannot do but also what it must do to meet legal or constitutional obligations'.[40] Although the courts in other countries such as Australia, Canada, Japan and West Germany have some power of judicial review, their impact on policy has been much less than the SC of the USA. This is because the American SC has formal authority in many areas not usual in other countries. In the case of India, the relative importance of the SC and the High Courts has been increasing. The Indian courts have become increasingly involved in prescribing specific policies in economic and social areas.

---

[37] See *The Tribune* (Chandigarh), 15 October 2008 and 20 August 2011.
[38] 1997 (6), SCC 241.
[39] See *The Tribune* (Chandigarh), 10 February 2015.
[40] Anderson, *Public Policy-making*, 41.

There are some areas in which judicial decision-making does contribute to the formulation of public policies. The elements of this complexity are as follows: First, a degree of independence is secured for the judiciary by the constitutional rules, for example, judges' salaries (charged upon the Consolidated Fund, i.e. salaries are not open to discussion by the legislature), service conditions and dismissal procedure (under Judges Inquiry Act, 1968). Judges have been appointed until retirement and can only be dismissed by resolution of both Houses of Parliament. Such action has never taken.[41] Judges are also protected from legal action in their administration of justice so that it may be carried out without fear and favour. Second, the judiciary is expected to function as an independent arbiter in a parliamentary democracy. Its role is to administer the law when conflicts arise in a neutral and impartial way.

The judiciary in India is now under severe attacks for its slow pace in deciding the cases. In many incidents, people have taken the law into their own hands. Although the country's judicial system is based on the Anglo-Saxon legal tradition, the process of delivery of justice to the common person is long and tortuous. Of the 3 crore cases pending in courts, 62,794 are in the SC, 45 lakh in 24 High Courts and a whopping 2.7 crore in lower courts. 'Some of the major reasons for the high pendency of cases in subordinate courts are the poor judge–population ratio, prolonged and costly litigation caused by procedures and lawyers' interests, poor infrastructure, shortage of judicial personnel and weak alternative dispute resolution mechanisms', the Standing Committee on Law and Personnel, in its report on 'Infrastructure Development and Strengthening of Subordinate Courts', stated.[42]

Concerned over alarming backlog and to ensure expeditious disposal of cases, Chief Justice of India (CJI) H.L. Dattu had asked the chief justices of all high courts to look into the dockets of cases pending for five or more years in subordinate judiciary of all states. The CJI has set up a special 'social justice bench' to deal with the situation besides emphasizing on the disposal of petty, compoundable (cases which can be compromised) criminal matters and other civil disputes through Lok Adalats as an alternative dispute resolution mechanism.

It may be pointed here that in the UK, the SC hears only 55 appeals in a year. In the USA, of the 5,000 petitions for leave to appeal every year, only 185–195 are admitted and the rest are rejected even without any oral hearing. Each SC judge in the USA handled a mere 9 cases (every year) against disposal of 2,600 cases by every judge on an average in the SC, High Court or trial court in India, every year. The American SC decides 81 cases in one full year compared with addition of 114 cases every day to pending cases in the SC

---

[41] The dismissal of a judge of the High Court and Supreme Court is a complex process, and since 1773 no judge has ever been dismissed. For example, the process to impeach Justice Soumitra Sen of the Calcutta High Court on charges of misappropriation of several lakh rupees began in September 2008 on the advice of the Chief Justice of India. The motion, passed by the Rajya Sabha in August 2011, was not taken in by the Lok Sabha as Justice Sen resigned in September 2011. In May 1993, a motion to impeach Justice V. Ramaswami, a judge of the Supreme Court, was moved, but the Congress under P.V. Narasimha Rao government did not issue the whip and Congressmen stayed away, enabling the motion to collapse. The frequency of executive–judiciary turf war and procedural delays in removing a judge of doubtful integrity raise a question whether the present system needs a change. Judges accused of malpractices no longer resign on their own to maintain the dignity of the office they hold.
[42] See also *The Financial Express* (Chandigarh), 15 May 2015.

in India.[43] On the contrary, the Union Law Ministry statistics show there are 4,600 vacancies in the subordinate judiciary, 470 vacancies of judges in 24 High Courts (sanctioned strength of 1,050 judges) and 6 in the SC as on 20 April 2016. Thus, there is an urgent need of reforms in the judiciary that would speed up the judicial process.[44] India's current judge–population ratio stands at 17 on its sanctioned strength, that is, one judge for a population of over 58,800. Nearly, 3.38 crore cases were pending before the judiciary.

Conclusion

Thus the role of the judiciary in responding to administrative action has been to protect the rights of the citizens against the growing state power. The increasing governmental interference in citizens' lives, the failure of governmental action on social and economic problems and the willingness of the judiciary to play a more constructive role all tend to ensure a continuation of judicial activism in policy formation. 'Independence of the judiciary is an important basic structure of the Constitution. To strengthen it, one does not have to weaken Parliamentary sovereignty which is not only an essential basic structure but is the soul of our democracy'.[45]

POLICYMAKING PROCESS IN A PARLIAMENTARY DEMOCRACY

The study of public policy is an important aspect of the politico-administrative science. So it is useful to understand the process of policymaking. Policymaking in a federal country such as India is a vital function of the government. In one way or another, each of us has the task of helping our government to determine its goals and objectives. As we do this, we try to develop policies. Our lives in the country are vitally affected by what we are able to achieve in the policymaking field. Since Independence (1947), our country has struggled a great deal with the problem of effective national policymaking and implementation. For example, the term 'policy process' suggests that there is some sort of system that converts policy ideas or demands into actual policies that have positive and negative effects when they are implemented. The policy process describes how policy is shaped by social, political, economic, institutional and other contexts.

In a democratic country such as India, the process of policymaking begins with the ideas people have about the actions they want the government to undertake. In other words, these are the demands or proposals made by civil society organizations or interest groups (private or official) upon the political system for action or inaction on some perceived problem. People with demands, which may be either supported or opposed by interests groups, seek to achieve some commitments from government to put their ideas into action. When the government undertakes such a commitment, it has the legal authority to do something that individuals cannot do. A governmental decision may be made on

---

[43] Law Commission in its report on 'Manpower Planning in the Judiciary' has recommended that the present strength of 10.5 judges per million of population be increased to 50 judges per million of population. See also *The Indian Express* and *The Tribune* (Chandigarh), 25 April 2016.

[44] The NJAC Act, 2014 was struck down by the Supreme Court on 16 October 2015, thereby reverting to old collegium system. See *The Tribune* (Chandigarh), 20 November 2015.

[45] Arun Jaitley (Union Finance Minister) on the 'Supreme Court verdict on JNAC'. See *The Financial Express*, 19 October 2015.

the demands of the people. The governmental and administrative processes comprise a vast mass of decisions made almost daily. Some of these have an immediate effect, while others may involve further lines of action and/or a further continuum of decision-making coming from that first decision. How can one distinguish a policy decision from others? Policymaking involves decision-making, but every decision is not a policy decision. For policymaking is the making of decisions, as much as all other decisions that are made by individual ministers, the Council of Ministers or by administrators. A policy decision involves action by some line officials, or body to reject, alter or accept a preferred policy alternative. If positive, it takes the shape of a legislation or the issuance of an executive order. Thus, policymaking is a difficult 'process to which there is no beginning or end'.

The Rules of Business (Article 77 of the Indian Constitution) govern the procedure for decision-making, and within the ambit of these rules, policy decisions are taken by the Council of Ministers, particularly by the Cabinet. But nowhere in the rules does there seems to be any distinction drawn between those decisions which are concerned with policy and those that are not. Policy and administration are intimately related and are an integral part of executive government. For the convenience of treatment only, it may be said that policy decisions are decisions made by public officials that authorize or give direction and content to public policy actions. A decision may be taken formally or informally if it is to be implemented. For example, the Union Cabinet in June 2016 gave its approval for raising the age of superannuation of government doctors from 60 or 62 to 65 years to enable the state and central governments to retain the services of experienced doctors, thereby bolstering medical profession and research activities in the country. The policy decision by the Union Cabinet was not placed before the Parliament for approval. Indeed, it may be said that some important decisions on policy are often taken informally. The PM or a particular colleague, if he is confident of being able to carry a particular policy through, may announce a decision, either in the Parliament or in public. For example, Union Food Minister in a communication on 4 May 2016 urged state governments to offer subsidies besides what it offers to make foodgrains available to targeted beneficiaries at prices lower than under the National Food Security Act, 2013.[46] Similarly, in Rajya Sabha, the Minister for Commerce and Industry said, 'India has ratified Trade Facilitation Agreement (TFA) of the World Trade Organization (WTO) and the instrument of Acceptance for Trade Facilitation Agreement was handed over to WTO director-general by India on 22 April 2016'.[47]

It may be noted that the Cabinet makes use of the committee system to facilitate decision-making in specific areas.[48] Depending upon the membership of any Cabinet committee, its decision is either final on behalf of the government or may be placed before the full Cabinet committee for ratification. A vast number of decisions are, of course, taken by individual ministers within the ambit of the rules for the business of the government. It

---

[46] See *The Financial Express* (Chandigarh), 5 May 2016. On 29 July 2015, the Cabinet approved amendments to the GST Bill to compensate states for revenue loss for five years on introduction of the uniform nationwide indirect tax regime as has been suggested by the Rajya Sabha, Select Committee (see *The Tribune*, 30 July 2015).

[47] See *The Financial Express* (Chandigarh), 5 May 2016.

[48] After a long struggle, the Appointment Committee of the Cabinet (ACC), headed by PM Narendra Modi, has finally approved a cadre change for Ramon Magsaysay Award, Indian Forest Service (IFS) officer Sanjiv Chaturvedi from Haryana to Uttarakhand. See *The Tribune* (Chandigarh), 17 August 2015.

often depends upon the personality and political image of a minister as to what matters he will decide, and what he will refer to the PM or to the Cabinet. But the Cabinet as a whole has to be persuaded of the rightness of most decisions. It is therefore argued that Cabinet decisions are taken by the PM together with the responsible minister so that the PM is in all important decisions. The job of the PM is to seek to harmonize collective rule with the individual responsibility of ministers.

Further, most of the decisions in various matters involving policy issues of less importance are taken by the administrative secretaries or committee of secretaries, some of which service a Cabinet committee. The secretary to government in the particular ministry, senior civil servants of the ministry, heads of government departments and other officials at levels below the departmental heads are vested, in particular matters, with delegated authority. For the conduct of government business, there are large volumes of departmental rules of procedure and of guidance in the making of decisions in each particular agency. Where a matter is seen to be of concern or interest to a ministry or department other than the one in which it is being considered, it is incumbent upon the former to consult the affected ministry or department at the appropriate level.

In a complex system, such as the government of a country, a vast number of social, political, economic and administrative forces influences the choice of a policy. The election manifesto of the political party in power, civil service organizations, the administrative and judicial courts, the Goods and Services Tax (GST) Council, a system of IGR, international bodies (such as WHO, ILO, UNESCO, UNDP, WB, IMF) and many other institutions, all these have functions bearing directly or indirectly on policymaking. Thus within the constitutional area, these institutions and factors may, and frequently do, exercise a profound influence on government policy. They bring influence to bear on those entitled to take and enforce policy decisions.

CONCLUSION

Policymaking in the public sphere seems to be tawdry to many people. Clearly, there are concerns about the motivations and honesty of those who are vested with the power of policymaking. The influence of interest group money, especially from big business and organized labour, is a matter of great concern. The legislative process often seems to be tardy and complex so that ordinary people cannot understand or participate in politics. As Lindblom rightly points out that policymaking is 'an extremely complex analytical and political process to which there is no beginning or end, and the boundaries of which are most uncertain'.[49] Somehow, a complex set of forces engage in 'policymaking', and taken as a whole, produce effects called policies. The Parliament is charged by the Indian Constitution with the function of representing the people in making policy through the passing of laws. The legislative process is a fundamental mechanism for expressing public policy. In India, all basic policies have to be determined by the legislative enactment, although legislation also permits more specific policymaking by the executive branch of the government within the legislative and constitutional framework, and the review functions of the judiciary. It is briefed that the real business of policy decision in

---

[49] Lindblom, *The Policy-making Process*, 4.

the government takes place in Cabinet committees rather than the full Cabinet and that a vast majority of policies sanctioned by the Parliament are initiated by the responsible ministers in consultation with the PM after having been planned within the departments in consultation with the affected interests. But as a government comes to the completion of its term of office and an election looms large, it generally finds cooperation from interest groups and industry organizations. Thus the study of public policy is the study of how we translate the (policy) problems of the people into actual policies.

Review Questions

(i) What do you think is the most outstanding feature of policymaking under the constitutional provisions in a democracy such as India? How far has India been able to reap the benefits of such a feature since the inception of the Indian republic?

(ii) Briefly discuss the structure of policymaking in the IGR in India.

(iii) Neither devolution nor delegation of legislative authority infringes the supremacy of … Parliament. How far is this statement true for India?

(iv) Discuss in detail the sources of executive power of a government.

(v) What do you understand by the term 'judicial review'? Explain its significance with examples from contemporary times.

POLICY ANALYSIS AND THINK TANKS

INTRODUCTION

The term 'think tank' is generally associated with policy research institutes engaged in the analysis of a particular policy area or a cluster of policy issues.[1] The think tank could be any institution undertaking policy-related, technical or scientific research and analysis. This could be an international agency, an NGO, a commercial research enterprise or policy analysis units inside government. Increasingly, the boundaries between think tanks and other groups are blurring. Interest groups and NGOs such as Amnesty or Transparency International have their own capacity or policy analytic research. But in any case, think tanks are repositories of information and ideas that provide valuable inputs into the policy process. An important function which they perform is the specialized research activity that leads to policy analysis. To Stone, think tanks have become key actors in a thickening web of global/regional institutions, regulatory activities and policy practices.[2]

Some of the well-known think tanks include the Brookings Institution in the USA, Adam Smith Institute in London and NITI Aayog in India.[3] Employing scholars and policy experts, these organizations provide information that policymakers and other influential people can use to make better policy. Many think tanks are involved in a particular ideological position (such as Brookings Institution); others are affiliated with business corporations (such as the Mitsubishi Research Institute, a profit-making institute founded in 1970). Despite this increasing divergence in legal constitution, the think tanks generally aim to make connection between policy analysis and policymaking. Some think tanks are associated with universities and research organizations that provide useful policy inputs. Such centres tend to be more scholarly and less ideological than some politically oriented think tanks, and state and local governments often rely on them for expert advice.

However, there is considerable diversity among think tanks in terms of size, ideology, resources and the quality or quantity of research output. In tandem, think tank modes of policy analysis range, at one end of the spectrum, from being highly scholarly or technocratic in style, to overtly ideological, partisan and advocacy oriented, at the other end, with vastly different standards of quality throughout.[4] As such, think tank policy analysis is

---

[1] Stella Ladi, *Globalization, Policy Transfer and Think Tanks* (Cheltenham: Edward Elgar, 2004).
[2] Diane Stone, 'The Knowledge Bank and the Global Development Network', *Global Governance* 9 (2003): 43–61.
[3] NITI Aayog was established on 1 January 2015 by the GOI.
[4] Stone, 'The Knowledge Bank and the Global Development Network'.

not simply an intellectual exercise providing policy documents or expert advice. Instead, policy analysis is also action oriented, reliant on policy entrepreneurship, institution building and the competitiveness of think tanks in the marketplace of ideas.

The pluralist nature of think tanks operating at national and international levels in their advocacy towards governments and international bodies is, however, complicated by understandings of the influence of think tanks. Consequently, the strategies to directly affect the course of legislation or the language of the policy initiatives must be considered alongside the longer-term capacity and effective influence over discourse of governance. There are practical guides and manuals on how to start and manage think tanks.[5] Apart from workshops regularly convened by the World Bank (WB), United Nations Development Programme (UNDP) and some other well-known institutes, specialist consultants and firms cater to both think tanks that need management advice and their donors who require evaluation of the think tank analysis they have funded.

MODES OF POLICY ANALYSIS

As think tanks provide expert advice to the policy analysts, their primary targets include legislators, executive officials including bureaucrats and politicians at all levels of governance. Further, their distinctive features lie in clearing house capacity advocacy involvement, networks incorporation and intellectual base.

One of the most important functions of think tanks is to provide policy inputs—draft legislation, working papers, training manuals, e-forums and other policy products. In this way, think tanks act as a clearing house representing a repository of independent and scholarly information and expertise.

Second, as advocates, think tank experts or activists are driven by ideological or professional principles to propagate specific practices or policies. In general, think tanks who are in the private sector domain seek to press their ideas in public domains such as radio/television, through newspapers or journals to draw public attention towards their 'public goods'.

Third distinctiveness of think tanks lies in their incorporation in domestic (insiders) and transnational (outsiders) policy networks (policy communities). These networks are a sectoral mode of governance incorporating actors from inside and outside government to facilitate decision-making and implementation. As providers of expertise and analysis, think tank staff can be co-opted into policy deliberation either informally through personal interactions or more formally through appointment to advisory bodies. In such circumstances, there is a relationship of trust between a think tank and a government ministry official where the think tank's expertise is recognized in return for some policy access.[6] Tata Institute of Fundamental Research (Mumbai), for instance, has a strong and long-standing relationship with the state government of Maharashtra for policy analytic research and policy access.

---

[5] Raymond J. Struyk, *Managing Think Tanks: Practical Guidance for Maturing Organisations* (Washington DC: Urban Institute, 2002).

[6] Heidi Ullrich, 'European Union Think Tanks: Generating Ideas, Analysis and Debate', in *Think Tank Traditions: Policy Research and the Politics of Ideas*, eds. Diane Stone and Andrew Denham (Manchester: Manchester University Press, 2004).

Fourth, by and large, think tank staff members are highly qualified and enjoy professional credibility. Although think tanks have the prime function of production of policy analysis, they provide opportunity to recruit new talents and impart policy training. Indeed, they produce human capital in the form of specialized analysts who, in return, provide rigorous policy analysis.

TRANSNATIONALIZATION OF THINK TANKS

The dynamic of globalization and regionalization has compelled the think tanks to look beyond primarily local and national matters to address global policy issues such as environment, health, security, trade and human rights. In conjunction with academics in universities, a notable number of think tank researchers have been leading commentators on globalization. Their transnational research agendas have been complemented by global dissemination of policy analysis via the Internet.[7] The Global Development Network is an extensive international federal network primarily of economic research institutes. There are many more. These networks provide an infrastructure for global dialogue and research collaboration, but institutes generally remain committed to the nation state in which they are legally established. Nevertheless, think tanks have become key players in a thickening web of global institutions and policy practices.

International organizations such as the WB, European Union (EU), the World Trade Organization (WTO) or UNDP are important financiers and consumers of research and policy analysis. They have provided capacity-building and training programmes throughout the world for local elites to establish new think tanks and policy networks. Global public policy networks are neocorporatist arrangements that act alongside international organizations, government officials, business representatives and stakeholders to a policy area to provide policy analysis.[8] Within these networks, selected think tanks have become key actors in building the infrastructure for communication between transnational policy actors, that is, websites, organizing international meetings and managing the flow of information coming from numerous sources. Consequently, think tanks can be called 'an excellent barometer of the transnationalization of policy analysis'.[9] It is pointed out that think tank activity within the EU has been considerable, reflecting the deepening of European integration.[10] In spite of notable differences between think tanks in relation to specific policy issues, structural and membership profiles and ideological perspectives on European integration, they have common features such as close relations with European Commission and a research focus on distinctively European issues.[11] Further, think tanks have also been key players in European harmonization of national structures through

---

[7] Ladi, *Globalization, Policy Transfer and Think Tanks*.
[8] Wolfgang Reinicke and Francis Deng, *Critical Choices: The United Nations, Networks and the Future of Global Governance* (Ottawa: International Development Research Centre, 2000).
[9] Diane Stone, 'Public Policy Analysis and Think Tanks', in *Handbook of Public Policy Analysis*, eds. F. Fischer, G.J. Miller and Mara S. Sidney (Boca Raton, FL: CRC Press, 2007), 153.
[10] Stephen Boucher et al., 'Europe and Its Think Tanks; A Promise to Be Fulfilled: An Analysis of Think Tanks Specialized in European Policy Issues in the Enlarged European Union', *Studies and Research* 35 (2004).
[11] Ullrich, 'European Union Think Tanks: Generating Ideas, Analysis and Debate'.

cross-national processes of policy transfer, where they go beyond detached policy analysis to highlight certain European standards and benchmarks.[12]

POLICY IMPACT AND CRITICISM

Notwithstanding extensive growth, think tanks research and analysis do not escape criticism. The question to examine is whether they contribute to policymaking in local, national or regional global fora. If so, to what extent they have relevance and utility if not direct policy influence.

In the first place, think tanks appear to have focused on the rigorous and professional analysis of policy issues. Many use their presumed apolitical status and look at them as civil society organizations equipped with knowledge and intellectual authority on policy concerns. However, a recent empirical survey of European policy issues indicated critical and cautious perceptions of influence of think tanks.[13]

Despite the fact that some think tanks have acquired political credibility by performing services for states and for non-state actors, many, however, respond to demand for high-quality research and policy analysis. Further, they provide services such as ethics or policy training for civil servants, or by organizing conferences or seminars. For governments concerned about evidence-based policy, think tanks potentially help create a more rational policy process by augmenting in-house research capacities and circumventing time and institutional constraints. For instance, state-owned Power Finance Corporation on 5 October 2015 witnessed an overwhelming subscription of its public issues of tax-free bonds to the tune of over 12 times (₹8,461 crore against an issue size of ₹700 crore).[14] Indeed, a number of think tanks in India that enjoy the trust of government have played a quiet but effective role behind the scenes. In this way, they provide intellectual advice on policy concerns.

Some think tanks also contribute to governance and institution-building by facilitating exchange between official and other private actors as interlocutors and network entrepreneurs. Networks are useful to think tanks in creating relationship with more powerful actors, thereby potentially amplifying their impact. However, such relationships also pull think tanks towards advocacy of certain political ideology or practices, thereby defeating the objective for which the research institutes were legally set up. Rather than organizations for rational knowledge utilization in policy, think tank development is also indicative of the wider politicization of policy analysis.[15] But a more informed, knowledge-based policy process—a role that think tank experts help fulfil—could enlighten policy analysis.[16]

---

[12] Ladi, *Globalization, Policy Transfer and Think Tanks.*

[13] Boucher et al., 'Europe and Its Think Tanks; A Promise to Be Fulfilled: An Analysis of Think Tanks Specialized in European Policy Issues in the Enlarged European Union', 85.

[14] See *The Financial Express*, 7 October 2015, accessed 16 November 2016, http://www.financialexpress.com/markets/indian-markets/despite-low-yields-public-issue-of-rec-tax-free-bonds-evokes-good-response/157637/

[15] Andrew Denham and M. Garnett, 'A Hallowed Out Tradition? British Think Tank in the Twenty-first Century', in *Think Tank Traditions: Policy Research and the Politics of Ideas*, eds. Diane Stone and Andrew Denham (Manchester: Manchester University Press, 2004).

[16] Carol Weiss, *Organizations for Policy Analysis: Helping Government Think* (London: SAGE Publications, 1992).

Some elite studies of think tanks such as the Brookings Institution in America adopted power approaches and indicated that think tanks were key components of the power elite where decision-making was concentrated in the hands of powerful individuals.[17] On the contrary, some scholars argued that 'establishment think tanks' are consensus-building organizations. As the common economic interests and social cohesion among the power elite or ruling class is insufficient to produce consensus on policies, agreement on such matters requires 'research, consultation and deliberation' to form a coherent sense of long-term class interests[18] and maintain hegemonic control.[19] However, these studies direct analysis towards such policy institutions which have solid links with political parties or the corporate sector.

In their edited work, Stone and Denham argued that contemporary analysts are sceptical of think tanks exerting consistent direct impact on politics.[20] Instead, they see think tank's roles as agenda setters who create policy narratives that capture the political and public organizations. This ability to set the terms of debate, define problems and shape policy perception has been described elsewhere as 'atmospheric' influence.[21] Moreover, the changing influence of think tanks has much to do with the way in which think tanks interact over time in epistemic community (that focuses on specific role of experts in the policy process),[22] advocacy coalitions (an approach that emphasizes the role of beliefs, values and ideas in policymaking) and discourse coalitions (an approach that emphasizes the role of language and political symbolism) in the definition and perception of the problem. In these perspectives, it is in the *longue duree* that think tank policy analysis and activity have achieved wider social relevance and shaping patterns of governance and moving paradigms.[23] As centres of policy analysis, think tanks need to sustain their intellectual credibility as repositories of policy knowledge.

Review Questions

(i) Define the term 'think tank'.
(ii) What are the main functions of think tanks?
(iii) How has the formation of EU affected think tank activity in the region?
(iv) Does think tank activity play a crucial role in mainstream policy formulation? If yes, how? If not, why?
(v) Do you think 'think tanks' need to have a positive relationship with the government to carry out active and effective research work?

---

[17] See, for example, Thomas Dye, 'Oligarchic Tendencies in National Policy Making: The Role of Private Planning Organisations', *Journal of Politics* 40 (1978): 309–31.

[18] William G. Domhoff, *Who Rules America Now? A View for the '80s* (New Jersey: Prentice Hall, 1983), 82.

[19] Radhika Desai, 'Second-hand Dealers in Ideas: Think Tanks and Thatcherite Hegemony', *New Left Review* 203 (1994): 27–64.

[20] Stone and Denham (eds.), *Think Tank Traditions*.

[21] Simon James, 'Influencing Government Policymaking', in *Banking on Knowledge: The Genesis of the Global Development Network*, ed. Diane Stone (London: Routledge, 2000), 163.

[22] Ullrich, 'European Union Think Tanks: Generating Ideas, Analysis and Debate'.

[23] Diane Stone, 'Public Policy Analysis and Think Tanks', 156.

CHAPTER 5

APPROACHES TO AGENDA ANALYSIS AND POLICY FORMATION

INTRODUCTION

For pluralists (such as Truman[1] Dahl and Lindblom[2]), setting of policy agenda is the outcome of a process of competition between and among different groups. The power to influence issues for the policy is seen as something which is open to public debate (here power is seen as dispersed rather than concentrated). In a free society, it is felt that all can influence policy agenda. Structural-functionalist (Almond's model), for example, represents the liberal democratic political system which converts inputs into outputs in the 'black box'. However, from the 1960s onwards, pluralistic assumptions about the openness and neutrality of the policymaking process in terms of agenda setting were challenged by Schattschneider and Cobb and Elder in their works.

A few approaches to agenda setting are briefly discussed in this chapter.

SCHATTSCHNEIDER AND POLITICS OF AGENDA SETTING

Schattschneider criticizes the pluralist assumptions of the neutrality of the policymaking process and focuses on the way in which public policy is made in the context of processes that are biased in favour of some groups.[3] For him, an essential power of government is to manage conflict before it starts. He argues that the domain of the political game is not as open and pluralistic as liberal democratic theory has maintained. Politics as a conflict of values and interests is thus displaced by the management of conflict.

From Schattschneider's model, it follows that public policy is an activity which is driven by public demands and opinions. It is an activity in which issues go up and down the policy agenda and often bias is mobilized to ensure that conflict is managed and contained. As Schattschneider writes,

> All forms of political organizations have a bias in favour of the exploitation of some kinds of conflict and the suppression of others because organization is the mobilization of bias. Some issues are organized into politics while others are organized out.[4]

---

[1] D. Truman, *The Governmental Process* (New York, NY: Alfred A. Knopf, 1951).
[2] Robert Dahl and C.E. Lindblom, *Politics, Economics and Welfare* (New York, NY: Harpers, 1976).
[3] E.E. Schattschneider, *The Semisovereign People* (Hinsdale, IL: Dryden Press, 1975).
[4] Ibid., 71–3; 69.

From the Schattschneider model, it follows that public policy is an activity in which definition of issues and alternatives is the supreme instrument of political power. And he writes, 'He who determines what politics is about runs the country, because the definition of alternatives is the choice of conflicts'. His theory of issue expansion explains how ingroups retain control over problem definition and the way such problems are suppressed by dominant actors in policymaking. These actors form what Baumgartner and Jones call policy monopolies which attempt to keep problems and underlying policy issues low on the agenda.[5]

COBB AND ELDER: EXPANSION AND CONTROL OF AGENDA

The Schattschneider model was developed further in subsequent years by Cobb and Elder.[6] Their focus is on how the agenda process provides a linking level of analysis between the social system as a whole and decision-making. According to Cobb and Elder, the formation of a policy/decision issue depends upon some 'triggering devices' such as natural or unanticipated human events, technological changes (internal triggers) and patterns of world alignment act of war, international conflicts (external triggers). Obviously, there has to be a link between a trigger and a problem which then transforms the issue into an agenda item.

According to Cobb and Elder, the agenda is of two types: systemic and institutional.

(i) Systemic agenda: The systemic agenda is composed of 'all issues that are commonly perceived by members of the political community as meriting public attention and as involving matters within the legitimate jurisdiction of existing governmental authority'.[7]

(ii) Institutional agenda: The institutional agenda, on the contrary, is defined as 'that set of items explicitly up for the active consideration of authoritative decision makers'.[8] The issue will get on to the institutional agenda if it has first found a place on the systemic agenda.

Agenda-building sets in as a result of the expansion of an issue from a specific interest group to an attentive public and finally to the general public.[9]

But the problem may arise when there is expansion of an issue. Group strategies (focusing on discrediting the group or its leader) and issue strategies (focusing on symbolic rewards or reassurance) are suggested for containing conflict and issue expansion.

In the process of expansion and containment of an issue, Cobb and Elder argue for the use of symbols. In the use of symbols (e.g. language), the role of mass media is crucial

---

[5] Baumgartner and Jones, *Agendas and Instability*.
[6] Cobb and Elder, *Participation in American Politics*.
[7] Ibid., 85.
[8] Ibid., 86.
[9] The gang rape and death of a 23-year-old student in December 2012 in New Delhi sparked public outrage which led to the appointment of Justice J.S. Verma Committee to suggest ways to make India safer for women.

in arousing concern, provoking action, dissuading the opposition, showing a strength of commitment and affirming support. A wider interested or attentive public will force the policy community to bring the issue on the policy agenda. Conflicts or issues that are confined to the attentive public are likely to attain the formal agenda through a brokerage channel or groups.

In brief, Schattschneider and Cobb and Elder provide models of agenda-building which may be used to show how an issue must be expanded if it is to impact on the policy-/decision-making process. Agenda setting in this sense is therefore to manage conflict in which institutions have a central role to play. As already mentioned, 'All forms of political organization have a bias in favour of the exploitation of some kinds of conflict and the suppression of others because organization is the mobilization of bias'.

Thus, politics of agenda setting and bias mobilization is seen in this model as the process in which issues and priorities are defined through the management of conflict.

BACHRACH AND BARATZ: AGENDA AND NON-DECISION-MAKING

Public policymaking agenda is generally driven by the cry of general public. The agenda setting occurs when issues or conflicts are confined to the attentive or general public and identification groups. But it should be noted that there is the politics of agenda setting and often 'some issues get organized into politics while others are organized out'.[10] For example, in the study of policymaking, Saggar shows how the issue of race was kept out of the policy agenda. He observed that 'race-specific policy proposals were not heard largely because they were perceived as illegitimate threats to the established policy framework'.[11]

In the pluralist accounts of democracy, public policy was seen as the outcome of a competition between ideas and interests. For example, in Robert Dahl's views, 'power' involved in control of behaviour (e.g. 'A' has the power (capacity) to make 'B' do something which 'B' would otherwise not like to do), and as it (power) was widely fragmented and distributed between different groups, the policy process was driven by public demands and opinions in the political system. Dahl argued, 'The independence, penetrability and heterogeneity of the various segments of the political stratum all but guarantee that any dissatisfied group will find a spokesman'.[12]

In the pluralist approach, participation in the game of politics (public policymaking process) was open to all. However, this view of liberal democracy was challenged by Schattschneider when he argued, 'It is not necessarily true that people with the greatest needs participate in politics most actively—whosoever decides what the game is about will also decide who gets in the game'.[13] He argues that an essential power of government is the power to manage conflict before it starts. The scope and extent of conflict is limited and determined by the dominant players—pressure groups, parties

---

[10] Schattschneider, *The Semisovereign People*, 71.

[11] Shamit Saggar, *Race and Public Policy* (Aldershot, Hants: Avebury, 1991).

[12] Robert Dahl, *Who Governs? Democracy and Power in an American City* (New Haven, CT: Yale University Press, 1961), 91–93.

[13] E.E. Schattschneider, *The Semisovereign People* (New York, NY: Holt, Rinehart, 1960), 105.

and institutions—in the political game. The game of politics is not something which is as open and pluralistic as liberal democratic theory had maintained (supported by Robert Dahl, Charles Lindblom and D. Truman). From Schattschneider's thesis, it follows that public policy is essentially an activity in which issues are included and excluded with a view to ensuring that conflict is contained and managed. The definition of issue is at the centre of politics. Because people cannot agree as to what the real issues are, 'He who determines what politics is about runs the country, because the definition of alternatives is the choice of conflicts'.[14]

The Schattschneider mobilization of bias theory was greatly enhanced by the work of Bachrach and Baratz,[15] whose approach addressed a different aspect of the pluralist case: the definition of power. Bachrach and Baratz argued that the pluralist approach failed to appreciate the extent of power of those who can actually exclude issues and problems from the policymaking agenda.

In the policy process, non-decisions do carry importance. Non-decisions are just as significant as decisions and policies which initiate some new relationship between government and the people. Therefore, attention should not only focus on decisions which produce change but also must be sensitive to those which resist change. Non-decisions are difficult to observe because they are not represented in the policymaking process by legislative enactment. There are situations in which people with power can actually exclude issues and problems from the policymaking agenda.

Non-decision-making involves the construction or containment of decision-making so as to be focused on 'safe issues by manipulating the dominant community values, myths, and political institutions and procedures'.[16] Bias against certain interests in society may be routinized, thus making it very difficult for certain demands to penetrate the 'black box' of the political system. What Bachrach and Baratz were arguing was that power was not simply the control of behaviour, as Dahl, for example, had argued, it (power) also consisted in the realm of 'non-decisions'. Bachrach and Baratz argued,

> A non-decision, as we define it, is a decision that results in the suppression or thwarting of a latent or manifest challenge to the values and interests of the decision maker. To be more clearly explicit, non-decision-making is a means by which demands for change in the existing allocation of benefits and privileges in the community can be suffocated before they are even voiced, or kept covert; or killed to gain access to the relevant decision-making arena; or failing all these things, maimed or destroyed in the decision-implementing stage of the policy process.[17]

Non-Decision explained

---

[14] Ibid., 69.

[15] P.S. Bachrach and M.S. Baratz, *Power and Poverty, Theory and Practice* (New York, NY: Oxford University Press, 1970). This empirical study in Baltimore showed how business leaders and politicians sought to ensure that the demands of black people in the city were excluded from the decision-making processes by various means, including force, sanctions, co-options and manipulation of symbols.

[16] P.S. Bachrach and M.S. Baratz, 'Decisions and Non-decisions: An Analytical Framework', *American Political Science Review* 57 (1963): 632.

[17] Bachrach and Baratz, *Power and Poverty*, 7.

In other words, the policymakers with power can keep decision issues off the agenda which they control. Non-decisional power is a powerful approach in that it shapes the policy agenda and seeks to confine scope and extent of conflict. However, it is not without its critics. Crenson, for example, argues there is a grossly inaccurate and simplistic conception of how issues get on or are kept off the agenda. Crenson suggests that political issues are determined by policymakers and organizations in terms of costs and benefits.

> In general, a political issue tends to be ignored if there is a mismatch between the kinds of benefits that it is likely to create and the kinds of inducements that influential community organizations need in order to survive and grow.[18]

Moreover, Crenson contends that concerns for political issues may lead to the issue of governmental reforms. Significantly, Crenson sees this exercise of inactivity power as operating at an 'ideological' level in which 'political forms and practices' serve to 'diffuse content and promote selective perception and articulation of social problems and conflict'.[19] And he argues, 'The issues on a political agenda may be rationally linked, not to one another, but to some comprehensive political ideal or principle that transcends the agenda—an ideological vision of the political system'.[20]

McCOMBS AND SHAW: MEDIA AND POLICY AGENDA

There is also the relationship between media and public policy and public opinion. According to McCombs and Shaw, media also influence the policy agenda.[21] They argue that media have had a key role in agenda setting, that is, in the power to determine what topics are discussed—public welfare, fiscal policy, civil rights, law and order and corruption. The model suggested by McCombs and Shaw was that the media order what publics regard as important issues. The high attention that the issue draws, the public regards it as being a high-agenda item and vice versa. Critics of the model have, however, challenged its empirical standing as well as the danger of simplistic and broad application. For example, Protess et al. concluded that the influence of the media in setting policy agendas was far more complex than had been thought in the 1970s.[22]

Rogers and Dearing also advanced a comprehensive model which focuses on the range of processes involved in agenda setting.[23] They argue that we must make distinction between three kinds of agenda: media, public and policy. For them, agenda setting is a more interactive process. The mass media do indeed influence the public agenda, as

---

[18] M.A. Crenson, *The Unpolitics of Air Pollution: A Study of Non-Decision Making in the Cities* (Baltimore, MD: Johns Hopkins University, 1971), 156.

[19] Ibid., 23.

[20] Ibid., 173.

[21] M.E. McCombs and D.L. Shaw, 'The Agenda Setting Functions of the Mass Media', *Public Opinion Quarterly* 36 (1972): 176–87.

[22] D.L. Protess et al., 'The Impact of Investigative Reporting on Public Opinion and Policy-making', *Public Opinion Quarterly* 51 (1987): 166–85.

[23] E.M. Rogers and W. Dearing, 'Agenda-setting Research', *Communications Yearbook* II (1987): 555–94.

McCombs and Shaw maintain, but the public agenda has an impact on the policy agenda, as the media agenda has an impact on the policy agenda. However, on certain issues, the policy agenda has a high impact on the media agenda. The media agenda also gets shaped by the impact of real-world issues and events.

According to McQuail and Windahl, this model represents the different kinds of effect and of feedback. It reminds us that 'mass media, the public, and elite policy makers all inhabit more or less the same wider environment when it comes to highly significant events and that each of the three separate worlds indicated are connected and permeated by networks of personal contacts and influenced by personal experience'.[24]

PUBLIC OPINION AND POLICY AGENDA

The study of public opinion is important as it contributes to policy agenda. That something (issue) which attracts the attention of policymakers and media is related to public opinion. In a democracy, the influence of public opinion does not go unnoticed. Expressing his empathy for the public protests that rocked the national capital after the brutal gang rape and murder of a 23-year-old physiotherapist on 16 December 2012, the President of India, Pranab Mukherjee, in his speech on the eve of Republic Day (25 January 2013) said the incident had left young Indians 'outraged' and shattered the nation's complacency.

Earlier, Justice J.S. Verma Committee appointed in December 2012 to suggest ways to make India safer for women recommended (report submitted on 23 January 2013) sweeping changes in the criminal and electoral laws to ensure a safer society.[25]

The fact that public opinion draws the attention of media and policy community gives weight to the argument that the policy agenda is set by the interplay of public opinion and public power.

The influence of public opinion on government should also be viewed in the context of power to shape public opinion. With the introduction of new techniques to measure public opinion on social issues, it is possible for policymakers to study the relationship between public opinion and policy. Thus, it is observed that policy agenda is set by the interplay of public opinion and public power.

---

[24] D. McQuail and S. Windahl, *Communication Models for the Study of Mass Communications* (London: Longman, 1993), 109.

[25] The Verma Committee (January 2013) sought Bill of Rights for Women to guarantee them the rights promised by the Indian Constitution. It rejected populist calls for death penalty and chemical castration of rape accused and proposed 20 years to rest of natural life as punishment for gang rape. The Committee has for the first time proposed a new Indian Penal Code (IPC) offence on human trafficking, prescribing minimum punishment of seven years rigorous imprisonment (RI) up to 10 years for traffickers of one person and 10 years RI up to life for those who traffic more than one person. For trafficking of minors, 14 years to life is the bracket of punishment suggested. It has sought changes to the IPC to make marital rape illegal and introduces a range of non-penetrative sexual offences from eve-teasing and stripping to stalking and voyeurism. Further, it recommends changes to the Representation of People's Act to disqualify politicians from their positions right when a court takes cognizance of the crime.

KINGDON: POLICY STREAMS APPROACH AND AGENDA SETTING

John Kingdon is a leading contributor to the study of agenda setting.[26] He finds 'garbage can' model (as propounded by Cohen et al.) an attractive framework to approach an agenda-setting process in which solutions search for problems.[27] The garbage can model stresses the anarchical nature of organizations as 'loose collections of ideas' as opposed to rational 'coherent structures'.

Kingdon approached the policy as comprising of four components: (i) agenda setting, (ii) alternative specification, (iii) policy choice and (iv) implementation components. His main concern was on how issues come to be issues; how they come to the attention of the public officials and policymakers; and how issues and solutions did or did not move from the specialized agenda of particular issue networks and policy community to the governmental agenda; and finally to the policy/decision agenda from which particular policies are adopted or aborted by making issues, solutions and politics. He framed question as to why ideas 'have their time'. He argued that incremental models were more accurate as descriptions of the federal policy process than models presuming comprehensive rationality and systematic, top-down analysis. Ideas for policies, he observed, can come from a variety of sources, such as interest groups, the media, political parties, elected members, bureaucrats, academics and other professional researchers and public. In fact, he contended that the garbage can model was more apt descriptively for characterizing the diverse origins and development of policies in a fragmented government with its diffuse and complex flows of information.

Agenda Process Streams

Kingdon argued that the agenda process may be conceived as composed of three distinct and partially independent streams: (i) problem (recognition), (ii) policy (formulation) and (iii) (electoral) politics. The government agenda is set by the political stream, while the policy stream shapes and modifies policy alternatives.

Problem Stream

First, people must recognize that there exists a problem. The problem stream consists of those problems on which policymakers fix their attention, as opposed to those which they refuse to entertain. Kingdon argues that there are three means which serve to bring problems to the attention of policymakers:

   (i) Indicators: Government data and reports are used to evaluate the scale and change in problems.
   (ii) Events: Events serve to draw attention on problems, such as disasters, personal experience and crises.
   (iii) Feedback: Feedback provides information on current performance and points to unanticipated consequences.

---

[26] Kingdon, *Agendas, Alternatives and Public Policies*.
[27] M. Cohen, J. March and J. Olsen, 'A Garbage Can Model of Organizational Choice', *Administrative Science Quarterly* 17 (1972): 1–125.

Problems are formulated by normatively redefining observed conditions. In keeping with the original formulation of the garbage can model, problems can go away even if they are not solved, including through inattention or calculated neglect.

Policy Stream

Kingdon develops the idea of the policy stream in terms of a 'primeval soup'. Policies emerge from the primeval soup of ideas floating around in policy communities of issue-area specialists (such as bureaucrats, analysts, consultants and professional researchers, who generate and evaluate solutions in the evolving primeval soup of the policy stream). Among the participants in policy communities are policy entrepreneurs who advocate particular policy solutions for problems in question. Policies are more likely to emerge from the soup and rise to the public decision agenda if they are matched with problems. In this soup stream, some ideas go to the top of the agenda, while others fall to the bottom. In this soup are policy entrepreneurs 'who are willing to invest resources of various kinds in hopes of a future return in the form of policies they favour'.[28] These people are crucial to the survival and success of an idea. In order that the idea gets to the top, it has to be technically feasible and acceptable to the dominant values of the community. Eventually, in the soup struggle emerges a list of proposals which form the base of governing agenda.

Political Stream

The government agenda is set by the political stream. The political stream determines the status of the agenda item. Kingdon argues that political stream is broadly composed of four elements: national mood (public opinion), organized political forces (such as electoral and legislative politics, pressure groups), government (jurisdictions among branches) and consensus-building (including bargaining and logrolling). The agenda-setting subprocess, concludes Kingdon, is driven primarily by (i) the emergence of problem, (ii) the course of politics and (iii) the activities of the process's visible participants—elected officials and their key appointees, the media and the political parties.[29]

Kingdon uses another metaphor, namely, 'policy windows', to describe the agenda-setting process when three streams merge. Once a window opens, it affords an opportunity to the policy entrepreneurs to join the three streams to move bundles of problems and solutions onto the decision agenda for action, inaction or rejection. When all three streams (problem, proposal and political receptivity) come together to form a single package, then the item has a high probability of gaining acceptability for policy agenda.

Kingdon's multiple streams model of agenda setting has been examined and formalized by Zahariadis who concluded that 'ambiguity is a fact of policy making'[30] that presents both costs and benefits for policy design/choice. Ambiguity renders the importance, meaning and value of solutions and problems difficult to ascertain precisely and invariantly. Thus, 'choice becomes less an exercise in solving problems and more an attempt

---

[28] Kingdon, *Agendas, Alternatives and Public Policies*, 151.
[29] Ibid., 174.
[30] N. Zahariadis, 'Ambiguity, Time, and Multiple Streams', in *Theories of the Policy Process*, ed. P. Sabatier (Boulder, CO: West View, 1999), 89.

to make sense of a partially comprehensible world'.[31] Further, Zahariadis suggested that there are very real advantages to policymakers of choosing solutions first rather than trying to solve problems directly.[32]

POLICY COMMUNITY AND NETWORK APPROACHES TO POLICY AGENDA

Introduction

'Policy community' and 'policy network' are new approaches which are concerned with more formal and informal aspects of the policymaking. They seek to focus on contacts and relationships which shape policy agenda and decision-making in contrast to the interactions within the formal policymaking institutions. They play critical roles in policy processes, among which the most important ones are those related to integration tasks performed. In all, variations of these terms direct attention away from formal institutional structures and towards the relations of power, political action, political conflict and coalition-building as additional loci of meaningful activity.[33] Activities in policy network and policy communities may precede policy formulation, on the one hand, and may influence policy enactment and administration, on the other.

Definition of Policy Community and Networks

The term 'policy community' is defined as 'a grouping of interrelated policy actors pursuing a matter of public policy important to them for instrumental reasons'.[34] The term seems to point towards something discernible. The 'community' metaphor implies people, close interaction and strong ties.[35] Stone et al. define policy communities as stable networks of policy actors from both inside and outside government, echoing an echo-prone literature that frequently notes the integrated character of policy communities.[36] Policy communities are based on common understandings of problems within a particular policy domain. The community label reflects the emphasis placed on strong and close relationships built among participants. These close relationships prevent conflict from becoming dysfunctional or unmanageable.

Policy community can include policy analysts, journalists, as well as influential politicians and bureaucratic officials. In addition, researchers, experts and professors from universities, think tanks or the law are likely to gain membership in a policy community if their values and ideas conform to the normative orientation of the group. 'The important point is that the policy community provides the institutional mechanism to resolve differences

---

[31] K.E. Weick, *The Social Psychology of Organizing*, 2nd ed. (New York, NY: Random House, 1979), 175.

[32] Zahariadis, 'Ambiguity, Time, and Multiple Streams', 83.

[33] Hugh Miller and Tansu Demir, 'Policy Communities', in *Handbook of Public Policy Analysis*, eds. Frank Fischer, Gerald Miller and Mara Sidney (Boca Raton, FL: Taylor & Francis Group, 2007), 145.

[34] Ibid., 137.

[35] M.M. Atkinson and W.D. Coleman, 'Policy Networks, Policy Communities and the Problems of Governance', *Governance* 5(2) (1992): 154–80.

[36] D.S. Stone et al., *Bridging Research and Policy* (London: UK Department for International Development, Radcliffe House, Warwick University, 2001).

of interests between regular actors'.[37] Hence, policy communities have become identified with stability and normal politics. Because of the strength of its practices and the durability of its norms, a policy community is perhaps the most institutionalized iteration among the policy network concepts.[38]

Policy communities indicate a policy process in which organized interests and governmental actors play a major role in shaping the direction and outcome of public policies. A policy community is neither market nor hierarchy.[39] In policy communities, one finds political administration, not neutral administration, and one finds a multidirectional pattern of interactions.[40]

Network analysis rests on the idea that a policy is framed within a context of interconnectedness and dependencies. Benson defines policy networks in terms of a 'complex of organizations connected to each other by resource dependencies'.[41]

Smith describes the idea of policy networks as a 'meso-level concept which is concerned with explaining behaviour within particular sections of the state or particular policy areas'.[42] The problem in comparing policy communities with related concepts is the increasing ambiguity.

Wilks and Wright suggested a threefold typology including 'policy universe', 'policy community' and 'policy network'.[43] For the scholars, 'policy universe' is the large population of actors and potential actors who share a common interest in industrial policy, and may contribute to the policy process on a regular basis. 'Policy community', on the other hand, refers to a more disaggregated system involving those actors and potential actors who share an interest in a particular industry and who interact with one another to mutual benefit. Finally, 'policy network', in their thinking, becomes a linking mechanism between and among policy communities.[44]

Propositions in Policy Community and Network Models

Smith advances the following six propositions about the relationship of state autonomy and networks:

(i) The type of network and community relationships varies across time, policy sector and states.

---

[37] G. Jordan and W.A. Maloney, 'Accounting for Subgovernments: Explaining the Persistence of Policy Communities', *Administrative & Society* 29(5) (1997): 574.

[38] E.H. Klijn, 'Policy Networks: An Overview', in *Managing Complex Networks: Strategies for the Public Sector*, eds. J.M. Walter et al. (London: SAGE Publications, 1997).

[39] O.E. Williamson, *Markets and Hierarchies* (New York, NY: Free Press, 1975).

[40] A.B. Cigler, 'Public Administration and the Paradox of Professionalism', *Public Administration Review* 50(6) (1990): 637–53.

[41] J.K. Benson, 'A Framework for Policy Analysis', in, *Interorganizational Coordination*, eds. D.L. Rogers and D. Whetten (Amsterdam, IA: Iowa State University Press, 1982), 148.

[42] Martin J. Smith, *Pressure, Power and Policy* (Hempstead: Harvester Wheatsheaf, 1993), 7.

[43] S. Wilks and M. Wright, eds., *Comparative Government–Industry Relations: Western Europe, the United States, and Japan* (Oxford: Clarendon Press, 1987).

[44] Ibid.

(ii) State actors have interests which shape the development of policy and policy networks.

(iii) The autonomy of the state in making and implementing policy is affected by the types of policy networks which exist.

(iv) Types of policy networks affect policy outcomes.

(v) The type of policy networks provides a context for understanding the role of interest groups in policymaking. Networks are the 'enstructuration' of past policies, ideologies and processes.

(vi) The types of network will affect the way in which policy changes.

Smith also sets out four propositions about the comparative context of policy networks/communities in the USA and Britain:

(i) policy communities are more likely to develop where the state is dependent on groups for implementation;

(ii) policy communities are more likely to develop where interest groups have important resources they can exchange;

(iii) issue networks will develop in areas of lesser importance to government, of high political controversy, or in new issue areas where interests have not been institutionalized;

(iv) policy communities are more likely in Britain than in the USA.[45]

Applications of Network and Community Ideas

One of the earliest users of the idea was Heclo, who compared 'issue networks' with 'iron triangles' in the context of the US executive.[46] Later, the idea was applied in Britain by Richardson and Jordan, who suggested that the policymaking map of Britain was characterized by a fragmented collection of subsystems: a 'series of vertical compartments or segments, each segment inhabited by a different set of organized groups and generally impenetrable by "unrecognized groups" or by the general public'.[47]

After applying the idea of network analysis in his study of local–central relationships, Rhodes suggested that policy networks had become the main feature of policymaking in Britain and lie at the 'heart of one of the major problems of British government.... The failure to appreciate that service delivery systems are complex, disaggregated and indeterminate has led to the failure of policies'.[48] Rhodes contrasts policy communities with issue networks along four dimensions such as membership, integration, resources and power. As compared to issue networks, in policy communities, the number of participants is very limited and some groups are consciously excluded.

---

[45] Smith, *Pressure, Power and Policy*, 10.

[46] H. Heclo, 'Issue Networks and the Executive Establishment', in *The New American Political System*, ed. A. King (Washington: American Institute for Public Policy Research, 1978), 87–124.

[47] J.J. Richardson and A.G. Jordon, *Governing Under Pressure: The Policy Process in a Parliamentary Democracy* (Oxford: Martin Robertson, 1979), 174.

[48] R.A.W. Rhodes, *Beyond Westminster and Whitehall: The Sub-Central Government of Britain* (London: Unwin Hyman, 1988), 85.

In 1982, Richardson et al. developed the idea of policy communities on a comparative level through the idea that different countries exhibit a variety of patterns—or styles—of policy formulation and decision-making.[49] Richardson suggested two main dimensions of policy style: an anticipatory style (a tendency to anticipate problems) or a reactionary style (a tendency to react to events and circumstances as they arise) and (ii) a consensus-seeking style (a tendency to make decisions through getting agreement between interested parties).

This model by Richardson suggests that although the modes of policymaking in industrialized countries are exhibiting a shift towards more 'community', 'network' structures, there will be considerable differences in the way in which policy communities interact. In the case of a well-organized and powerful policy community, policymaking takes place with a good deal of negotiations and bargaining. On the other hand, in policy community in which policymakers face a loose, diffuse network, government may opt for a more robust approach and impose its decisions without too much by way of consultation or negotiation with a policy community. However, policy issues pertaining to defence, for example, may be dealt with in secrecy and without very much consultation with a wider policy community.[50]

Smith uses several case studies and shows how the idea of policy networks may be applied in a range of theoretical macroframeworks which define different relationships between state autonomy and policy networks. In the case of Marxist frames, policy communities are characterized as dominated by capital; in elitist models, communities are viewed as dominated by privileged interests; state-centred theorists envisage networks as dominated by the state; and pluralists envisage networks as having no dominant group.

With the help of his case studies, Smith argues how policy networks do indeed affect state autonomy and structure interests in the policy process. He concludes by arguing,

> Policy communities do develop where the state needs highly resourced groups to assist in policy implementation, and issue networks develop in areas of lesser importance or where there is a high level of political controversy. Although policy communities do seem more likely in Britain than in the United States, the book did identify some policy communities in the US. Perhaps the most important point to emerge from this book is the complexity of the policy process. Notions of the state, pressure groups, state autonomy and policy networks are highly problematic. Consequently, it is difficult to make general claims about any of these concepts. The relationships between the state and groups have to be examined in a context that is historical, ideological and institutional. It also has to be remembered that the relationships between state and groups are relationships of dependence and therefore simplistic society- and state-centred approaches say little about empirical reality.... The state has advantages but ultimately it exists in an intricase relationships with civil-society and so state-actors cannot ignore group pressures.[51]

---

[49] J.J. Richardson, 'The Concept of Policy Style', in *Policy Styles in Western Europe*, ed. J.J. Richardson (London: Allen & Unwin, 1982).

[50] A.G. Jordan and J.J. Richardson, *British Politics and the Policy Process: An Arena Approach* (London: Unwin Hyman, 1987), 180.

[51] Smith, *Pressure, Power and Policy*, 234–5.

More recently, Denhardt and Denhardt proposed a model that sought to bring administrators and citizens together to work out solutions to pressing policy problems.[52]

CRITICISMS OF COMMUNITY AND NETWORKS APPROACHES

Atkinson and Coleman find the policy network and community approach significant as it takes us beyond the bureaucratic–political models and offers the possibility of bridging the boundaries between disciplines. However, the authors are critical of three aspects of the approach. First, that models have a problem of getting influenced by the macro-political institutions and political discourse. Second, that they have difficulty with the issue of the internationalization of many policy domains. And third, that the networks/community approach has failed to address the problem of policy innovation and change. They conclude on an optimistic note by arguing,

> These approaches appear to serve as a kind of conceptual crossroads for ongoing theoretical and empirical research… they provide a useful junction for the converging fields of international political economy and comparative public policy. They also invite discussions between those studying executive and legislative structures of government, those focusing on interest intermediation, and those analysing party politics and party government. More broadly, insights from such important branches of sociology as network analysis and the sociology of ideas and from the studies in economics on industrial organization, the structure of the firm, and institutional transactions have also been examined and, in some studies, incorporated into the analysis of networks and communities.[53]

It may be pointed here that policy communities are highly integrated within the policymaking process in contrast to issue networks which are less stable and have much weaker points entry into actual policymaking.

Some case studies use Rhodes's model as point of departure. Atkinson and Coleman point to the discriminatory nature of policy communities in contrast to issue networks in which anyone can gain membership.[54] Similarly, Bache states that the nature of linkages between organizations can range from tightly integrated policy communities to loosely coupled issue networks. 'If the ideal types of policy communities and issue networks are on extreme ends of the study spectrum, in between lie typologies of networks with some features of both'.[55]

Atkinson and Coleman further criticize approaches by arguing that if every policy community represents a specialized segment, what is the role of broader institutions? They

---

[52] R.B. Denhardt and J.V. Denhardt, 'The New Public Service: Serving Rather Than Steering', *Public Administration Review* 60(6) (2000): 549–59.
[53] Atkinson and Coleman, 'Policy Networks', 176.
[54] Atkinson and Coleman, 'Policy Networks, Policy Communities and the Problems of Governance'.
[55] I. Bache, 'Government within Governance: Network Steering in Yorkshire and the Humber', *Public Administration* 78(3) (2000): 576.

caution, 'proceedings to analyze the policy process as if broad state institutions are irrelevant is a misuse of the concepts network and community'.[56]

As a model of policymaking, studies on policy networks and policy communities have drawn considerable attention and support. However, this model has also attracted considerable criticism. Hogwood, for example, is not completely convinced as to its usefulness when it comes to understanding how issues are taken on to the policy agenda. Moreover, issues do not exist in well-defined communities and they tend to overlap and get mixed up in one policy network or another policy community. But this does not mean that we should give up the concepts, but he thinks that we should be more subtle in the way in which we define the boundaries between policy communities and policy areas. Policy communities will consist of a core set of issues, but at the boundaries, there will be many 'peripheral' issues which will overlap with the interests and concerns of other communities. But, the 'garbage can' model presents a picture which is altogether different from the one described in the policy community or policy network approach. Hogwood argues,

> Suppose we view a choice activity as a garbage can into which various problems and solutions are dumped by participants. The mix of garbage in a single can depends partly on the labels attached to the alternative cans; but it also depends on what garbage is being produced at the moment, on the mix of cans available, and on the speed with which garbage is collected and removed from the scene.[57]

PUBLIC ADMINISTRATION AND NETWORKS AND COMMUNITIES APPROACHES

A few scholars point to the long-term negative consequences of the trend towards policy community and network styles of politics. According to Skok, for instance, they are 'displacing political parties, chief executives and other political institutions that once served to centralize power in our fragmental governmental system'.[58] However, Fox and Miller do not agree with Skok's thesis. Instead of looking at policy and administrative processes as a series of power transactions between walled institutions, think as an energy field.[59] A public energy field is composed of a multiplicity of malleable, discursive social formations. Discourse formations such as policy communities, policy networks, adhocracies and the like are in abundant practice, but political and administrative scholars have only begun to theorize this phenomenon.

The complex web of relationships arising out of the use of networks bears major implications on the dichotomy of politics and administration. The conception of public administrators as neutrally competent and efficiency-guided public employees fails the admissibility test in political–administrative life. These administrators might engage in network-style policy communities due to administrative knowledge and experience on substantive policy

---

[56] Atkinson and Coleman, 'Policy Networks, Policy Communities and the Problems of Governance', 168.

[57] Quoted in Hogwood, *From Crisis to Complacency?* 23.

[58] J.E. Skok, 'Policy Issue Networks and the Public Cycle: A Structural–Functional Framework for Public Administration', *Public Administration Review* 55(4) (1995): 330.

[59] C.J. Fox and H.T. Miller, *Postmodern Public Administration: Toward Discourse* (Thousand Oaks, CA: SAGE Publications, 1995).

problems without being identified with party politics. Yet, as participants in policy communities, public administrators are political administrators. Public administrators maintain an activist role in policymaking process in that they freely put their knowledge and expertise into use to achieve certain policy goals. With different agendas, some scholars in public administration spoke up on behalf of a more active role of the administrators. New Public Management (NPM) expresses itself as managerialism which has the aim of controlling and managing policy communities for administrative purposes.

Public administrators mobilize key actors and effect policy outcomes. With knowledge and skills, they lead others to value their expertise and understanding of the important dimensions of the problem.[60] Knowledgeable people, along with others in need of answers, join efforts and work together. In the process of interaction and reciprocal influence, the issues become clarified, relevant evidence shared and alternative solutions suggested.

CONCLUSION

In brief, the functional utility of policy communities and policy networks is both political and administrative. In a political context, members of policy communities are instrumental in the process of getting funds from the larger political system. Policy communities are also administrative because critical management functions such as coordination, communication and integration are facilitated through them. Professional or intellectual interests represented by the players in the networks help link various policy actors located at different levels of government. At the same time, it is important to check the evil designs of the policy communities to assure that they do not usurp the vague yet pressing demands of the larger political community.

Review Questions

(i) Discuss the pluralist view of policy agenda setting.
(ii) Critically explain Schattschneider's argument regarding public policy agenda setting.
(iii) How did Cobb and Elder develop on Schattschneider's model of policy agenda setting?
(iv) The definition of issue is at the centre of politics. Elucidate.
(v) How did Bachrach and Baratz criticize the pluralist approach to policymaking agenda?

---

[60] Ibid.

POLICY DESIGN AND TOOLS
Approaches and Framework

INTRODUCTION

Policy formulation and implementation (including its consequences) need a policy design to anticipate and address policy gaps and distortions. Relatively, we know little about what constitutes a well-designed policy. Rather than a 'random and chaotic product of a political process', policies have underlying patterns and logics.[1] A policy design is seen as an institutional structure consisting of components such as problem definitions, goals, target groups, an implementation structure, tools, rationals and rules. The perspective in this chapter is that the policy process problems can be partially overcome with the crafting of an appropriate policy design. But the crafting of the policy is not easy. It typically entails a long process of analysis of problems and choices and an authoritative decision to enact a policy. Given the vagaries of the policy process, a policy design does not result from a single blueprint as in the case of a design of a building. Policy design shapes the implementation processes and outcomes.

Policy Design Defined

John Dryzek defines 'policy design' as 'the process of inventing, developing and fine-tuning a course of action with the amelioration of some problem (in mind)'.[2] In a recent article, May defines, 'policy design is both an art in identifying and working through feasible options and a science in analyzing the costs and impacts of different options'.[3] In democratic countries, the design perspective calls attention to matching content of a given policy to the political context in which the policy is formulated and implemented. Policy design is not simply an administrative or technocratic task. Rather, policy design is an activity of policy and political problem-solving strategies that are subject to a variety of forces. Political and social environment does play its role in fostering implementation as well as shaping choices about policy instruments and implementation structures.[4]

---

[1] Anne Larason Schneider and Helen Ingram, *Policy Design for Democracy* (Lawrence, KS: University Press of Kansas, 1997), chap. 3.

[2] John S. Dryzek, 'Don't Toss Coins in Garbage Cans: A Prologue to Policy Design', *Journal of Public Policy* 3(4) (1983): 346.

[3] Peter J. May, 'Policy Design and Implementation', in *Handbook of Public Administration*, eds. B. Guy Peters and Jon Pierre (London: SAGE Publications, 2003), 224.

[4] Steven Maynard-Moody, 'Beyond Implementation: Developing and Institutional Theory of Administrative Policy Making', *Public Administrative Review* 49 (1989): 137–42.

APPROACHES TO POLICY DESIGN

Policy formulation involves not only an administrative exercise but also, to a substantial degree, the political intervention. In recent times, the literature on the policy process uses the concept of 'policy design' as a framework for policymaking, policy implementation and policy evaluation. The works on policy designs and tools figured in the analytical studies in response to policy implementation failure. In many of implementation studies, policy failure was attributed to 'limits to human cognition' and 'limits to our knowledge about the social world'.[5] Research on policy formulation aims to bring 'awareness of the "boundaries" of rationality to the design process in order to expand the search for solutions, in hopes of improving the policies that result'.[6]

Some scholars approach policy design from the perspective of professional policy analysts. They think that improving the search for and generation of policy alternatives will lead to more effective and successful policies. Alexander, for example, proposes a 'deliberate design stage' in which policymakers search for policy alternatives. Usually, designing policy involves rational process of search, but Alexander argues that 'a conscious concern with the systematic design of policy alternatives can undoubtedly effect a significant improvement in decisions and outcomes'.[7] Linder and Peters also recommend a framework for use by the policy analysts. To them an effective framework would enable the analyst to analyse, compare and match the characteristics of problems, goals and instruments.[8]

Some scholars have written on policy designs from the perspective of academic research. Their works typically seek to develop a framework that can improve our understanding, analysis and evaluation of policy processes and their effects. They draw on institutional approaches that suggest laws, constitutions and the organizations of the political process channel, political behaviour and choices. That is, institutions shape actors' preferences and strategies by recognizing the legitimacy of certain claims over others.[9] Fischer argues that local contextual knowledge has an important role to play both in improving policy solutions and in advancing democracy.[10] On the other hand, Ingraham considers environment in terms of institutional setting. She argues that there is an interaction among various institutional settings. For example, legislative settings often require compromise among diverse issues which may lead to the blurring of a policy's purpose and content. On the other hand, bureaucratic settings enable technical expertise to be brought to bear on the design process, but at the expense of democratic legitimacy.[11]

---

[5] Herbert Simon, 'Human Nature in Politics', *American Political Science Review* 79(2) (1985): 293–304.

[6] Mara S. Sidney, 'Policy Formulation: Design and Tools', in *Handbook of Public Policy: Theory, Politics and Methods*, eds. Frank Fischer, Gerald J. Miller and Mara S. Sidney (Boca Raton, FL: CRC Press, 2007), 80.

[7] Ernest R. Alexander, 'Design in the Decision-making Process', *Policy Sciences* 14 (1982): 289.

[8] Stephen H. Linder and B. Guy Peters, 'From Social Theory to Policy Design', *Journal of Public Policy* 4 (1985): 237–59.

[9] Ellen M. Immergut, 'The Theoretical Core of the New Institutionalism', *Politics and Society* 26 (1998): 34.

[10] Frank Fischer, *Citizens, Experts and the Environment: The Politics of Local Knowledge* (London: Duke University Press, 2000).

[11] Patricia Ingraham, 'Toward a More Systematic Consideration of Policy Design', *Policy Studies Journal* 15 (1987): 611–28.

Weimer urges policy designers to think policies in terms of institution-building.[12] That is, policies as institutions that can shape behaviour and perceptions. So, he argues, that policies can be structured in such a way as to bring about desired changes in problematic conditions, but also the political coalitions to support them. Bobrow and Dryzek also advocate contextual designs that explicitly incorporate values, and urge policy analysts to draw from a range of perspectives on policy analysis, from welfare economics, public choice and structural approaches to political ideology when searching for policy alternatives for the policy design.[13]

May argues that political environment has a significant influence on the policy design process. For example, on forest preservation or child labour issues, many organized interests will take an active part in defining the problem and suggesting alternatives, and they may offer an array of opposing ideas. The design challenge in such a scenario is to find solutions that will be acceptable to participants but also will achieve desired outcomes, 'A dilemma arises when policy proposals that balance the competing interests do not necessarily lead to optimal outcomes'.[14] On the other hand, on some issues, few groups participate in defining the problem and offering policy alternatives. The dilemma here involves concerns about democratic process, but also the policymakers may have trouble capturing the attention of the policy community. For example, the Land Acquisition Bill (2015) could not get parliamentary approval as the ruling NDA did not have a majority in the Rajya Sabha.[15] Here the challenge is sometimes to mobilize public opinion to care about policies.

Schneider and Ingram: Integrative Approach to Policy Design

The basic idea in the policy formulation is that any given policy incorporates a variety of means or tools for accomplishing objectives that include mandates, incentives, penalties and provisions of sharing of information. In their work, *Policy Design for Democracy*, Schneider and Ingram present a policy design that departs from the stagist model by conceptualizing an iterative process.[16] The key feature of their framework is a shift from the discrete stages of the policy process into a single model that emphasizes the connections between problem definition, agenda setting, and policy design on the one hand, policy design, implementation and impact on target groups and democratic society, on the other. This framework of theirs is primarily an integrative approach as exhorted by Lasswell and other policy scientists. The policy design perspective presents a framework to guide empirical research that integrates these three dimensions: Ideas and interests interact within an institutional setting to produce a policy design. This policy design then becomes institution-building in its own right, structuring the future interaction of ideas and interests. Sidney proposes that this model can be used to guide empirical research; and also studies can be undertaken to refine their predictions about policy designs and their impact on society.

---

[12] David L. Weimer, 'The Craft of Policy Design: Can It Be More Than Art?', *Policy Studies Review* 11(3–4) (1992): 370–88.

[13] Bobrow and Dryzek, *Policy Analysis for Design*.

[14] Peter May, 'Reconsidering Policy Design: Policies and Publics', *Journal of Public Policy* 11 (1991) 197.

[15] See *The Financial Express*, 12 May 2015.

[16] Schneider and Ingram, *Policy Design for Democracy*, 53.

With their framework, Schneider and Ingram, in their study, explore how government and policy create and maintain 'systems of privilege, domination, and quiescence among those who are the most oppressed'.[17] Moreover, as already pointed out, policy designs influence not merely policy implementation, but also political mobilization and the nature of democracy. They call public policies 'the principal tools in securing the democratic promise for all people'. However, they are concerned about the impacts of policy designs that result from 'degenerative' political processes.[18] During such processes, political actors sort target populations into 'deserving' and 'undeserving' groups as justification for channelling benefits or punishments to them. Clearly, politics is involved not only in the understanding of the problem but also in the choice of a political solution to solve it. For example, the Punjab government passed in 2014 a law against damage to public and private property but uses it when politically convenient. Farmers are spared because they constituted a large vote base, but smaller groups of protesters who can cause little political damage are very often dealt with brutally.[19]

APPROACHES TO POLICY TOOLS

When considering to the discussion on approaches to the policy tools or instruments, the literature is somewhat disconnected. Policy tools are used to achieve the goals set out in a policy. According to Lester Salamon and Michael Lund, a policy tool is 'a method through which government seeks a policy objective'.[20]

Anne Schneider and Helen Ingram define policy tools as 'elements in policy design that cause agents or targets to do something they would not do otherwise or with the intention of modifying behaviour to solve public problems or attain policy goals'.[21] James Anderson calls policy instruments or tools 'techniques of control' that are 'by one means or another, overtly or subtly,… designed to cause people to do things, refrain from doing things, or continue doing things that they would otherwise not do'.[22]

Along with the study on policy designs, there is also found a change in focus from the study of policy context as a whole to the study of policy instruments. The basic assumption is that any given policy incorporates a variety of tools for achieving objectives that include incentives and mandates (e.g. grants, loans), penalties (such as fines) and provision for sharing of information.

In his framework of policy analysis, Bardach offers a range of eight tools: taxes, regulation, grants, services, budgets, information, rights and other policy tools. For each tool,

---

[17] Ibid.

[18] Helen Ingram and Anne Schneider, 'Introduction: Public Policy and the Social Construction of Deservedness', in *Deserving and Entitled: Social Construction and Public Policy*, eds. A.L. Schneider and H.M. Ingram (Albany, NY: SUNY Press, 2005), 2.

[19] From 7–10 October 2015, on a call by eight farmer bodies, rail services were badly affected in various parts of Punjab as farmers began their 'rail roko' (disruption of train services) agitation against government policies.

[20] Lester M. Salamon and Michael S. Lund, 'The Tools Approach: Basic Analytics', in *Beyond Privatization: The Tools of Government Action*, ed. Lester M. Salamon (Washington: Urban Institute Press, 1989), 29.

[21] Schneider and Ingram (1997), *Policy Design for Democracy*, 93.

[22] James E. Anderson, *Public Policy-making*, 5th ed. (Boston, MA: Houghton Mifflin, 2002).

he suggests why and how it might be used, and what some of the possible pitfalls could be, aiming to stimulate creativity in designing policy.[23] Hood examines a variety of government tools with the aim of making sense of government complexity, generating ideas for policy design and enabling comparisons across governments.[24]

Salamon notes that in recent years there has developed 'a set of theories that portrays government agencies as tightly structured hierarchies insulated from market forces and from effective citizen pressure and therefore free to serve the personal and institutional interests of bureaucrats instead'.[25] Salamon maintains that in the changed situation 'a massive proliferation has occurred in the tools of public action, in the instruments or means used to address public problems'. These arrangements provide government parties (private sector actors and NGOs) much greater discretion than the close supervision and regulation of the past. He identifies the following tools: direct government provision, governmental corporations and sponsored enterprises, economic regulation, social regulation, government insurance, public information and charges and special taxes, contracting, purchase-of-service contracting, grants, loans and loan guarantees, tax expenditures, vouchers and tort liability. The clear limitation of this type of classification is the *ad hoc* nature of the listing of tools.[26]

As in the case of policy design, work on policy tools highlights the political consequences of particular tools, as well as their underlying assumptions about problems, people and behaviour. Salamon characterizes the choice of tools as political as well as operational: 'What is at stake in these battles is not simply the most efficient way to solve a particular public problem, but also the relative influence that various affected interests will have in shaping the program's post enactment evolution'.[27] Thus the choice of tools is important because it affects not only the nature of public management but also the policy outcome. Study by Salamon and Lund offers four dimensions according to which tools may be compared.[28] These are:

(i) *Nature of government activity* (money payments, provision of goods and services, legal protections, restrictions and penalties).

(ii) *Structure of delivering system* (direct or indirect service delivery). For example, the central government approved ₹50,000 crore for the Pradhan Mantri Krishi Sinchayee Yojana (PMKSY) for 2015–20 for providing irrigation facilities in every village. But the cost of implementing PMKSY would be shared at 75 per cent grant by the centre and 25 per cent by the state government.[29]

(iii) *Degree of centralization* (more directly service is provided, e.g., the more the administration of the programme is centralized).

[23] Eugene Bardach, *A Practical Guide for Policy Analysis: The Eightfold Path to More Effective Problem Solving* (Washington: CQ Press, 2005).

[24] Christopher Hood, *The Tools of Government* (Chatham: Chatham House Publishers, 1986), 115.

[25] Lester M. Salamon, 'The New Governance and the Tools of Public Action: An Introduction', in *The Tools of Government: A Guide to the New Governance*, ed. Lester M. Salamon (Oxford: Oxford University Press, 2002), 1.

[26] Ibid., 1–2.

[27] Ibid., 11.

[28] Salamon and Lund, 'The Tools Approach: Basic Analytics', 28–30.

[29] See *The Financial Express*, 3 July 2015.

(iv) *Degree of automaticity* (detailed administrative action). For example, foreign firms that do not have a permanent establishment in India will be/are exempt from paying minimum alternate tax (MAT) on profits from April 2001 that are covered under double taxation avoidance agreement (DTAA); Section 115JB of the Income Tax Act, 1961.[30] This exemption is a virtually effortless encouragement for foreign institutional investors (FIIs).

In addition to Salamon and Lund's typology of policy tools, some other scholars have also sought useful types of tools for policy. Elmore, for instance, draws a distinction among authority tools that are intended to produce compliance, inducements as conditional transfers of money for provision of specified services, capacity-building tools that invest in development of future services and system changing tools that transfer authority with a view to changing service delivery.[31] Schneider and Ingram also classify instruments and provide a related analytic distinction among authority tools that prescribe desired behaviours, inducements and sanctions that alter calculated behaviours, capacity-building tools that enhance abilities and hortatory tools that are used to produce effect.[32]

Howlett and Ramesh provide two broad categories of policy tools: 'economic models' and 'political models'.[33] Economic models of policy tools focus on individual freedom, initiative and choice (focus on non-coercive tools). However, they also note that welfare economists, whose focus is on overall societal well-being rather than the aggregation of individual well-being, do acknowledge the need for more coercive tools, such as an income tax, to correct some of the flaws of laissez-faire economics. In both cases, however, economists look at the choice of a policy tool on a rational consideration in order to find the best possible solution to a policy problem.

On the other hand, political models of policy tools focus on political feasibility. Howlett and Ramesh write, 'Any instrument [or tool] can theoretically accomplish any chosen aim, but governments prefer less coercive instruments unless forced by either recalcitrance on the part of the subject and/or continued social pressure for change to utilize more coercive instruments'.[34] Clearly, politics is involved not only in the understanding of the problem but also in the choice of a political solution to solve it. For example, the decision by the Haryana government to provide reservations to Jats and four other castes under the Specially Backward Class (SBC) was seen as a political solution in response to a political pressure, although the Punjab High Court on 26 July 2015 stayed this decision of the Haryana government.[35]

Although there are important shortcomings to thinking about policy tools or instruments from a solely political angle, again, while the typology of tools is useful to achieve certain goals, it does not explain much about the relative strengths and weaknesses of these techniques. Levine, Peters and Thompson provide a scheme for assessing the strengths

---

[30] See *Hindustan Times* (Chandigarh), 25 September 2015.
[31] Richard Elmore, 'Instruments and Strategy in Public Policy', *Policy Studies Review* 7(1) (1987): 174–86.
[32] Schneider and Ingram, *Policy Design for Democracy*, 93.
[33] Michael Howlett and M. Ramesh, *Studying Public Policy: Policy Cycles and Policy Subsystems* (Toronto: Oxford University Press, 1995), 157–63.
[34] Howlett and Ramesh, *Studying Public Policy: Policy Cycles and Policy Subsystems*, 158.
[35] See *The Tribune*, 27 July 2015.

and weaknesses of each tool.[36] They acknowledge the tentative nature of these criteria, and their limitations, but they are helpful in thinking about what tools might be useful to achieve specific goals. The managerial approach to the study of instrument fails to adequately address the policy context.[37]

May contends that implementation prospects are enhanced through sets of policy provisions[38]:

(i) *Capacity-building of intermediaries* through instruments of education and training, funding and technical assistance;

(ii) *Commitment-building of intermediaries* through instruments that include publicity about policy goals, authorization for citizen suits against inadequate implementation and incentives to carry out programmes; and

(iii) *Procedural policy instruments for intermediaries* that help to signal desired courses of action.

FRAMEWORK FOR POLICY DESIGN

It is undisputed that different policy designs either hinder or facilitate implementation. Therefore, a well-structured design is needed that enhances implementation prospects. The basic contention is that poorly framed statutes and complex implementation structures are a source of implementation problems.[39]

Here in this section, much of the discussion focuses on elements of policy design that decision-makers must consider while preparing to design policies.

Context of Policy Formulation

Often a policy has a particular design for its formulation and implementation. The framework suggested by Schneider and Ingram, for example, draws on institutional and decision-making theories (such as bounded rationality). Policymaking is seen to take place in a distinct socio-politico-economic environment. Institutional arenas such as legislature, executive, judiciary, bureaucracy and non-officials (interest groups, political parties, etc.) have rules, norms and procedures that affect actors' choices in favour of particular solutions and their preferences when they take specific policy decisions. Analysis of a particular context might lead to broad predictions about the policy design that will come from this design. But because designs have so many components (such as goals, target groups and tools), such analysis cannot specify in advance the particular package of dimensions that actors will build at a particular point in time. Further, prediction also is complicated by the human dimension of policymaking.

---

[36] Charles Levine, B. Guy Peters and Frank Thompson, *Public Administration: Challenges, Choices, Consequences* (Glenview: Scott, Little Brown, 1990).

[37] May, 'Policy Design and Implementation', 225.

[38] Ibid., 225.

[39] Deborah McFarlance, 'Testing the Statutory Conference Hypothesis', *Administration and Society* 20 (1989): 395–422.

Problem in Question

At the initial point, it is important to understand whether something really is a problem, and, if it is so, who it affects. It may be noted that the definition of the problem often shapes the way the problem is treated throughout the policy process.[40]

Whether there exists a problem could be ascertained through two mechanisms. In one, we know about public problems through changes in the indicators of a problem over time, rather than all of a sudden. For example, farmers' suicide gained attention as a public policy problem when upon hearing a PIL by a Punjab-based NGO (namely, Youth Kamal Organisation), the SC (through Social Justice Bench) on 21 August 2015 asked the central government to review the National Policy for Farmers (2007) to bring down the number of such incidents.[41] The farmers' suicide did not strike all at once; rather, the problem has been already in existence.

Other problems that gained attention as a public policy problem relate to sudden events such as earthquakes, terrorist attacks, flood furies or industrial accidents. Attention is also paid to the kind of event (e.g. death due to dengue) that affects a particularly influential member of a policy community than would ordinarily be paid.

Formulating Policy Goals

Once a problem is understood, the question arises as to how to eliminate or alleviate the problem or hold the problem from getting worse. Policies are created or made to meet a particular challenge or achieve progress towards specific goals.

It would be useful to categorize policy goals. Deborah Stone, for instance, lists four major categories of goals: equity, efficiency, security and liberty. In many cases, Stone argues, these goals clash: Most prominently, security often conflicts with liberty, while efficiency conflicts with all these goals.[42] Then there are different approaches to define goals. For instance, it is difficult to judicially define as to what constitutes the notion of equality. Generally, we believe that everyone should have equal opportunity for success but no guarantee of equal outcomes—particularly when the opportunities themselves are not equal. The current debate in India over reservation policy is a case in point.[43]

Moreover, such terms as equity, liberty and security are political terms and hard to define. But this does not mean that one cannot or should not use such terms to make a case for or against moves to create socio-economic viability and political balance. What is appropriate to examine is the extent to which conflicts exist and how they are resolved.

An important point is that government policies and goals are often vague, because they are created and made on political considerations. Therefore, it is sometimes difficult for the agencies charged with implementation to satisfy the demands of everyone involved

---

[40] E.E. Schattschneider, *The Semi-sovereign People* (Illinois: Dryden Press, 1975), 71–3.

[41] See *The Tribune* (Chandigarh), 22 August 2015. In its affidavit, the central government had maintained that the number of suicides among farmers had come down from 17,368 in 2009 to 11,772 in 2013.

[42] Deborah Stone, *Policy Paradox: The Art of Political Decision Making* (New York, NY: W.W. Norton, 2002), 83.

[43] Rajinder Chaudhry's article in *The Tribune* (Chandigarh), 25 September 2015.

in formulating and approving the broad policy. For example, there are many ways to stop female foeticide. One commonly cited method is to provide family planning services, promoting morality, spreading awareness among the people and motivating doctors to avoid female foeticide. The second method is to enforce implementation of the Pre-Conception and Pre-Natal Diagnostic Techniques (PCPNDT) Act, 1994. For example, in the state of Haryana, it was reported that under the PNDT Act, registration of 53 private centres had been either cancelled or suspended. During investigations of about 2,400 cases, 41,000 ultrasound machines were sealed and 28 cases were registered in lower courts.[44]

Advocates of these policies believe that these will yield the outcomes. The disagreement comes later when the decision is implemented, that is, when an agency takes specific steps to lower female foeticide rates. But when the legislature has specified the method for implementing a programme, these post-enactment goal conflicts are less likely, because they are explicitly stated in the legislation or at least strongly embedded in the policy design. Nevertheless, because legislation is usually the product of compromise, sometimes the means are not clear, and the targets remain only in files. For example, the National Health Profile (2015) of India revealed that the maternal mortality ratio (MMR) stood at 140 per one lakh live births as against the goal of 109 till September 2015 global deadline for targets.[45] The goal and how attainment is measured are clear: reduce the MMR. There may be other goals, such as reducing welfare dependency, increasing educational attainment, promoting morality and other benefits that derive from this, but the main goal is to reduce the MMR.

Developing a Casual Theory

Often government policies are vague and complex, and in the course of their implementation, they pose questions to the implementing agency for necessary intervention. The point is without good causal theory, and it is unlikely that a policy design will be able to deliver the desired outcomes. A causal theory or a model is a theory about what causes a problem and what particular response or intervention would alleviate that problem.

But developing causal theories in response to complexity of social problems is a very difficult exercise. On the other hand, if one develops the wrong causal theory, no policy, no matter how well designed, can have a good effect on the problem under consideration. For example, 'reservation policy' on the basis of castes has led to numerous protests and agitations in the country. 'Different legal treatment of SC/ST reservation and OBC reservation itself is indicative of something being seriously amiss'.[46] For example, National Scheduled Castes Alliance (NSCA), a conglomerate of non-general category communities, on 4 October 2015 slammed Rashtriya Swayamsevak Sangh (RSS) chief Mohan Bhagwat's statement about putting an end to reservation, saying such a trend would polarize society.

Stone finds that isolating the causes of problems is a complex issue. Stone makes a distinction between cause and effect in the natural world and in the social world: 'The natural world is the realm of fate and accident, and we believe we have an adequate understanding of causation when we can describe the sequence of events by which one

---

[44] See *The Tribune* (Chandigarh), 5 October 2015.
[45] Ibid., 25 September 2015.
[46] Ibid.; See also *Hindustan Times*, 5 October 2015.

thing leads to another'. On the other hand, 'in the social world we understand events to be result of will, usually human but perhaps animal. The social world is the realm of control and intent. We usually think we have an adequate understanding of causation when we can identify the purposes or motives of a person or group and link those purposes to their actions'.[47] Because of these different ways of causation, one can attribute a problem to an act of God or to acts of human causation, either purposive or negligent. For example, one can argue that when a climatic disaster damaged a part of Kashmir Valley (Jammu and Kashmir) in August 2014, it was seen as an act of God that we cannot avoid and we should simply feel compassion for victims, give aid to recover from the disaster and move on. Another view is that hurricanes (or earthquakes, or floods, or other disasters, for that matter) do not *cause* anything but high winds, heavy rains or too much water. It is the consequence of human activities that causes the damages, such as building houses too close to rivers or beaches or in such a way that they do not stand up to shaking ground or high winds and floods. In this context, human decision has an important role to play. It can change policy to induce better decisions that help reduce or avert human, animal or crop loss from such events.

A causal theory that a problem is caused by carelessness and omission means that policies are likely to be crafted regulating the activities in question, to prevent or at least penalize these actions. On the other hand, if a causal theory purports that a problem is caused by undesirable effects such as accidents (e.g. industry's carelessness), in such situations and cases different sets of policies are adopted which may emphasize self-regulation over government action. It has been observed, for example, that most industries in states have not come out strongly to comply with provisions of the EPA, 1986 and the Water (Prevention and Control of Pollution) Act, 1974. Industry management hesitates to comply with conditions imposed by the State Pollution Control Boards, such as treating the effluents and discharging them in an appropriate manner. In this way, the owner of the industry is evading liability, implying that rules and regulations are not being observed. These causal theories imply what sorts of policy instruments will be applied to address the problems in question.

Choice of Instruments and Politics

Differing perspectives have been offered for thinking about choice of policy instruments. Peters, for example, suggests that five factors come into play: ideas (including ideologies), institutions, interests, individuals and the international environment.[48] Schneider and Ingram and also Peters focus on relevant interests in considering the role of policymakers' perceptions of the target groups of a policy.[49] From this perspective, 'advantaged groups' such as farmers that are powerful are more likely to be selected for subsidies or other inducements. In contrast, 'deviant groups' such as drug users that are powerless are more likely to be chosen for penalties and coercive programmes. Donovan shows that legislators sometimes obscure intended beneficiaries by crafting legislation that has hidden gains.[50]

---

[47] Stone, *Policy Paradox: The Art of Political Decision Making*, 189.
[48] B. Guy Peters, 'The Politics of Tool Choice', in *The Tools of Government: A Guide to the New Governance*, ed. Lester Salamon (New York, NY: Oxford University Press, 2002).
[49] Schneider and Ingram, *Policy Design for Democracy*, 129–40.
[50] Mark Donovan, *Taking Aim: Target Populations and the Wars on AIDS and Drugs* (Washington: Georgetown University Press, 2001).

Scholars such as Bressers and O'Toole focus on the source of policy ideas as an impor-tant basis for the selection of policy instruments.[51] They argue that policy communities in which ideas evolve will advocate those instruments that help to maintain the existence of the community.

These differing perspectives in the choice of instruments suggest how different interests and ideas influence policy designs. The reverse of this is the way in which policy instru-ments affect various target groups.

POLICY DESIGN AFFECTING IMPLEMENTATION

After the policy is designed, it requires enactment and implementation, at which point the implementing agencies translate the will (objects and goals) of the political executive and legislature into actual policy outcomes (inducing changes in the target population and altering policy targets).

The success of public administration for development can be measured only in relation to the implementation of policies. Policy implementation is of critical importance to the success of government. However good the political system, however noble the goals, however sound the organizational system, no policy can succeed if the implementation does not bear relationship to the intentions of the policymakers. Implementation is a pro-cess of putting policy, law or authoritative decision into action. It is a process which is mainly concerned with coordinating and managing various elements—personnel, finan-cial, equipment resources, administrative capability to marshal resources and judicial and political support—required to achieve the desired goals.

Much has been said that policy designs and implementation structures are messy and often result in policy failure. Recognizing these facts, it is relevant to consider how choices made when designing policies potentially shape policy implementation.

Policy Intentions and Goals

In the first place, it is relevant to analyse whether the policy intended would provide benefits for particular segments of society, restrict behaviours in preventing a harm or mobilize action on the part of groups to address a problem. Policy intentions, in main, lead to formation of goals that are put in place. But even in the formation of intentions, that also shapes policy directions, one cannot rule out the obvious roles of political ideology and social learning.

Second, how does policy intention affect implementation? Instead of setting forth explicit direction for policy, it sets boundaries around choices of policy instruments and implemen-tation structures. Thus, for instance, the BJP-led government at the centre offered one-time opportunity to holders of hidden overseas wealth to avoid prosecution under the Black Money (Undisclosed Foreign Income and Assets) and Imposition of Tax Act, 2015 by paying 60 per cent of such wealth in taxes and penalty (in return for immunity from prosecution).[52]

---

[51] Hans Bressers and Laurence O'Toole, 'The Selection of Policy Instruments: A Network-based Perspective', *Journal of Public Policy* 18(Part III) (1998): 213–39.
[52] Under this amnesty scheme (special three-month compliance window), only 635 Indians declared unaccounted overseas assets of ₹4,160 crore which ended on 30 September 2015. See *The Financial*

An important lesson for policy design is to fashion instruments and approaches to implementation that are consistent with the policy goals (intentions). Failing which the policy seems to be working at cross purposes. A second important lesson is that the political environment, that is the target groups and field staff that implement the policy, must be supportive of the policy goals (intentions). Failing which the field staff and target groups may not follow the principled agreements of the policy, and also work to weaken or thwart it.

Targets of the Policy

Parliament's enactment of a law or its approval of the public policy does not result in a simple translation from Parliament's will to actual action on the part of implementing agencies, or actual compliance on the part of the people whose behaviour the policy seeks to change. For example, public education campaigns, such as encouraging villagers to send their children to schools, could be successful in inducing behavioural change among a large enough proportion of the village population. Such campaigns can also become problematic in the face of old customs and poverty factors. Some difficulties are involved in altering public behaviour or attitudes when new information becomes available. The resource question is also involved in operating a programme. Obviously, establishing or operating any public programme is likely to face much more problems if adequate manpower, financial and infrastructure resources are lacking.

Policy targets may be people, organizations or animals whose behaviour the policy seeks to alter. The selection of the policy tool is a function of the assumed behaviour of the target. It may be coercive or non-coercive. The more coercive a policy, the more likely compliance with the policy can be achieved. But coercion needed to create compliance requires considerable financial resources. In contrast, non-coercive policies such as incentives and hortatory policies are much easier to administer because of their design and assumed behaviour, but the likelihood of policy success is likely to vary. Thus, there is a link between policy target and policy tool. This linkage falls under a broader category that Salamon and Lund call 'effectiveness'. According to them, this effectiveness can be assessed on two levels: the 'supply effectiveness' of the programme in providing a necessary level of output to induce changes in the target population, and the 'targeting effectiveness' of the programme in altering policy targets.[53]

Policy Instruments Influencing Target Groups and Intermediaries

Needless to emphasize that for delivering governmental services to segments (target groups) of society entail choices about the appropriate means of intervention (use of instruments). And in this context, ideology, strategy and politics do influence the ways in which different instruments are combined into policy mixes.[54] The strategic issues revolve around policy analysis relate to appropriate role of the government, the potential means of intervention and the costs and feasibility of implementing the programmes. One key

---

Express, 6 October 2015. Total tax receipt from black money is reported to be ₹2,500 crore (31 December 2015).

[53] Salamon and Lund, 'The Tools Approach: Basic Analytics', 40–42.

[54] David Weimer, 'Claiming Races, Boiler Contracts, Heresthetics, and Habits: Ten Concepts for Policy Design', *Policy Sciences* 25(2) (1992): 135–59.

lesson for policy design and implementation is that the mix of instruments needs to adhere to an overall strategy for which the elements do not work at cross purposes. For example, it makes little sense when the government encourages production of tobacco on the one hand, while it, on the other hand, discourages smoking cessation policies.

Apart from influencing groups, policy instruments affect intermediaries who are charged with carrying out policy programmes. Weimer strongly recommends that policies should contain features that encourage or compel intermediaries to carry out requisite actions for implementing the policy. Similarly, May also writes, 'Commitment- and capacity-building provisions are best thought of as interactive features that reinforce each other in facilitating policy implementation'.[55] These features also serve important functions in signalling what is expected of implementing intermediaries.

Implementation Structure

Although much of the literature focuses on intended targets or outcome of policy, implementation structure choice to carry out a policy is also relevant. The intermediaries that are charged with carrying out policy and how they share responsibilities are important aspects that constitute the implementation structure for a given policy. According to O'Toole, policy implementation is shaped by many variables, and therefore it is necessary to understand the dynamics and operations of a host of other types of institutions and how they relate to each other.[56] What is necessary is a structure that both reflects the philosophy of the policy and engages entities that are committed to and have the capacity to carry out the policy. Stoker refers to this as the development of constructive patterns of cooperation.[57] It is of utmost importance to give attention to the existing implementation structure when it is deficient or too rigid to adapt to new requirements. Under such circumstances, Elmore suggests that 'system changing' can be a useful policy tool. Changing the service delivery or regulatory responsibilities provides an opportunity to put in place a new, and hopefully more constructive, set of relationships.[58]

The policy design should also include oversight mechanisms not only for encouraging cooperation among reluctant partners but also for identifying and addressing problems occurring in implementing the policy.[59] Perhaps an important function of oversight is provision of repeated signals about the importance of specific policy goals. Oversight may not only occur through governmental mechanisms. The media, trade groups, investors, and interest organizations can potentially play important roles in monitoring progress of a given policy or policy sector. For example, a National Mission for Clean Ganga (NMCG) has been set up under the Ministry of Water Resources, River Development and Ganga Rejuvenation (GOI) for water quality monitoring.[60]

---

[55] May, 'Policy Design and Implementation', 229.
[56] Laurence J. O'Toole, 'Interorganizational Relations in Implementation', in *Handbook of Public Administration*, eds. B. Guy Peters and Jon Pierre (UK: SAGE Publications, 2003), chap. 18.
[57] Robert P. Stoker, *Reluctant Partners, Implementing Federal Policy* (Pittsburgh, PA: University of Pittsburgh Press, 1991).
[58] Elmore, 'Instruments and Strategy in Public Policy', *Review of Policy Research* 7(1) (1987):174–86.
[59] Stoker, *Reluctant Partners, Implementing Federal Policy*, 186.
[60] See *Hindustan Times*, 1 October 2015.

The intermediaries tasked for policy implementation are also faced with problems of discretion and accountability. Lipsky's seminal work on street-level bureaucrats, points out that field-level personnel, on the one hand, often need discretion in interpreting rules and implementing policy programmes to be responsive to the special needs of diverse clientele. On the other hand, inconsistent use of discretion can result in *de facto* policies that differ greatly from policy intentions as well as inequitable policy implementation. But any programme for which those at the frontlines of service delivery must have discretion to deal with complex situations. Thus, for example, Sunita Narain discusses how regulatory inspectors' choices about the style of enforcing regulations affect regulatory compliance.[61]

Here it may be noted that it is impossible to separate the process of designing policies from their implementation—much as all the stages of the policy process are hard to separate. Design and implementation are closely linked as the choices made in the design of a policy will greatly influence the way a policy is implemented, which in turn influences the outcomes of these policies. In fact, policy designers often base their policy designs on experience with similar policies that have already been put into effect. Moreover, separation of design and implementation is hard from the rest of the policy process because the policy design process continues even during the design and implementation stages. Parliament's approval of a policy or enactment of a law does not result in actual action on the part of government agencies, or actual compliance on the part of the people whose behaviour the policy seeks to modify. Staff agencies or implementing agencies must take what Parliament has passed and figure out what it requires or allows them to do. The process of translating vague legislative commands into rules and regulations can be a very difficult task in the entire policy process.

But the experience with the implementation of the policy helps change the policy design, even when the policy and its goals are supposedly in place and operating. Often the target policy is replaced by blocking financial grants because, to a considerable extent, implementation was not successful as was hoped.

CRITICISM AND OPTIMISM

The stagist model as proposed by a host of scholars does have certain limitations. The specification of policy alternatives and the selection of policy tools do not follow neatly from agenda-setting process nor lead into implementation. On the other hand, Schneider and Ingram offer an integrative approach that pushes past a simple stage model by conceptualizing an 'iterative process'. With their integrative framework that places policy design at its centre, they offer a theory of public policy that directly addresses 'the question of who gets what, when, and how from government'.[62] Critics charge that this approach lacks a clear mechanism of policy change that can be tested across cases. The case in point is the judiciary which is the governmental sphere most absent from scholarship on public policy analysis. Although many scholars have undertaken the research on the role

---

[61] Sunita Narain, 'The Great Indian Sale', *Business Standard* (Chandigarh), 23 September 2013.
[62] Anne L. Schneider and H.M. Ingram, eds., *Deserving and Entitled: Social Constructions and Public Policy* (Albany, NY: SUNY Press, 2005).

of judiciary in public policymaking and implementation, the study is largely disconnected from theoretical work on the policy process in general, and policy formulation in particular. On the other hand, many scholars argue that the work of the courts by nature constitutes policymaking. For example, the SC on 11 August 2015 restricted the use of Aadhaar card for getting subsidies on foodgrains under the public distribution system, kerosene and cooking gas. After the Attorney General and other law officers pleaded that governance had been hit following the curbs, a Constitution Bench was set up to consider the plea for allowing the use of Aadhaar cards on a voluntary basis for effective implementation of welfare schemes and regulation of financial, telecom and other sectors.[63]

Certainly, courts represent a distinctive institutional setting, whose actors, procedures, language and processes of reasoning differ from those that prevail in legislatures and bureaucracies.[64] Yet it is possible to conceptualize court cases as processes of policy formulation. Courts thus offer a productive comparative case for studies of the impact of institutions on policymaking. In India, many policy issues are decided by the judiciary.

Attention is already drawn to the increased role of the NGOs in policy formulation and selection of tools. Research about the kinds of policy designs that NGOs formulate is emerging, or at least they provide sufficient data about the problems in question. For example, Green NGO Navdanya, led by environmental activist Vandana Shiva, accused genetically modified (GM) seed companies of 'luring' farmers with 'false' promises and demanded fair compensation and promotion of local varieties of seeds to prevent another 'catastrophe'.[65]

More recently, neighbourhood organizations have designed many innovation policies and successfully implemented them.[66] In Baltimore's poor neighbourhoods, organizations targeted their policies to the most needy, framing individuals as redeemable. Sidney says, 'More attention to policy formulation outside the bureaucracy, and below the national level can broaden our theories and substantive knowledge of this important function'.[67] Such efforts by organized interests together with government officials make up policy communities.[68]

CONCLUSION

Much of the discussion in this chapter is on interplay of policy design and implementation with focus on the extent to which glaring policy distortions can be anticipated and addressed as part of the policy design, policy instruments and policy implementation. Such policy designs seek to build the capacity of intermediaries to effect requisite actions and to foster increased commitment to the policy intentions. However, it may be clarified that policy design and implementation are tasks of political and administrative

---

[63] See *The Tribune*, 10 October 2015.
[64] Sidney, 'Policy Formulation: Design and Tools', 86.
[65] See *Hindustan Times*, 9 October 2015.
[66] Padmalaya Mahapatra and Niranjan Pani, 'Gender, Poverty and Globalization in India', *South Asian Journal of Socio-political Studies* 14(2) (2014): 46–49.
[67] Sidney, 'Policy Formulation: Design and Tools', 86.
[68] Hugh T. Miller and Tansu Demir, 'Policy Communities,' in Sidney, 137–147.

problem-solving that are subject to a variety of pressures. However, there is an ample evidence to suggest that little is known about the interplay of a mix of instruments that emerge as a result of variety of policy and political compromises.

Review Questions

(i) What do you understand by the term 'policy design'?

(ii) Discuss various approaches to the concept of policy design.

(iii) How does policy design influence the nature of democracy? Explain with an example from recent times.

(iv) Discuss the dimensions according to which policy tools can be classified (ref: Salmon and Lund's work).

(v) Explain the basic framework of policy design with an example from contemporary times.

PUBLIC POLICY AND INTERGOVERNMENTAL RELATIONS

INTRODUCTION

Policymaking and policy implementation in a system of multilevel government confront a basic problem of governance—how to resolve policy conflicts and compete claims between and among central, state and local governments. The basic question is, 'How to relate area and function?'[1] The link between constitutional arrangements (policy requirements) and intergovernmental units implementation (administration) is primarily an issue of IGR.[2] Managing IGR has become all the more important in the wake of growing federalism. They involve consultation, cooperation and coordination of the relationships among governments for the purpose of achieving specific policy goals.

As a concept, IGR[3] originated in the 1930s, but the person who popularized the term, however, was William Anderson.[4] IGR, for Anderson, 'designates an important body of activities or interactions occurring between governmental units of all types and levels within the federal system'.[5] Consequently, 'IGR is generally characterized by reciprocal activity and interdependent choices among multiple governmental units and political interests'.[6] In a sense, there are no IGR but only relations among officials who perform different roles in diverse units of government.

The term 'intergovernmental relations' refers to the working relationships between and among all levels of government. Technically speaking, the study of IGR is concerned with how the multiplicity of types of governmental units interact with one another. IGR involve a series of political, administrative and financial relationships among all units of government

---

[1] J.W. Fesler, 'The Basic Theoretical Question: How to Relate Area and Function', in *The Administration of the New Federalism: Objectives and Issues*, ed. L.E. Grosenick (Washington: ASPA, 1973), 4–14.

[2] IGR as a phrase describing the character of federalism was initially used by Snider in 1937. (See C.F. Snider, 'County and Township Government in 1935–1936', *American Political Science Review* 31 (1937): 909–16.)

[3] A landmark book in the field is an edited collection of papers on interorganizational policymaking by Hanf and Scharpf (1978), which surveys the rising interest in how central and local governments in both unitary and federal systems interact and limit control and coordination. See K. Hanf and F.W. Scharpf, eds., *Interorganizational Policy Making* (London: SAGE Publications, 1978).

[4] William Anderson, *Intergovernmental Relations in Review* (Minneapolis, MN: University of Minnesota Press, 1960).

[5] Ibid., 3.

[6] D. Krane and D.S. Wright, 'Intergovernmental Relations', in *International Encyclopedia of Public Policy and Administration*, Vol. 2, ed. J. Shafritz (Boulder, CO: Westview Press, 1998), 1168–76.

that possess varying degrees of authority and jurisdictional autonomy. In federal systems, sub-national governments refer to states or provinces and local-level units such as village panchayats, counties and councils. However, in unitary systems, there are two levels of government usually.

IGR include relations between (i) the national (usually called one central or federal) government and local units of government, (ii) two or more states, (iii) each state and its own subordinate (local) governments and (iv) two or more governments at the local level. Regardless of the country, the design of IGR has important implications for the public policy.

Reasons for and Objectives of IGR

As a matter of public concern and policy, effective governmental relations and cooperation have become all the more important in a federal polity. Although IGR are an essential aspect of federal systems such as the USA,[7] Canada[8] and India,[9] they are also an essential aspect of all multi-tier or multi-sphere political systems, including constitutionally decentralized unitary systems in Britain[10] and France. Tensions between central-, state- and local-level officials may not be inevitable but may result when federal or central programme requirements and regulation interfere with the policy and political preferences of diverse state and local constituencies. Greater IGR between union, state and local result from several factors, some of which are

(i) conflict of interest among federal units,
(ii) unavoidable interdependence and interpenetration between levels and
(iii) increased role of government at all levels.

Interdependence between governments and the need for effective IGR are required particularly where the Constitution provides that a considerable portion of central legislation is to be executed or administered by the province or states as in India and South Africa. Hence in a federal country such as India, there is a need to make provisions for IGR. The experience of IGR in many federations points to the existence of a variety of arrangements (constitutionally prescribed, established by legislation, government resolution, etc.).

---

[7] First federation in modern times is the USA founded in 1787, though combined with presidentialism.
[8] Canada was the first country in the world to combine parliamentarism and federalism in 1867.
[9] India was the first country in the Afro-Asian world to combine parliamentarism and federalism with charter of rights in 1950 like the USA federation (in 1787) but unlike Canada (1867) which belatedly adopted the charter in 1982.
[10] British constitutionalism is a harmonious construction, consistent with democratization based on an amalgamation of three constituent elements: parliamentary sovereignty, rule of law and conventions of the constitution regarding executive prerogatives and parliamentary privileges. The three elements together represent a hierarchy of values, making the will of the House of Commons, and ultimately the will of the people supreme. See A.V. Dicey, *Introduction to the Study of the Law of Constitution* (Indianapolis, IN: Liberty Fund, 1982); first published in 1885 and the present 1982 edition is a reprint of the 1915 edition with a new Introduction by Roger E. Michner. With grant of transfer of powers to Scotland since 1999 when a Scot's Parliament was set up, now there is the beginning of the end of UK and heralding an eventual federalism.

Specifically, IGR are desirable as to

(i)   coordinate national and state policies in areas where jurisdiction is shared (concurrent subjects);
(ii) improve the information base in order to better policymaking and to reconcile policy differences;
(iii) attain national objectives in social and economic policy areas of state and local jurisdiction;
(iv) work towards a coordinated approach in the implementation of public policies at the national, state and local levels;
(v)   accommodate differences among states in policy capacity and fiscal resources for the exercise of their jurisdiction;
(vi) enable state and local governments to meet the specific needs of their people; and
(vii) contribute to stability through alternative channel of policymaking.

Thus by way of idealizing IGR, differences in policy areas can be ironed out. In this context, Henry observes,

All in all, federal systems of government and decentralized governance appear to be less corrupt, more efficient, less costly, more responsive, more innovative, and have more trusting citizens than do unitary systems and centralized governance.[11]

POLICY AND ADMINISTRATIVE ISSUES OF IGR

Forms of IGR

A federalist system generally consists of a centralized national government that has jurisdiction over the national as a whole. The subject matter of channels of IGR includes (i) legislation and policymaking area, (ii) administration, (iii) fiscal adjustment (which is a crucial area in most multi-sphere political systems) and (iv) information gathering (information exchange or joint collection).

Interaction is a prerequisite to effective IGR. Interaction between the three spheres of government or agencies of IGR on policy, legislative or administrative issues may take the following forms:

(i) **Coordination:** In this form of interaction, governments try to develop commonly acceptable policies and objectives which they will then each develop within their own jurisdiction.
(ii) **Conflict Resolution:** Conflict resolution on jurisdiction is another type of interaction between governments. Intergovernmental conflict may be resolved through intergovernmental negotiation or through appeal to the courts.

---

[11] Nicholas Henry, *Public Administration and Public Affairs*, 12th ed. (New Delhi: PHI Learning, Indian Reprint 2012), 412.

(iii) **Independent or Joint Policymaking:** Governments may take action without consulting others or considering their interests. In joint policymaking, governments are required to iron out differences on policy issues and act together. Shared-cost programmes on environment protection or population control are examples where joint policies can be made.

(iv) **Consultation:** In consultation, governments recognize that their actions affect others and therefore exchange views before making a policy. But it is not necessary that the central government acts on the advice of the state government.

Policy Issues in IGR Context

In all countries, be they federal or unitary, power is necessarily divided across governments. The extent of division of power has, however, important implications for the functioning of the IGR. Properly structured intergovernmental transfers provide support for policy objectives of sub-national governments. The legal and constitutional framework, therefore, should provide clarity to the role of intergovernments in public policymaking process. In countries where the system of IGR is guaranteed by the Constitution, sub-national policymaking power is not susceptible to shifts in the allocation of power. On the other hand, in countries where the legal basis for policymaking power lies in the enactment of simple laws, the changes in the political environment affect IGR. In countries where the legislative branch of government enacts simple laws for defining sub-national governments' revenue and expenditure assignments, central government has discretionary power over sub-national governments' policymaking domain. Some of the important issues concerning IGR in public policy are briefed in this chapter.

Decentralization Versus Centralization

Recent trends in IGR point to decentralization of policymaking among governments at various levels. As a general term, decentralization includes broader elements of political, fiscal and institutional arrangements, and can be characterized as devolution, deconcentration and/or delegation.[12] The clear distinction between three forms of decentralization practices is decision-making power of sub-national authorities. 'Devolution' is the fullest form of decentralization where independently established sub-national governments are given the responsibility for delivery of a set of services along with the authority to impose taxes and fees to finance services. 'Deconcentration' refers to decentralization of central government offices. 'Delegation' is mandating sub-national governments with certain services under the supervision of central government. The argument in favour of decentralization stems from motivation for enhanced efficiency, accountability and autonomy. Touching aspects of decentralization, a study on Denotified and Nomadic Tribes (DNTs) brings out some important facts: 'Though so much of the schemes and programmes are noticed in the documents, the condition of the Denotified and Nomadic Tribes has not improved much', despite budgetary allocations.[13]

---

[12] Robert D. Ebel and Karen Hotra, 'World Bank Supports Fiscal Decentralization', *Transition* 8(5) (1997): 11–12.

[13] D. Malli Gandhi, 'Development of Denotified Tribes Communities in India: Issues and Concerns', *South Asian Journal of Socio-Political Studies* 16(2) (2016): 32–43.

Monetary and Fiscal Issues

Granting of funds from the centre to the poor states for achieving policy goals is important. It is argued that assigning the stabilization function to sub-national governments is inappropriate because currency stability requires that monetary policy can be best pursued by central government. Central government is better equipped to deal with spillover effects of local spending inflationary pressures. But at the same time, price stability is a direct result independent of a monetary authority such as Reserve Bank of India or the US Federal Reserve Board. The question is whether fiscal decentralization mitigates the problem or not. In countries where sub-national governments' accountability is weak and the institutions of political control are immature, there may be a risk that sub-national governments may abuse the fiscal power. Therefore, Wildasin argues that 'effective fiscal decentralization requires an institutional structure that minimizes these adverse incentives'.[14] An effective decentralization initiative should also promote transparency, accountability and predictability in the system of intergovernmental fiscal relations. Although devolution of power to sub-national governments is a necessary condition for decentralization, it has to be accompanied with hard budget constraints. Hard budget constraints motivate responsible behaviour by sub-national governments also and eliminate bailout conditions. Nearly, all states in India are experiencing debt burden situations.

Further, there are issues of redistribution and resource allocation. In most of the federal countries, the Constitution explicitly assigns social welfare functions and redistributive taxing ability to sub-national governments. Even in some of the transition countries, such as India and Russia, sub-national governments are engaged in public health care and public education. In addition, the regulatory power of sub-national governments has distributional impact on land use, rent controls, user charges and the like.

As regards the resource allocation function, it is argued that policies of sub-national governments differ to reflect the preferences of their residents. Therefore, the argument in favour of fiscal decentralization is twofold: (1) fiscal decentralization will increase competition among the local governments which will ultimately limit the size of the public sector, and (2) decentralization will increase efficiency because local governments have better information about their residents' needs than the central government. Although macroeconomic management must be a concern of central government primarily, the arguments support the idea that decentralization would not endanger stability. In fact, if appropriately designed, fiscal decentralization may indeed help macrostability.

Making a compelling case for 'cooperative federalism', the 14th Finance Commission (FC) (GOI) (2016–20) suggested necessary institutional changes to minimize discretion and improve the design of fiscal transfers from the centre to states. Following the acceptance of the 14th FC recommendations, the centre on 24 February 2015 announced withdrawal of financial support to eight CSS (and this process could gradually be accelerated). The Modi government recently decided to reduce the CSS to 27 from 72. Of the 27 CSS, the centre would fully fund 10, and provide 60 per cent of the funds for the 17 others. However, he reiterated that the centre will continue to support national priority projects

---

[14] David E. Wildasin, 'Externalities and Bailouts Hard and Soft Budget Constraints in Intergovernmental Fiscal Relations', *Policy Research* (Washington: World Bank, 1997), 26. Working Paper No. 1843.

such as poverty elimination, Mahatma Gandhi National Rural Employee Guarantee Act (MNREGA), education, health and rural development and agriculture, among others.[15]

Expenditure and Revenue Responsibilities

The important components of an intergovernmental system are expenditure and revenue responsibilities. The legal framework defining IGR should assign revenues and expenditures to different levels of government without leaving a room for ambiguity and negotiations.

An effective decentralization requires a well-defined framework in the assignment of expenditure responsibilities. The underlying premise behind the expenditure assignment is avoiding 'government failure'. If market conditions do not prevent internalization of costs in the service provision, private provision of services, such as telecommunications, electricity and water, would alleviate the burden of expenditure assignment. Sub-national governments can provide public goods such as roads and transportation services. However, regional spillovers across sub-national governments are an important factor that needs to be taken into consideration in public goods service provision. Presence of benefit spillovers is the major argument in favour of central government intervention. However, horizontal cooperation among sub-national governments provides a solution spillover problem. Expenditure assignment is directly related to resource allocation.

Along with the issue of expenditure assignment, the legal framework should define clearly revenue responsibilities for different levels of government. Revenue assignments without a concrete assignment of expenditure responsibilities would weaken the decentralization process. The essence of decentralization is that sub-national governments have the authority and responsibility to finance local services at the margin. While criticizing the Central Food Ministry, the CAG of India in its report to Parliament on 29 April 2016 said, 'The stales were largely unprepared for handling the logistics of allocation, movements and storage of foodgrains which was necessary for efficient and successful implementation of the National Food Security Act, 2013', which envisages providing highly subsidized foodgrains to two-thirds of the country's population.

In revenue assignment, steep progressive tax rates can be problematic for sub-national governments. Especially if income redistribution function is assigned to the central government, progressive taxes at sub-national level would drive out investments. Uniform levy of taxes minimize locational distortions of economic activities.

Services provided by sub-national governments can be financed through user charges and other local fees and taxes that are related to benefits. Examples of benefit-related revenues include taxes levied on motor vehicles and fuels and construction fees.

Uniform levy of taxes minimize locational distortions of economic activities. If sub-national governments are assigned to provide redistributional services such as education and health care, they need to control a stream of revenues. Such revenue items include income tax, local general business taxes and the sales tax. The proper assignment of revenues

---

[15] See *The Financial Express* (Chandigarh), 25 February 2015. See also *The Financial Express*, 9 November 2015.

depends on the expenditure assignment. In the Indian context, the 14th FC (under the chairmanship of Y.V. Reddy) said, 'We recognize that some of the current centrally sponsored schemes relate to subjects and can best be handled entirely by the states and, hence, should be in the fiscal space of states alone'.

Most states allege that with inadequate sources of revenue, they are unable to meet social and economic obligations. Further, there are wide differences in the level of development of the people. To address the issues of this vertical and horizontal imbalance in the centre–state and inter-state relations, the constitution has provided for intergovernmental transfers through the mechanism of FC. In addition, there are two main channels of central transfers to states: (unlike five-year plans in the past, there would be no allocation of funds by NITI Aayog) GST Council and financial assistance under CSS. Along with the Commission, prescribed statutory grants, the total untied transfers to states, in the FY 2015–20 are said to be 47.7 per cent of the pool, up from over 39 per cent between FY 2010 and 2015, giving a tremendous boost to states fiscal space and spending flexibility. As per the Finance Commission award, the tax devolution and United grants to states would rise as per their growing demands. [16]

During the assignment of resources, it must be ensured that sub-national governments do not exploit the fiscal power. Decentralization is not a panacea for government failure; however, it provides a greater potential for an improved public administration system. Transparency and accountability should become the features of the fiscal devolution in order to ensure healthy IGR.

POLICY AND ADMINISTRATIVE IMPLICATIONS OF IGR

As a framework, IGR are diverse and multi-theoretic. IGR designate an important body of activities in all federal and unitary systems of the world. But they have several policy and administrative implications. A major issue relates to provision of IGR. The issue is whether provision of IGR should be constitutionally prescribed, established by legislation, or left to be developed by practice and convention? It is observed that practically in all constitutions where there has been multi-sphere government, constitutional provisions for some basic intergovernmental institutions and processes have been made, although rarely in detail.

The Indian Constitution specifically contains several provisions governing IGR but does not specify the scope or timing of such implementation. A second issue is whether different forms of IGR should be in terms of encouraging centralization or overemphasizing the states? This will depend on the extent to which IGR are based on mutual agreement or are used as a vehicle for imposing views by one sphere on another. A third significant issue is who manages or controls IGR? What are the appropriate roles of legislature, executive, judiciary, and independent commissions in facilitating intergovernmental coordination? This will depend on the extent to which IGR are managed or controlled by these bodies.

A fourth important issue is how to relate IGR to democratic accountability? Often, complex arrangements for intergovernmental coordination and decisions requiring consultation and negotiation between governments dilute or undermine the democratic accountability

---

[16] See *Economic Times*, 25 February 2015.

of each government. Some mechanisms have to be devised for linking IGR to democratic accountability. A fifth issue is how to secure balance between intergovernmental coordination on the one hand and the diversity and policy innovation made possible by state initiatives on the other?

Public demands for doing more with less, promoting public organizations that are effective and bolstering citizen trust are issues of IGR. Many systems of IGR focus just on two tiers of spheres, leaving local government totally within state or provincial jurisdiction. The Indian Constitution has accorded constitutional status to the local governing institutions (under the 73rd and 74th Constitution Amendment Acts, 1993; inserted on 1 June 1993). The Indian Constitution in Parts IX (Panchayats) and IX A (Municipalities) appropriately recognizes the importance of local government as a third sphere, but this does make IGR more complex and gives to them a triangular rather than hierarchical character.

STRUCTURES AND PROCESSES OF POLICYMAKING

Constitutionally, India is a Union of States (Article 1 of the Indian Constitution) but organized on federal lines[17] with power vertically divided between the union, state and local governments. The Constitution contains also detailed provisions governing IGR which would promote harmonious functions of the whole political structure—union, state and local governments. In the federal structure of India, the nation is divided into 29 states and 7 UTs.[18] The latter are administered as if they were parts of a unitary state. Predominantly, therefore, India is federal. In certain circumstances, federalism may be suspended by the imposition of the President's rule. But in normal times, the centre has more authority than the states, but the spheres of both are clearly demarcated in such matters as legislation, policymaking, administration, finance, trade and commerce. Like the centre, the states have their own governmental machinery—legislature, executive and services, functioning within the sphere guaranteed to them. Sharing internal services is ideal when the service function requires little interaction with the people.

Distribution of Legislative Subjects

The Constitution has divided powers between the union and the states (Articles 245–252 and Schedule VII). Three lists of powers and functions have been constitutionally prescribed. The Union List comprises now 100 subject matters after a gain of 3 entries (addition of entries 2A, 92A, 92B, 92C and deletion of entry 33) during recent years. These subject matters are considered to be of national importance or scope—for example,

[17] The term 'federation' has not been used in the Indian Constitution as the erstwhile semi-autonomous provinces (later designated as states) were merged together by the decision of representatives of people in the Constituent Assembly, to form the Union. There was therefore no formal agreement among these entities to form any federation. The constituent units of the Union have therefore no constitutional right for secession. The Union has both federal and unitary features.

[18] The number of states within the Union has increased from 14 in 1950 to 29 at this instant. This has been mostly due to reorganization of boundaries of the states and upgrading political status of the UTs. The erstwhile princely states were also merged into these states. There are also at present 7 UTs under the direct control of the union government. Two of these, namely, Delhi and Puducherry, have a higher political status than the other territories.

defence, international relations, major means of transport and communication, credit institutions and currency. The Union Parliament may legislate on these subject matters and the union government may exercise executive powers in co-extension with the legislative powers. The State List includes 61 subject matters now after the deletion of 5 over the years. These matters are considered to be of regional and local concern—for example, public order, public health, agriculture and water supplies. The State Legislature may make laws in respect of these subject matters. The executive power of the state extends also to such matters. The Concurrent List contains 52 subject matters now after a gain of 5 entries during the past few years.[19] These matters are considered to be of both national and regional interest and scope. Both the Union Parliament and State Legislature may make laws in respect of these—for example, population control, criminal law and procedure, economic and social planning, education, electricity and factories. The executive power in regard to these matters normally belongs to state government, but it is subject to being limited by any law specifically passed by the Parliament for this purpose (Article 162). In case of any inconsistency between laws and policy made by Parliament and the ones made by State Legislatures in respect of these matters, normally the former would prevail.[20] Only if the state law has acquired the assent of Parliament when reserved for his consideration, the state law would prevail. But Parliament may pass a new law for amending or repeating the state law concerned (Article 254).

The Constitution vests the residuary power (i.e. the power to legislate with respect to any matter not enumerated in any of the three lists) in the Parliament (Article 248) and the final determination as to whether a particular matter falls under the residuary power or not is that of the courts.[21]

Expansion of the Union Legislative Powers

The Parliament may assume powers on certain occasion to make laws in regard to subject matters included in the State List. First, the Council of States (Rajya Sabha) may pass a resolution by a two-third majority that it is necessary in national interest for Parliament to pass such a law or laws. The resolution is to remain in force for a period not exceeding one year (Article 249). Second, two or more State Legislatures may pass a resolution inviting the Parliament to pass a law in respect of a specified state subject matter. This law can also be extended to other states if their legislatures pass resolutions to that effect (Article 252), for example, the Water (Prevention and Control of Pollution) Act, 1974 and the Transplantation of Human Organs Act, 1994.

Third, the Parliament is competent to enact laws in respect of any matters included in the State List for the whole or part of the country if a Proclamation of Emergency has been put into operation. Such laws would cease to operate within a period of six months after the expiry of the Emergency Proclamation (Article 250). If there is any inconsistency between

---

[19] The addition of five entries are administration of justice, population control, weights and measures, forests and education.

[20] The notification creating 92 universities by the Chhattisgarh State under Entry 32 of List II was quashed by the SC as the State Act undermined the University Grants Commission Act, 1954. See Dr Yashpal versus State of Chhattisgarh, 2005 (5) SCC 420.

[21] The residuary powers are reserved to the states under the American Constitution.

law made by the Parliament during Proclamation of Emergency or in accordance with Rajya Sabha resolution and the law made by State Legislatures, the former is to prevail.

The Parliament may pass an Amendment Bill for making a change in any of the three lists in the Seventh Schedule. But it has to be ratified by the legislatures of not less than half of the states before being made into law after receiving the President's assent. The Union Parliament has been constitutionally empowered (Article 3) to admit or establish new states and reorganize and rename the existing ones.

Union's Power to Give Directions to the State Government

The states are to ensure compliance with the Union laws within their respective territory (Article 256). The union government is competent to issue directions, if need be, for this purpose. Also, states are not to impede or prejudice exercise of the Union executive powers. Directions can be given by the union government if necessary in this connection (Article 257). Moreover, the Union can issue directions to a state on certain other matters: protection of railways, construction and maintenance of means of communication of national importance (Article 257), implementation of Scheduled Tribe Welfare Schemes (Article 339), development of Hindi language (Article 351), provision of adequate primary education facilities in mother tongue to linguistic minorities (Article 350A) and, more importantly, that the state government is carried on in accordance with the provisions of the Constitution (Article 355).

It is to be noted that the Constitution prescribes a coercive sanction for the enforcement of the directions (Article 365) issued by the union government during a Proclamation of failure of constitutional machinery in a state (Article 356) and during a Proclamation of Emergency under Article 353. Further, during a Proclamation of Financial Emergency, state governments are required to observe canons of financial propriety, as may be specified in the directions under Article 360.

Delegation of Functions

Besides division of powers between the Union and states, the Constitution makes certain provisions for coordination between the Union and states and also between the states. There can be mutual delegation of executive functions between the Union and states. With the consent of a state government, the President may entrust to that government or its officers any executive functions of the Union. Parliament may also do the same when making a union law applicable to a state (Article 258). Similarly, a state government with the consent of union government may entrust certain state functions to that government (Article 258A). Also Parliament may make financial grants to give financial assistance to a state in need of it.

Creation of All India Services

Administrative coordination between the states and the Union is also being promoted by the constitutional provision for All India Services. These services are common to both the Union and states and are moved between them. At present, there are three such services in operation. These are Indian Administrative Service (IAS), Indian Police Service (IPS) and Indian Forest Service (IFS). More services can be created, if need be, according to the

Constitution (Article 312).[22] The object behind the provision for the All India Services is to impart a greater cohesion to the federal system and to maintain standards of administration throughout the Union. Recently, a committee on National Education Policy which submitted its report to the HRD Ministry on 27 May 2016 recommended the creation of an All India Education Service.

Local Government System in the Constitution

The country has local government system in the urban areas (municipalities) and in rural areas (panchayats). These are governed by laws passed by the State Legislatures and function under the supervision of state governments. Article 40 in the Constitution on Directive Principles of State Policy has directed the state to organize village panchayats and empower them to function as units of self-government. Panchayat institutions and municipalities have expanded considerably in number and spatial coverage. With the 73rd and 74th Constitution Amendment Acts (1992), these local governing institutions have been accorded constitutional status. The state governments have now passed new laws or are amending existing ones in context of these new provisions incorporated in Parts IX and IXA of the Constitution on account of these Acts. Schedule XI (Article 243G) and XII (Article 243W) of the Constitution provide 29 and 18 subjects to the panchayats and *nagarpalikas*, respectively, which may be considered by a State Legislature for devolution to the panchayats and the municipalities, respectively. Article 243ZD mandates the constitution of a District Planning Committee to consolidate the plans between those prepared by the panchayats and municipalities in the district and to prepare a draft development plan for the district as a whole. Under Article 243 ZE, Metropolitan Planning Committee would prepare a draft development plan for metropolitan area as a whole.

Further, a State FC has been provided in every state for reviewing financial position of the panchayats and municipalities and making recommendations to the state government concerned for strengthening it (Article 243 I&Y).

Unified System of Judiciary

The Constitution also makes provision for a unified system of judiciary. In the hierarchy of courts, there is SC at the apex, High Courts at state level and subordinate courts at the lower level. The Constitution stipulates the main provisions for their organization and jurisdiction and powers.

The SC has original, appellate and advisory jurisdictions. The original jurisdiction relates to determination of a dispute between the GOI and any state or states on one side and one or more states on the other or between two or more states (Article 131). However, any

---

[22] Until 1961, no additional All India Services were created, but several new services have been added to the list of All India Services, namely, the Indian Engineering Service, the Indian Forest Service and the Indian Medical Service. See the All India Services (Amendment) Act, 1963. The SC has directed the GOI in 1992 for the setting up of an All India Judicial Service, but so far this service remains uncreated. For higher judiciary appointments (Judges of the High Courts and the SC), the SC on 16 October 2015 struck down the NJAC Act, 2014 (99th Constitutional Amendment) as 'unconstitutional and void' and restored the 22-year-old collegium system.

disputes regarding treaty, and foreign arguments and so on, as well as certain other matters (e.g. river water dispute) are excluded from its jurisdictions. The original jurisdiction of the Court also covers cases of violation of fundamental rights of individuals. The SC is the highest court of appeal from all courts in the country. Its appellate jurisdiction covers cases involving interpretation of Constitution, civil and criminal cases. Further on a reference by the President, it may be asked to express its opinion on a question of law or fact of public importance (Article 143).

In the hierarchy of judicial system, a High Court is constituted in each state or else a common High Court may be constituted for two or more states as decided by Parliament. The High Court has appellate jurisdiction in civil cases from the decisions of district judges and subordinate judges. It has also appellate jurisdiction in appeals from the decisions of sessions judges, additional and assistant sessions judges and in certain cases from decisions of judicial or metropolitan magistrates. It also exercises superintendence in relation to all district and subordinate courts and tribunals other than military tribunals, which are under its jurisdiction.

At the district level, the district and sessions judge is the top judicial authority in both civil and criminal matters in a district. He tries serious criminal cases and hears appeals from the decisions of magistrates and subordinate civil judges.

The judiciary (through the functioning of the SC and High Courts) has been playing an active role as the guardian of the Constitution. Judiciary is vested with the power of judicial reviews and has struck down several laws as violative of the Constitution. It has declared several cases of executive action as unconstitutional or illegal. For example, following the Delhi High Court's direction to treat women officers at par with their male counterparts in armed forces, the central government in 2008 took a policy decision to grant permanent commission to serving women officers in defence forces.[23]

Also the judiciary decides all disputes arising between the Union and the states and between different states, and generally among different units of the constitutional edifice. The SC and the High Courts decide on the constitutionality of issues brought before them, besides interpreting specific provisions of a statute or an executive order. Judicial decisions provide legitimacy to policies of the government. For example, in a landmark judgement the SC held on 10 July 2013 that (Parliament has exceeded its powers conferred by the Constitution in enacting Sub-Section (4) of Section 8 of the Representation of the People Act, 1951 that protected the sitting lawmakers against immediate disqualification upon conviction) from onward (10 July 2013) MPs, Member of Legislative Assembles (MLAs) and Member of Legislative Councils (MLCs) would automatically lose their membership if sentenced to jail for not less than two years by the trial court.[24] The SC in 2002, and subsequently in 2003, made it mandatory for all candidates contesting elections to disclose criminal, financial and educational background prior to the polls by filling an affidavit with the Election Commission. Recently, the Apex Court ruled the centre has

---

[23] In a petition to the Delhi High Court, it was submitted: 'Female officers cannot be discriminated against by declining to grant them permanent commission and by releasing them from service after just 10 years when they are physically fit.' See The Tribune, 24 November 2008.

[24] The SC verdict came on two PILs filed by Lily Thomas and Lok Prahari (NGO) challenging the provision saying it was against the constitutional provisions under Article 102 (1) relating to Parliament and Article 191 (1) pertaining to legislative assemblies and Councils of States.

primacy over state's right to grant remission to convicts who were tried under central laws (verdict of the SC on 2 December 2015).

General Observations

This unique system of political organization as envisaged in the Indian Constitution, it is believed, would promote IGR and thereby facilitate cooperative and competitive policymaking. But at the same time, the Constitution makes the centre more powerful than the states in legislation and policymaking. As stated already, in the case of division of powers, the Constitution ensures the Union's legislative supremacy over the Union List, Concurrent List and the Residuary legislative jurisdiction. Over the State List, the Parliament can legislate in specified and exceptional circumstances as per Article 249. It ensures the supremacy of Parliament in matters of taxation, constitutionally anticipated emergencies, judicial administration, constitutional amendments and so on. In practice, analysis of the application of emergency provisions of the Constitution of India, role of the State Governor and financial dependence of the states upon the centre endorses the unitary tilt to federalism in India. This creates conflicts and tensions in the functioning of the states and local-level machinery. There are also disputes within and outside public sector entities. For example, in a dispute between the Indraprastha Gas Ltd (IGL) and the Petroleum and Natural Gas Regulatory Board (PNGRB) over gas price fixation, the SC on 1 July 2015 pronounced its verdict upholding the Delhi High Court order (2013) ruling in favour of IGL. Apex Court says, 'The PNGRB has no power to fix or regulate the maximum retail price at which gas is sold by city gas distribution entities'.[25]

Given predominant role to executives in parliamentary form, administrative channels of IGR are crucial to achieving effective cooperative government in policy areas. But despite constitutional provisions in respect of Union–State relations, some problems continue to persist in policy and governance areas. For example, while states in India raise issues of law and order as being their subject, terrorism operates in a seamless world and states do not have the wherewithal to deal with the situation. States turn to the Ministry of Home Affairs (GOI) which deploys central forces and at times calls in the army to deal with such situations. Large-scale deployment of central forces leads to complaints of human rights violations.[26]

Efforts at cooperative federalism have commenced, but they need to be strengthened. The acceptance of the 14th FC's recommendations, apart from significantly enhanced devolution, enables states to design and implement programmes better suited to their needs.

ROLE OF INTERGOVERNMENTAL AGENCIES

Theoretically, it sounds good to distribute powers between the federal structure and its units for legislation and policymaking. But overlap and interpenetration of jurisdictions are inevitable. A few non-statutory bodies have been established for one purpose or the other

---

[25] See *The Financial Express* (Chandigarh), 3 July 2015.
[26] There is a demand for repeal of the Armed Forces Special Powers Act as issues to which solutions have not been found in Jammu and Kashmir and Northeast (except Tripura). See *The Tribune*, 12 July 2015.

for the common interest of the Union and states. One of these was the PC (abolished in August 2014), another is the NDC and third is the National Integration Council (NIC).

Apart from these, there are extra-constitutional agencies set up by the union government which further the coordination of state policy and eliminate difference as between the states. Besides, the Indian Constitution establishes FC (under Article 280) and GST council for facilitating intergovernmental financial cooperation and Inter-State Council (ISC) (under Article 263) for discussing subjects of common interests between and among states and the Union. Administrative coordination between the states and the Union is also being promoted by the constitutional provision under Article 312 for All India Services. These services are common to both the Union and states and are moved between them.

Policy Planning Machinery

The Indian Constitution originally did not contain any provisions relating to the planning machinery, such as the PC (established in 1950) and the NDC (established in 1952). Nor were these agencies established under a statute.[27] The PC, seen as an extra-constitutional and non-statutory body, was set up by a resolution on 15 March 1950 of the Union Cabinet by PM Jawaharlal Nehru with himself as its first Chairman to formulate an integrated Five-Year Plan for economic and social development. From the terms of reference, it will be apparent that the PC was thought of as a staff agency to prepare national plans for social and economic development within the framework of a federal state, a parliamentary democracy and a welfare state. The Commission was to suggest, coordinate and evaluate policies and programmes, although the final responsibility to the people's representatives and to the people remained with the political institutions. Although the states had no PCs of similar status, they had special planning departments and boards (advisory boards) to do the planning work. The 74th Constitutional Amendment Act, 1992 (w.e.f. 1 June 1993) provides for setting up of District Planning Committees and Metropolitan Planning Committees (Articles 243ZD and 243ZE).[28] These committees are now being associated with the formulation and implementation of plans within the range of responsibilities assigned to them.

On 13 August 2014, the Union Cabinet of the Modi government approved the repeal of the Cabinet resolution of 15 March 1950 by which the PC was set up. Speaking at his first meeting with CMs on 7 December 2014, PM Narendra Modi stressed that 'it was impossible for the nation to develop' unless states develop and have a greater role in the new body (think tank) which reflects the true spirit of 'cooperative federalism'. To Modi, the PC symbolized centralized planning of the Nehruvian era and ruled out incremental steps and proposed a 'bottom to top' approach in policy planning to be implemented by a 'think tank'.

---

[27] The 74th Constitutional Amendment Act provides for the setting up of District Planning Committees and Metropolitan Planning Committees at the local level. In his first Independence Day address, PM Narendra Modi had announced that a new institution would be created to replace the Planning Commission in order to respect the country's federal structure.
[28] Recently, the PMO has asked NITI Aayog to work on some kind of planning under the heads: Vision Document (for 15 years), Strategy Department (for 7 years) and Macro Framework (for 3 years). See *The Tribune* (Chandigarh), 14 May 2016.

Experiences by several state governments had shown that the PC and the Union Cabinet exercised greater control over the formulation of policy in the state sphere than the Constitution warranted.

A 14th FC (FY 2015–20) member Govinda Rao remarked, 'Centrally planning is a negation of federalism—nor does it make any sense for approving the plans of the States'. In his first meeting with the CMs on 7 December 2014, PM Narendra Modi, citing remarks of former PM Manmohan Singh towards the end of his term on 30 April 2014, said, 'Dr. Singh, who had been associated for a long time with the PC, had noted the body has no futuristic vision in the post-reform period and that it would have to reinvent itself to remain more effective and relevant in the present situation'.[29] PM Modi ruled out incremental steps and called for a total replacement of the PC by a 'think tank' of independent experts, CMs and the PM.

India's Finance Minister Arun Jaitley made the following observation on the necessity of creating NITI Aayog:

> The 65-year-old Planning Commission had become a redundant organization. It was relevant in a command economy structure, but not any longer. India is a diversified country and its states are in various phases of economic development along with their own strengths and weaknesses. In this context, a 'one-size-fits-all' approach to economic planning is obsolete. It cannot make India competitive in today's global economy.[30]

The PC was finally scrapped on 13 August 2014 by a Union Cabinet decision, and it was replaced by a new body called the NITI Aayog.

NITI Aayog

NITI Aayog was created through a Union Cabinet resolution on 1 January 2015 in place of the PC.[31] The NITI Aayog is tasked to serve as a policy 'think tank' of the government and as a 'directional and policy dynamo' and would provide the governments at the centre and in states with strategic and technical advice on key policy matters, including economic issues of national and international importance.[32]

As per the policy statement of the government, NITI Aayog will create a knowledge, innovation and entrepreneurial support system through a collaborative community of national and international experts, practitioners and partners. It will offer a platform for resolution of inter-sectoral and inter-departmental issues in order to accelerate the implementation of the development agenda. In addition to being the incubator of ideas for development, the NITI Aayog will provide a critical directional and strategic input into the development process. Noting that progress is not possible without all states advancing in tandem, Modi called upon CMs to work with the centre to forge a model of cooperative federalism,

---

[29] See *The Tribune* (Chandigarh), 8 December 2014.
[30] OPEN magazine, 'We Will Use Every Provision in the Constitution to Push Reforms', accessed 16 November 2016, htt://www.openthemagazine.com/article/nation/we-will-use-every-provision-in-the-constitution-to-push-reforms
[31] See *The Financial Express* (Chandigarh), 2 January 2015.
[32] Ibid.

whereby the centre and the states can come together to resolve differences. He termed this partnership as 'Team India'.[33] Through the mechanism of the NITI Aayog, India would move away from 'one size fits all' schemes and forge a better match between various schemes and the needs of states. One of the objectives of NITI Aayog will be to ensure that the interests of the national security are incorporated in economic strategy and policy.

Organization of the NITI Aayog

The NITI Aayog comprises the following:

(i) PM of India as the Chairperson.
(ii) Governing Council comprising the CMs of all the states and UTs with legislatures and Lieutenant Governors of other UTs.
(iii) Regional Councils will be formed to address specific issues and contingencies impacting more than one state or a region. These will be formed for a specified tenure. The Regional Councils will be convened by the PM and will comprise the CMs of states and Lt Governors of UTs in the region. These will be chaired by the Chairperson of the NITI Aayog or his nominee.
(iv) Experts, specialists and practitioners with relevant domain knowledge as special invitees nominated by the PM.
(v) Full-time organizational framework (in addition to PM as the Chairperson) comprising:

    (a) Vice-Chairperson: Arvind Panagariya.
    (b) Full-time members (2): Economist Bibek Debroy and former DRDO chief V.K. Saraswat.
    (c) Part-time members: Maximum of two from leading universities research organizations and other relevant institutions in an ex officio capacity. Part-time members will be on a rotational basis.
    (d) Ex officio members: Maximum of four members of the Union Council of Ministers to be nominated by the PM.
    (e) Chief Executive Officer (CEO): To be appointed by the PM for a fixed tenure, in the rank of Secretary to the GOI. Sindhushree Khullar appointed as the CEO.
    (f) Secretariat as deemed necessary.[34]

According to a statement, the Regional Councils will be formed to address specific issues and contingencies impacting more than one state or a region. These will be formed for a specified tenure. The Regional Councils will be convened by the PM and will comprise the CMs of states and Lt Governors of UTs in the region. These will be chaired by the Chairperson of the NITI Aayog or his nominee.

The NITI Aayog will also have experts, specialists and practitioners with relevant domain knowledge as special invitees nominated by the PM. The two part-time members of the new body would be from leading universities and research organizations.

---

[33] *The Tribune* (Chandigarh), 9 February 2015.
[34] 'Cabinet Resolution for NITI Aayog'. *Gazette of India*. Accessed 10 January 2015. http://www.egazette. ni.in/WriteReadData/2015/162317.pdf

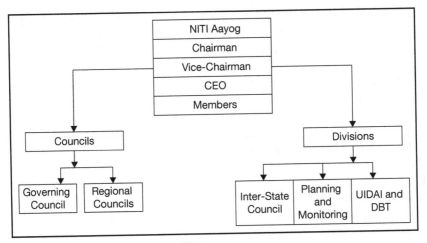

■ Figure 7.1: Structure and Composition of NITI Aayog
Source: NITI Aayog (GOI), New Delhi.

The structure and functions of the NITI Aayog replacing PC is shown in Figure 7.1.

Explanatory Notes

NITI Aayog has been set up on 1 January 2015.

(i) PM is the Chairman; *Vice-Chairman* (VC) is appointed by the PM; CEO is an officer of secretary rank.

(ii) *Members* include: (a) four to five domain experts to assist VC; (b) two part-time members from institutes/universities, appointed on rotational basis; and (c) four council ministers (ex officio) nominated by the PM.

(iii) *Governing council* comprising all state CMs and Lt Governors of UTs (headed by the PM) to ensure genuine and continuing partnership of all states in policymaking.

(iv) *Regional councils* to address specific issues within a specific time frame.

(v) *ISC* will carry the development agenda to the states forward to finance and other central ministers (headed by a Secretary). It will move from Home Ministry to Yojana Bhawan to oversee development works by the states. Thus, the states will have a greater role in planning.

(vi) The Planning and monitoring division will work on a long-term plan for the government and evaluate the flagship social sector schemes (headed by a Secretary).

Objectives and Functions of the NITI Aayog

The NITI Aayog (established on 1 January 2015) will serve as a 'think tank' of the governments as 'a directional and policy dynamo' and would provide the government at the centre and in states with strategic and technical advice on key policy matters including economic issues of national and international importance.[35]

---

[35] See *The Financial Express* (Chandigarh), 2 January 2015. While chairing the first meeting of the NITI Aayog on 8 February 2015, PM Narendra Modi said, 'We will move away from 'one size fits all' schemes and forge a better match between these schemes and the needs of states'.

NITI Aayog will seek to provide a critical directional and strategic input into the development process. The centre-to-state-one-way flow of policy, that was the hallmark of the Planning Commission era, is now sought to be replaced by a genuine and continuing partnership of states.

NITI Aayog will merge as a 'think-tank' that will provide Governments at the central and state levels with relevant strategic and technical advice across the spectrum of key elements of policy.

The NITI Aayog will also seek to put an end to slow and tardy implementation of policy, by fostering better Inter-Ministry coordination and better Centre–State coordination. It will help evolve a shared vision of national development priorities, and foster cooperative federalism, recognizing that strong states make a strong nation.

The NITI Aayog will develop mechanisms to formulate credible plans to the village level and aggregate these progressively at higher levels of government. It will ensure special attention to the sections of society that may be at risk of not benefiting adequately from economic progress.

The NITI Aayog will create a knowledge, innovation and entrepreneurial support system through a collaborative community of national and international experts, practitioners and partners. It will offer a platform for resolution of inter-sectoral and inter-departmental issues in order to accelerate the implementation of the development agenda.

In addition, the NITI Aayog will monitor and evaluate the implementation of programmes, and focus on technology upgradation and capacity-building.

The NITI Aayog aims to enable India to better face complex challenges through the following functions:

(i) Leveraging of India's demographic dividend, and realization of the potential of youth, men and women, through education, skill development, elimination of gender bias, and employment;

(ii) Elimination of poverty, and the chance for every Indian to live a life of dignity and self-respect;

(iii) Redressal of inequalities based on gender bias, caste and economic disparities;

(iv) Integrate villages institutionally into the development process;

(v) Policy support to more than 50 million small businesses, which are a major source of employment creation and

(vi) Safeguarding of our environmental and ecological assets.

The second meeting of the Governing Council of the NITI Aayog called by PM Narendra Modi on 15 July 2015 who sought support for rural development through the passage of the Land Acquisition Bill, 2015 (Amending to Right to Fair Compensation and Transparency in Land Acquisition, Rehabilitation and Resettlement Act, 2013) was boycotted by over a dozen CMs. The Union Finance Minister Arun Jaitley observed, 'An overwhelming section said either the Centre must build a consensus and pass amendments…quickly or give flexibility to states to make their own laws'.[36] The PM said, 'The political deadlock

---

[36] See *The Financial Express* (Chandigarh), 16 July 2015.

over land acquisition is seriously impacting rural development, including the creation of schools, hospitals, roads and irrigation projects'.[37]

In the context of new developments in the NITI Aayog, it is said that

- **15-year Vision Document:** Will be in sync with global trend and the nation's ambition to retain its status as the world's growth engine. Will cover aspects of internal security and defence.
- **7-year Strategy Document:** Will spell out policies for 'achieving the desire goals' while also factoring in the 15-year vision.
- **3-year Macro Framework:** Will deal with issues of 'immediate concerns' and will be taken up on a priority basis.

A Critical Evaluation of Policy Planning Machinery

The government's move to replace the PC with a new institution called 'NITI Aayog' was criticized by opposition parties of India. The Congress sought to know whether the reform introduced by the BJP-led government was premised on any meaningful programme or if the move was simply born out of political opposition to the party that ran the PC for over 60 years. 'The real issue is do you (the government) have a substantive meaningful pro-gramme to reform the Planning Commission?' Congress spokesperson Abhishek Manu Singhvi said. 'If you (the BJP government) simply want to abolish it (the commission), because it is something which (Jawaharlal) Nehru created for this country and you don't like Nehru or simply because it was run by the Congress for 60 years and you don't like the Congress, that is pitiable', he said.

Arun Maira, the former PC member, said,

> The idea to create an institution where states' leaders will be part and parcel of the collective thinking with the Centre and other stakeholders in formulating a vision for the development of the country is right on as compared with the previous struc-ture, where a handful of people formulated the vision and then presented it to the National Development Council (NDC). This was not entirely absorbed and adopted by the latter.

In fact, a recent survey of expert opinions in the magazine *Business World* shows that either a very clear distinction of roles of NDC, Governing Council and ISC or a merger of one or two with a vibrant and functional ISC can serve the two key goals of such forums: policy development and conflict resolution.[38]

The thrust behind the setting up of the NITI Aayog is to coordinate states for identify-ing specific problems and devising mechanisms to resolve them through the spirit of cooperative federalism.[39] Sharma in his writing on federalism makes a strong case for

---

[37] *Hindustan Times* (Chandigarh), 16 July 2015.
[38] Chanchal Kumar Sharma, 'NITI's Destiny and the Federal Question', *Business World*, 8 April 2015.
[39] Union Finance Minister Arun Jaitley's comments on the nature of NITI Aayog. See *The Financial Express* (Chandigarh), 9 February 2015.

collaborative federalism, but also adds that this outcome can be realized only in the context of 'a balanced, transparent and distortion free system of intergovernmental fiscal relations'.[40]

With a view to seeing that this NITI institution plays an effective role in intergovernmental policymaking and conflict resolution among and between Union and state governments, it is important for the union government to ensure that this institution is insulated from partisan pressure. In an article, Rao argues that the 'NITI Aayog be given statutory status, and powers' if it has to play an effective 'role in promoting intergovernmental bargains, resolving issues and coordinating policies between the Union and States in the spirit of cooperative federation'.[41]

National Development Council

NDC was set up as an extra-constitutional and non-statutory body by a Union Cabinet resolution on 6 August 1952 on the initiative of first PM Jawaharlal Nehru. In the first meeting of the NDC held on 8–9 November 1952, the PM observed that the NDC was essentially a forum for intimate cooperation between the state governments and the central government for all the tasks of national development (GOI).

Following functions were assigned to the NDC (GOI, 2005):

(i) to review the working of the National Plan from time to time;
(ii) to consider important questions of social and economic policy affecting national development;
(iii) to recommend measures for the achievement of the aims and targets set out in the National Plan. In 1967, the functions of the NDC were redefined:

    (a) to prescribe guidelines for the formulation of the National Plan;
    (b) to consider the National Plans as formulated by the PC;
    (c) to assess resources required for implementing the plan and to suggest ways and means for raising them.

The NDC, as reconstituted in 1967 on the acceptance of the Administrative Reforms Commission's recommendations (1967), is composed of the PM (as Chairman), all Union Cabinet Ministers, CMs of all states, CMs/administrators of all UTs and the members of the PC (now replaced with the NITI Aayog on 1 January 2015).

A Critical Evaluation of NDC

The NDC appeared to be a useful instrument of intergovernmental policy cooperation. It has served as an apex forum not only for the approval of the Five-Year Plans but also for achieving policy coordination on the matters of national significance. However, of late, it has become a body of partisan forum. Santhanam observed, 'The position of NDC has

---

[40] C.K. Sharma, 'Reimagining Federalism in India: Exploring the Frontiers of Collaborative Federal Architecture', *Asia-Pacific Social Science Review* 15(1) (2015): 1–25.
[41] M. Govinda Rao, 'Getting NITI Aayog to Work', *The Financial Express* (Chandigarh), 21 July 2015.

come to approximate to that of a super cabinet of the entire Indian federalism, a cabinet functioning for the government of India and the governments of all the States'.[42]

The Sarkaria Commission (1988) lamented that the NDC had not been able to act as an effective instrument for developing consensus and commitment to national policies. It recommended that it should be renamed as National Economic and Development Council.

The first Administrative Reforms Commission, constituted on 5 January 1966, in its 13th Report recommended replacement of the NDC with an ISC which should be established under Article 263 (b) and (c) of the Constitution.

Although the NDC is an important device for IGR, it is seen as a rubber stamp. In the last 10 years, there were only two meetings of NDC.

INTERGOVERNMENTAL FINANCIAL RELATIONS

The prospects of cost savings and improved services have prompted the founders of the Constitution to establish funding streams that encourage IGR. Intergovernmental financial relations are critical to the financial health of the country. The degree to which three spheres of government—central, state and local—can each perform their constitutional responsibilities effectively depends upon the financial resources available to them. Here there are both vertical and horizontal dimensions. There is the vertical distribution of revenue raised nationally to match the expenditure responsibilities of central, state and local spheres of governments. There is also the horizontal dimension: the allocation of equitable spheres of financial resources to each state and local government taking account of disparities in resources and needs. Articles from 264 to 290 govern the financial relations between the Union and the states.

After making provisions for the transfer of resources from the Union to the states in the form of shared taxes and the grants, the Constitution provided for the Constitution of a FC at five-year intervals (Article 280), to suggest the principles and the amount of such sharing. Other similar matters could also be referred to such a Commission by the Presidential Order.[43]

At the state level, a State FC has been provided in every state for reviewing financial position of the panchayats and municipalities and making recommendations to the government concerned for strengthening it (Article 243 I & Y). These Finance Commissions operating at the central and state levels facilitate intergovernmental financial cooperation.

Among the objectives for the operations of the Commission that need to be emphasized is the desirability of focusing on maximizing the scope for economic growth and minimizing complexities that would arise from the inevitable pressures to consider every possible

---

[42] K. Santhanam, *Union-State Relations in India* (Bombay: Asia Publishing House, 1960), 47.
[43] The First Finance Commission was constituted in 1951 with Sri K.C. Niyogi as the Chairman, and the 14th Finance Commission has been constituted in 2012 whose operational duration is 2015–20. The duty of the FC is to make recommendations to the President as to (a) distribution of taxes between the Union and the states, (b) principles governing the grants-in-aid of revenues of the states, (c) measures needed to augment the Consolidated Fund of the state for supplementing the resources of the panchayats and municipalities in the state and (d) any other matter that may be referred by the President.

variable. To secure healthy cooperation among all the three spheres of the government, it is necessary to devise some procedures for consultation between governments prior to financial transfers from central tax revenue to state and local spheres of government in order to support their constitutional expenditure responsibilities. The Punchhi Commission (2010) recommended the introduction of GST to be levied by the centre and states.

By means of grants-in-aid under Article 275, the Union would be in a position to correct inter-state disparities in financial assistance. Special grants may be given for promoting the welfare of the scheduled tribes and for raising the level of administration of the scheduled areas. Under Article 282, the Union or a state gives grant for any public purpose, such as National Literacy Mission and Polio Eradication. Besides, under MPLAD (Members of Parliament Local Area Development) Scheme, an MP is allowed to recommend expenditure every year up to the ceiling fixed for any work for public purpose.[44] The Union has claim to immunity in respect of its property (Article 285). Analogous to this, the property and income of the state are exempt from Union taxation.

INTER-STATE COUNCIL

Conflicts of interest and disputes between two or more states are inevitable. Although states have their own sphere of powers and enjoy a certain degree of independence, they cannot remain in complete isolation from each other.

Accepting the recommendation of the first Commission on Centre-State Relations (the Sarkaria Commission which submitted its report in January 1988), the GOI constituted an ISC under Article 263 on 28 May 1990.

The composition of the Council as per the Presidential Order dated 28 May 1990 is as follows:

(i) PM as Chairman
(ii) CMs of all States
(iii) CMs of UTs having a Legislative Assembly and Administrators of UTs not having a Legislative Assembly
(iv) Six ministers of Cabinet rank in the Union Council of Ministers to be nominated by the PM.

The second Administrative Reforms Commission (2005–09) recommended that the ISC must be given the power to resolve inter-state and Union–State conflicts. However, it also recommended that the Council need not exist in perpetuity. It should be constituted as and when the need arises.

The Punchhi Commission on Centre–State Relations (2010) recommended functional independence and quasi-judicial status for the ISC. It also recommended that ISC should be made a vibrant negotiating forum for policy development and conflict resolution.

[44] The SC held that MPLAD Scheme is constitutional under Article 275 and 282. Refer to Bhim Singh versus Union of India, 2010 (5), SCC 538.

The Constitution of India empowers the President of India to establish a constitutional body for inquiring into and advising upon inter-state disputes under Article 263 (a) and for achieving better coordination of policy and action, under Article 263 (b) and (c), regarding subjects of common interest to some or all of the states, or the Union and one or more of the states.[45]

However, the following issues may not be brought up before the Council:

(i) Any issue which can be resolved at the official/ministerial level.
(ii) Any issue which has to be dealt with by the NDC, the NIC and the FC.
(iii) Any issue which is sub judice or is under consideration in either House of Parliament.
(iv) Any other issue the discussion of which may, in the opinion of the Chairman, create discord between the states or otherwise be against the public interest or against the interests of the sovereignty or integrity of India, the security of the state, friendly relations with foreign state or public order.

It is mentioned here that there is no provision making it mandatory for the Council to hold its meetings on a regular basis with a constitutionally specified frequency. Ten members including the Chairman form the quorum for a meeting of the Council. Although the Council was set up in 1990, it has so far not been very active. Its first meeting was held on 10 October 1990. The Council had taken a view on all the 247 recommendations made by Sarkaria Commission. Out of 247 recommendations, 65 have not been accepted by the ISC/administrative ministries, 180 have been accepted and 2 are at different stages of implementation.[46]

The National Commission (under Justice M.N. Venkatachaliah) to Review the Working of the Constitution (NCRWC) (2002) as well as the second Commission (under Justice M.M. Punchhi) on Centre-State Relations (2010) in their respective reports recommend that the ISC need to be substantially strengthened and activized as the key player in IGR. The Punchhi Commission also suggested equal representation of states—small or big—in the Rajya Sabha to alter the balance of power in favour of smaller states in federal governance. It strongly expressed itself in favour of removal of 'factors inhibiting the composition and functioning of the Second Chamber as a representative forum of States' by constitutional amendment.

The ISC is the only constitutional body to deal with federal disputes in a comprehensive manner. It has a high potential to strengthen vertical and horizontal cooperation in Indian federalism. However, this potential remains untapped. It was made to languish while the PC flourished. But it is only the 'constitutional entity for harmonizing the actions of the Centre and States. Its effective utilization would lend legitimacy to cooperative federalism'.[47]

---

[45] Article 263 of the Indian Constitution. It may be mentioned here that ISC has not been assigned the function envisaged in clause (a) of Article 263 as recommended by the Sarkaria Commission.
[46] K.P. Mishra, 'Management of Centre–State Relations in Indian Federation', *Management in Government* April–June (2013): 28.
[47] N.K. Singh, 'An Unfinished Agenda of Federalism', *Indian Express*, 4 November 2015.

NATIONAL INTEGRATION COUNCIL

Besides the NITI Aayog and the ISC, there is the NIC for deliberation and facilitating policymaking. As a forum, the NIC was created by the Nehru government in the backdrop of the Chinese aggression in 1962 that goes beyond the intergovernmental scope and includes non-governmental agencies also. The NIC is a 103-member forum of union ministers, CMs, political leaders, heads of national commission and eminent public figures. The body can be used to gauge broader opinion of the intelligentsia on sensitive matters. It discusses such issues as banning on extremist organizations, communal violence, imposition of Article 356 in the state and related matters.

Recently at the first Roundtable organized by the Tribune National Security Forum in association with the Indian Council of World Affair, Jammu and Kashmir governor N.N. Vohra advocated, 'There is a need for a bipartisan National Security Policy evolved after consultation between the Centre and the States. We need federal laws and federal investigation and prosecuting agencies that are accepted by the States'. He re-emphasized the need for an 'all-India National Security Administrative Service with a specialized cadre of trained officers' to manage the national security system.[48]

OTHER INTER-STATE COUNCILS AND BODIES

In addition to these bodies, there have already grown a large number of structures which are playing an important role in the policy areas. The CMs' Conference, Governors' Conference,[49] DGP/IGPs' Conference, Inter-governmental Ministerial Conference, Chief Secretaries' Conference, five Zonal Councils, Inter-State Tribunals, National Water Resources Council, Transport Development Council, Central Council of Health, Central Council of Local Self-Government, Central Council of Indian Medicine, Central Family Welfare Council, Central Council of Homeopathy, National Commission on Population, National Commission on Women, National Commission for Protection of Child Rights, NHRC (1993), and so forth are active bodies which play a crucial role in formulation of policies in the context of IGR. In 2009, the central government set up a National Investigation Agency to deal with terror across the country.[50]

EXTRA-JUDICIAL TRIBUNAL

While Article 131 provides for the judicial determination of disputes between states by vesting the SC with exclusive jurisdiction in the matter, Article 262 provides for the adjudication of one class of disputes by an extra-judicial tribunal. Under the Article, the

---

[48] A Roundtable on National Security was organized by the ICWA in collaboration with the *Tribune* in New Delhi on 2 December 2014. See *The Tribune* (Chandigarh), 3 December 2014.

[49] The CMs' Conference includes not only the CMs but also key union ministers. Similarly, the Governors' Conference includes not only the Governors but also the President of India who is its Chairman. At a meeting of CMs on 6 January 2009, the Home Minister suggested the setting up of 24×7 control rooms in the states and UTs to receive and disseminate information pertaining to terrorism and other forms of organized violence.

[50] The Union Ministry has taken the decision after the SC ruled that the Kerala government has no jurisdiction to prosecute the two Italian marines—Massimiliano Latorre and Salvatore Girone—allegedly involved in the killing of the fishermen.

Parliament has enacted the Inter-State Water Disputes Act, 1956 to provide for adjudication of disputes relating to waters of inter-state river and river valleys.[51] Under the aforesaid Act, the union government has constituted several water disputes tribunals.

The NCRWC noted that on several occasions the parties to the disputes approached the SC for judicial review both against the interim orders of the Tribunal and against the final decision.[52] Further in the implementation of decision of the Tribunal, the oustees seek financial compensation and often resort to agitation for enforcing their fundamental right under Article 21 of the Constitution consequent on the submergence of their lands due to construction of reservoirs.

In the context of the water disputes involving one or more states, the NCRWC made certain suggestions. First, it observes that it is not necessary to exclude inter-state water disputes from the original jurisdiction of the SC under Article 131. Second, the NCRWC has recommended that appropriate parliamentary legislation should be made for repealing the River Boards Act, 1956 and replacing it by another comprehensive enactment under Entry 56 of List 1. Third, the NCRWC is of the view that as water disputes are important, they should be heard and disposed by a bench not less than three judges and if necessary, a bench of five judges of the SC for the final disposal of the suit. In December 2016, the Union Cabinet decided to set up a single permanent tribunal to adjudicate all inter-state river water disputes subsuming existing tribunals. It also proposed to float benches by amending the Inter-State Water Disputes Act, 1956.

INTER-STATE COMMERCE COMMISSION

For promoting coordination between states in public interest, Article 307 of the Indian Constitution provides for appointment of an authority. The NCRWC and the second Commission on Centre-State Relations (constituted on 27 April 2007 under the Chairmanship of Justice Madan Mohan Punchhi) recommended the setting up of an Inter-State Trade and Commerce Commission under Article 307 read with Entry 42 of the List I for carrying out objectives of Articles 301–304 and other purposes relating to the needs of inter-state trade and commerce.

As a constitutional body and similar to the Inter-State Commerce Commission in the USA for regulating trade and commerce throughout the territory of India, no such Commission has been constituted so far.

ZONAL COUNCILS AND GST COUNCIL

Five Zonal Councils (Northern, Southern, Eastern, Western and Central) have been established under the States Reorganisation Act, 1956 to advise on policy and matters of

---

[51] The process under the Act, including the giving of the award by the Tribunal, takes normally 7–10 years. The delay at times has been causing bitterness and friction between the states involved in the disputes.
[52] On the recommendations of the Sarkaria Commission, the ISC and the Ministry of Water Resources, Section 6 of the Inter-State Water Disputes Act, 1956 has been amended to provide that the decision of the Tribunal, after its publication in the *Official Gazette* by the central government shall have the same force as an order or decree of the SC.

common interest (economic and social planning, border disputes and inter-state transport and the like) to each of the five zones into which the territory of India has been divided. If properly worked, these Councils would foster the federal sentiment by resisting the separatist tendencies of linguism and provincialism.

Besides the five Zonal Councils, there is a North-Eastern Council established under the North-Eastern Council Act, 1971 to deal with the common problems of Assam, Meghalaya, Manipur, Nagaland, Tripura, Arunachal Pradesh and Mizoram. Even these Regional Councils representing the common interests in their dealing with the union governments have failed in this task.

Besides Zonal Councils, the GST Council was set up on 16 September 2016 under article 279A of the Indian Constitution. The Council comprises the Union Finance Minister (as Chairman), the Union Minister of State in charge of Finance and Taxation and the Minister in charge of Finance or Taxation or any other Minister, nominated by each state government. This Council will make recommendations on GST rates, the business turnover threshold for the new tax, the exemption list, the contours of the model GST laws and other related matters.

Amalgamating several central and state taxes into a single tax would mitigate problems of double taxation and check inflation. GST rates have been finalized with a four-tier structure of 5, 12, 18 and 28 per cent while basic consumption items, such as foodgrains will be taxed at zero per cent. GST could potentially bring economic dividends for the country. Further, for reaching a decision, the GST Council gives the centre one-third voting power and the states two-third, while a resolution will need three-fourth majority.

A survey conducted by Sharma shows that there is an overwhelming consensus that the FC and the ISC are the two constitutional bodies which have the potential to strengthen federalism in India.[53] The NITI Aayog and GST Council are specifically designed to promote cooperative federalism.

Such bodies as discussed earlier facilitate cooperation and interaction between intergovernmental agencies. The interaction and recommendations reached help in the formulation of policies governing IGR. These must ensure that changes envisaged in policy matters are brought about smoothly, and that national and regional interests do not clash with each other. This relationship has certain dimensions in policymaking, that is, legislative, administrative and financial.

CONDITIONS FOR EFFECTIVE IGR

The study of intergovernmentalism has been equally significant as a line of inquiry for both federal and unitary states in recent decades. The subject of IGR has, however, gained grounds among governments especially experiencing federation. The federal structure of governance in India may become democratically unsustainable if the union government fails to ensure a decisive role for state governments in the framing of policies and implementation of development programmes. As such, there is a need for examining conditions required for effective IGR.

---

[53] Sharma, 'Reimagining Federalism in India'. Also see Sharma, 'NITI's Destiny and the Federal Question', *Business World*, 8 April 2015.

A first condition for effective intergovernmental interaction and cooperation is the constitutional provision. But experience suggests that more than legal provisions, there are two fundamental prerequisites for effective IGR. The first is the establishment of a political culture of cooperation, mutual respect and trust. And to develop a sense of trust requires tolerance towards diversity and a willingness to consult and take account of the concerns of other state governments before policymaking. Imposed relations do not work and breed resentment and distrust.

Speaking at the first meeting of the CMs chaired by PM Narendra Modi on 7 December 2014, Punjab CM Parkash Singh Badal welcomed and said that the 'plan panel had been imposed on country's constitutional structure through an administrative order violating the federal spirit, as it placed excessive powers regarding planned development in the hands of centre'.[54]

Second, a political culture fostering cooperation requires recognition of the need for intergovernmental consultation and interaction in a political partnership emphasizing mutual assistance and support, regular exchange of information and consultation, cooperation and coordination in areas of overlapping and complementary jurisdiction. In his first meeting with CMs on 7 December 2014, PM Narendra Modi said that 'States must have a greater role in the "think tank" and reflect the true spirit of cooperative federalism'.[55]

A second condition for effective IGR is the development of a capacity within each government in terms of human and financial resources and technological facilities. The three All India Services (IAS, IPS and IFS) have been constitutionally accepted in India to engage effectively in IGR. These services are expected to coordinate developmental activities in the states and the centre and keep divisive forces, if any, at bay.[56] An important task will be to develop the All India Services through training programmes, enabling them to preserve administrative unity and uniformity in the country's governance. The SC in India has directed the GOI for the creation of an All India Judicial Services on the lines of IAS and IPS. But several states were apprehensive about its viability, mainly citing the need for using regional languages in lower court proceedings.[57]

For effective IGR between all levels of government in the polity, there would be the need for provision of adequate financial resources and communication and e-governance infrastructure to enable frequent informal exchange of views. A scholar in the study of IGR urges 'the need to install and improve mechanisms for dissemination of information about service delivery and development of a Database and a Research Cell to assist intergovernmental interactions'.[58]

Much more attention has to be paid towards improving the functioning of mechanisms engaged in IGR. Constitutional and institutional bodies such as the FC (Article 280),

---

[54] See *Hindustan Times* (Chandigarh), 8 December 2014.
[55] *The Financial Express* (Chandigarh), 8 December 2014.
[56] U.C. Agarwal, 'Public Services in India: Achievements and Disappointments', *Indian Journal of Public Administration* LII(3) (2006): 308.
[57] See *The Tribune* (Chandigarh), 8 April 2013. A joint conference of CMs and Chief Justices on 7 April 2013 failed to arrive at a consensus on the creation of an All India Judicial Services.
[58] C.K. Sharma, 'Intergovernmental Coordination Mechanisms in India', *South Asian Journal of Socio-Political Studies* 15(2) (2015): 48.

ISC (Article 263), NITI Aayog, Central Council of Health, GST Council and NIC should hold annually or more frequently meetings to share information, discuss problems and contemplate joint action. They are expected to sustain relationships, recommend policy measures and facilitate intergovernmental legislative cooperation. In this way, federal structure of governance will become democratically sustainable.

CONCLUSION

Improving IGR system through better services is the need of the hour. Functioning of various constitutional bodies and executive-created institutions facilitating IGR in most federal countries including India indicates that they do contribute to the policymaking process. However, it is observed that the development of a political culture of coopera-tion, mutual respect and trust is much more important for effective IGR than the establish-ment of formal structures and legal procedures.[59] In this way, danger of monopoly to the policymaking in a federation can be warded off. We can only be losers if we try to temper with the federal structure as envisaged in the Indian Constitution.

In step with the times, both the Parliament and the intergovernmental forums (especially the ISC under Article 263) in their respective domains must ensure opportunity of delib-erative as well as participatory democracy. This can be achieved by expanding the scope and practice of interaction with the civil society, the media and all the stakeholders in the processes of policy management and federal governance.

Review Questions

(i) Briefly discuss the fundamental reasons behind the requirement for IGR.
(ii) What are the forms of interaction that generally take place between the three spheres of the government when public policymaking is considered?
(iii) Elaborate on the expenditure and revenue responsibilities of the IGR system.
(iv) Present a critical account of NITI Aayog.
(v) Which basic conditions are vital for the smooth functioning of the IGR system?

---

[59] D.S. Wright and C.L. Cho, 'State Administration and Intergovernmental Interdependency', in *Handbook of State Government Administration*, ed. J.J. Gargin (New York, NY: Marcel Dekker, 2000), 33–66.

INSTITUTIONALISM
Its Impact on Policy Process

INTRODUCTION

In recent times, there has been a growing awareness of the significance of placing public policy in the context of institutions. The fact that policymaking takes place in the context of institutions, the impact of institutional arrangements, cannot be ignored in understanding the process of policy formulation. Institutions are now described as organizations as well as systems in which individuals interact and achieve political and policy goals through explicit or implicit rules that evolve over time through cooperative means.[1] The institutional approach attempts to study the relationships between public policy and governmental institutions. Institutionalism, with its focus on the legal and structural aspects of institutions, can be applied in policy analysis. The structures and institutions and their arrangements and interactions can have a significant impact on public policy.

The study of institutions and the people who compose them are important. In a democratic society, a state is a web of government structures and institutions. The state performs many functions. It strives to adjudicate between conflicting social and economic interests. It is regarded as the guardian of all sections of the community. It does not defend the predominance of any particular class or community. No organization has ever been able to succeed in its objectives across the whole range of public policies, and policy issues tend to be resolved in ways generally compatible with the preferences of the majority of the public.[2] In a democratic society, the activities of individuals and groups are generally directed towards governmental institutions such as the legislature, executive, judiciary and bureaucracy. Public policy is formulated, implemented and enforced by governmental institutions. In other words, a policy does not take the shape of a public policy unless it is adopted and implemented by the governmental institutions. Government institutions give public policy three different characteristics.

Characteristics of Public Policy

First, the government gives *legal authority* to policies. Public policy is the result of certain decisions and is characterized by the use of legal sanctions. It is regarded as a legal obligation which commands the obedience of affected people. Second, the application

---

[1] Elinor Ostrom, 'Institutional Rational Choice', in *Theories of the Policy Process*, ed. Paul A. Sabatier (Boulder, CO: Westview, 2007).
[2] C. Hewitt, 'Policy-making in Post-war Britain: A Nation-level Test of Elitist and Pluralist Hypotheses', *British Journal of Political Science* IV(2) (1974): 187–216.

of public policy is extended to citizens or people who are objects or for whom the policy is meant. Third, public policies involve *coercion*. It is applied to the acts of government in backing up its decisions. A policy conveys the idea of capacity for imposing penalties, through coercion of a kind usually reserved to the government itself. Only the government can legally impose sanctions on violators of its policies. Since the government has the ability to command the obedience of all its people to formulate policies governing the whole country and to monopolize the coercion, the individuals and groups generally work for the enactment of their preferences into policies.

According to the institutional theory, there is a close relationship between public policy and governmental institutions. It is not surprising, then, that political scientists would focus on the study of governmental structures and institutions. The institutional study has become a central focus of public policy. Thus, one of the models of the policymaking system might be called the institutional theory because it depends on the interactions of those institutions created by the constitutions, government or legislature.

In the institutional model, power is exercised by different individuals and groups such as the PM, MPs, bureaucrats or leaders of interest groups. Each exercise of power constitutes one of the influences which, in totality, go to make up the policymaking process.[3] This is to say that there is a process through which public policy is enacted. The process generally comprises a sequence of related decisions made under the influence of powerful individuals and groups, which together form what is known as state institutions. The institutional approach is concerned with explaining how social groups and governmental institutions bring influence to bear on those entitled to take and implement legally binding decisions. Such decision-makers include those who hold office within the formal and constitutional system of rules and regulations which give formal authority and power to the various positions within the governmental structures and institutions.

The institutional approach attempts to study the behaviour of actors within institutions and the interactions between institutions. The structures and institutions and their arrangements and interactions can have a significant impact on public policy. Governmental institutions are structured patterns of behaviour of individuals and groups which persist over a period of time.[4] The renewed interest in institutions has taken place broadly in three major categories: (i) sociological institutionalism, (ii) economic institutionalism and (iii) political institutionalism.

SOCIOLOGICAL INSTITUTIONALISM

Sociological institutionalism comprises contributions that focus on institutional arrangements within a society that shape human behaviour, ideas and interests. Key contributors to sociological institutionalism are Phillip Selznick[5], and J. March and J. Olsen.[6]

---

[3] Birkland, *An Introduction to the Policy Process*, 301–05.
[4] Thomas Dye, *Understanding Public Policy*, 3rd ed. (New Jersey: Prentice Hall, 1980), 21.
[5] Phillip Selznick, *TVA and the Grass Roots* (California: UCP, 1949).
[6] J.G. March and J.P. Olsen, *Rediscovering Institutions: The Organizational Basis of Politics* (New York: Free Press, 1989).

March and Olsen maintain that problems and solutions happen within political framework, rather than outside the 'black box', because human activity and ideas are fundamentally bounded by the institutions within which they are set. The political framework (institutions and rules) provides the parameters of how conflict takes place, how participants interact and how citizens relate to governing bodies. Thus an explanation of how and why a given policy emerged in relation to a 'problem' requires that we first analyse the structure, historical development, personal networks and decisions over time of the institutions involved in finding a solution to a problem.

According to Selznick, formal structures 'never succeed in conquering the non-formal dimensions of organizational behavior'. The decision-making which takes place in organizations is, therefore, influenced by its dependence on the environment in which it is situated, rather than by formal or rational considerations. Selznick argues,

> Every formal organization ... attempts to mobilize human and technical resources as means for the achievements of its ends. However, the individuals within the system tend to resist being treated as means. They interact as wholes, bringing to bear their own special problems and purposes.... As a result, the organization may be significantly viewed as an adaptive social structure, facing problems which arise simply because it exists as an organization in an institutional environment, independently of the special ... goals which called it into being.[7]

As such, people are dependent on the organization to fulfil certain needs, and in turn the organization is dependent on the environment in which it is located. In other words, decision-making in organizations may be driven by an inner logic, the interests and values of its members, by its need to adapt or displace goals, rather than by rational considerations. The policymaking process may consequently subvert formal policy and institutional arrangements.

Criticism

The institutional theory in terms of structural-functionalist explanation advocated by Selznick offered much insight into the organizational context of decision-/policymaking, and it does not however take account of power within and around organizations. Second, it is possible that some organizations may be more powerful to shape their environment than others. In this case, more powerful organizations will have an ability to shape their own agendas, whereas the less powerful will be far more the product of the external environment. The limited amount of time or resources available to any institution or society means that only a limited number of issues are likely to reach the institutional agenda.[8] In his criticism to the Selznick's model, Perrow contends that 'the dominant organizations or institutions of our society have not experienced goal displacement and have been able to institutionalize on their own terms'.[9]

---

[7] Phillip Selznick, *Leadership in Administration* (Illinois: Row and Peters, 1957), 251.
[8] James Hilgartner and Charles Bosk, 'The Rise and Fall of Social Problems: A Public Arenas Model', *American Journal of Sociology* 94(1) (1988): 53–78.
[9] C. Perrow, *Complex Organizations: A Critical Essay* (New York, NY: Random House, 1986), 175.

Third, Selznick's model neglects the way in which power operates within organizations. However, in the functioning of organizations, Perrow argues that elites clearly have an important role in defining the environment.[10]

But the formation of policy agendas has increasingly been influenced by institutionalized policy analysis in modern think tanks. The predominance of institutions in the making of policy, and the setting of policy agendas, in particular, has meant that, as Lindblom argues, participation in policymaking has become an exclusive preserve of those interests which are powerful and well resourced.[11] And having been invented, institutions which exist within wider environments are subject to the pressures of more powerful, better-resourced, better-connected organizations.[12]

ECONOMIC INSTITUTIONALISM

In comparison to sociologists who envisage decision-making in institutions involving environmental impact and interests, economic institutionalists argue that human beings are driven by self-interest and are self-regarding. Economic institutionalism comprises theories derived from 'transaction cost economics' and 'principal–agent' theories (agency theory).

Transaction Cost Economics

Transaction cost economics (TCE) reasons that the markets involve costs in locating buyers (customers) and sellers (suppliers) in getting information, in negotiating over price, terms and conditions and also in monitoring agreed contracts. In all of this, we are involved in trying to reduce uncertainty and increase control over our transaction. The institutionalist model derived from TCE is one composed of buyers and sellers in which there is little trust, much uncertainty, bounded rationality, opportunism, moral hazard (sellers being dishonest) and where contracts impose on human transactions discipline and control. The issue of costs in economic transaction was developed into a theory of 'how firms grow' by Oliver Williamson in his work.[13]

Theory of How Firms Grow

In his work, Williamson argued that the costs of buying and selling with outside firms which involved high transaction costs might best be reduced by buying a supplier and placing it within a hierarchy of other departments or divisions. In other words, a firm grows by incorporating firms within its own structure by adopting a hierarchy of activities and divisions so as to reduce transaction costs by substituting an internal market or price

---

[10] Ibid., 172.

[11] C.E. Lindblom and E.J. Woodhouse, *The Policy-making Process*, 3rd ed. (New Jersey: Prentice Hall, 1993), 104–13.

[12] P. DiMaggio and W. Powell, 'The Iron Cage Revisited: Institutional Isomorphism and Collective Rationality in Organizational Fields', in *The New Institutionalism in Organizational Analysis*, eds. W. Powell and DiMaggio (Chicago, IL: University of Chicago Press, 1991).

[13] O.E. Williamson, *Markets and Hierarchies* (New York, NY: Free Press, 1975); *Economic Organizations* (Brighton: Harvester Wheatsheaf, 1986).

system for an external arrangement. From this model, Williamson deduces that hierarchies replace markets when the costs of transactions are such as to make for lower efficiency. As the firm incorporates within its structure departments and divisions where once it did business with them as external firms, the cost of monitoring contracts falls also. For Williamson, the core of the theory is that reduced transaction costs resulting from more control and more capacity to monitor the opportunism of individuals and subordinates will create greater efficiency for the firm. Williamson argues that hierarchies are often a more efficient solution than markets in cases of information-related market failures or 'organizational failures'. He says that hierarchies grow as markets fail to keep transaction costs down. Complexity and the higher costs of dealing with factors such as uncertainty moral hazard, little trust and opportunism mean that the firm must grow with a view to reducing the costs which impair inefficiency. It may be far more efficient to replace a market relationship with a supplier with a better control or authority relationship. Williamson argues that the longer the term of the contract, the greater the uncertainty involved and the greater the costs of monitoring that contract.

Principal–Agent Theory

Organizational economic theory strives to ensure that worker (rank-and-file employees) interests coincide with the organization interests. Agency theory or popularly known as principal–agent theory also emerged in the 1970s as an alternative to the behaviour tradition. Stiglitz[14] and Alchian and Demsetz[15] are the key contributors to the development and popularization of the principal–agent theory. It holds that an organization's principals—owners, CEOs, government agency heads—look for achievement of organizational goals. From a public sector's perspective, this could include more efficient and effective service delivery or improved citizen satisfaction. Principals need help from agents. Agents usually represent an organization's employees, but they also include external players that provide services to the organization. Like the TCE's analysis, the formulation of the agency theory focuses on the problem of the relationship between principals (buyers of services), contracts and agents (sellers of services). It has served as a tool for examining interest–conflict problems in aligning the choices of principles and agents in the face of inadequate information and bounded rationality that tend to weaken principal's abilities to form judgements about the knowledge, traits and performance of agents. The point is that relationship between principal and agents in the marketplace is problematic for the reason that the principal is highly dependent on (and at the mercy of) agents. Employees will be after their own interests, and outside firms will be more interested in their profits than those of the purchaser. Cheating and an eye to the main chance (opportunism) therefore form the essential considerations of principals in monitoring and controlling their agents.

Advocates of the agency theory argue that costs of monitoring the relationship will, in conditions of high uncertainty, a small number of agents, poor information, an opportunistic behaviour of agents, be higher in dealing with outside agents than with intra-organizational agents. The answer to this troublesome relationships, in which agents seem to have the

[14] J.E. Stiglitz, 'Principal and Agent', in *The New Palgrave: A Dictionary of Economics*, eds. J. Eatwell et al. (London: Macmillan, 1987).
[15] A.A. Alchian and H. Demsetz, 'Production, Information Costs and Economic Organization', *American Economic Review* 62 (1972): 777–95.

upper hand, lies in the selection of institutions—markets or hierarchies—so that contracts can be monitored at lower cost. According to these advocates, outside agency will do it for less and contract can be given on short-term basis so that if it does not deliver services, the relationship can be terminated. But in awarding the task of implementing the policy to outside agents, the contract has to be such that it maximizes the ability of the provider to control the agent qua individual and 'firm'. In other words, the agency model proposes that in making decisions, we should also be in the business of choosing those institutional arrangements which best provide for contractual (monitorable) relationships between purchasers and providers. Like public choice theorists, economic intuitionalists who propounded agency theory advocated the idea that markets should be brought into play so as to improve the efficiency of the public sector. The theory attempts to reconcile the inherent conflict between principal's and agent's interests.

For the proponents of TCE and principal–agent theory as a model of political life, the answer appears to be to improve the way in which contractual arrangements can keep tabs on actors who are involved in the policymaking process. One approach, of course, is to infuse public services with a consumerist ethos so that the voter/citizen is seen as a customer whose relationship to public services is mediated through quasi-contracts such as performance targets and 'mission statements'.[16] In main, the principal–agent theory deals with the inherent challenges of motivating employees and controlling cooperative action.

Criticism

Halachmi raises certain issues in the application of agency theory.[17] As Moe noted, there are certainly significant problems in translating economic approaches to organizational analysis to the distinctive operating and task environment of the public sector.[18] What Moe explains as a great strength of 'new economics of organization'—promoting assumptions of neoclassical economics—can also be seen as less realistic descriptively and so somewhat less useful prescriptively in a world of multiple principals, ambiguous goals and labile preferences.

Reviewing the use of quasi-markets as social policy, Le Grand and Bartlett offer a conclusion in terms of TCE that it has pushed up TCEs in the delivery of welfare services: 'Overall, the issue of appropriate institutional design to minimize transaction costs is one which will undoubtedly require a long period of experimentation and disruption in the evolving quasi-market system'.[19] Lane also comments that basis to the operation of the bureau is a principal–agent relationship between politicians on the one hand and civil servants on the other hand.[20]

[16] W. Parsons, *Public Policy* (Cheltenham: Edward Elgar, 1996), 332.
[17] A. Halachmi, 'Principal-Agent Perspective', in *Encyclopedia of Public Administration and Public Policy,* Vol. 2, ed. J. Rabin (ed.) (New York, NY: Marcel Dekker, 2003), 956–58.
[18] T.M. Moe, 'The New Economics of Organization', *American Journal of Political Science* 78 (1984): 739–77.
[19] J. Le Grand and W. Bartlett, eds., *Quasi-markets and Social Policy* (London: Macmillan, 1993), 211–12.
[20] J.E. Lane, *The Public Sector: Concepts, Models and Approaches* (London: SAGE Publications, 1993), 188.

POLITICAL INSTITUTIONALISM

Political institutionalism is most closely associated with the works of Theda Skocpol[21] and Peter Hall.[22] Skocpol and Hall's approaches to political institutionalism come from theories of state–society relations, and consequently their definition of institutions goes far beyond that of either of the sociological or economic institutionalism.

Political institutionalism approach argues that policymaking is the outcome of the internal agenda of state institutions rather than the result of external pressures and influences. Contrary to the Marxist idea of the state as an instrument of the dominant class, Skocpol in her review of the research argues that the state in both liberal democratic systems (such as France, Britain and Sweden) and the developing world has the capacity to be relatively insulated from social and economic forces.[23]

Hall's model gives a macro view of the relationships of institutions to society and state, rather than single organizations or the mechanisms of individual rational choice. For Hall, focusing on institutions/organizations refers to 'an analysis of the formal rules, compliance procedures, and operating practices that structure the relationship between individuals in various units of the polity and economy'.[24] His approach is fundamentally opposed to the factionist sociological framework of Selznick.

Both Skocpol and Hall argue that the analysis of policymaking must be set within the context of the capacity which state institutions have for shaping policy. In their view, state institutions have a dominant role in shaping key areas of policymaking over a long period of time. However, institutions do not exist in isolation from the wider relationship of the state to society. Further, Hall argues that, unlike the approach taken by economic institutionalism, a state–society approach must take account of specific historical experiences.

Hall's conclusion of the detailed study of economic policymaking in Britain and France is that economic policy has been the result of institutional structuring of state–society relations. Hall's political institutionalism approach provides a framework for the analysis of decision-making in historical and comparative terms. It requires that we understand how institutions constrain decision-making in government outside the formal constitutional arrangements that also shape and often determine decisions that are made. Hall says that institutions exist and have an impact on how decisions are made as they provide the context within which judgements are made, but they do not eliminate the 'free will of policy-makers'. Hall does not accept the central assumption of the economists, that we are free to choose and reform institutional structures. On the other hand, policymakers in the political institutionalism approach are free to make choices (within the constraints of institutional arrangements). The view which runs through TCE and agency theory is that,

---

[21] Theda Skocpol, 'Bringing the State Back In', in *Bringing the State Back In*, P.B. eds. Evans et al. (Cambridge: Cambridge University Press, 1985).

[22] P.A. Hall, *Governing the Economy* (Cambridge: Polity Press, 1986).

[23] See T. Skocpol and K. Finegold, 'State Capacity and Economic Intervention in the New Deal', *Political Science Quarterly* 97 (1982): 255–78. This work on the agricultural policy shows how policy was the result of administrative innovation, rather than simply farming pressure groups.

[24] Hall, *Governing the Economy*, 19.

as Chandler argues, structures follow strategy.[25] However, in the case of political decision-makers, Hall doubts that, on the strength of historical evidence, ~~structures follow strategy: It is more usual in politics for the structures to shape strategy.~~[26] History shows that political arrangements are far less manipulable than the organization of firms, however big.

CONCLUSION

Arguments of the institutionalists have gained wide recognition. As Almond and others conceded that such issues were grossly neglected in the 1960s and 1970s.[27] The impact of March and Olsen and of Skocpol and others have done much to redress the balance in favour of taking more account of the institutional context within which problems and policy are formulated. Political institutionalism also offers a critique of the kind of arguments advanced by Sabatier and Jenkins-Smith in regard to policymaking as the product of 'advocacy coalitions'. Skocpol and Hall, for example, argue that the analysis of policy-making must be set within the context of the capacity of the state institutions. Sabatier argues that this idea of state autonomy is 'highly dubious' and misleading.[28] However, the approaches advocated by institutionalists cannot be easily discarded. To them, 'institutions do make a difference when explaining public policy outcomes'.[29]

Review Questions

(i) Discuss the basic characteristics of public policy that derives from institutional approaches.
(ii) How has Selznick's sociological institutionalism been criticized?
(iii) Propose with examples how principal–agent theory applies to public policymaking.
(iv) Discuss the basic principles of political institutionalism in policy formulation.
(v) Argue with illustrations if or not institutionalism affects public policy process.

---

[25] Hall, *Governing the Economy*, 259.

[26] A.D. Chandler, *The Visible Hand* (Cambridge, MA: Harvard University Press, 1977).

[27] Almond et. al., *Comparative Politics: A Theoretical Framework* (New York, NY: Harper Collins, 1993), 133.

[28] P.A. Sabatier, 'Policy Change over a Decade or More', in *Policy Change and Learning*, eds. Sabatier and H. Jenkins-Smith (Boulder, CO: Westview, 1993), 37.

[29] B. Dan Wood, 'Federalism and Policy Responsiveness: The Clean Air Case', *Journal of Politics* 53(3) (1991): 851–59.

CHAPTER 9

POLICY ANALYSIS
Processes and Tools

INTRODUCTION

As an academic field, public policy is the study of government decisions, actions and non-actions designed to deal with values, needs and problems of the people. The study of public policy prepares and helps us to cope better with the future. It improves our knowledge about the state and society. An important part of the study of public policy is concerned with society's future.

Questions of policy ultimately rest on the application of knowledge to political decisions. Such knowledge is generated both within and outside the government agencies and other public affairs institutions. An understanding of the causes and consequences of policy decisions permits us to apply the knowledge of social sciences to the solution of practical problems. The acquisition and dissemination of information about public policies have become a major theme in social sciences, especially in the disciplines of public administration and political science. The use of such knowledge for making, managing and evaluating public policy is generally termed as 'policy analysis'. In spite of the importance of the public policy, thinking about the future is quite primitive, among both social scientists and policymakers in developing countries, especially India.

Policy analysis owes its origin to the development of social sciences (which probably emerged in an environment of social reforms). In the early 20th century, there was a general retreat from any sort of the policy advocacy. Much of the focus in study of social sciences shifted to the adoption of scientific objectivity. As the state grew in power and intellectual technology became more available, particularly in the 20th century, so the need for application of rationality as a basis for policy increased. Many of the analysis techniques of policy analysis had their origins in the decision sciences developed during the war, particularly operations research.[1]

In the 1960s through 1970s, policy study centres and think tanks were set up in many developed countries. For example, in Britain, the Central Policy Review Staff (CPRS) was set up in 1970 whose aim was to provide a more strategic long-term analysis of problems in terms of policies in specific areas. However, there has been considerable growth in the research and training in policy analysis since the early 1970s in many developed countries.[2] In most developed countries, policy analysis has been substantially stimulated

---

[1] P. DeLeon, *Advice and Consent: The Development of the Policy Sciences* (New York, NY: Russell SAGE Foundation, 1988).

[2] See, for example, E. Stokey and R. Zeckhauser, *A Primer for Policy Analysis* (New York, NY: Norton, 1978).

by the government's increased concern for public problems. The attractiveness of the government as a research sponsor has also been enhanced.

Definition and Issues of Policy Analysis

According to Patton and Sawicki, the term 'policy analysis' was probably first used in 1958 by Charles Lindblom.[3] According to Wildavsky, 'policy analysis' is both art and craft, rather than a science. Analysis is about exercising 'imagination' and conducting 'thought experiments'. He says, 'Policy analysis, to be brief, is an activity creating problems that can be solved'.[4] Wildavsky sees the role of analysis as contributing to the improvement of politics, rather than as a substitute for it.

Edward Quade is often considered a pioneering proponent of the policy analytical approach. In his *Analysis for Public Decisions*, Quade asserts that policy analysis remains a 'reasonable strategy for discovering good solutions'. Its main purpose is to 'help a decision-maker a better choice than he would otherwise have made. It is thus concerned with the more effective manipulation of the real world'.[5]

In Dunn's words, policy analysis is 'an applied discipline which uses multiple methods of inquiry and argument to produce and transform policy-relevant information that may be utilized in political settings to resolve public problems'.[6] Patton and Sawicki observe that policy analysis is 'a systematic evaluation of the technical and economic feasibility and political viability of alternative policies, strategies for implementation, and the consequences of policy adoption'.[7]

Public policy analysis is thus nothing more than estimating the impact of public policy on the government programmes. The *Dictionary of Public Administration* defines policy analysis as 'a systematic and data-based alternative to intuitive judgements about the effects of policy or policy options'. It is used '(a) for problem assessment and monitoring, (b) as a 'before the fact' decision tool, and (c) for evaluation'.[8]

Policy analysis encourages social scientists and policymakers to examine policy issues and decisions with scientific tools. Thomas Dye labels policy analysis as the 'thinking man's response' to demands. He observes that specifically public analysis involves

(i) *A primary concern with explanation rather than prescription.* Policy recommendations—if they are made at all—are subordinate to description and explanation. There is an implicitly judgement that understanding is a prerequisite to prescription, and that understanding is best achieved through careful analysis rather than rhetoric or polemics.

[3] Charles E. Lindblom, 'Policy Analysis', *American Economic Review* 48(3) (1958): 298–312.
[4] A. Wildavsky, *Speaking the Truth to Power: The Art and Craft of Policy Analysis* (Boston, MA: Little, Brown, 1979), 16–17.
[5] E.S. Quade, *Analysis for Public Decisions* (New York, NY: Elsevier, 1976), 21, 254.
[6] William Dunn, *Public Policy Analysis: An Introduction* (New Jersey: Pearson, 2004).
[7] Carl Patton and David Sawicki, *Basic Methods of Policy Analysis and Planning* (New Jersey: Prentice Hall, 1993).
[8] Ralph C. Chandler and Jack C. Plano, *The Public Administration Dictionary* (New York: John Wiley, 1982), 88.

(ii) *A rigorous search for the causes and consequences of public policies.* This search involves the use of scientific standards of inference. Sophisticated quantitative techniques may be helpful in establishing valid inferences about causes and consequences, but they are not really essential.

(iii) *An effort to develop and test general propositions about the causes and consequences of public policy and to accumulate reliable research findings of general relevance.* The object is to develop general theories about public policy that are reliable and that apply to different government agencies and different policy areas. Policy analysts clearly prefer to develop explanations that fit more than one policy decision or case study—explanations that stand up over time in a variety of settings.[9]

Generally speaking, policy analysis is a technique which puts data to use in, or deciding about, estimating and measuring the consequences of public policies. Its purpose is two-fold. It provides maximum information with minimal cost about (i) the likely consequences of proposed policies and (ii) the actual consequences of the policies already adopted.

To achieve these two purposes, various methods or approaches are applied. Among the principal methodologies are (i) cost–benefit analysis (CBA), (ii) economic forecasting, (iii) systems analysis and simulation, (iv) financial planning, (v) policy evaluation and impact assessment and (vi) social indicators.[10]

As we have seen, policy analysis is an inter-discipline drawing upon data from other disciplines. It is essentially impact research.

A number of trends have occurred in policy analysis research since the early 1970s. Stuart Nagel has identified four key elements to it,[11] which have been undergoing a change over the past 50 years. These are:

(i) the goals with which policy analysis is concerned,
(ii) the means for achieving those goals,
(iii) the methods for determining the effects of alternative means on goal—achievement and
(iv) the profession of policy analysis which is applying these methods in relating means to goals.

Goals refer to the societal benefits minus the societal costs that one is seeking to achieve through public decisions. The crime reduction field provides a good example of the need for an approach to this problem. On the means elements, there is a growing need for means that are politically and administratively feasible. The environmental policy provides a good example of this approach. As regards the methods, they refer to the procedures whereby one can determine the effects of alternative policies on given goals. How to provide counsel to the poor in civil cases is a good example to illustrate this point.

---

[9] Dye, *Understanding Public Policy*, 6–7.
[10] Lineberry, *American Public Policy*, 120–33.
[11] Stuart Nagel, 'Policy Analysis', in *Making and Managing Policy*, ed. G. Ronald Gilbert (New York: Marcel Dekker, 1984), 87–106.

As already said, understanding public policy is both an art and a craft. It is very much art because it requires insight and creativity in identifying societal problems and describing them, in devising public policies that might reduce them. It is a craft because these tasks require some knowledge of economics, political science, public administration, sociology and law. Policy analysis is a subfield of all of these traditional disciplines. Finally on the element of the profession of policy analysis, there is a substantial growth in the policy analysis training programmes, research centres, funding resources and other professional institutions.

POLICY ANALYSTS AND CONCERNS

There are varieties of groups and people (academics, independent research institutions, interest groups, political parties, mass media) who are involved in policy analysis and are concerned with

   (i) the relationship of public policies to societal problems,
   (ii) the content of public policies,
   (iii) what the policymakers do and
   (iv) the likely future consequences of policy in terms of outcomes.

Some analysts, for example, may be interested in the role of political parties in shaping public policy, while others in the impact of bureaucracy on policymaking or the role of professionals in policy delivery. Analysts again may focus on different stages of the policy process, such as policy formulation, implementation or evaluation.

Policy analysts, therefore, study how the actors in the policy process make decisions, and what goals are developed by the group interests. They study the methods by which problems are identified, goals are specified, options evaluated and selected and performance measured. They attempt to apply rational analysis to the effort to produce better policy decisions. However, it should be noted that policy issues are decided not by analysts but by political actors—elected and appointed government officials, interest groups and occasionally even citizens as voters.

POLICY ANALYSIS TYPOLOGY

As with models of the policymaking process, types of policy analysis vary. In main, there are two types of policy analysis.

Prospective and Retrospective Analysis

Policy analysis is ex ante (prospective) analysis which takes place before a decision is taken. On the other hand, policy analysis is ex post (retrospective) analysis which takes place after to assess or evaluate policy. The focus of prospective policy analysis is on the future outcomes of the proposed policy. In this case, the policy analyst endeavours to predict the future results of given policy alternatives. The retrospective policy analysis focuses on the analysis of past policies.

Normative and Positive Analysis

Normative policy analysis is directed towards studying what public policy ought to be (normative) to resolve public issues. Policy analysis is prescriptive rather than descriptive when it recommends action to be taken rather than merely describing policy processes. Normative policy analysis deals with some sort of statements involving value judgements about what should be (the future course of action for a given problem). For example, the statement that cost of education for primary school-going children is too high cannot be confirmed by referring to data. The cost is based on a given criterion. One may agree on the facts of education cost but disagree over one's ethical judgement regarding the implications of the education cost.

Positive policy analysis excludes values in its policy analysis. It tries to understand public policy as it is. It strives to explain how external forces would change policy. It endeavours to pursue truth through the process of testing hypothesis by measuring them against the criterion of real-world experiences. Positive policy analysis usually deals with cause-and-effect assertions. In case of disagreement over the analysis, matter could be resolved by examining the facts.

But positive policy analysis is not without effects. First, by excluding values, the focus reduces the relevance of policy analysis for policymakers who are concerned with preferred goals and objectives. Second, the focus reduces the importance of values in policy debates by shifting the discussion to CBA. Third, the attempt to become more scientific by excluding such values as justice and fairness means favouring business interests and social conservatives to tout the values of right to property, virtues of self-reliance and so on.

As a professional, a policy analyst attempts to apply rational analysis to the effort to produce better policy decisions. Thus through rational analysis, a body of research findings is produced which provides valuable input for improving and promoting good policy decisions. Policy analysis is thus seen as a technique to public policy which aims to contextualize research from those disciplines which have a problem and policy orientation.

POLICY ANALYTICAL FRAMEWORKS AND VARIETIES

Public policy is a field which tends to be defined by policy areas or sectors. Some of the key areas of public policy include education, health, environment, housing, agriculture, transport, urban planning and economic and social contexts.

Policy Analytical Frameworks

In the classification of policy field, Bobrow and Dryzek suggest five main frames of policy analysis: (i) welfare economics, (ii) public choice, (iii) social structure, (iv) information processing and (v) political philosophy.[12] However, the analytical frameworks are not necessarily exclusive as policy analysis tends to range across them. Within each of these policy areas and frameworks, there exist specialized research networks and communities which address problems and advocate public policies. Analysts may focus on different stages of the policy process, such as policy formulation, implementation and/or evaluation.

---

[12] Bobrow and Dryzek, *Policy Analysis by Design*.

Variety of Policy Analysis

Policy analysis has different varieties comprising a range of activities in the policy process. Gordon et al., for example, set out five varieties of policy analysis.[13]

(i) **Analysis of policy determination:** Analysis of policy determination is concerned with how policy is made, why, when and for whom.

(ii) **Analysis of policy content:** Analysis of policy content may involve a description of particular policy and how it developed in relation to other earlier policies, or it may seek to offer a critique of policy.

(iii) **Policy monitoring and evaluation:** This analysis examines how policies have performed against policy objectives and what impact a policy may have had on a specific problem.

(iv) **Analysis for policy information:** This analysis provides feed into policymaking activities in the form of detailed research, advice or policy options.

(v) **Analysis for policy advocacy:** This analysis involves research and arguments which are intended to influence the policy agenda of the government.

As a term, *policy analysis* is most closely associated with the use of a variety of techniques to make or improve rational decision-making process.

POLICY ANALYSIS PROCESSES AND STAGES

The effort to provide an abstract framework for the decision/policy process was probably first presented by Harold Lasswell in 1956. David Easton in 1965 provided an input–output model for the entire policy process.[14] Since 1965, effort has concentrated on presenting several stagist models. However, public policy analysis has not progressed in developing scientifically law like propositions.

Policy analysis models and techniques aim at providing a more rational basis for decisions. However, policymaking frameworks of rational analysis vary.

For Lasswell, following categories of functional analysis act as the base: (i) intelligence, (ii) promotion, (iii) prescription, (iv) invocation, (v) application, (vi) termination and (vii) appraisal.[15]

To Jenkins, seven stages are critical to policy analysis: (i) initiation, (ii) information, (iii) consideration, (iv) decision, (v) implementation, (vi) evaluation and (vii) termination.[16]

Likewise, Hogwood and Gunn set out the following stages for rational policy analysis: (i) deciding to decide (issue search or agenda setting); (ii) deciding how to decide (issue

---

[13] I. Gordon, J. Lewis and K. Young, 'Perspectives on Policy Analysis', *Public Administration Bulletin* 25 (1977): 26–35.

[14] David Easton, *A Systems Analysis of Political Life* (New York: John Wiley, 1965).

[15] H.D. Lasswell, *The Decision Process: Seven Categories of Functional Analysis* (Maryland: University of Maryland, 1956).

[16] W. Jenkins, *Policy Analysis: A Political and Organizational Perspective* (London: Martin Robertson, 1978).

filtration); (iii) issue definition; (iv) forecasting; (v) setting objectives and priorities; (vi) options analysis; (vii) policy implementation, monitoring and control; (viii) evaluation and review; and (ix) policy maintenance, succession and termination.[17]

For Quade, the decision-making process involves five key stages which he defines in terms of

(i) Formulation: clarifying and constraining the problem and determining the objectives;
(ii) Search: identifying, designing and screening the alternatives;
(iii) Forecasting: predicting the future environment or operational context;
(iv) Modelling: building and using models to determine the impacts and
(v) Evaluation: comparing and ranking the alternatives.[18]

Rational analysis maintains that a decision is the result of a series of logical steps. The role of analysis is to facilitate a rational choice of means and ends, within the limitations recognized by Quade. To him, in real world, decision-making is often constrained and bounded by interests and involves clashes of values and beliefs.

Simon's decision-making comprises four stages:

(i) Intelligence: that is finding occasions called for a decision;
(ii) Design: that is identifying, developing and analysing possible courses of action;
(iii) Choice: that is selecting a particular course of action from those available and
(iv) Evaluating: that is comparing programmed and non-programmed decision-making.

Patton and Sawicki lay down a six-step process for the policy analysis: (i) verify, define and detail the problem; (ii) establish evaluation criteria; (iii) identify alternative policies; (iv) evaluate alternative policies; (v) display and distinguish among alternative policies and (vi) monitor the implemented policy.[19]

Policy-/decision-making in the modern policy context is a complex exercise. It involves the question of rationality which appears to be compatible with the real world of decision-making in which there is considerable uncertainty.

Here in this chapter, the discussion would be devoted to ex ante analysis, that is, analysis which takes place prior to decision. This involves the utilization of ex post evaluation of existing policies and programmes. Here it needs to be stressed that analysis for decision-making necessarily involves analysis of the existing policies which impact upon the 'new' or future policy decisions.

The rational analysis depends upon the use of information, advice and knowledge. The data for analysis comes from formal and informal sources. Formal information consists of data on the economy and society. These are compiled in the form of official statistics. This formal data constitutes the basis of official problem formulation. However, informal

---

[17] B.W. Hogwood and L.A. Gunn, *Policy Analysis for the Real World* (London: Oxford University Press, 1984).

[18] Quade, *Analysis for Public Decisions*, 45.

[19] Patton and Sawicki, *Basic Methods of Policy Analysis and Planning*.

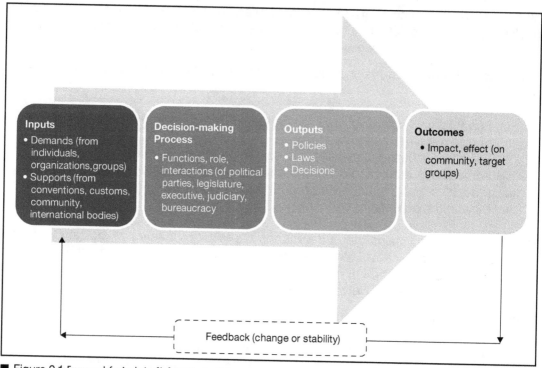

■ Figure 9.1: Framework for Analysis of Information for Policy
Source: Author's own.

source of information is also employed. Non-formal channels and forms of information may in reality prove far more determining than the official data in shaping the decision-making process.

Since policy analysis makes use of the required information in examining, deciding about and, finally, measuring the consequences of public policies, a framework for policy analysis is required. Such a policy analysis framework would identify both the kinds of information used to define policy and the analytic processes.[20]

Figure 9.1 indicates the basic linkages of a framework for the systematic analysis of information and its use in a policy-related context. The basis to the framework is a process of information for policy analysis which is derived from systems or programme performance in terms of the interaction among

   (i) *Inputs* that indicate needs and demands;
   (ii) *Processes* related to the provision of long-term care services;
   (iii) *Outputs* in terms of the use of services and costs of care and
   (iv) *Outcomes* that identify the end results of certain courses of action.[21]

---

[20] M.R. Burt, *Policy Analysis: Introduction and Applications to Health Programmes* (Washington: Information Resources Press, 1974).

[21] S. Katz and J.A. Papsidero, 'Information, Evaluation and Policy for Long Term Care', in *Operations Research and National Health Policy Issues*, eds. H.E. Emlet et al. (Operations Research Society of America and the National Centre for Health Services Research, 1977).

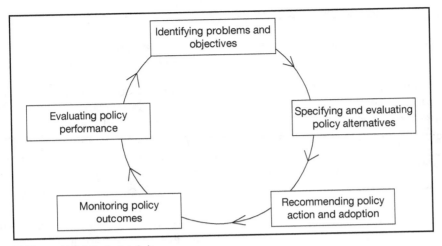

Figure 9.2: Policy Analysis Cycle
Source: Author's own.

Based on the appraisal of systems performance using the previous linkages, issues for various goals can be identified. Once these issues are identified, information is analysed in terms of how it pertains to the larger issues (Figure 9.2).

For example, in the context of the National Health Policy for India (2002), the inputs (in term of needs and demands) comprise health, illness and the quality of life, expressed in physical, psychological, social and environmental terms. Needs are the conditions that ask for action. They are among the most important predictors of utilization, and are mostly described in terms of diagnosis, perceived illness, symptoms or poor health status. On the other hand, demands are expressed as desires in relation to the services sought, whether they are needed or not.

Other inputs include resources, such as manpower, facilities and equipment and performance standards. On the processes linkage, it is concerned with the delivery of services to meet the needs and demands of clients and professionals. Services are described in such terms as their kinds, delivery, management and controls of cost and quality. Other services include supports such as legal aid, income support, consumer education and professional development. The outputs of service-related programmes are described in terms of the use of those services, the costs and the quality of care. Finally, the outcomes are the responses to the services expressed in terms of the levels of well-being and health, and client and professional satisfaction. Thus, based on the appraisal of performance using linkages, issues for various goals can be identified.

The process, stages or cycle involved in policy analysis is discussed here. Rational decision-making continues to be the basis for policy analysis which comprises the following steps:

(i) Identifying problems and objectives,
(ii) Specifying and evaluating policy alternatives,
(iii) Recommending policy action and adoption,
(iv) Monitoring policy outcomes and
(v) Evaluating policy performance.

Identifying Problems and Objectives

Public policy begins when a problem is perceived and gets on the policy agenda. The first stage in the policy process is a prerequisite for all the stages that follow.

It may be pointed out here that the society faces many problems but all may not cause policy response. Success in getting on the policy agenda requires intense lobbying by special interest groups, political support in the legislature and earnest attention of the authoritative actors in the government. Often a systemic agenda emerges which is made up of those issues perceived by the political community as meriting public attention and resolution.[22] For example, shaken by the massive protests against the gang rape of a 23-year-old woman in the national capital (Delhi) on 16 December 2012, the government constituted a commission of inquiry for suggesting measures including the safety of women. The Home Minister promised that 'the government would take immediate steps for amendment of the criminal law for more effective punishment in the rarest of rare cases of sexual assault'.[23]

On the contrary, the institutional agenda is made up of those issues and items that receive the powerful attention of policymakers and that are actively pursued through the various institutions of government. For instance, the government took up the issue of foreign direct investment (FDI) in multi-brand retail and got it approved from the Parliament in December 2012. Some issues get on the policy agenda yet drift along for years without getting the first stage. For example, the institution of Lokpal at the centre has not been created despite the fact that Lokpal Bill was introduced nine times (first in 1968 and the last time in 2012) in the Lok Sabha.

Dearth of political focus on issues concerning women is evident from the fact that the new anti-rape draft law, which the Union Cabinet cleared in July 2012, was not placed for discussion in Parliament. In December 2012, a commission of inquiry was constituted to suggest amendments to law for quicker trial and more stringent punishment in 'aggravated sexual assault' cases amid demands for death penalty. On 2 April 2013, the President gave his assent to the Anti-rape Bill, and it is now called the Criminal Law (Amendment) Act, 2013.

The first stage is the most important stage, because many times the objectives of the problem analysis are not clear and in some cases the objectives are contradictory. Policy analysis requires clarity in identifying the problems to be sorted out. Defining the problem involves moving from mundane descriptions to a more abstract, conceptual plane. Here, an attempt should be made to diagnose the form of market failure, that is, confronted. For example, an environmentalist who is investigating alternative pollution control measures

---

[22] In the wake of mounting pressure from various interest groups, the Modi government at the centre was able to get the undisclosed foreign income and assets (Imposition of Tax) Bill, 2015 approved from the Parliament providing for heavy penalties for stashing away black money in foreign accounts. Seeking to unearth unaccounted funds and assets stashed by Indians abroad, it provides for 120 per cent tax and penalty in additions to 10- year jail term. See *The Tribune*, 14 May, 2015. Under Amnesty Scheme that ended on 30 September 2015, some 638 Indians declared overseas assets of ₹3,770 crore, accessed 16 November 2016, http://images.tribuneindia.com/news/nation/ls-clears-bill-to-crack-down-on-black-money/79432.html

[23] See *The Tribune* (Chandigarh), 23 December 2012, accessed 16 November 2016, http://timesofindia.indiatimes.com/india/Govt-mulling-over-amendment-to-rape-law/articleshow/17723551.cms

for the Ganges will find that the water is being polluted by the dumping of industrial wastes and untreated sewages into river.

Having identified the context of the problem, the next step is to determine what objectives are to be achieved confronting it. Too often, we lose sight of the rational objectives. Paying careful attention to the objectives is important. For example, the *Right of Children to Free and Compulsory Education Act* promulgated in 2010 is merely a means to the end of improving children's knowledge.

Specifying and Evaluating Policy Alternatives

Once a policy problem has been clearly identified and placed on the policy agenda, the policy analyst is required to specify and generate alternative policies. The analyst will determine which kind of alternative is good if not best in terms of efficiency and effectiveness. For example, consider the following possibilities in the case of pollution of the river Ganges in India:

(i) Contractors in some areas of the river might be granted rights by the government to clean water. They would then have the right to sue a polluter.

(ii) The government may require the concerned industrialists and cities and town dwellers to stop dumping wastes and untreated sewage into river. It may prescribe such specifics as enforcement stringency of standards.

(iii) The government may permit polluters to purchase rights to discharge a certain amount of pollutants. Polluters may be required to pay effluent charges and to install pollution control devices.

(iv) The government itself can directly undertake the work of cleaning and removing the pollutants that others dump. On 13 August 2014, the SC (India) asked the Modi government to come up with a road map for making the 2,500-km-long river Ganga pollution free as the issue of cleaning Ganga is very important.

These are some of the alternatives for pollution control. As difficulties are identified and additional information becomes available, refinement of alternative courses of action will continue throughout the analysis. Determining alternatives for policy choice is a difficult task. Often, the process is treated merely as a mechanical exercise, and consequently, attractive policies are not paid adequate attention. It rarely proceeds in a straightforward fashion from the identification of the problem to the choice of the preferred action. Rationalists select the alternative that maximizes utility. However, there is not even a basis for constructing a satisfactory list of criteria to determine which goals or options are the most reasonable and which could be left out.

Evaluating Policy Alternatives

Evaluation is an important aspect of policy analysis. Once a policy problem has been clearly stated and alternatives for policy choice have been determined, it is important to forecast the consequences of each of the alternatives. For this, this policy analyst will turn to a relevant model for forecasting consequences. In the case of the pollution control problem, the models needed would be far more complex. Here, the analyst would have to build a model of how the quality of water in the Ganges responds to the various types of pollution. Only then can he forecast the consequences in terms of quality of water and the alternative measures of pollution control. In such a case, a model based on computer simulation is the most appropriate. It is necessary here for the analyst to predict all the effects of the proposed policies, not just the economic effects desired by the decision-maker. If required, additional data may be collected for analysing the different levels of influence on the economic, social and political dimensions of the problem.

If the consequences of an alternative course of action are uncertain or the possible outcomes differ widely from one another, the analyst may develop a decision tree and evaluate the probability of each outcome. For example, in the Ganges pollution case, it is difficult to predict with complete accuracy either the weather or future developments in pollution control measures, or the vagaries of the political executive. The analyst should seek the advice of experts in the field, but at the same time, he should look for independent corroboration before depending on those whose past experience may commit them to particular policies. This precaution is needed to avert any kind of biasness.

The step in the sequence of policy analysis also relates to evaluating the policy alternatives. It is difficult to have a rational policy choice unless the relative merits of alternative options are compared. The question of measuring success in pursuit of each objective is a difficult one. However, if the analyst is to recommend a policy decision, he must find some way to evaluate the possible degrees of improvement of policy option. Improvement in water quality, for example, will be achieved only at a very high cost, while the benefits of pollution control may be enjoyed by one section of the community, and the government may have to bear a substantial portion of costs in administering the pollution control. These costs therefore must be discounted. In view of such conflicting objectives, it becomes difficult for an elected or appointed policymaker to make these tough policy choices. However, evaluation of the outcomes is of great importance as it reminds us to look carefully at the CBA of a particular policy choice.

Further, it is important to bear in mind about the difference between technically superior alternative and politically feasible alternative. If an alternative is technically superior, its political feasibility should also be weighed by the policy analyst. For example, when we frame a health policy, it has to be for all and not just the poor.

Recommending Policy Action and Adoption

The next and important stage in policy analysis relates to making the preferred choice. The situation may be so simple for the policymaker that he can simply look at the consequences predicted for each alternative and select the one that is best. In contrast, it may be so complex that he will have to think of his preferences among the various possible outcomes. Rational analysis selects the alternative that maximizes utility.

Policy analysts are asked to explain the causes and consequences of public policies. They are involved to recommend policy actions (e.g. to recommend policies to reduce crime). When they are explaining why crime rate has increased, they act as policy analysts, and when they are proposing policies to reduce criminal activity, they act as non-official policymakers. Getting a proposed policy passed at the legislative or executive level is not an easy task. It must follow a standardized procedure. The bill may not be placed at appropriate forum for its clearance. Political entrepreneurs try to redraw dimensions of the dispute so that they can gain a winning edge. Party leaders and senior members of the legislative committees considering the issue often hide their time and move when they sense the time is ripe for action. The actors involved here are clearly political elites and must be persuaded not of the wisdom of the proposed policy, but of its chances of success politically. The proposed policy must convince the authoritative actors in the government that it is in their own interests to promote the policy through their votes.

Monitoring Policy Outcomes and Evaluating Policy Performance

For better results, the policy is required to be monitored. Generally, the policy/decision analyst is not involved in the implementation and monitoring of policy. However for better policy, it is important that policy analysts should be involved in the maintenance, monitoring and evaluation of the implemented policy. In this context, Patton and Sawicki observe, 'Even after a policy has been implemented there may be some doubt, whether the problem was resolved appropriately and even whether the selected policy is being implemented property'.[24] These concerns require that policies and programmes are maintained and monitored during implementation stage to assure that they do not change form unintentionally; measure their impact; determine whether they have the intended impact; and decide whether they should be continued, modified or terminated. Similarly, evaluation of the programme is important to improve the quality of programme analysis. It must be realized that the policy could fail because the programme was not implemented as it was designed or failed to produce the intended results because the underlying assumptions were either incorrect or irrelevant.

As a whole, the rational policy analysis involves five key stages and each stage has its own complexity of exercises. But the experience shows that countless policy studies have led nowhere. Sometimes the fault is attributed to the public decision-makers who do not take advantage of readily accessible data. Too often, it is the producers of the analysis who are to blame. Most policy analyses are gathering dust because they have not been properly understood. The analysis should be brought out in such a way that the essential points can be easily grasped and communicated. The choice among competing policy alternatives is complex, as the future is always uncertain. But, by enhancing capability of the analysts to forecast the consequences of the policy alternatives and providing a framework for valuing those consequences, the techniques of policy analysis lead them to better policies. Despite all this, the policy analysis based on rational considerations has not been accepted as an effective tool of management.

TOOLS OF RATIONAL POLICY ANALYSIS

Policy decisions have to be rationally grounded on scientific norms. Yet many of decisions are not, and 'science remains a social activity as fraught with weaknesses as many other human enterprise'.[25] Some decisions turn on values as much as on the facts. In this section, an attempt is made to discuss tools for rational policy analysis. Among others

---

[24] Patton and Sawicki, *Basic Methods of Policy Analysis and Planning*.
[25] Clinton Andrews, 'Rationality in Policy Decision-making', in *Handbook of Public Policy Analysis*, eds. F. Fischer, Gerald Miller and Mara Sidney (Boca Raton, FL: CRC Press, 2007), 161.

include welfare maximization, public choice, multi-agent simulation and decision support systems.

Welfare Maximization

CBA is extensively used to quantify costs and benefits of policy outcomes and thus identifying the outcome providing the greatest net benefit. Thus, this tool endeavours to guide policymakers to welfare-maximizing choices. Kaldor–Hicks decision criterion that directs the social planner to choose the alternative providing the 'greatest net social benefits'. It rests upon two assumptions: First, that it is reasonable to add gains and losses across individuals when enumerating the societal benefit; and second, that the things individuals gain or lose are easily substitutable so that the winner can at least compensate the losers.

In contrast, the Pareto decision criterion[26] that promotes fairness and efficiency requires unanimous and voluntary participation in transactions to ensure that decisions have no losers, only mutual gains. The Kaldor–Hicks criterion is formally coercive and involves majority rule at best, and dictatorship by the social planner at worst. Yet this tool attempts to impose costs on a few in order to reap broad social benefits. Examples include public health, jails, income taxation, sewage treatment plants and highways.

As a decision aid, CBA offers progressive insights that help reduce alternatives. But it requires a comprehensive calculation of costs and benefits. It has challenged public managers to examine both sides of a service or programme, to look at the long-term consequences and more so to articulate its effect in quantitative as well as qualitative terms.

Public Choice

Public choice, rational choice and political economy are some names which have acquired growing importance in the rationalist paradigm of policy decision-making. Under the rubric of public choice, a variety of contributions show how individual interests influence both marketplace and public policy outcomes. It is also strongly argued that collective decision-making methods are deeply flawed so that neither markets nor politics on their own serve the public adequately. As such, formal democratic decision-making mechanisms need to be supplemented sometimes.

In one sense, rationalist choice is concerned with 'Pareto optimality' (no-loser principle), but because optimality is supremely difficult to achieve in any context, rational choice concerns a 'Pareto improvement', or 'a change in economic organization...that makes one or more members of society better off without making anyone worse off'.[27]

Some important extensions to the microeconomic approach are game theories. Game theories have usefully characterized responses to governmental interventions as 'mixed-motive' (competitive cooperative) negotiations.[28]

---

[26] The economist Pareto (1848–1923) provided an important model to explain welfare problems.
[27] E.J. Mishan, *Economics for Social Decisions* (New York: Praeger, 1972), 14.
[28] R. Axelrod, *The Evolution of Co-operation* (New York: Basic Books, 1984).

Some rational choice theorists have introduced concepts of risk preference and multi-criteria trade-offs. By trade-off, they mean what value is being exchanged (and the social costs and benefits incurred in such an exchange) for what other value.[29]

Psychologists, on the other hand, say that individuals who rely on heuristics suffer from systematic biases, thereby weakening the policy optimality claims of microeconomic analysts, and highlighting the roles of communication and perception of public management.[30]

It may be added here that most of these contributions have the effect of making the science more effective in explaining and prescribing changes in public decision-making in accord with rationality norms.[31]

Decision Support Systems

Another innovative tool for the policy analysis is the decision support systems. Decision support systems reserve key decisions for decision makers, and plan for repeated interactions between analysts and decision-makers. It is a refined approach, but its analytics are often more complex. An example of a decision support system is the power grid in India. Its purpose is to help break an impasse among utility companies, regulators and other interested parties regarding public utility investment policy. Under the support systems, the analysts built a complex scenario analysis tool for simulating the operation of the regional power system under various assumptions over a multi-decade time horizon, and then they convened a planning process that involved all of these parties.

In the context of Britain's EU membership, the British PM David Cameron said, 'If we can't reach such an agreement, and if Britain's concerns were to be met with a deaf ear, which I do not believe will happen, then we will have to think again about whether this European Union is right for us'.[32] And on 23 June 2016, Britain voted to leave the EU but its membership would remain until 2019.

Under this approach, when, for example, stakeholders disagree among themselves about the assumptions placed by analysts, the stakeholders may suggest policy alternatives and the analysts again evaluate their multi-attribute impacts. The stakeholders evaluate these simulated impacts and draw their own conclusions about which solution would be optimal from their point of view. Out of this interaction between stakeholders and analysts emerges broad consensus on a net set of policies for the region.

Decision support systems have found application in an increasing number of fields spanning urban planning, environmental policy, health policy, energy policy, international relations and military policy, among others. In comparison to traditional policy analysts, the decision support systems have an explicit procedural component. Decision support analysts devote much effort to shifting the practice of policy analysts away from a major focus on substantive rationality to giving equal consideration to procedural rationality.

---

[29] R. Keeney and H. Raiffa, *Decisions with Multiple Objectives: Preferences and Value Tradeoff* (New York: John Wiley, 1976).

[30] A. Tversky and D. Kahneman, 'Judgement under Uncertainty: Heuristics and Biases', *Science* 185 (1974): 1124–31.

[31] Andrews, 'Rationality in Policy Decision-making', 165.

[32] See *The Financial Express* (Chandigarh), 9 November 2015, accessed 16 November 2016, http://www.bbc.com/news/uk-politics-34759063

Multi-agent Simulation

Lasswell argues that simulation exercises may be utilized in decision seminars as they may succeed in 'conferring a vivid sense of reality' on the participant.[33] Multi-agent simulation is relatively new modelling approach that seeks to generalize from microeconomic game theory by incorporating more actors, imbuing them with knowledge about limitations of bounded rationality. In policy decision simulations, preferred governmental interventions often differ dramatically from those identified as optimal under microeconomic assumptions.

The multi-agent approach has been useful in the innovation, anti-trust, environmental, and security policy domains, among others.[34] One early application shows how modelling with adaptive agents can yield results that are at variance with those of neoclassical economics. In particular, in perfectly competitive markets, regulation is either distorting and inefficient or irrelevant.[35]

It is pertinent to note here that the tools of rational policy analysis have evolved over a century towards a richer conception of rationality that acknowledges substantive and procedural dimensions and rational applications of reasonable decision rules.

Public Participation

In addition to the brief description of four tools of rational policy analysis, public participation has several potential roles in policy decision-making. Public participation is itself a policy when pursued as a normative perception. Because in the words of Susskind and Elliott, it promotes democratization, decentralization, deprofessionalization and demystification of public policy.[36] One can pursue participation as a strategy, as a means for achieving other ends. Participation can serve as a means of communication, leading to improved information flows that produce better decisions. Participation can operate as conflict resolution, so that participation may lead to reduced tensions and stable outcomes in controversial decisions. More intuitively, the best way to find out what people value is to cultivate public participation as a strategy or policy.

Public participation has many forms and mechanisms. Federal Environmental Assessment Review Office (FEARO), for example, categorizes the spectrum of participation mechanisms into

  (i) public information (ads, newsletters, exhibits);
 (ii) public information feedback (polls, focus groups, surveys);
(iii) consultation (hearings, workshops, panels, games);
(iv) extended involvement (advisory committees, charrettes, task forces);
 (v) joint planning (arbitration, conciliation, mediation, negotiation, partnership) and
(vi) delegation (citizen control, home rule).[37]

---

[33] H.D. Lasswell, *A Preview of Policy Sciences* (New York: Elsevier, 1971), 153.
[34] N. Gilbert and K.G. Troitzsch, *Simulation for the Social Scientist* (Milton Keynes: Open University Press, 1999).
[35] D. Teitelbaum, *An Adaptive Agent Approach to Environmental Regulation* (Pittsburgh, PA: Carnegie Mellon University, 1998).
[36] L. Susskind and M. Elliott, *Paternalism, Conflict, and Coproduction* (New York: Plenum Press, 1983).
[37] Federal Environmental Assessment Review Office (FEARO), *Public Involvement: Planning and Implementing Public Involvement Programs* (Hull, Quebec: FEARO, 1988).

Steps in choosing a mechanism typically include (i) informal consultation to identify major issues and actors; (ii) confirmation of an organizational mandate to proceed; (iii) identification of potentially interested participants; (iv) setting objectives for the participation; (v) determining information exchange requirements; and (vi) planning the length of the activity and the complexity of involvement, implementation and evaluation of how it worked.[38]

As with other decision-making mechanisms, public participation is not without flaws. It is often termed as a potential tyranny of the majority. Other flaws include fractured decisions, adverse reactions to perfunctory involvement, and the non-representativeness of participants in any small group process, and poor information apathy. However, much success in public participation can be achieved through measures of fairness and competence.[39] While a fair process gives all interested parties equal opportunities to participate in the discourse, a competent process operates in direct tension with fairness. Like other tools of policy analysis, participation does contribute to the rationality of public decision-making but to the extent that it overcomes failings of politics and markets as well as its own weak points.

LIMITATIONS OF RATIONAL POLICY ANALYSIS

There are severe limitations on the use of policy analysis as a tool of policy decision-making.

No Substitute for Politics

Politicians often look for policies which strengthen their positions rather than information to help guide policy. The major concern is whether the proposed policy is politically viable and meets the needs of the people in a dynamic society based on democratic values.

The usefulness of the idea of policy analysis as involving a series of logical stages, problem identification, goal setting, analysis of alternatives, decision-making and implementation, appears to be weak vis-à-vis political and bureaucratic interests.[40] Political realists view policy analysis as a threat to politics. For them analysis is not a substitute for politics or 'anti-political', but essentially supplementary and subordinate to the political process.[41]

Lindblom and Woodhouse also argue, 'The quality of public policy depends on a vast network of thought and interaction, in which professional policy analysts play a small role.... In principle, those who analyze public policy can help to deepen political debates about problems, opportunities, and policy options'.[42] Lindblom has argued that the real issue is not rationality so much as improving the capacity of societies to cope flexibly with uncertainty.

---

[38] Ibid.

[39] T. Webler and O. Renn, 'A Brief Primer on Participation: Philosophy and Practice', in *Fairness and Competence in Citizen Participation*, eds. O. Renn, T. Webler and P. Wiedemann (Dordrecht: Kluwer Academic Publishers, 1995), 17–33.

[40] R.A. Heineman et al., *The World of the Policy Analyst* (New Jersey: Chatham House, 1990), 62–4.

[41] T.A. Smith, *Anti-politics: Consensus, Reform and Protest in Britain* (London: Charles Knight, 1972).

[42] Lindblom and Woodhouse, *The Policy-making Process*, 137.

Wildavsky sees the role of analysis as contributing to the improvement of politics, rather than as a substitute for it.[43] Policy analysis is thus an art and a craft, rather than a science. The idea that policy analysts can be neutral is a myth.

Distorting Democratic Values

Whereas Lasswell viewed the future of the policy sciences as being directed towards improving the practice of democracy and a fuller utilization of human dignity,[44] in practice, the idea of policy analysis has been criticized for undermining democratic society. There is a criticism that analysis inhibits political initiatives. It is argued that it reduces the impact which political participation may have on the decisions which are taken by government. Policy analysis in certain contexts appears to be more a form of democratic distortion than enlightenment.[45] Analysis affects the democratic legitimacy.

Weak in Policy Implementation

Heineman notes that the analysis may be strong on the diagnosis of problems and formulation of policy but weak in terms of how a policy should be implemented.[46] A policy analysis is of no use if it cannot be communicated to others. Too often, the policy analysis deals with subjective topics and must rely upon the interpretation of results. Professional researchers often interpret the results of their analysis differently and come out with different policy recommendations. Often administrators are unhappy to find that the policy analysis research hinders the pursuit of policies on which they have already embarked. Moreover, the policy analysts lack a power base. The experience of analysts in the policy process tends to be of being weak vis-à-vis political and bureaucratic interests.

Poor in Resolving Social Conflicts

Policy analysis cannot provide solutions to problems when there is no consensus on what the problems are. It is incapable of resolving societal value conflicts. At best, it can offer advice on how to accomplish a certain set of end values. It cannot determine what those end values should be. Furthermore, social science research cannot be value-free.

It is also very difficult for the government to cure all or even most of the maladies of society. The government is constrained by many forces, both from within and from outside—such as population growth, patterns of family life, class structure, religious beliefs, diversity of cultures and languages and financial resources, and cannot be easily managed by the government. Some social ills are very complex. Moreover, the policy analysis cycle ignores the real world of policymaking which involves multiple levels of government and interacting cycles. In such a situation, the decision-makers choose the decision which is already made and plausible.

---

[43] Wildavsky, *The Art and Craft of Policy Analysis*.
[44] Lasswell, 'The Policy Orientation', 15.
[45] C.H. Weiss, 'Research for Policy's Sake: The Enlightenment Function of Social Research', 531–46.
[46] Heineman, *The World of the Policy Analyst*, 62–64.

Difficult to Predict the Impact

Another limitation of policy analysis is the fact that society's ills are so complex that analysts are incapable of predicting the impact of proposed policies. Social scientists largely fail to give proper advice to the policymakers owing to lack of knowledge about individual and group behaviour. The fact that social scientists offer many contradictory recommendations indicates the absence of reliable scientific knowledge of social problems. Most of society's ills are shaped by so many forces that a simple explanation of them is hardly possible. As Majone notes, 'As politicians know only too well but social scientists often forget, public policy is made of language. Whether in written or oral form, argument is central in all stages of the policy process'.[47]

CONCLUSION

With all the limitations, the idea of analysing policymaking and policy analysis is not without its advantages, and as such, it should not be abandoned lightly. Those who advocate abandoning the stagist model argue for a different framework to take its place (see e.g. the work of Lindblom and Woodhouse, 1993). Stewart's ideas about policy analysis, for example, acknowledge the centrality of the rational model in policy justification but suggest that its role is to 'break down the constraints of organizational thought'. In practice, it is a means of improving decision-making by facilitating a learning process in public sector.[48]

On the whole, it seems safe to say that social scientists can at least attempt to measure the impact of present and past public policies and make this knowledge available to policymakers. Reason, knowledge and scientific analysis are always better than the absence of any knowledge. Robert Lineberry notes that 'policy analysis rests on the assumption that information is better than no information, and that right questions are better than no questions asked, even when the answers may not be definitive'.[49]

It may be noted that policy analysis may not provide solutions to society's ills, but it is still an appropriate tool in approaching policy questions. Policy analysis enables us to describe and explain the causes and consequences of public policy. In broad terms, this framework does allow us to analyse the complexities of the real world. The strength of the analytical approach is that it affords a rational structure within which we may consider the multiplicity of reality. Policy analysts study all the issues that are of interest to policymakers, which means that policy analysis is wide ranging. The criticism of the policy analysis approach in the rational policy decision-making has prompted the search for other approaches to the frameworks for policy analysis.

---

[47] G. Majone, *Evidence, Argument and Persuasion in the Policy Process* (New Haven: Yale University Press, 1989), 1.

[48] J. Stewart, *The New Management of Local Government* (London: Allen & Unwin, 1986), 72–92.

[49] Lineberry, *American Public Policy*, 135.

Review Questions

(i) Define policy analysis. Write a short note on how Thomas Dye has substantiated on the concept.

(ii) What are the two major subtypes of policy analysis?

(iii) Present a comparative analysis of decision-making processes and stages as proposed by different theorists.

(iv) Briefly discuss the various stages involved in rational policy analysis.

(v) Discuss three major limitations of policy analysis as a tool of policy decision-making. Give examples to support your argument.

10

EASTONIAN, VICKERIAN, ELITIST, GROUPTHINK AND MARXIST MODELS FOR POLICY PROCESS

INTRODUCTION

The study of policymaking owes much to the contribution of political scientists, psychologists and sociologists. They provide models or frameworks in which the insights of systems, power and communication are combined. The systems approaches rely on concepts of information, knowledge and institutions and conceive of the policy process as being cyclical and unending. The contribution of David Easton and Geoffrey Vickers who had most influence in the development of models for analysing the policymaking process in systems thinking is discussed here in this chapter. Further, power models which view policymaking or decision-making as something which is shaped and determined by the structures of power are also discussed in this chapter.

EASTONIAN MODEL OF POLICY ANALYSIS

In contrast to institutional approaches which looked at politics purely in terms of executive, legislature and constitution, David Easton's little 'black box' offered the prospect of analysis in favour of the policy 'process' as a whole.[1] Easton's work, although on political analysis, is regarded as a significant contribution to the development of the policy approach (Figure 10.1).

Characteristics of the Eastonian Model

In the Eastonian model, the policymaking process is regarded as a 'black box' which converts the demands (inputs) of the society into policies (outputs). Easton in his *Analysis of Political System* argued that the political system was that part of the society engaged in the 'authoritative allocation on values'.[2] The main characteristics and elements of the Eastonian model of policy analysis are briefly discussed here.

(i) **Inputs:** Inputs are viewed as the physical, social, economic and political products of the environment which are received into the political system in the form of demands, supports and apathy.

---

[1] David Easton, *The Political System* (New York: Alfred Knopf, 1953); David Easton, *A Framework for Political Analysis* (New Jersey: Prentice Hall, 1965).
[2] David Easton, 'An Approach to the Analysis of Political Systems', *World Politics* 9 (1957): 384.

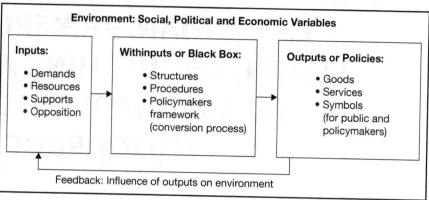

■ Figure 10.1: Eastonian 'Black Box' Model
Source: Adapted from Easton (1965).

(ii) **Demands:** Demands arising from the public and interest groups form part of the inputs. Demands are the claims made on the political system by individuals and groups to effect public policy. The flow from the environment mediated through input channels (parties, media, interest groups) becomes the basis of demands.

(iii) **Environment:** The environment is any condition or event defined as external to the boundaries of the political system. It comprises physical, social, economic and political variables in the polity. These variables influence the internal and external environment of the political system.

(iv) **Supports:** Supports consisting of rules, laws and customs provide a basis for the existence of a political community and the authorities. Supports are rendered when individuals or groups accept the decisions or laws (such as obeying laws, paying taxes or even respecting the national flag). They constitute the psychological and symbolic or material inputs of a political system.

(v) **Withinputs:** The 'black box', or the 'conversion process', or 'withinputs' comprising structures, procedures and policymakers' psycho-social framework are all involved in translating inputs into policy outputs. In the political scientists' version, it is the 'black box' crowded with personnel and institutions that can be called decision-makers.

(vi) **Outputs:** Outputs are the goods, services and symbols to public and other policymakers. They are the authoritative value allocations of the political system, and these allocations constitute public policy or policies. The systems theory portrays public policy as an 'output of the political system'. Policy outputs may generate new demands and new supports, or withdrawal of the old supports for the system.

(vii) **Feedback:** Feedback mechanisms are the means by which an organization collects and analyses data in regard to the impact of its outputs. Feedback plays an important role in generating suitable environment for future policy. The concept of feedback indicates that public policies may have a modifying effect on the environment and the demands generated therein, and may also have an effect upon the character of the political system.

Thus, the main features of the 'black box' model is that of viewing the *policy process* in terms of received (i) inputs, in the form of flows from the (ii) environment, mediated through

(iii) input channels (individuals, pressure groups, political parties), (iv) demands within the political system (withinputs) and their (v) conversion into policy outputs (laws, services, etc.) and (vi) outcomes (effects of policy). This framework which has dominated the field from the 1960s onwards is derived from the combination of the stages approach. The text-books which provided the 'normal science' of policy analysis were, for the greater part, derived from the fusion of Lasswell, Simon and Easton's approach to decision-making.

Criticisms and Limitations of the Systems Approach

Easton and the systems theorists argue that the public policy process as the product of a system is influenced by and influences the environment in which it operates. The systems model is a useful aid in understanding the policymaking process. Thomas Dye says that the value of the systems model to policy analysis lies in the questions that it poses:

1. What are the significant dimensions of the environment that generate demands upon the political system?
2. What are the significant characteristics of the political system that enable it to transform demands into public policy and to preserve itself over time?
3. How do environmental inputs affect the character of the political system?
4. How do characteristics of the political system affect the content of public policy?
5. How do environmental inputs affect the content of public policy?
6. How does public policy affect, through feedback, the environment and the character of the political system?[3]

The systems model is thus concerned with such questions as: What constitutes the black box? What are the inputs, withinputs, outputs and feedback of the policy process? Despite the fact that the systems theory attempts to conceptualize the relationship between policymaking, policy outputs and its wider environment, the theory is constrained owing to several factors. The major criticism of the Eastonian model is that it treats the political system as a 'black box' (in which the actual workings of that system are unclear). The challenge in thinking about public policy is how policymakers translate sets of inputs (demands) into policy outputs (laws).

The traditional input–output model ignores the fragmentary nature of the 'black box'. The missing ingredients in the systems approach are the 'power, personnel, and institutions' of policymaking. Lineberry observes that in examining these, 'we will not forget that political decision-makers are strongly constrained by economic factors in the environment in the political system'.[4] The model is accused of employing the value-laden techniques of welfare economics which are based on the maximization of a clearly defined 'social welfare function'. Broadly, policy analysis involves the application of models of welfare economics to improving the rationality of decision-making.

This systems model also ignores an important element of the policy process, namely, that the policymakers (including institutions) have also a considerable potential in influencing the environment within which they operate. The traditional input–output model would see the decision-making system as 'facilitative' and value-free rather than 'causative', that

---

[3] Dye, *Understanding Public Policy*, 39.
[4] Lineberry, *American Public Policy*, 47.

is, as a completely neutral structure.[5] In other words, structure variations in the systems are found to be having no direct causal effect on public policy.

Further, the extent to which the environment, both internal and external, is said to have an influence on the policymaking process is influenced by the values and ideologies held by the decision-makers in the system. It suggests that the policymaking involves not only the policy content but also the policymaker's perceptions and values. The values held by the policymakers are fundamentally assumed to be crucial in understanding the policy alternatives that are made.

Further, it is argued that this input–output model appears to be too simplistic to serve as a useful aid to understanding the policymaking process. In a developing polity such as India, both the political and bureaucratic elite fashion mass opinion more than masses shape the leadership's views. The concept of 'withinputs' as opposed to inputs has been created to illustrate this point.[6] Thus, policy changes may be attributed more to the political and administrative elite's redefinition of their own views than as a product of the demand and support from the environment. Quite often, policy initiation does emerge from the bureaucracy. Under certain situations, the bureaucracy becomes a powerful institution not only in formulating but also in legitimizing public policies. In a developing country such as India where the state's objectives are not fully articulated and clear, the bureaucracy easily capitalizes on the process of policy selection out of alternative policy strategies. It does participate in the formulation of public policy in addition to performing purely technical tasks.

Easton's work has made a vital contribution to the establishment of a policy approach, in that it provided a model of that political system which greatly influenced the way in which the emerging study of policy in the 1960s began to conceptualize the relationship between policymaking, policy outputs and its environment.[7]

VICKERS AND ANALYSIS OF POLICYMAKING

Geoffrey Vickers, a British theorist, has been also regarded as a great contributor to the development of models for analysing the policymaking process. His work The *Art of Judgement* is important but had far less influence on the way in which the policy approach evolved. Vickers's model addresses policymaking as a complex activity in which values and reality judgements are modified and adjusted, and in which problems are never solved in the way goal-setting conceptualizations suggest.[8] His work stresses the importance of analysing the interaction of value judgements and reality judgements, and represents synthesis of psychological, cybernetic and political ideas. Much of his work is devoted to the analysis of judgement in the terms of what be called 'appreciative behaviour'. He believed that 'social institutions are best analysed in terms of systems and

---

[5] F. Cortses et al., *Systems Analysis for Social Scientists* (New York, NY: Wiley, 1974), 11.
[6] J. Stonecash, 'Politics, Wealth and Public Policy: The Significance of Political Systems', in *The Determinants of Public Policy*, eds. Thomas R. Dye and V. Gray (Toronto: Heath, 1980), 24.
[7] Parsons, *Public Policy*, 23–24.
[8] Sir Geoffrey Vickers, *The Art of Judgement* (London: Chapman & Hall, 1965).

his published work... made far-reaching contributions to systems thinking in its application to human society'.[9]

Vickers's model on human decision-making is derived from two sources: cybernetics and systems analysis and psychology. According to Vickers, the model of human regulation and control devised by systems engineers needs to be adapted to take account of the behaviour, cognition and psychology of human beings as individuals and groups and as segment of society. His notion of regulation as it occurs in mechanical systems when applied to institutional policymaking suffers from limitations such as (i) the number of multiple relations and norms is more numerous and complex; (ii) the means of regulation are far less dependent on past experience; (iii) implementing responses to judgements requires time and cooperation between many people built up over decades.[10]

Furthermore, for unlike the engineer who behaves as a controllable in a mechanical system, the politician makes intervention in the system with the limited object of making its course more acceptable or less repugnant to his human values.[11]

Vickers's model of decisional analysis is shown in Figure 10.2.

Vickers argues that the study of human regulation is an activity which must be predicated on the notion that 'the mental activity and the social process are indivisible'.[12] His contribution to the study of human decision-making covered the same kind of ground as done by Simon, especially in terms of the limitations on human rationality and cognition. However, there are major differences in certain areas between Vickers and Simon. Among other differences, major ones include

  (i)   the conceptualization of human decision-making in terms of 'systems' and 'subsystems',
  (ii) the rejection of the notion that decision-making is about 'goal setting' and 'best' choices in favour of the system's operation,
  (iii) the belief that facts and values are 'interlinked',
  (iv) the centrality of 'appreciative systems' to understanding the decision-making process and
  (v)   the way in which appreciative systems are changed by the exercise of judgement.[13]

In a concise summary, Vickers offers his arguments,

> An appreciation involves making judgments of facts about the 'state of the system', both internally and in its external relations. I will call these reality judgments.... It also involves making judgments about the significance of these facts to the appreciator or to the body for whom the appreciation is made. These judgments I will call value judgments. Reality judgments and value judgments are inseparable constituents of appreciation... for facts are relevant only in relation to some judgments of value

---

[9] N. Johnson, 'Sir Geoffrey Vickers', in *The Dictionary of National Biography 1981–1985*, eds. Lord Blake and C.S. Nicholls (London: Oxford University Press, 1990), 400.

[10] Vickers (1965), *The Art of Judgement*, 107.

[11] G. Vickers, *Value Systems and the Social Process* (London: Tavistock Publications, 1968), 77.

[12] Vickers (1965), *The Art of Judgement*, 150.

[13] Ibid., 22.

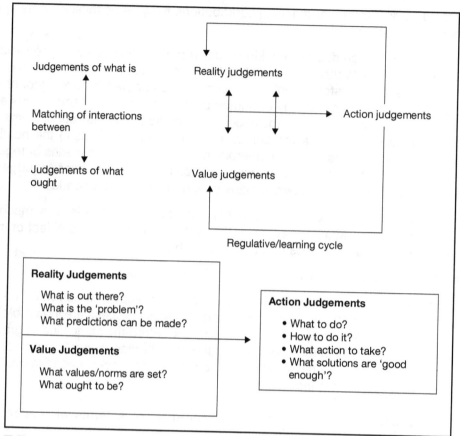

■ Figure 10.2: Vickers's Model of Decisional Analysis
Source: Adapted from Vickers (1965).

and judgments of value are operative only in relation to some configuration of fact. Judgments of value give meaning to judgments of reality, as a course gives meaning to a compass card. Information is an incomplete concept; for it tells us nothing about the organization of the recipient which alone makes a communication informative.[14]

Vickers's concise observation is that human systems are different to mechanical systems because they are informed by appreciation and the 'art of judgement'. The world is not a set of data, but a 'construct, a mental artifact, a collective work of art'.[15] He further argues that facts are judgements about reality and in themselves carry no meaning without value judgements. The choices which confront policymakers are multivalued, and therefore in analysing the decision-making process, Vickers's framework emphasizes the importance of understanding the way in which 'appreciation' constructs 'reality' and 'value' and sets the context within which judgements are made about action in the light of the reality and value judgements.

---

[14] Ibid., 40.
[15] Vickers (1968), *The Art of Judgement*, 85.

Action judgements or judgements about what to do and how, when and with what and by whom are to be understood as the outcome of an interaction between the appreciation of reality and value. Judgements as to the outcomes of actions must form Vickers's perspective, take into account how unobjectives 'objective' tests and criteria actually are. Since 'the appraisal of judgment is itself an act of judgement. In particular judgements are logically incapable of being validated by any objective test. They can only be approved as right or condemned as wrong by the exercise of another value judgment'.[16]

From this argument, it is clear that Vickers departs significantly from the notion that decision-making is about 'goal setting' or of evaluating decision-making in terms of how goals have been met. He says, 'I have described policymaking as the setting of governing relations or norms, rather than in the more usual terms as the setting of goals, objectives or ends....' To explain all human activity in terms of

> goal-seeking...raises insoluble problems between means and ends and leaves the most important activities, the ongoing maintenance of our ongoing activities and their ongoing satisfaction, hanging in the air.... I believe (that) a more fundamental and more neglected aspect of our activities (is) the maintenance of relationships in time.[17]

Owing to the limitations on human rationality and cognition, Vickers's model addresses policymaking as a complex multivalued activity in which values and reality judgements are adjusted. Furthermore, this process is not seen as an activity of individual rationality, so much as how decision-making, in an institutional setting, involves the interaction between the appreciation of reality and value judgements. Consequently, the Vickers model directs our attention to the learning processes that take place when decision-makers endeavour to regulate social, economic and political systems. Despite the mechanical nature of its discourse, the Vickers model postulates that focus of policy analysis should be the study of the 'appreciative' dimensions of human behaviour.

Vickers's Framework for Policy Analysis

To facilitate the making of judgements, Vickers's methods involve four analytical contexts or dimensions: mental, institutional, situational and ecological.

(i) **Mental activity:** In the first place, the first task is to map the appreciative system involved in the decision. The analysis of the process involves understanding how the network frames the 'mental' artefact which constitutes an important dimension of the policymaker. The next aspect of the analysis of the appreciative system is a consideration of its key skills, namely (a) prediction, (b) valuation and (c) innovation.

(ii) **Institutional setting:** This phase involves the examination of the institutional setting of the appreciative system.

(iii) **Situational context:** The next phase is the placement of decisions in their situational context, that is, in the context of ideas and events.

---

[16] G. Vickers, 'Judgement', in *Creative Management*, ed. J. Henry (London: SAGE Publications, 1991), 179.
[17] Vickers (1965), *The Art of Judgement*, 33.

(iv) **Ecological context:** The final Vickerian analysis may be viewed as a process of placing the policy decision in a wider network of communication/ecological context. These four contexts or dimensions may be used in actual case study material.

In brief, the Vickers's framework may be seen as a process of examining policy decisions in terms of focusing first on the psychological dimension of policy, and concluding with placing the decision in the ecological context.[18]

Prescriptions for Improving Policymaking Process

Since Vickers's work stresses the importance of analysing the interaction of value and reality judgements, he was sceptical as to potential of rational techniques such as planning, programming and budgeting systems (PPBS) and CBA in policymaking. Vickers argued that costs and benefits are inadequate to the task of making decisions in the context of multiple values, since values cannot be proved correct, so much as approved or condemned.[19] With a view to improving policymaking process, Vickers prescribed certain suggestions, including

(i) The first task in this sphere would be to develop the skills and arts of judgement, while recognizing that the capacities of individuals to handle, arrange and combine information vary, as do moral qualities, courage and endurance. Organizations should be schools in which all are learners and teachers.[20]

(ii) Second, Vickers says that improvements in policymaking analysis can be brought about by the development of society which can 'learn not primarily new ways of responding...but new ways of appreciating a situation which is new and new through our own making'.[21]

(iii) Third, Vickers stresses the use of systems analysis to improve the capacity of organization and society as a whole to learn. Here, Vickers's work is seen as contributing to the development of 'soft systems' approaches.[22]

(iv) Finally, as Vickers's model addresses policymaking as a complex multivalued activity, he stresses the need to recognize that policy decisions involve multiple values. Vickers's approach in this respect is seen as more closer to the approaches of Lasswell and Lindblom than to other systems models.

Vickers's work *The Art of Judgement* (1965) still remains a seminal contribution to the study of policy and decision. With the rise in interest in the role of values in the policy process, his work will receive wide recognition for the study of public policy in the 21st century. In his foreword to the 1983 edition, Boulding argued that it is a classic volume to be read by all those concerned with the analysis of policymaking, as it contains 'critique of the more academic models of human behaviour, both from economics and from psychology, inspired by a reflection on a large and varied experience of it'.[23]

---

[18] Vickers (1965), *The Art of Judgement*, 173.
[19] Ibid., 71.
[20] Vickers (1991), 189–91.
[21] Vickers (1965), 233.
[22] See P.B. Checkland and J. Scholes, *Soft Systems Methodology in Action* (London: Wiley, 1990).
[23] K. Boulding, 'Foreword' in G. Vickers, *Human Systems Are Different* (London: Harper & Row, 1983), 8.

ELITE–MASS MODEL (ELITE THEORY)

Much of the current literature on political power adopts the elite theory perspective. Elite–mass model suggests that power is concentrated in the hands of a few elites. Policymaking, according to the elite theory, is a process which works to the advantage of these elites. The theory argues that in the society there are those at the top 'with power' and the mass 'without power'. The theory also holds that the elite, whose members share common values and have more money, education and power, governs the masses who are apathetic and ill-informed about public policy. In an environment which is characterized by apathy and information distortion, elites influence mass opinion on policy issues more than masses influence elite opinion. Policy flows downward from the elite to the mass.

Thus, one way to study policymaking is through the power approach. The power approach views decision-making as something which is influenced and determined by the structure of power: class, interest groups, bureaucratic and political arrangements and so on. According to Birkland, policymaking under the influence of elites is 'dominated by the best educated, wealthiest and most powerful elites'.[24] In the elitist perspective, public policy is viewed as 'the preferences and values of a governing elite'.[25] Public officials and bureaucrats merely implement the policies decided on by the elites. An illustration of the elite theory is shown in Figure 10.3.

Although this theory is associated with sociologist C. Wright Mills,[26] it has its origins in the work of Mosca and Pareto.[27] They argued that, contrary to Marx, elitism is inevitable and that classless society is a myth. Later, Mosca modified his view and argued that democracy could be viewed as a form of politics in which elites compete for the people's

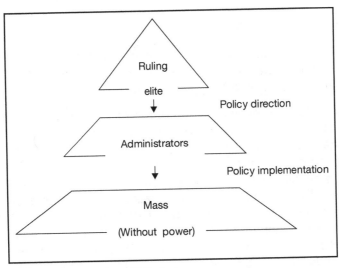

■ Figure 10.3: Elite Theory of Policy Process

---

[24] Birkland, *An Introduction to the Policy Process*, 169.
[25] Elite theory is, explained at length, in Thomas R. Dye and L. Harmon Zeigler, *The Irony of Democracy* (Ft Worth, TX: Harcourt Brace, 2000).
[26] C.W. Mills, *The Power Elite* (New York, NY: Oxford University Press, 1956).
[27] Mosca and Pareto were two Italian theorists in social science.

vote in order to secure legitimacy for the elite rule. Drawing upon Mosca's ideas, Robert Michels in a study of political parties argues that there was an 'iron law of oligarchy' which operated in organizations.[28] Over time, organizational elites generate their own interests and goals which are different from those of the masses. The decision-making process, according to Dahl and Lindblom in their revised view, is biased in favour of the powerful, and functions to the disadvantage of the less powerful and less well resources.[29]

Propositions of the Elite–Mass Theory

Some of the important propositions of the elite theory are as follows:

(i) In the society, there are those at the top 'with power' (elite group) who govern and have the power to decide on public policies, and those at bottom 'without power' (the masses) who are governed and do not have power to decide on public policies.

(ii) Elite members are drawn disproportionately from the higher socio-economic strata of the society. They share common values and have money, education and power than the masses who are apathetic and ill-informed.

(iii) The bases of elites, who share consensus on the common values of the social system, are the sanctity of private property, limited government and individual liberty.

(iv) Public policies do not reflect what the masses (the governed class) demand but rather the preferences and values of the governing elite (the ruling class).

(v) Elites shape mass opinion on policy issues more than masses shape elite opinion.

(vi) The elite theory recognizes the scope of elite–mass conflict.

Lasswell's Contribution to Elitism

Lasswell has also made a substantial contribution to the development of the elite theory. He took the view, 'the influential are those who get the most of what there is to get.... Those who get the most are elite, the rest are mass'.[30]

For Lasswell, the study of politics is the study of influence. Accepting Pareto's idea, Lasswell argued that different 'skill groups' had emerged from the class struggle in the democracy.[31] These skill groups included those skilled in the use of violence (such as military and police elites), those with communication and propaganda skills, those with business and commercial skills, technocrats who possess specialist technical knowledge and bureaucrats with administrative or organizational skills. His apprehension was that the combination of these new elites posed a dangerous threat to democracy and raised the prospect of the development of the 'garrison state' in which military, bureaucratic and technocratic elites rule. According to Lasswell, the policy sciences have a vital role to play in enhancing democracy by seeking to promote a wider distribution and pluralism of power. Merelman believes, however, the Lasswell's prescription to prevent the 'garrison

---

[28] Robert Michels, *Political Parties*, trans. Eden and Cedar Paul (London: Constable, 1915; Reprint 1959).
[29] Dahl and Lindblom, *Politics, Economics and Welfare*, Preface.
[30] Lasswell, *Politics: Who Gets What, When, How*, 13.
[31] Ibid.

state' is pretty 'weak tea'. 'Apparently Lasswell believed that in the hands of the policy scientist social science would become so compelling, so inexorable, so powerful, that the sheer strength of its ideas would sweep all before it'.[32]

However, the Lasswellian approach for controlling elites is indeed very weak if we do not read it in the context of his writings on human rights and dignity.[33] To some extent, it is said that Lasswell had a somewhat naïve faith in the possibility of policy analysis.

Mills and the Elitism

Another line of development in the elite theory was that placed by C. Wright Mills. Like Lasswell, his analysis led him to view intellectuals, scholars, scientists and others as having a vital role to play in checking the growth of elite power.[34] His book *The Power Elite* written in 1956 sought to show how a military-industrial bureaucratic elite becomes the main force in shaping key areas of US decision-making during the Vietnam War.[35] The growing power of military elites in the USA and elsewhere during the Cold War confirmed Lasswell's analysis of the 'garrison state'.[36]

Schumpeter's Contribution to Elitism

Joseph Schumpeter, an economist, applied an economic approach to the problem of reconciling the elitism of the society with the need of democratic legitimacy.[37] For Schumpeter, 'government by people' will be unreal and idealistic if explained in terms of Mosca and Pareto's theses. He argued that elitism would be legitimated in a democracy by a political market composed of competing parties and rival elites. The people were involved in the decision-making process by the act of choosing between the policy programmes and promises of rival political firms. Schumpeter's model gave a fillip to the pluralist theories advocated by Dahl and other scholars in the 1950s.[38]

A Critical Evaluation of Elite Model

The elite–mass approach, like many other approaches to the policy process, is subjected to a lot of criticisms. First, decision-making, according to the elite–mass theory, is a process which works to the advantage of elites in whom power is concentrated. This theory holds that public policy does not reflect the demands of the masses so much as it does preferences of elites. Therefore, changes in public policy occur as a result of redefinitions by elites of their own values and choices. Because elites share a consensus in preserving the social system, changes in the public policy are brought about through reforms (incremental in nature) when events threaten the system. The stability of the system, therefore,

---

[32] R.M. Merelman, 'Harold Lasswell's Political World: Weak Tea for Hard Times', *British Journal of Political Science* II (1981): 495.

[33] Bobrow and Dryzek, *Policy Analysis by Design*, 173.

[34] C. Wright Mills, *Power, Politics and People* (New York, NY: Oxford University Press, 1963), 246.

[35] C. Wright Mills, *The Power Elite* (New York, NY: Oxford University, 1956.)

[36] Harold Lasswell, 'The Garrison State', *American Journal of Sociology* 46 (1941): 455–68.

[37] Joseph Schumpeter, *Capitalism, Socialism and Democracy* (London: Allen & Unwin, 1974).

[38] See Robert Dahl, 'A Critique of the Ruling Elite Model', *American Political Science Review* 52 (1958): 463–69.

depends on elites sharing in a consensus about basic values underlying the system, and only policy alternatives that fall within the shared consensus will be taken into account. For example, the welfare of the masses may be an important element in the elite decision-making, but the responsibility for the welfare rests on the shoulders of elites rather than masses.

Second, elitism views the masses to be apathetic and ill-informed about public policy. It is found that elites manipulate mass opinion and sentiments on policy questions more than masses manipulate and influence elite values and opinion. Further, for the most part, policy flows downward from the elite to the mass. Therefore, policy questions are seldom decided by the masses through popular elections or through the presentation of policy options by political parties. For the most part, these elections and political parties play their symbolic role. Elitism views the masses as largely apathetic having at best an indirect influence over the policymaking process of the governing elites.

Work by Bachrach and Baratz sought to provide evidence to support their theory that power had dimensions which extended beyond the open control by 'A' over 'B'.[39] Likewise in his study of the hidden dimensions of the elite power and domination, Gaventa notes that power is a dimension of politics as it may involve 'locating the power processes behind the social construction of meanings and patterns that serve to get 'A' to act and believe in a manner in which 'B' otherwise might not, to A's benefit and B's detriment'.[40]

MARXIST PERSPECTIVE OF THE POLICY PROCESS

Marx sought to show how power is exercised in capitalist society in ways beneath the surface levels of political institutions. For Marx, people who are socially and politically strong ignore the desires of the politically weak and exploit them. Marxists have come to accept a picture of class domination and the state as an instrument of class power. This so-called 'instrumentalist' approach has focused on the surface levels of decision-/policymaking. Miliband, for example, argued that the state in capitalist society was an instrument of a ruling class which ruled in the interests of that class (comprising politicians, civil servants and business and financial elites who came from the same social class and were educated at the same schools).[41]

But structural critics of this theory, such as Poulantzas, dispute this view of the state as an instrument of capitalism as it fails to take accounts of two factors.[42] First is the 'structural' power of capitalist (and not the ruling class) which ultimately structures the decision-/policymaking process. And, second is the state's autonomy from the capitalist system (capitalist interests) to make decisions.

This model of the state in capitalist society as autonomous from the capitalist interests has been widely applied in critical or radical approaches to the study of the policy process. In a sense, this model provides a form of Marxist pluralism, in that it argues that

---

[39] Bachrach and Baratz, *Power and Poverty*.
[40] J. Gaventa, *Power and Powerlessness, Quiescence and Rebellion in an Appalachian Valley* (Oxford: Clarendon Press, 1980), 15–16.
[41] R. Miliband, *Marxism and Politics* (Oxford: Oxford University Press, 1977).
[42] N. Poulantzas, *Political Power and Social Classes* (London: New Left Books, 1973).

decision-making in capitalist society is more complex than the one operating under the state as an instrument (instrumental model). Poulantzas, for example, maintains that the state in a capitalist society is engaged in multifarious activities. The state, on the one hand, is involved in a process of maintaining or managing different 'fractions'. And on the other, it appears as some kind of arbiter or neutral force so as to better serve the interests of capital and the capitalist class. 'Functionalists' have sought to show how, in order to maintain social order, the state promotes the interests of capital accumulation, and in order to secure legitimacy, the state manages public policy through allocating resources between 'social expenses', 'social investment' and 'social consumption spending'.[43]

This dual-state model, as maintained by Cawson and Saunders, argues that the state in a capitalist society seeks to structure policymaking to address the policy concerns of the capital at the higher reaches of state decision-making.[44] However, at the lower levels, where legitimacy is of prime concern, the state will permit a more pluralistic policymaking style. They argue that decision-making on a corporalist form at the level of central ruling-class (producer) interests and a more pluralist, open form at the level of working-class and middle-class (consumer) interests.

However, Goldsmith and Wolman maintain that this model is more appropriate to the UK and Scandinavian circumstances than to the USA. In particular, they observe that 'Saunders is wrong in assuming that the local level was not concerned with production issues' and that corporatist modes of decision-making do not take place at the local level.[45]

GROUP THEORY: POLICY AS GROUP POLITICAL ACTIVITY

Groups have long been a focus of study as political activity. Policymakers are viewed as constantly responding to group pressures. Individuals in a group sharing common interests band together formally or informally to pressurize the government for accepting their demands. According to David Truman, an interest group is 'a shared-attitude group that makes certain claims upon other groups in the society'; such a group becomes political if and when it makes a claim through or upon any of the institutions of government.[46] Individuals are important in politics when they act as part of the group interests. In this way, a group becomes the essential bridge between the individual and the government. Politics is really the struggle among groups to influence public policy.

Group theory of public policymaking is modelled on the 'hydraulic theory of politics'[47] in which the polity is viewed as a system of forces and pressures, pushing against one another in the making of public policy. The theory begins with the proposition that interaction

---

[43] I. Gough, *The Political Economy of the Welfare State* (London: Macmillan, 1979). For a critique, see P. Dunleavy and B. O'Leary, *Theories of the State: The Politics of Liberal Democracy.* (London: Macmillan, 1987), 252–53.

[44] A. Cawson and P. Saunders, 'Corporatism, Competitive Politics and Class Struggle', in *Capital and Politics*, ed. R. King (London: Routledge and Kegan Paul, 1983).

[45] M. Goldsmith and H. Wolman, *Urban Politics* (Oxford: Blackwell, 1992), 15–16.

[46] An exemplary work that represents the group theory is in Truman, *The Governmental Process*.

[47] L. Harmon Zeigler and G. Wayne Peak, *Interest Groups in American Society*, 2nd ed. (Englewood Cliffs, NJ: Prentice Hall, 1972), 12.

among groups is the main fact of politics.[48] For the ordinary citizen, the pressure group is certainly an important channel of influence and power.

For the most part, a group interest seeks to influence the policy decisions of the government. The group influence and power are dominant features of all democratic countries. Politics is indeed the struggle of power among different groups, although some are more likely than others to be concerned with political power. However, passive members in a group fail to resist conformity imposed by more assertive members.

Group Equilibrium

Advocates of the group theory argue that public policy is the equilibrium which is determined by the group struggle or relative influence of any interest groups. The group influence is determined by its numbers, wealth, organizational strength, leadership, access to decision-makers and internal cohesion. The public policy will move in the direction desired by the group which has gained more influence. From the group theory viewpoint, Latham described public policy in the following words:

> What may be called public policy is actually the equilibrium reached in the group struggle at any given moment, and it represents a balance which the contending factions or groups constantly strive to tip in their favour.... The legislature referees the group struggle, ratifies the victories of the successful coalition, and records the terms of the surrenders, compromises, and conquests in the form of statutes.[49]

Group theorists look at political activity of group in terms of the group struggle. Policymakers in this theory are viewed as responding to group pressures (negotiating and compromising) among competing demands of influential groups. Politicians and political parties attempt to form a majority coalition of groups. In doing so, they may select the groups, which have diverse interests, to form a majority coalition. The group theory holds that several forces contribute to maintaining equilibrium in whole interest group system. First, a large latent group in the society supports the constitutional system of the country. Second, overlapping group membership helps to maintain the equilibrium by preventing any one group from violating the constitutional system and prevailing values. The fact that individuals belong to more than one groups moderates the demands of groups who must avoid offending members of other group affiliations. And third, equilibrium results from group competition. The power of one group is checked by the power of other competing groups. However, it is found that passive members typically censor their ideas given the fear being criticized by the more assertive members of the decision-making team.

Groupthink Decision-making

Irving Janis probably is the scholar who gave the idea of 'groupthink'. According to Janis, groupthink is a particular form of conformity. It occurs in a highly cohesive group that operates in an environment where there is a feeling of security. The primary goal of this

---

[48] Truman, *The Governmental Process*, 37.
[49] Eral Latham, 'The Group Basis of Politics', in *Political Behaviour*, eds. Heinz Eulau, Samuel J. Eldersveld and Morris Janowitz (New York, NY: Free Press, 1956), 239.

particular decision-making group is to maintain its power and cohesiveness. Groupthink is characterized by

(i)   directive leadership,
(ii) group homogeneity in terms of ideals and background and
(iii) isolation from outside influences.

The groupthink process as explained by Janis is given in Figure 10.4.

The groupthink approach discourages anyone from conveying a dissenting view. If any member argues against any of the group's decisions, pressure is brought upon that individual by the other members. The point is that group loyalty stands paramount, and dissenting opinion or criticism, if any, is discouraged. Even though several group members may have reservations about a decision, each member is, however, directed to be in agreement with that decision. If failure occurs after a decision is implemented, it amounts to be a group failure (as in the case of a cabinet decision under the parliamentary form of government).

Some of the classic symptoms of groupthink can be identified easily if we examine France's (under French president Francois Hollande's leadership) decision to carry out military operations against Islamic State of Iraq and Syria (ISIS) in Syria. Similarly, no one in the White House dared challenge President John F. Kennedy's decision to invade Cuba's Bay of Pigs. One White House aide, Arthur Schlesinger, expressed a desire to question the president before the plan was put into action, but he was met by this response from Attorney General Robert Kennedy. 'You may be right or you may be wrong, but the President has made up his mind. Don't push it any further. Now is the time for everyone to help him all they can' (quoted by Janis in 2nd ed. 1982, p.40). That same groupthinking group brought about disaster in Vietnam, as the war effort kept growing despite evidence that further escalation would not enable the USA to achieve its military objectives.

Another symptom of groupthink can be identified if we analyse the then PM Indira Gandhi's decision. Under her order military Operation Blue Star was carried out from 3 to 8 June 1984 in order to establish control over Harmandir Sahib Complex in Amritsar.

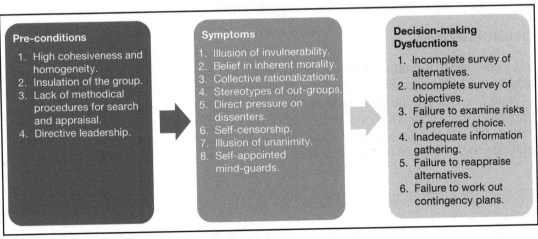

■ Figure 10.4: The Groupthink Process
Source: Adapted from Janis (1982).

Prescriptions for Improving Group Decisions

Research on the influence of groups on individuals has, however, shown how powerful the group can be in distorting judgements and decision-making. Individuals in groups are under pressure to conform to group norms and perception of information. But the cohesiveness of a group is a major factor in the achievement of tasks.[50] In this context, Janis has propounded groupthink theory: 'the psychological drive for consensus in cohesive decision-making groups'.[51] Janis argues that because the members of a group are loyal to a group's viewpoint, consensus blinds decisions-makers to the realities. The pressures to conform to what the group thinks, in contrast to what other individual members think, can lead to a total misinterpretation of judgements.

Janis on the basis of his research prescribes a number of measures to combat the group-think decision-making process:

1. Leader has a role in encouraging critical evaluation in all members and the expression of doubts and objections.
2. Key leaders should not state preferences when assigning policy-planning and analysis.
3. Decision-making should be conducted through the setting up of several policy-planning and evaluation groups.
4. From time to time the policymaking group should divide into subgroups and meet under different chairpersons.
5. Members of policymaking groups should discuss deliberations with trusted associates outside the group.
6. Experts and others not in the policymaking group should come in and be encouraged to challenge core members.
7. Alternatives should be evaluated at very meeting. Someone should play devil's advocate.
8. If the policy issue involves a rival nation or organization, ample time should be given to surveying the signals and intentions of the rival.
9. After arriving at a consensus, a 'second-chance meeting' should be convened to allow the expression of outstanding doubts.[52]

Critical Observations

It is observed that group theory has been applied to situations in which a policy or decision is made by a small group which develops a strong commitment to a certain line of thought. The groupthink model with Janis's prescriptive measures has been widely applied in policy analysis. The evidence provided by research in group theory model is very mixed. There is the general notion that groups can distort decision-making. Group theory purports to describe all political activities in terms of the group struggle and policymakers

---

[50] D.S. Wright et. al., *Introducing Psychology: An Experimental Approach* (Harmondsworth: Penguin Books, 1970).

[51] I.L. Janis, *Groupthink: Psychological Studies of Policy Decisions and Fiascos* (Boston, MA: Houghton Mifflin, 1982), 8.

[52] Ibid., 262–71.

are viewed as constantly responding to demands of the influential groups. However, Esser and Lindoerfer find some evidence of illusions of invulnerability, pressures on dissenters to conform, and distortion of information.[53] Thus, the scientific and analytical status of the study is still not very clear.

CONCLUSION

A model is merely an abstraction or representation of some aspects of the real world. It may be used by a researcher or a policy analyst to show its worth. It should be able to simplify and clarify our thinking about politics and public policy. It should offer explanations for public policy. It should suggest hypotheses about the causes and consequences of public policy. The model should identify not only significant aspects of public policy but also its irrelevant variables. Certainly, the usefulness of a model lies in its ability to order and simplify political life so that we can understand the relationships we find in the real world. In brief, the model should communicate what is relevant about the worth of a public policy.

Review Questions

(i) Critically elaborate the 'black box' approach to policymaking process as proposed by Easton.
(ii) Discuss Vickers's model of decisional analysis.
(iii) How did Vickers relate policy analysis with psychological dimensions in his framework for policy analysis?
(iv) What are the basic propositions of elite–mass theory?
(v) Explain groupthink process and how it is related to public policy process.

---

[53] J.K. Esser and J.S. Lindoerfer, 'Groupthink and the Space Shuttle Challenger Accident: Towards a Quantitative Case Analysis', *Journal of Behavioural Decision Making* 2 (1989): 167–77.

CHAPTER 11

CRITICAL POLICY RATIONALISTS
Simon, Lindblom, Dror, Etzioni and Cohen, March, Olsen

INTRODUCTION

There are severe limitations to the rational approach to policymaking. The critical rationalists have taken on board the criticisms of the rational approach and offer modified models which seek to take account of its deficiencies.

SIMON'S RATIONAL APPROACH TO POLICY DECISION-MAKING

Herbert Simon (1916–2001) stands out as a leading contributor to the development of the policy approach. His work *Administrative Behaviour* is central to the analysis of rationality in decision-making. His concern with human decision-making has centred on the idea of rationality which is limited but not irrational as 'bounded rationality'.

Decision-making Process

Simon's idea of examining decision-making has formed a central element of policy analysis. Simon sees decision-making as a 'problem-solving' activity. When human beings engage in making decisions, they are endeavouring to fill a gap: Given a goal, how can this be achieved?

Simon believes, therefore, that we should direct our attention to the behavioural manifestations of decision-making and its cognitive limits, rather than to its subconscious dimension. He says, 'Behaviour is purposive in so far as it is guided by general goals or objectives; it is rational in so far as it selects alternatives which are conducive to the achievement of the previously selected goals'.[1]

Simon identifies four phases of the decision-making process in the organization (Figure 11.1):

(i) *Intelligence activity*, that is, finding occasions calling for a decision.
(ii) *Design activity*, that is, identifying, developing and analysing possible courses of action.
(iii) *Choice activity*, that is, selecting a particular course of action from those available.[2]
(iv) *Evaluating activity*, that is, evaluating past choices to compare programmed and non-programmed decision-making in the organization.[3]

---

[1] Herbert A. Simon, *Administrative Behaviour*, 2nd ed. (New York, NY: The Free Press, 1957), 5.
[2] Herbert A. Simon, *The New Science of Management Decision* (New York, NY: Harper & Row, 1960), 1–4.
[3] Ibid., 40–41.

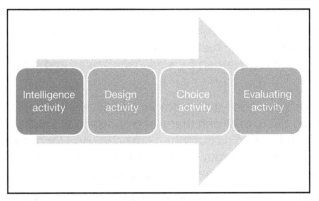

■ Figure 11.1: Phases of Decision-making Process
Source: Adapted from Simon (1960, 1977).

Simon argues that decision-making is a complex exercise involving both technical and political determinants. In the sequence, each stage in itself can be a complex decision-making process. The design stage may call for new intelligence activities. Problems at one stage can create several sub-problems for the other stages. Decision-making process is not only restricted to taking a decision but also includes carrying out the decision. Thus, after a policy decision has been taken, the management having to implement it is faced with a wholly new set of problems involving decision-making. And this process continues.

For Simon, human behaviour involves conscious or unconscious selection of a particular alternative or choice. The selection of a choice refers to preference of a course of action over other courses of action. Both the choice and action are directly related. Simon places great stress on the processes and methods that ensure action. The question of determination of 'what to do' rather than 'doing actually' did not receive sufficient attention. Decision-making deals with the process of choice which creates action. Simon points out that without a deep understanding of this aspect, which is rooted in the behaviour of man in the organization, the study of administration would not throw much light.

Programmed and Non-programmed Decisions

Human beings face two kinds of problems: well-structured problems and ill-structured problems. To deal with these problems, Simon suggests programmed and non-programmed decisions.

Both programmed and non-programmed decision-making start with a 'definition of the situation' which includes the decision-maker's perception of happening of future events, the possible range of alternatives and their consequences and rules for ordering the preferred consequences.

One can also make a distinction between routine and non-routine decision types. Herbert Simon defines the two types as 'programmed' and 'ill-structured' decisions. He views routine decisions as those that can be made in a prescribed manner.[4] Often of

---

[4] Herbert Simon, 'The Structure of Ill-structured Decision Processes', *Artificial Intelligence* 4 (1973): 181–201.

an administrative or procedural nature, these decisions are governed by the traditional mores of the organization. The public agency has historically operated in a particular manner, and the clients or constituent groups have grown to expect a fixed pattern of behaviour, or the agency is governed by established rules and legislative mandates that limit its operations.

Programmed decisions are those that are more repetitive and routine, or a definite procedure has been worked out to deal with them. In organizations, mathematical techniques of operations research and electronic computers may be used for handling the programmed decisions. On the contrary, non-routine or ill-structured decision types involve complex problems and issues for which no precedent or pattern exists.

Non-programmed decisions are new, instructed or where there is no 'cut-and-dried' method for handling the problem. Examples are the decisions to introduce a new method or a product, or to order staff retrenchment, or setting up a new venture. All these decisions would be non-programmed because the organization would have no detailed strategy to deal with these situations.

As a whole, machine and administrative systems are appropriate in dealing with programmed decisions. However, in decisions that cannot be easily programmed (non-programmed), into routine stages, problem-solving requires ways in which complex problem can be simplified by breaking down into various stages which enable us to use our limited cognitive powers to their maximum. These methods are termed 'heuristics' in the cognitive approach.

Thus, decision-making is effective when the problem is well structured. So, Simon argues, the real challenge in decision-making is the division and simplification of a problem into its component parts which can be well structured.[5] Where a problem is well structured, a top-down structure would suit (programmed decision-making). On the contrary, ill-structured and messy problems require commitment to the long-term strategy to deal with activity, and high levels of motivation. Decision-making may be looked on a continuum on which 'programmed decisions' are placed at one end and 'non-programmed decisions' at the other (Figure 11.2).

Although Simon's approach to decision-making provides a set of heuristics to improve on the way in which we approach a complex and uncertain world, it is not without criticism. The major difficulty in public decision-making is that problems do not offer solutions nor are they best served by implications.

Simon's Rationality Model

Simon was somewhat critical of the rational model. He raises the question, On what basis does the administrator makes his decision? He disputes the assumptions of total rationality underlying the theories of choice in economics, game theory and statistical decision-making. For example, the classical theory of the economists assumed complete rationality with its 'economic man' model. After studying various models of decision-making man, Simon proposes a new model of decision-making man which he refers to as

---

[5] Ibid., 190.

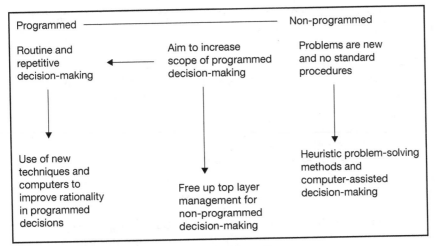

■ Figure 11.2: Programmed and Non-programmed Decision-making
Source: H. Simon, 'The Structure of Ill-structured Decision Processes'. (1973).

Satisficing Man, that is, a decision-maker who, because of the limits on his cognitive and analytical abilities, accepts alternatives that are merely satisfactory or sufficient in regard to his aspiration levels.[6] Goals under this model are satisfactory and achievable.

Simon rejects the concept of *Economic Man* and other traditional theories as they are founded on three unrealistic assumptions:

(i) The decision-maker is omniscient, that is, he has knowledge about all possible alternatives as well as their future consequences.
(ii) The decision-maker has unlimited computational ability.
(iii) The decision-maker has the capacity to put in order all possible consequences.

Simon argues that these models promoted by economists do not really help us to understand the actuality of decision-making. Simon argues that the economic model cannot sufficiently account for behaviour and, consequently, cannot effectively predict decision-making outcomes.[7] Furthermore, he argues that the model of *Satisficing Man* is a better description of decision-making behaviour and thus has better predictive power. Goals under Simon's administrative man are not optimal but acceptable.

Simon asserts that any theory based on these assumptions is fundamentally wrong. He maintains that actual human rate rationality is neither perfectly rational nor irrational. Rather, it involves 'bounded rationality' or limited rationality. It is in the concept of bounded rationality, Simon proposes a model of *Administrative Man* (in place of 'Economic Man').[8] While the Economic Man maximizes (i.e. selects the best course from those available to

---

[6] Simon, *Administrative Behaviour*, xxiv.
[7] Herbert A. Simon, 'Rational Decision-making in Business Organizations', *American Economic Review* 69(4) (1979): 497.
[8] Quoted from D.S. Pugh, D.J. Hickson and C.R. Hinings, *Writers on Organizations* (Harmondsworth: Penguin, 1971), 109.

him), the *Administrative Man* 'satisfices'—he looks for a course of action that is satisfactory or 'good enough'. Simon observes

> Most human decision-making, whether individual or organizational, is concerned with the discovery and selection of satisfactory alternatives; only in exceptional cases is it concerned with the discovery and selection of optimal alternatives.

To illustrate Simon's concept of 'satisficing', Pugh and his colleagues write, 'Most decisions are concerned not with searching for the sharpest needle in the haystack but with searching for a needle sharp enough to sew with'.[9] Thus the *Administrative Man*, because of limited rationality, can make decisions without looking for all the possible alternatives and can pick a course of action that is satisfactory or good enough.

Here, it may be mentioned that in making decisions, *Satisficing Man* does not examine all possible alternatives; he ignores most of the complex interrelationships of the real world and makes decisions by applying relatively simple rules of thumb or heuristics.[10] In short, *Satisficing Man* simplifies and satisfices because he operates in an area of 'bounded rationality' with bounds imposed by the limits on available information and his own computational capacity. In business terms, he does not look for 'maximum profit' but 'adequate profit'; not 'optimum price' but 'fair prices'. He makes his choices taking into account just a few of the factors that he regards as most relevant.

Consequently, Simon argues that the definition of rationality should be expanded to incorporate a wider range of human behaviour. He defines rationality as 'the selection of preferred behavioral alternatives in terms of some system of values whereby the consequences of behavior can be evaluated'.[11] This enlarged definition of rationality is consistent with his claim that all human behaviour has a rational component and his insistence that we look beyond the rather narrow bounds of economic rationality in analysing and assessing human behaviour. Given the concept of bounded rationality, decision-maker chooses the decision that is most satisfactory.

Herbert Simon's work *Administrative Behaviour* is central to the analysis of rationality in decision-making. His concern in this book is to explain organizations in real, rather than ideal, terms. At the centre of this is the issue of rationality in decision-making. Simon criticizes the flaws of classical politics—administration dichotomy as well as the contradictions in the 'proverbs' of the classical theory. He recognizes efficiency as the primary objective of administration, but he also recognizes the limits of individuals in organizations to behave rationally. In this seminal work, Simon seeks to show how human behaviour, although not rational in the economist's sense (Economic Man is driven by rational calculation and has a set of preferences from which he can select the best alternative), is 'in good part intentionally so'. Simon also does not agree with the Freudian view of the human condition (that people are not nearly as rational as they thought themselves to be). Simon argues that these models do not help us to explain the actuality of decision-making. What economists or Freudians might term 'irrationality' is not, from Simon's point

[9] Ibid., 110.
[10] Simon, *Administrative Behaviour*, xxvi.
[11] Ibid., 75.

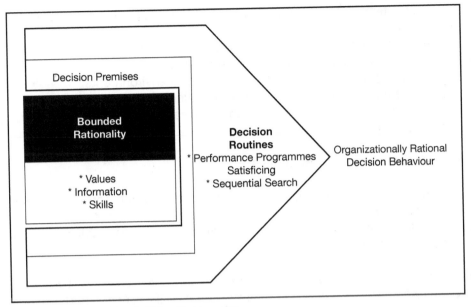

■ Figure 11.3: Simon's Bounded Rational Decision-making
Source: C.W. Choo, *The Knowing Organization,* 2nd ed. (New York: Oxford University Press, 2006).

of view, a satisfactory explanation of the way in which rationality is limited. The concept that he develops to describe a rationality which is limited but not 'irrational' is 'bounded rationality' (Figure 11.3).

Simon characterizes decision-making by *Administrative Man* as operating in a world of rationality. Simon says,

> It is impossible for the behaviour of a single, isolated individual to reach any high degree of rationality. The number of alternatives he must explore is so great, the information he would need to evaluate them so vast that even an approximation to objective rationality is hard to conceive.[12]

Actual behaviour falls short of rationality in at least three ways:

(i) Complete knowledge of the consequences of choice is necessary for rational behaviour, but knowledge is always incomplete.
(ii) Our valuation of future consequences is imperfect.
(iii) Rationality requires a choice among all possible alternative behaviours, but in reality, only a few alternatives even come to mind.

According to Simon, human rationality is limited in terms of

(i) the incomplete and fragmented nature of knowledge,
(ii) imperfect valuation of future consequences,

---

[12] Simon, *Administrative Behaviour,* 79.

(iii) limits of attention (decision-makers cannot think about too many issues at the same time),

(iv) the existence of multiple values and the large measure of uncertainty,

(v) limits on the storage capacity of the human mind,

(vi) human beings as limited by their psychological environments,

(vii) human beings as creatures of habit and routine and

(viii) decision-making also bounded by an organizational environment that frames the process of choice.

In his work *Models of Man*, Simon argues,

> The capacity of the human mind for formulating and solving complex problems is very small compared with the size of the problems whose solution is required for objectively rational behavior in the real world or even for a reasonable approximation to such objective rationality.[13]

Given these limitations, therefore, decision-making is very difficult to be rational. He contends that an organization may be held to be behaving rationally if it is concerned with attaining or maximizing its values in a given situation. In order to clarify what he means by rationality in decision-making, he talks of two models: *Economic Man* and *Administrative Man*.

> While economic man maximizes—selects the best alternative from among all those available to him;...administrative man satisfices—looks for a course of action that is satisfactory or 'good enough'.

In a world of bounded rationality, *Administrative Man* in the organization is motivated by factors of satisficing, rather than maximizing. This means that *Administrative Man* makes decisions which are not derived from an examination of all the alternatives. Simon argues that in decision-making in the organization, the problem is that of understanding the limitations on rationality. Further, it is not possible for a decision-maker to analyse all the information and operations when considering a problem. In the real world, decision-makers do not confront organizations devoid of values, prejudices and experience. So, for Simon, rational decision-making has to be understood in terms of the organizational and psychological environments within which decisions are taken. As decision-makers cannot make a calculation with regard to the outcomes of decisions or policies, there cannot be in practice a straightforward relationship between the outcomes of a policy or decision and means which are used to achieve the goal. A decision-making process is concerned with a satisfactory outcome, in contrast to an outcome which is the maximum or optimal result. In other words, decision-makers are concerned with what is essentially satisficing: a compromise of values and goals.

For Simon, decision-making involves two tasks: theory and practice. At a theoretical level, decision analysis involves the study and recognition of the limits of human rationality in organizational contexts. In practical terms, it entails designing the organizational

---

[13] Herbert A. Simon, *Models of Man: Social and Rational* (New York, NY: John Wiley, 1957), 198.

environment so that 'the individual will approach as close as practical to rationality in his decisions'.[14]

Techniques for Improving Rationality

In his 1960 work *The New Science of Management*, Simon views how decision-making could be improved in the context of new techniques, including the use of computers

Simon is an exponent of an optimistic rational approach to human affairs. He advocates the use of rational techniques and computers in order to improve situation. To him, rationality can be a goal in decision-making. However, while he emphasizes the use of rational techniques, Simon notes in a series of lectures in 1983 at Stanford University that rationality is tempered with a realism. He argues that 'self-interest' is a powerful human motivator and reason can only be an enlightener of interests; it cannot solve conflicts.

In his lectures (Reason in Human Affairs), Simon argued for some arrangements for attaining a more rational decision-making process.[15]

(i) *Creation of specialist group*: With a view to reducing elements of irrationality, Simon advocates creation of specialist groups and organizations which can deal with routine and repetitive decisions.

(ii) *Restrictive use of market mechanisms*: Simon argues that market mechanisms provide a way of limiting how much information we need to operate and reach 'tolerable', if not 'optimal', arrangements.[16] But he notes that they do not provide an independent mechanism for social choice. They can only be used in conjunction with other methods of social control.

(iii) *Use of adversary proceedings*: According to Simon, adversary proceedings (judicial or legal methods of procedural fairness) are like markets in reducing the information that participants must have in order to behave rationality. 'They provide a useful mechanism for systems in which information is distributed widely and in which different system components have different goals'.

(iv) *Use of technical tools for decision*: Simon advocates the use of rational techniques, operations research and computers as aids to improving the rationality of decision-making. Although there are problems in their quantification, he has faith in the potentials of management and artificial intelligence.

(v) *Knowledge of political institutions:* To Simon, institutions help in changing human behaviour. But he has no prescription for how institutions may be changed, apart from better political education. Similarly, improvement in the level of public information enhances rational decision-making process, yet Simon has doubt about its real impact due to the distorting effects of the mass media on the one hand and the role of experts on the other.

(vi) *Knowledge as facilitating rational problem-solving*: Simon has an unbounded faith in human progress through knowledge. Although knowledge is a key component in human progress, Simon is too aware of its limitations as facilitating more

---

[14] Simon, *Administration Behaviour*, 241.
[15] Herbert A. Simon, *Reason in Human Affairs* (California: Stanford University Press, 1983).
[16] Ibid., 105.

rational problem-solving in a complex and uncertain world. Reason, he argues, is instrument; it cannot help in selecting goals, so much as it 'helps us to reach agreed-upon goals more effectively'.[17]

Here the contrast between Simon and Lasswell is most telling. Simon's work leads, inexorably to the management approach to public policy, whereas Lasswell's directs us to a more critical form of policy analysis. In brief, the decision-making processes elaborated by Simon are likely to be rational only in a limited, bounded and subjective sense and that too may not be rational in the true sense. Lasswell views the policy sciences as offering the prospect of greater freedom than rationality.

A Critical Appreciation

Although Simon's contribution to theory of decision-making in terms of 'bounded rationality' has brought him name and fame, his work is criticized on several grounds. Simon's approach to administration in terms of decision-making activity is a valuable contribution to administrative theory, yet it alone is not adequate to explain the totality of an organization. Decision-making is one of the managerial or administrative activities and is an important variable for the organizational effectiveness, but it fails to explain the organization phenomenon.

Simon asserts that all human behaviour has a rational component, but the logical implication of that contention is that human behaviour also has a non-rational component. In this way, Simon's definition of rationality provides little basis for distinguishing between the two. In addition, his model of *Satisficing Man* has limited predictive value. The model, as is acknowledged by Simon, does not provide unique solutions on precise predictions.

Simon's concepts of authority and rationality seek to explain human behaviour from an idealistic point of view. His approach is general and of little practical relevance. Chris Argyris observes that Simon, by insisting on rationality, has not recognized the role of intuition, tradition and faith in decision-making.[18] Simon's theory uses satisficing to rationalize incompetence. Likewise, he has not taken into account the material conditions and historical and cultural factors which largely govern human behaviour. Similarly, the productive forces and general human relations factors which largely determine the value judgements and choice of behaviour have not been properly analysed. His work leads invariably to the management approach to public policy.

In criticizing the rational model as advocated by Simon and others, Lindblom rejected the idea that decision-making was essentially something which was about defining goals, selecting alternatives and comparing alternatives. Lindblom contended that rational decision-making was simply 'not workable for complex policy questions'.[19] To Lindblom, constraints of time, intelligence, cost and politics prevent policymakers to identify societal goals and their consequences.

Notwithstanding these criticisms, Simon's contribution to administrative theory, especially his contribution to decision-making, is well recognized. His views on efficiency,

---

[17] Ibid., 106.

[18] Chris Argyris, 'Some Limits of Rational Man Organization Theory', *Public Administration Review* 33(3) (1973): 255.

[19] Charles Lindblom, 'The Science of Muddling Through', *Public Administration Review* 19(2) (1959): 79–88.

authority, centralization, rationality, communication, training and computer simulation of problem-solving processes have often been quoted in textbooks. 'Specializing in the computer simulation of individual decision-making', Gross says, 'he has become one of the world's outstanding pioneers in psychological research and theory on the cognitive aspects of thought processes and in the development of thinking machines'.[20] His efforts in developing—including programming computers to play chess, prove mathematical theorems, distinguish between geometrical shapes and even create abstract art designs—have made him a leader in the field of artificial intelligence.

Herbert Simon's contribution to the development of the policy approach is well recognized. His work on *Administrative Behaviour* has impacted on a range of social sciences—including economics, public management, computer sciences and political science—means that Simon is studied as a writer and critic who crosses several disciplinary boundaries. His concern with decision-making has centred on the idea of rationality as 'bounded'. This theme he has examined and explained both theoretically and practically. Simon's approach to decision-making in terms of a sequence of rational stages has formed a central element of policy analysis. Thus, Simon is certainly a believer in rationality in decision-making, but his rationality is known to be 'bounded rationality'.

LINDBLOM'S ANALYTICAL POLICYMAKING MODEL

Introduction

Charles Lindblom (1917) was not content with the rational choice model. The rational comprehensive or synoptic model assumes that decision-makers possess full information and can select the best alternative to realize known objectives. The decision process in the rational model is based on non-partisan and scientific analysis that is not 'contaminated by ethical issues' (as in Harold Lasswell's version of scientific policy analysis). Elevated to the policy process, the decision process is linear, that is, proceeding from problem definition to identification of alternatives, to selection of an alternative, to implementation and, finally, to evaluation.

Problems Confronting Synoptic Model: For Lindblom, this stagist model is simply tidy and 'not workable for complex policy questions'. The rational decision-making fails to describe the messy business that constitutes real-life decision- and policymaking. Specifically, the synoptic model suffers from seven problems caused by its lack of adaptation to

   (i) people's limited problem-solving capability,
   (ii) constraints of time and intelligence,
   (iii) costliness of analysis,
   (iv) inability to limited satisfying evaluation techniques,
   (v) bridging fact and value,
   (vi) analyst's need for strategic sequences of analysis and
   (vii) various forms wherein policy problems actually occur.[21]

---

[20] Bertram M. Gross, *The Managing of Organizations* (New York, NY: *The Free Press*, 1964), 182.
[21] David Braybrooke and Charles Lindblom, *A Strategy of Decision* (New York, NY: Free Press, 1963), 48–54.

Broadly, synoptic model confronts two fundamental problems: (i) uncertainty and (ii) multiple decision-makers.

First, in the context of uncertainty, the decision-maker may be uncertain about objectives, about the alternative means of achieving objectives, about the relationships between alternatives and their consequences and about the consequences of those alternatives.

Second, the involvement of multiple decision-makers causes conflicting interests. The synoptic model yields little practical guidance of dealing with this type of collective decision environment. The model suggests the formation of public preference functions, but it fails to provide a preference measure which helps interpersonal comparison of utilities.

Preceding Lindblom's work, Herbert Simon also attempted to deal with the problem of uncertainty (limited information and capabilities) by offering his concept of *Satisficing Man*, that is, one who satisfies for he has not the wits to maximize. However, Simon avoided the problem of collective decision environment by resorting to a hierarchical solution.

Lindblom, in contrast, has attempted to deal with these problems of the synoptic model by offering concepts of incrementalism and bargaining. The problem of uncertainty is addressed by introduction of simplifications in both the bargaining and incremental elements of Lindblom's approach. And the problem of collective decision environment, in which individuals share power and have conflicting interests, is dealt within the bargaining (mutual adjustment) portion of his approach. Lindblom's concept of incrementalism had much in common with Popper's 'piecemeal social engineering'.[22]

Lindblom's Incremental Approach

As an alternative to traditional rational model decision-making, Charles Lindblom presented the 'incremental model' of the policymaking process. His article on the *Science of Muddling Through*,[23] published in 1959, gained wide recognition in the development of policy analysis as concerned with the 'process' of making policy. Since then Lindblom's thought has evolved beyond his original argument.

Initially, Dahl and Lindblom described 'incrementalism' as 'a method of social action' that takes existing reality as one alternative and compares the probable gains and losses of closely related alternatives by making relatively small adjustments in existing reality, or making larger adjustment about whose consequences approximately as much is known as about the consequences of existing reality, or both.[24]

A few years later, Lindblom described 'incrementalism' as a method of 'successive limited comparison' that would allow the decision-maker to easily revisit earlier decisions

---

[22] See Robert Dahl and Charles Lindblom, *Politics, Economics and Welfare* (New York, NY: Harper & Row, 1953).

[23] Charles Lindblom, 'The Science of Muddling Through', *Public Administration Review* 19 (1959): 78–88.

[24] Dahl and Lindblom, *Politics, Economics and Welfare*, 82.

and correct them if necessary.[25] What Lindblom called 'successive limited comparison' resembles Polanyi's notion of problem solving through 'successive approximations'.[26]

In 1958, Lindblom spoke for the first time of 'muddling through'—a label that featured prominently in the *Public Administration Review* in 1959.[27] 'Muddling through', he argues, is a method or 'science' which advocates of policy analysis.

In 1963, Lindblom added the qualification 'disjointed' to the concept of incrementalism,[28] to make the repetitiveness of events more incremental. In 1965, Lindblom wrote that disjointed incrementalism should be seen as an instrument not for solving social problems but merely for helping to deal with social problems.[29] In 1979, Lindblom again refined the concept of incrementalism[30] in response to the criticism about the confusion he had created by not distinguishing incremental politics from incremental analysis. In the 1993 edition of his textbook on the *Policy-making Process*, Lindblom writes,

> Deliberate, orderly steps... are not an accurate portrayal of how the policy process actually works. Policy-making is instead, a complexly inter-active process without beginning or end.[31]

In criticizing the rational model as advocated by Simon and others, Lindblom rejected the idea that decision-making was essentially something which was about defining goals, selecting alternatives and comparing alternatives. Lindblom wanted to show that rational decision-making was simply 'not workable for complex policy questions'. To Lindblom, constraints of time, intelligence, cost and politics prevent policymakers to identify societal goals and their consequences. He drew briefly the distinction in terms of comprehensive (or root) rationality as advocated by Simon and what he regarded as the operative mode of decision-making as 'rational' activity: successive limited comparisons (or branch) decision-making.

Two Models of Decision-making

The incremental approach (branch method) of decision-making involves a process of 'continually building out from the current situation, step-by-step and by small degrees' (Table 11.1).

The 'root' approach as favoured by the policy analysts would have to start from 'fundamentals anew each time, building on the past only as experience embodied in a theory,

---

[25] C. Lindblom, 'Policy Analysis', *American Economic Review* 48(3) (1958): 301–02.
[26] See M. Polanyi, *The Logic of Liberty: Reflections and Rejoinders* (Chicago: University of Chicago Press, 1951) 141.
[27] Lindblom, 'The Science of Muddling Through', 79–88. This article has been voted a 'top three policy piece' in A *History of Political Economy* 37(1) (2005): 36.
[28] Braybrooke and Lindblom, *A Strategy of Decision*, 61.
[29] Charles Lindblom, *The Intelligence of Democracy* (New York, NH: Free Press, 1965), 148.
[30] Charles Lindblom, 'Still Muddling Through', *Public Administration Review*, 39(6) (1979): 517–25.
[31] Charles Lindblom and E.J. Woodhouse, *The Policy-making Process*, 3rd ed. (Englewood Cliffs, NJ: Prentice Hall, 1993), 11.

■ Table 11.1: Lindblom's Two Models of Decision-making

	Rational Comprehensive (root) Approach	Successive Limited Comparison (branch) Approach
(i)	Identification of societal values or goals is necessary to empirical analysis of alternative policies	Selection of values or goals and empirical analysis of the needed action are interlinked
(ii)	Policymaking is approached through means–ends analysis	Means–ends analysis is often inappropriate or limited
(iii)	The test of a 'good policy' is that it is a means to desired ends	The test of a 'good policy' is that various analysts find themselves directly agreeing on a policy
(iv)	Analysis is comprehensive involving every relevant factor	Analysis is limited and important possible outcomes and alternatives are neglected
(v)	Reliance on theory	A successive limited comparison reduces dependence on theory

Source: Adapted from Lindblom (1959).

and always prepared to start from the ground up'. In contrast, the branch method of decision-making involves a process of 'continually building out from the current situation, step-by-step and by small degrees'. Lindblom proposes that 'successive limited comparison' is both more relevant and more realistic in such a condition of 'bounded rationality'. To Simon's problem, Lindblom's answer is that we do not need to search out new techniques; we need to be more appreciative of the benefits of 'non-comprehensive analysis':

> In the method of successive limited comparison, simplification is systematically achieved in two principal ways. First, it is achieved through limitation of policy comparisons to those policies that differ in relatively small degree from policies presently in effect. Such a limitation immediately reduces the number of alternatives to be investigated and drastically simplifies the character of the investigation of each.... The second method of simplification of analysis is the practice of ignoring important possible consequences of possible policies, as well as the values attached to the neglected consequences.[32]

Features of Incremental Decision-making

The incremental model is a more realistic approach to public decision-making because it provides greater flexibility in coping with time-sensitive policy problems. The following features characterize the decision-making in terms of muddling through:

(i) First, only a few policy alternatives can be considered at one time. It proceeds through a succession of incremental changes. Policymakers accept the legitimacy of existing policies because of the uncertainty about the consequences of new or different policies.

(ii) Second, it involves mutual adjustment and negotiation. Agreement is arrived at through a process of adjustment and compromise. Thus, incrementalism is of significance in reducing political stress.

---

[32] Lindblom, 'The Science of Muddling Through', 84–85.

(iii) Third, incremental approach involves the trial-and-error method. Objectives under this approach are set in terms of existing policies and resources. Existing policy serve the base for change. Change occurs through decisions that have an incremental effect.

(iv) Fourth, policy is not made once and for all. As Lane observes, 'Incrementalism is thus more satisfactory from a theoretical point of view as it scores high on criteria like coherence and simplicity'.[33] The incremental model is thus a more realistic approach in decision-making.

Advocates of incrementalism defend the muddling through process as more realistic, as being able to respond to the interests of many groups, as being able to respond to crisis pressures and as not requiring the massive investments of time, money and effort that logical decisions require. Decisions to implement policy are usually made in small steps, incrementally, rather than through an all-encompassing rationality which is not practically achievable. As a method of successive limited comparisons, the incremental model would allow the decision-maker to easily revisit earlier decisions and correct them if necessary.

Incremental Analysis

In his work *Politics and Markets*, Lindblom conceded much to Etzioni's critique of his theory of incremental pluralism.[34] The work recognized that pluralist decision-making was biased: not all interests and participants in incrementalist politics were equal in the sense that some had considerably more power than others. Business and large corporations, he analysed, occupied a predominant position in the policymaking process. Lindblom in his work proposes the need to improve *mutual partisan adjustment* by 'greatly improved strategic policy-making'.[35]

Subsequently, in 1979, he published his article 'Still Muddling Through'. Lindblom makes clear that the core idea in an incrementalist approach is the belief in skill in solving complex problems, and that his aim is to suggest 'new and improved' ways of 'muddling through'. To do this, he draws a distinction between (i) incrementalism as a political pattern (step-by-step changes) and (ii) incrementalism as policy analysis.[36] In this article, he makes the case for 'analytical incrementalism' as a method of securing the balance of power in a pluralist polity in which business and large corporations tend to exercise a powerful influence over the policymaking process. Lindblom argues that there are three main forms to incremental analysis: (i) simple incremental analysis, (ii) strategic analysis and (iii) disjointed incrementalism.

Simple Incremental Analysis

It is a form of analysis in which only those alternative policies which are marginally different to the existing policy are analysed. According to Lindblom, simple incremental analysis is a useful tool of proceeding to make decisions. 'Focusing on small variations from present

[33] Jan-Erik Lane, *The Public Sector* (London: SAGE Publications, 2000), 75.

[34] A. Etzioni, 'Mixed Scanning: A 'Third' Approach to Decision-making', *Public Administration Review* 27 (1967): 385–92.

[35] Charles Lindblom, *Politics and Markets* (New York, NY: Basic Books, 1977), 346.

[36] Lindblom, 'Still Muddling Through', 517–25.

policy... makes the most of available knowledge'. Thus, this method allows the decision-maker to consider and profit from feedback from previous experiences and decisions.

Strategic Analysis

Lindblom argues that since completeness of analysis is not possible because of many constraints, an analyst should take a middle position: 'informed, thoughtful' use of methods to 'simplify problems' so as to make better choices. These methods include 'trial and error learning; systems analysis; operations research; management by objectives; and programme evaluation and review technique' (PERT). In using these methods, Lindblom says that analysis should not aim for the 'synoptic/root' ideal, but should aspire to deploy them in the development of strategies to guide and direct 'something to be done, something to be studied and learned, and something that can be successfully approximated'.[37]

Disjointed Incrementalism

In his work *A strategy of Decision* with David Braybrooke, Lindblom developed his ideas on the non-comprehensive approach to decision-making. This work places incrementalism in a continuum of understanding and scale of change. In this work, he introduced the notion of *disjointed incrementalism*. Lindblom sees this as a method of decision-making in which comparison takes place between policies which are only 'marginally' different from one another and in which there is no 'great goal' or vision to be achieved. It is disjointed because decisions are not subject to any control or coordination. Disjointed incrementalism is an analytical strategy which involves 'simplifying and focusing' problems by six methods: (a) the limitation of analysis for a few familiar alternatives, (b) intertwining values and policy goals with empirical analysis of problems, (c) focusing on ills to be remedied rather than on goals to be sought, (d) trial-and-error learning, (e) analysing a limited number of options and their consequences and (f) fragmenting of analytical work to many partisan participants in policymaking.

In 1977, Lindblom called 'disjointed incrementalism' as Model II which focuses on a limited but calculated and thoughtfully chosen set of stratagems to simplify complex policy problems, thus avoiding large, irreversible errors.

In the third edition of *The Policy-making Process*, he and his new co-author, E.J. Woodhouse, distinguished between incrementalism as an analytic strategy, as a political process for supporting a strategy of disjointed incrementalism and as a policy outcome that consists of small steps.[38]

In brief, incrementalism as a paradigm serves to simplify the decision process in the following ways:

  (i) Limiting the number of alternatives that are considered (only those that are marginally different from the previous practice);
  (ii) Allowing the decision-maker to rely on feedback from previous experience; and
  (iii) Managing risk by making the process serial and remedial (to avoid large errors).

---

[37] Lindblom, 'Still Muddling Through', 318.
[38] Lindblom and Woodhouse, *The Policy-making Process*, 7.

Partisan Mutual Adjustment

The notion of 'mutual adjustment', which Lindblom designated as the 'hidden hand in government', also figures in his writings.[39] In the *Intelligence of Democracy*, he argues that decision-making involves a process of bargaining and negotiation between decision-makers: partial mutual adjustment. In other words, decision-making is a process of adjustment and compromise which facilitates agreement and coordination. Partisan mutual adjustment, Lindblom argues, is the democratic and practical alternative to centralized decision-making. The process of mutual adjustment is open-ended and is fed by ideas from all participants. Subordinates have power over supervisors through the information and analysis they provide. To him, the criterion of a 'good policy' is simply agreement.

Lindblom argues that bargaining encourages the representation of general interests. It strengthens the democratic process. It does so because the act of participation encouraged by the bargaining process creates a greater sense of citizenship and empowerment in the polity. The point is that, Lindblom argues, though bargaining and incrementalism may not constitute the best of all conceivable worlds, they may represent the best of all possible worlds in a polyarchal political system.

Although Lindblom is deeply pessimistic about experts and analysts, he is optimistic about the potential of wider social learning and greater participation in decision-making by citizens. The decision or policy process, he defends, would not be limited to experts nor would it be based on scientific information. Instead, the policy process would assign a central role to ordinary citizens employing ordinary knowledge. Practitioners of professional social inquiry may be non-partisan experts, but their major activities are to provide information and analysis suited to the interactive roles of participants in interaction. They should not strive for independent authoritativeness, but instead facilitate in the policy-making process. He warned against the exclusion of the recipients and beneficiaries of policy, and deplored the possibility that policy substance would be determined by the so-called experts only. He insisted that scientific analysis must be considered only supplementary to other knowledge sources. With Cohen, he observed that 'a scientific theory of decision-making can make a significant contribution only by not attempting to wholly displace the ordinary knowledge'.[40] Policymaking as a problem-solving process can only succeed, in Lindblom's observation, when both ordinary and scientific knowledge are applied. After all, he argues, policy is made not by policymakers but by interaction among a plurality of citizens.[41]

Conclusion and Critical Evaluation

Lindblom is a key contributor to the development of policy analysis. Since 1959 when Lindblom advocated incremental decision-making, there had been an apparent 'VOTLE face' in his arguments. In 1977 and 1979, Lindblom attacked the idea of pluralism, offered a radical critique of the business and expressed the need for policy analysis. He believes

[39] Charles Lindblom, 'Bargaining: The Hidden Hand of Government', in *Democracy and Market System*, ed. Charles Lindblom (Oslo: Norwegian University Press, 1988), 139–70.
[40] Charles E. Lindblom and D.K. Cohen, *Usable Knowledge* (New Haven, CT: Yale University Press, 1979), 90.
[41] Ibid., p. 64.

that there is a need for drastic radical change in a whole range of policy areas, and that the whole world is in dire need of more than simply incremental change. But societies 'seem incapable, except in emergencies, of acting more boldly than in increments'.[42] Such are the constraints on decision-makers and on the way in which policy agendas are narrowly formulated. In 1959, we have Lindblom, the pluralist, advocate of incremental decision-making as the most effective mode of policymaking, yet Lindblom of the 1970s through 1990s is indeed a more radical critic of incrementalism as a 'political ideology'. He has developed his ideas about the policymaking process as moving slowly, but has continued to maintain that it can be improved. He proposed a model which took account of power and interaction between phases and stages.

Despite his substantial contribution to theory-building in the policy arena, Lindblom's work attracted quite a bit of critical attention. The most general criticism of his work is that Lindblom presents sweeping generalizations but does not support them adequately with empirical evidence. For example, Harsanyi charged that Lindblom made 'little use of precisely defined theoretical concepts or clearly specified analytical models'.[43]

Both Dror and Etzioni also are not convinced that incremental model is either realistic or satisfactory normative accounts of decision-making. To Dror, this model is profoundly conservative and is suitable in those situations where policy is deemed to be working or is satisfactory, where problems are quite stable over time, and where there is availability of resources. Further, Dror observed that incrementalism justifies status quo and ignores the possibility of fundamental change. It reinforced the pro-inertia and anti-innovation forces in society.[44]

Several authors also observed that incrementalism lacked good orientation. For example, Kaplan argued that incremental adjustment would lead to blind policy alternatives. Tullock feared that incrementalism disregards long-term outcomes, while Etzioni noted that nothing in incrementalism would guide the small steps' accumulation towards a large step. Dror observed that incrementalism represented a 'complacent approach'. It is difficult to bring about a fundamental change via incrementalism.

Lindblom's response to the critique of incrementalism is summarized in his introduction to *Democracy and Market System* (1988): '...incrementalism was weak, inefficacious, inadequate to problems at hand, often controlled by the wrong people, and yet...usually the best possible course of action'.[45]

Despite the lack of empirical evidence cited in support of his generalizations and for the ideological slant in his later work, there has been ample attention to his ideas and scholarship. Lindblom has surely made his mark. Possibly his most lasting contribution consists of incrementalism in policymaking and mutual adjustment as instruments of social coordination.

---

[42] Charles Lindblom, *Democracy and Market System* (Oslo: Norwegian University Press, 1988), 11.
[43] John C. Harsanyi, 'Review of the Intelligence of Democracy by Charles Lindblom', *American Economic Review* 55(5) Part I (1965): 1191.
[44] Y. Dror, 'Muddling Through 'Science' or Inertia', *Public Administration Review* 24(3) (1964): 153–57.
[45] Lindblom, 'Bargaining: The Hidden Hand of Government', 11.

DROR'S NORMATIVE OPTIMUM MODEL OF POLICY ANALYSIS

Yehezkel Dror presented a modified form of the rational model of policy analysis. He argues that policy analysis must acknowledge that there is a realm of world which involves values and personal experiences. He thus creates an approach which combines core elements of the rational model with extra-rational factors which are not included from the 'pure rationality' model.

In comparison to Lane's observations, Dror finds Lindblom's 'incrementalist model' of decision-making quite conservative and unsatisfactory.[46] He believes that incremental approach is unjust as it creates a gap between those who have more power and those who have little power. The latter category of people will find it difficult to bring about change. In place of incremental and rational models, Dror offers an alternative. His model in main seeks to accept

(i) the need for rationality (in Simon's definition);
(ii) the need for introduction of management techniques for enhancing rationality of decision-making at low levels;
(iii) the policy science approach (Lasswell's term) for dealing with complex problems requiring decisions at the higher levels; and
(iv) the need to take account of values and irrational elements in decision-making.

Here it may be mentioned that Dror's aim is to (i) increase the rational content of government and (ii) to build into his model the 'extra-rational' dimensions of decision-making. Dror calls this 'normative optimalism' which combines core elements of the 'rational' model (such as the measurement of costs and benefits) with 'extra-rational' factors which are excluded from the 'pure rationality' model. He argues, 'What is needed is a model which fits reality while being directed towards its improvement, and which can be applied to policymaking while motivating a maximum effort to arrive at better policies'.[47] He thus puts forward alternative to the rational policy approach. As such, Dror attempts to present a modified form of rational model which can move policymaking in a more rational direction. Policy analysis, he argues, must acknowledge that there is a realm of extra-rational understanding based on tact knowledge and personal experience.[48] He argues that the aim of analysis is to induce decision-makers to expand their frameworks to deal better with a complex world. Thus, in place of a purely rational model, Dror offers a more complex model of some 18 stages.[49]

I. Meta-policymaking stage:
1. processing values;
2. processing reality;
3. processing problems;
4. surveying, processing and developing resources;

---

[46] Y. Dror, *Public Policymaking Re-examined*, 2nd ed. (New Brunswick: Transaction Publishers, 1989), 143–47.
[47] Y. Dror, 'Muddling Through – 'Science' or Inertia?', *Public Administration Review* 24 (1964): 164.
[48] Dror, *Public Policymaking Re-examined*, 15–16.
[49] Ibid., 163–64.

5. designing, evaluating and redesigning the policymaking system;
6. allocating problems, values and resources;
7. determining policymaking strategy.

II Policymaking stage:
8. sub-allocating resources;
9. establishing operational goals, with some order of priority;
10. establishing a set of their significant values, with some order of priority;
11. preparing a set of major alternative policies, including some 'good ones';
12. preparing reliable predictions of the significant benefits and costs of the various alternatives;
13. comparing the predicted benefits and costs of the various alternatives and identifying the 'best' ones;
14. evaluating the benefits and costs of the 'best alternatives' and deciding whether they are 'good' or not.

III Post-policymaking stage:
15. motivating the execution of policy;
16. executing the policy;
17. evaluating policymaking after executing the policy;
18. communication and feedback channels interconnecting all phases.

From the standpoint of analysis, Dror's model suggests that we should analyse public policy as being made at two interacting sub-phases. Thus, the 18-stage outlined must be seen as a cycle which has its rational and extra-rational aspects (see Figure 11.4) His model operates at two interacting phases.

In phase 1, 'the processing of values', decision-making will involve 'specifying and ordering values to be a general guide for identifying problems and for policy-making'. In phase 2, 'rational sub-phase', this involves 'gathering information on feasibility and

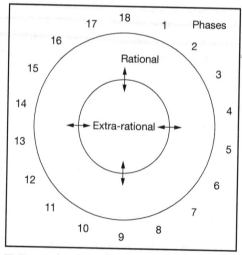

■ Figure 11.4: Dror's Policy Cycle
Source: Adapted from Dror (1989; appendix B).

opportunity costs', and at the 'extra-rational sub-phase', decision-making will involve 'value judgements, tacit bargaining and coalition-formation skills'.[50]

In Dror's 'normative–optimum' model which combines both descriptive (in the real world, decision-making is driven by rational and extra-rational influences) and prescriptive (improving both the rational and extra-rational aspects) approach, he envisages a radical reform of the public policymaking process. According to Dror, there is the need of bringing about changes in the personnel (politicians, bureaucrats and experts); in structures and process (to improve systematic thinking and integrating experts into policymaking); as well as in the general environment of policymaking.

Thus, Dror's model envisages decision-makers using rational analysis but also using intuition and feelings. He has created an approach which combines core elements of the rational model with extra-rational factors. Dror's aim is to increase the rational content of the government.

A Critical Appreciation

Dror views policymaking as a conscious awareness of choice between two main alternatives for steering societies. He is of the concerted view that a long-term strategy to improve public policymaking is necessary for human progress. Dror could be equated with Lasswell. But whereas Lasswell saw the policy sciences as having a 'role in enlightenment, emancipation and democratization', Dror seems to have very little regard for the people in policymaking. To quote Dror, 'But if the success of democracy depended on the people's ability to judge the main policy issues on their merits, then democracy would surely have perished by now'.[51]

It will be observed that his model of 18 stages is seen as a cycle which has its 'rational' and 'extra-rational' components. It may be of relevance to point out that the real strength of Dror's analysis is not to be seen in terms of the prescription dimension of his model, so much as in the framework it provides to analyse the policymaking process. Although agreeing with Lindblom that policymaking was a complex exercise, he was opposed to Lindblom's incrementalism position and advocated alternative paradigm of rational analysis.

ETZIONI'S MIXED SCANNING APPROACH

At the forefront of advocating 'communitarianism' as an approach to public policy is Amitai Etzioni, whose contribution to the development of the policy approach that has been without doubt noteworthy. Etzioni is another advocate for a modified form of the rational model of policy analysis. Like Dror, he has taken on board the criticisms of the rational approach and puts forward a third approach that he believes offers a realistic model which avoids the conservatism of the incrementalist position as articulated by Lindblom. Etzioni calls his model 'mixed scanning'.

---

[50] Ibid., 312.

[51] Ibid., 289.

A rationalistic approach to decision-making requires greater resources than decision makers command. The incremental strategy which takes into account the limited capacity of actors, fosters decisions which neglect basic societal innovations. Mixed scanning reduces the unrealistic aspects of rationalism by limiting the details required in fundamental decisions and helps to overcome the conservative slant of incrementalism by exploring long-run alternatives.[52]

For Etzioni, the mixed-scanning approach is a description of the reality of decision-making strategy. His idea of 'mixed scanning' is drawn from early weather forecasting and observation techniques. Etzioni's idea of mixed scanning has, however, to be placed in the context of his wider intellectual concerns and his work as a whole. After the publication of his 'mixed scanning' paper in 1967, Etzioni published a large work on *The Active Society*.[53] In the 1990s, he became most closely associated with 'communitarianism'.[54] But the work *The Active Society* remains, however, as possibly, the best introduction to his ideas for the policy analysis. Etzioni believes that personal transformation is rooted in the 'joint act of the community transforming itself'.[55] He says that the aim of public policy is ultimately to promote a society in which people are active in their communities and in which 'political action and intellectual reflection would have a higher, more public status'. This is to be achieved through raising individual and societal consciousness and a new emphasis on 'symbolization' as opposed to wealth. In *The Active Society*, Etzioni examines the social context of knowledge, the relationship between power and knowledge, the distribution of knowledge and 'societal consciousness'. His view is that the rational model and incrementalist approach are neither realistic nor satisfactory normative accounts of decision-making. These approaches cannot be the basis for promoting an 'active society'. This is a society in which people through social collectivities and social knowledge can transform the society in accordance with its values. In this context, Etzioni says, 'No man can set himself free without extending the same liberty to his fellow men and the transformation of the self is deeply rooted in the joint act of a community transforming itself'.[56] In common with Dror, Etzioni acknowledges that there is an information gap in government.

The emphasis on 'community', which has been central to his later writings, has therefore to be placed in the context of his belief in the role of knowledge in bringing about a more open and more 'authentic' public policy process.[57]

Etzioni uses the analysis to improve society and the self. For Etzioni, an active society is one which involves public in analysis. Moreover, in an active society, the knowledge elites—intellectuals, experts and politicians—should interact with publics in a form of 'collective reality testing'.[58] Rebuilding society, therefore, involves both a knowledge and a moral

---

[52] Etzioni, 'Mixed Scanning', 385.

[53] A. Etzioni, *The Active Society: A Theory of Societal and Political Processes* (New York, NY: Free Press, 1968).

[54] A. Etzioni, *The Spirit of Community: Rights, Responsibilities and the Communitarian Agenda* (New York, NY: Crown Publishers, 1993).

[55] Etzioni, *The Active Society*, 2.

[56] Ibid., 2.

[57] Ibid., 635.

[58] Ibid., 155–70.

dimension.[59] Etzioni's 'mixed scanning' approach tries to 'explicitly combine"(i) high-order, fundamental policy-making processes which set basic directions, and (ii) incremental ones which prepare for fundamental decisions and work them out after they have been reached'.[60]

For Etzioni, the mixed-scanning approach is a description of the reality of decision-making strategies, and it is also a model for better decision-making.[61] It recognizes that decision-makers have to consider the costs of knowledge (not everything can be scanned). Thus, policymakers should endeavour to scan key areas fully and rationalistically and can subject other areas to a more 'truncated' review. In a way, his approach is a long way removed from Dror's technocratic managerialism.

POLITICAL PROCESS APPROACH

The study of public policy is generally regarded as an important aspect of politics. Public policies address problems that are public, or more importantly, that some people think should be public. A significant departure from the rationality model is the political policy process approach espoused in policymaking. This approach has been described by writers such as Laurence Lynn[62] and Peter DeLeon.[63]

In this approach, public policymaking is viewed as a 'political process' instead of a 'technical process'. The approach emphasizes the political interaction from which policy derives. Lynn sees public policy as the output of government. He says,

> Public policy can be characterized as the output of a diffuse made up of individuals who interact with each other in small groups in a framework dominated by formal organizations. Those organizations function in a system of political institutions, rules and practices, all subject to societal and cultural influences.[64]

For example, Lynn argues that individuals in organizations function under a variety of influences and 'to understand policy-making it is necessary to understand the behaviour of interactions among these structures: individuals holding particular positions, groups, organizations, the political system, and the wider society of which they are all a part'.[65] Therefore, instead of involving particular methodologies, policymaking in this approach is a matter of adapting to and learning to influence political and organizational environments. The policymaking is constrained by such factors as institutions, interest groups and even 'societal and cultural influences'.

---

[59] A. Etzioni, *An Immodest Agenda: Rebuilding America Before the Twenty-First Century* (New York, NY: Free Press, 1983).
[60] Etzioni, 'Mixed Scanning', 385.
[61] Ibid.
[62] Laurence Lynn, *Managing Public Policy* (Boston, MA: Little, Brown, 1987).
[63] Peter DeLeon, *Democracy and the Policy Sciences* (Albany, NY: SUNY Press, 1977).
[64] Lynn, *Managing Public Policy*, 239.
[65] Ibid., 17.

The focus in this political process of policymaking approach is on understanding how particular policies were formed, developed and work in practice. Lynn argues that policymaking 'encompasses not only goal setting, decision-making, and formulation of political strategies, but also supervision of policy planning, resource allocation, operations management, programme evaluation, and efforts at communication, argument, and persuasion'.[66] According to Lynn, 'managers of public policy' operate under a variety of influences. He observes, 'Public executives pursue their goals within three kinds of limits: those imposed by their external political environments; those imposed by their organizations; and those imposed by their own personalities and cognitive styles'.[67] Rather than being technical experts, effective managers of public policy should, argues Lynn,

(i)   establish understandable premises for their organization's objectives;
(ii) attain an intellectual grasp of strategically important issues; identify and focus attention on those activities that give meaning to the organization's employees;
(iii) remain alert to and exploit all opportunities, whether deliberately created or fortuitous, to further their purposes;
(iv) consciously employ the strong features of their personalities as instruments of leadership and influence;
(v)   manage within the framework of an economy of personal resources to govern how much they attempt to accomplish and how they go about it.[68]

As such, this approach is a significant departure from the rationality model. Managers use any means to achieve their goals. They work in this way because their own positions are on the line.

Public policy is, therefore, more 'political' than 'public administration'. It is thus an effort to apply the methods of political science to policy areas (e.g. health, education, environment) but has concerns with processes inside the bureaucracy, so it is more related to public administration.

COHEN, MARCH AND OLSEN: GARBAGE CAN MODEL

Borrowing from rational comprehensive and incrementalist models of decision-making, Michael Cohen, James March and Johan Olsen developed the 'garbage can model' to explain decision-making in what they call 'organized anarchies'.[69]

They used universities as an example of organized anarchies to explain decision-making. To them, institutions of higher learning are not rigidly organized. In universities and colleges, faculty members usually have considerable autonomy in the management of their work and of their departments. Students too enjoy a degree of freedom in their choices of which courses and majors to take and what to do during free time. And administrative officials must manage the various interests—faculty, students and members of

---

[66] Ibid., 45.
[67] Ibid., 42.
[68] Ibid., 271.
[69] Michael Cohen, James March and Johan Olsen, 'A Garbage Can Model of Organizational Choice', *Administrative Science Quarterly*, 17 (1972): 1–25.

the broader community—without disregarding the traditional prerogatives of any of these groups.

There are three streams in the garbage can model: problems, solutions and participants. In each of these streams, various elements of decision-making float about. In this model, there are solutions searching for problems and participants floating about looking for a way to participate in putting together these problems and solutions. Cohen, March and Olsen call the decision opportunities 'garbage cans', in which the three streams are mixed together.

This is not a model in which problem is identified followed by people going out to find solutions and bring them back. On the contrary, solutions already exist, and the role of participants is to simply carry a solution in search of a problem.[70]

The garbage can model stresses the anarchical nature of organization as 'loose collection of ideas' in contrast to rational 'coherent structures'. These organizations qua 'garbage cans' are collection of choices which look for problems and seek decisional situations in which they may be advanced. Choices thus compose a 'garbage can' into which 'various kinds of problems and solutions are dumped by participants as they are generated'.[71]

The garbage can model maintains that there is essentially a condition in which some problems will have solutions attached to them, others will not and still other solutions may be looking for an issue in which to attach themselves. Decision-makers in this model may well dump a problem or solution into whatever can they have to hand. In a garbage can process, there are issues, problems and solutions which are messy and untidy sorts of things whose mode of identification by policymakers will depend on the time it was picked up, and the availability of cans to put them in.

The garbage can model is deduced from the assumptions that values are complex, knowledge is uncertain, rules are complex and that decision-making involves much that is symbolic.[72] The decision-making process, therefore, when viewed through a garbage can model, is far less rational than traditional economic and organization theories of decision-making suggest.[73]

However, it must be observed that not all organizations are as anarchic and unmanaged as universities. But John Kingdon finds this garbage can model an alternative framework to approach in which solutions search for problems and the outcomes are a function of the mix of problems, participants and resources.[74]

CONCLUSION

It is concluded here that the responses to the rationalist versus the incrementalist approaches have, in fact, given rise to a continuum of theories and models which advocate

---

[70] For example, the selection of a new dean is an opportunity for participants to come together in a garbage can and use the hiring to link perceived problems in the university with perceived solutions.
[71] Cohen et al., 'A Garbage Can Model of Organizational Choice', 2.
[72] R.M. Cyert and J.G. March, *A Behavioral Theory of the Firm* (Oxford: Basil Blackwell, 1992), 235–38.
[73] Ibid., 238.
[74] John Kingdon, *Agendas, Alternatives and Public Policies* (Boston, NY: Little, Brown, 1984).

ways in which policy and decision-making might be improved. Simon, Lindblom, Dror and Etzioni, in particular, have in their theories endeavoured to convince that there is a gap in the public and its problems which can be bridged simply by improving decision- and policymaking through changing the relationship of the political process to knowledge. Their writings express a belief in the notion that there is an alternative to the unrealistic concept of comprehensive rationality. In this regard, the contributions of Simon, Lindblom, Dror and Etzioni have a great deal in common. As a social science, public policy utilizes the scientific method in an effort to explain the causal relationships between people and their problems.

As a separate approach, it is useful in studying the interaction between government which produces policies and its people for whom the policies are intended. There are now two public policy approaches each with its own methods and emphases. The first is labelled as 'policy analysis' while the second, 'political public policy'.

From a policy analysis perspective, Putt and Springer argue,

> The functions of policy research is to facilitate public policy process through providing accurate and useful decision-related information. The skills required to produce information that is technically sound and useful lie at the heart of the policy research process, regardless of the specific methodology employed.[75]

Attempting to bring modern science and technology to bear on societal problems, policy analysis searches for good methods and techniques that help the policymaker choose the most advantageous action. There is another approach (taken by Lynn) which emphasizes the political interaction from which policy derives. Here it is rather more difficult to separate public policy from political science, and sometimes it becomes difficult to analyse whether a particular study is one of public policy or politics. Public policy is seen to be different from traditional model of public administration, in that it realizes that there are political processes in the domain of public administration, which leads to the emergence of policies. Public policy is, therefore, more 'political' than 'public administration'. As Henry argues,

> Public policy has been an effort to apply political science to public affairs; its inherent sympathies with practical field of public administration are real, and many scholars who identify with the public policy sub-field themselves in a twilight-zone between political science and public administration, pirouetting in the shadows of both disciplines.[76]

While the policy analysts use, as noted earlier, scientific methods with the mathematical focus on policymaking, the political public policy theorists, on the other hand, are more interested with the outcomes of public policy.

---

[75] Allen Putt and J. Fred Springer, *Policy Research: Concepts, Methods and Appreciations* (Englewood Cliffs, NJ: Prentice Hall, 1989), 10.

[76] Nicholas Henry, 'Root and Branch: Public Administration's Travail Towards the Future', in *Public Administration: The State of the Discipline*, eds. Naomi Lynn and Aaron Wildavsky (Chatham, NJ: Chatham House, 1990), 6.

Specialists in public policy issues may not always agree, for they have different scientific assumptions and models to simplify a complex world to provide greater understanding. They also disagree, for they have different value systems about what ought to be to improve society. The complexity of the problems in policy analysis has made the development of public policy theory difficult.

Review Questions

(i) What are the phases of decision-making process identified by Herbert Simon?

(ii) Decision-making is effective when the problem is well structured. Explain the statement with suitable examples.

(iii) What are the major criticisms against Lindblom's incrementalism?

(iv) Discuss Etzioni's mixed-scanning approach to decision-making.

(v) How is Cohen, March and Olsen's 'garbage can' model different from other conventional models of decision-making?

12

RATIONALIST PARADIGM AND PUBLIC CHOICE THEORY

INTRODUCTION

The interplay of numerous forces determines the formation of public policy in a democratic system. From a theoretical point of view, these forces which produce effects called 'policies' represent 'power' and 'rationality'. Policymaking is partly a manifestation of power, and partly a function of administration. Policymaking thus is a combination of 'politics' and 'administration'. It implies exercise of political as well as intellectual activity.

The first, that is 'power', is concerned with explaining how social groups and organizations (e.g. individuals and civil society organizations, political parties, members of the executive and legislature, leaders of organized interests) bring influence to bear on those entitled to take and enforce policy decisions. Such decision- or policymakers include those who hold office within the formal or constitutional system of rules which assigns formal powers to various positions within the governmental structure. Decision-making is also affected by non-official groups who seek to influence the decisions made by those in office. Such roles may be structured to form organized groups, parties and social movements.

The second dimension of policymaking is 'rationality'. In government, there are many large organizations seeking to impose upon policymaking process some of the characteristics of rational activity. Rationality in policymaking may be seen as the administrative component of government. It is within the administrative structure that, for the most part, techniques such as CBA and output budgeting are continually being developed to enhance the capacity of the government for rational policymaking.

This two dimensions of policymaking—(i) politics, involving power and ideology; and (ii) administrative, involving analysis, organization and planning—taken together produce effects (products) called policies.

In this chapter as well as in subsequent chapters, an attempt is made to deal with rational as well as political aspects of the policymaking.

RATIONALITY AND RATIONAL APPROACH

Meaning and Use of Models

With a view to understanding and analysing the complexity of issues involved in public policy, we construct models, maps or think in terms of approaches. These models not only simplify and clarify our thanking about forces shaping public policy but also offer explanations as to its causes and consequences. A model is, thus, an abstraction or representation of some aspects of the real world.

Rational Approach

The idea of 'rationality' has been the key factor in the study of policy- and decision-making in the post–Second World War era. The following two sources are mainly responsible for this rational approach:

(i) The idea of 'economic rationality' as it grew in economic theory.
(ii) The idea of 'bureaucratic rationality', as formulated by sociological theories of organization.

To begin with, rationality, as it has been applied in public policies, has its roots in the construction of 'economic man',[1] which is conceptualized in terms of 'calculating self-interested individual'. The Weberian model (formulated by Max Weber, a German sociologist) of the rational imperative in decision-making constitutes the starting point for the analysis of rationality in public policy. The rationality precept emphasizes that policymaking is making a choice among policy alternatives on rational grounds. Rational policymaking is 'to choose the one best option'.[2]

Robert Haveman observes that a rationality policy is one which is designed to maximize 'net value achievement'.[3] Thomas Dye equates rationality with efficiency. 'A policy is rational when the difference between the values it achieves and the values it sacrifices is positive and greater than any other policy alternative'.[4] He further says that rationalism 'involves the calculation of all social, political, and economic values sacrificed or achieved by a public polity, not just those that can be measured to dollars'.

Modern governments have come increasingly to expect that their administrative organizations and technical and expert bodies will provide the analytical capabilities necessary for the planning of public policies. Rationality is employed in the analysis of government since all organizations concerned directly or indirectly with government—NGOs, parties, legislatures and particularly executive departments—attempt to utilize the resources at their disposal to perform or achieve specific tasks or goals. They may be more or less successful in relating means to ends as their rationality may be limited.

Irrationality, to Sutherland, has become a major fact of public and private decision-making. As such, its results can be disastrous.[5] Irrationality can be caused by (i) the limitations of the capacity of the human brain to handle complexity of issues, (ii) failure to make use of new tools including computers for rational analysis, (iii) distorting reality to fit in with what is comfortable and (iv) lack of knowledge and capability to think.

---

[1] Economic man is driven by reason and rational calculation (in Simon's terms).
[2] Y. Dror, *Public-Making Re-examined* (New York, NY: Intext, 1968), 132–41.
[3] Robert Henry Haveman, *The Economics of the Public Sector* (New York, NY: John Wiley, 1970).
[4] Dye, *Understanding Public Policy*, (2004), 17.
[5] Stuart Sutherland, *Irrationality: The Enemy Within* (Harmondsworth: Penguin Books, 1994).

The muddled (Lindblom) and bounded (Simon) rationality is given up in favour of

(i) methodically assigning relative weights to all social values;
(ii) listing all policy alternatives and their consequences, costs and benefits and
(iii) selecting the most efficient and effective policy to implement.

The rationalist paradigm is concerned with the nature of public goods and services,[6] the relationships between formal decision-making structures and human propensities for action[7] and the broad implications of technological innovation.[8]

REQUIREMENTS AND STAGES FOR RATIONAL ANALYSIS

Rational decision-making model is 'a model of decision-making in which it is assumed that decision-makers have nearly all information about a problem, its causes, and its solutions at their disposal, whereupon a large number of alternatives can be weighted and the best one selected'.[9]

Thomas Dye prescribes certain requirements to policymakers in selecting a rational policy. They must

(i) know all the society's value preferences and their relative weights,
(ii) know all the policy alternatives available,
(iii) know all the consequences at each policy alternative,
(iv) calculate the ratio of benefits to costs for each policy alternative and
(v) select the most efficient policy alternative.[10]

Rational policymaking is a very difficult exercise. It requires capacity to foresee the consequences of alternative policies, and the intelligence to calculate correctly the ratio of costs to benefits.[11]

In a rational decision-making, instead of making an 'ideal' decision as Simon argued, policymakers will break the complexity of problems into small and understandable parts, choose the one option that is best and satisfactory and avoid unnecessary uncertainty.[12] This means that 'although individuals are intensely rational, their rationality is bounded by limited cognitive and emotional capacities'.[13]

---

[6] An example is L.L. Wade and R.L. Curry, *A Logic of Public Policy* (Belmont, CA: Wadsworth, 1970).
[7] An example is Gordon Tullock, *The Politics of Bureaucracy* (Washington: Public Affairs Press, 1965).
[8] An example is Nicholas Henry, 'Copyright, Public Policy, and Information Technology', *Science* 182 (1974): 384–91.
[9] Birkland, *An Introduction to the Policy Process*, 254.
[10] Dye, *Understanding Public Policy*, 17.
[11] Ibid., 16–17.
[12] Simon, *Administrative Behaviour*, (1957).
[13] Lynn, *Managing Public Policy*, 84.

Rational policymaking thus requires making hard choices among policy alternatives. It entails many stages:

(i)   The rationality assumes that the policymaker identifies the underlying problem. He formulates and sets goal priorities. This is necessary because one goal may be more important than another.

(ii) At the second stage, the rational policymaker identifies the range of policy alternatives and options that might attain some of the goals. He prepares a complete set of alternative policies and of resources with weights. The process of identifying policy alternatives is of critical importance as it affects both the range and quality of alternatives.[14]

(iii) The third stage requires the calculation of predictions about the costs and benefits of policy alternatives. The rational policymaker is required to calculate for each policy alternative, both the expectation that it will achieve the goal and also its cost. Here there is a question of calculation of the 'cost–payoff' ratios of each alternative.

(iv) Although simultaneously with calculating net expectation for each alternative, the rational policymaker is required to compare the alternatives with the highest benefits. It is possible that by comparing two alternatives, one may derive twice the benefits at lesser cost.

(v)   Now comes the stage of selecting the most efficient policy alternative. If the rational policymaker has done his work properly, the policy choice should be straightforward.

(vi) Finally, rational policymaking requires a decision-making system that facilitates rationality in the policy process.

An example of a rational approach to a decision system that facilitates rationality in policymaking is shown in Figure 12.1.

Once a select policy decision is implemented, the rational policymaker is required to monitor this implementation systematically to find out the accuracy of the expectations and estimates. If necessary, the policymaker will complete the gap in the policy or give it up altogether. This may be called the feedback stage of rational policymaking. If decision-makers make use of feedback to monitor and adapt policy, the policy system becomes self-correcting or cybernetic.

---

[14] Most alternatives and options can be drawn basically from four types of search processes:

(i)   *Experimental search process*: In the case of new problem, the past policy could serve as a guide to the range of alternatives.

(ii) *Analogical search process*: Analogous problems might have been dealt with in the past on a relatively new issue. For example, if the objective is to prevent and control air pollution, see what policies were used to prevent and control water pollution.

(iii) *Comparative search process*: In similar policy problems, policies of other governments could be adopted. For example, the housing policy of the central government could be adopted by other state governments.

(iv) *Advocacy search process:* Policy options advocated by organized or pressure groups on certain problems may be adopted.

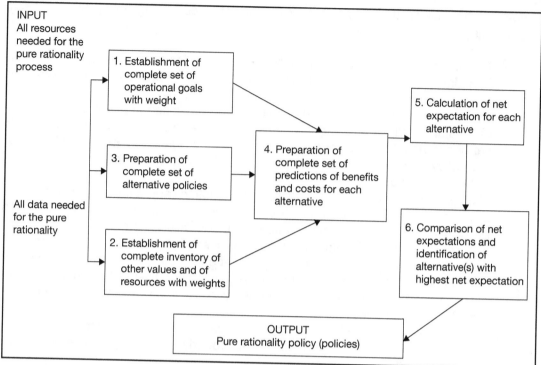

Figure 12.1: A Rational Model of a Decision System
Source: Adapted from Thomas Dye (2004).

A rational policy that achieves maximum social gain is espoused to such an extent that many types of rational decision models are to be found in the literature of social sciences.[15]

BUILDING BLOCKS OF RATIONAL CHOICE

Rational choice theory is a family of theories rather than a single theory[16] that has challenged orthodox accounts across a range of different contexts. It is best characterized as an approach to understanding the dynamics of public policy. A set of common building blocks that provide the foundations for the rationalist approaches is briefly discussed in this section.

Assumptions of Individuals as Rational Actors

One of the assumptions of rationality is that individuals in the policy process are rational. Rational individuals are characterized as instrumental actors pursuing courses of action 'not for their own sake, but only insofar they secure desired typically private ends'.[17] In

[15] See L.L. Wade and R.L. Curry, *A Logic of Public Policy: Aspects of Political Economy* (Belmont, CA: Wadsworth, 1970).
[16] D.P. Green and I. Shapiro, *Pathologies of Rational Choice Theory* (New Haven, CT: Yale University Press, 1994), 28.
[17] D. Chong, 'Rational choice theory's mysterious rivals', in *The Rational Choice Controversy*, ed. J. Friedman (New Haven, CT: Yale University Press, 1996), 39.

this sense, rational individuals are those actors who choose the feasible course of action or policy option which is most likely to maximize their own utility. Rationality thus emerges from an actor's capacity to calculate costs and benefits to available policy options, and to select the course of action that best maximizes his own utility.[18] Policy actors are constructed as egotistical, self-regarding instrumental actors, 'choosing how to act on the basis of the consequences for their personal welfare (or that of their immediate family)'.[19] As such, mainstream rational choice lends itself towards explanations of policy outcomes grounded in the goal-oriented action of individuals,[20] where the desires, beliefs and preferences of individual actors are identified as the causes of their actions.[21] Of course, rational utility-maximizing individual will and do deliver collectively unintentional outcomes or socially irrational outcomes[22] as the 'tragedy of the commons demonstrates'.[23] The point is that such rational behaviour by instrumental actors may not necessarily produce positive collective outcomes.

Rank-ordering of Preferences

Second, if the assumption of rationality is to hold, individual rational actors must possess preferences that are ranked-ordered and consistent in that they are both transitive and stable over time. This means that individuals are able to establish a hierarchy of preferences and a particular consistency of preferences that (preferences) are taken to be both stable over time and to be given.

Premises of Methodological Individualism

Rational choice builds its explanations of policy outcomes on the actions of individual actors who constitute social structures. Social structures are thereby conceptualized through the intentional behaviour of individual actors. Structures give rise to institutions which become 'instrumental products used by individuals to maximize their respective utilities'.[24] As such, rational choice stresses the production of causal mechanisms, underplayed in structural and functionalist explanations.[25] For, as Laver argues, 'the primitive motivational assumptions' of rational choice 'relate to the individual as a self-contained unit of analysis'.[26]

---

[18] P. Dunleavy, *Democracy, Bureaucracy and Public Choice: Economic Explanations in Political Science* (Hemel Hempstead: Harvester Wheatsheaf, 1991), 3.

[19] Ibid., 3.

[20] P.K. MacDonald, 'Useful Fiction or Miracle Maker: The Competing Epistemological Foundations of Rational Choice Theory', *American Journal of Political Science* 97 (2003): 552.

[21] Green and Shapiro, *Pathologies of Rational Choice Theory,* 20.

[22] M. Levi, 'A Model, A Method, and a Map: Rational Choice in Comparative and Historical Analysis', in *Comparative Politics: Rationality, Culture and Structure,* eds. M.I. Lichbach and A.S. Zuckermann (Cambridge: Cambridge University Press, 2003), 20.

[23] G. Hardin, 'The Tragedy of the Commons', *Science* 162 (1969) 958–62.

[24] M. Blyth, *Great Transformations: Economic Ideas and Institutional Change in the Twentieth Century* (Cambridge: Cambridge University Press, 2002), 19.

[25] Chong, 'Rational Choice Theory's Mysterious Rivals', 42–43.

[26] M. Laver, *Private Desires, Political Action: An Invitation to the Politics of Rational Choice* (London: SAGE Publications, 1997), 9.

Deductive Reasoning

Most approaches to policy analysis, Laver argues, simply extrapolate generalized propositions about political behaviour from 'systematic observations of what real people actually do', which 'in the last analysis more or less says that the world is as it is because that's how it is'.[27] Laver argues, however, that the very value of deductive reasoning in rational choice accounts lies in the fact that the explanation of political outcomes derives from motivational assumptions defined in another realm, that of the individual.

In sum, building blocks of mainstream rational choice theory offer is a 'convenient shortcut which makes possible a naturalist science of the political such as is capable of generating through a process of deduction, testable and predictive hypotheses'.[28] The complexity of both individual motivations and the decision-making process is thus necessarily mobilized out of rational choice accounts in the quest for universal explanation of the public policy.

LIMITATIONS OF RATIONAL CHOICE

When considering in purely abstract terms, few would deny the need for rationality in policymaking. Yet practically, there are many obstacles to the realization of the degree of rationality. Analysis of rationality in public policy is a difficult exercise. It suffers from many constraints.[29] Simon says, 'It is impossible for the behaviour of a single, isolated individual to reach any high degree of rationality'.[30] The concept of rationality is bandied about so much and so indiscriminately that it threatens to lose its meaning. It is more widely espoused than practised. The reason why the ideal rational model is a *straw man* as its several features render it an unrealistic model of decision-making. Some of the constraints to rational policy decision-making are briefly discussed here.

Difficulty in Specification of Goals

First, the clear specification of objectives required by pure rationality is very, very difficult in politics where goals are determined by the interaction of many different political structures. There is the problem of goal consensus. Often, rational policymaking is a very difficult exercise. The expectation that a rational policy will emerge is small. By the time the policymaker recommends a rational policy, the problem in question has become so complex that rational prescriptions become decisions which are made on the basis of societal goals. Instead, they try to maximize their own rewards, such as power, status, money and re-election. Therefore, making for more rational policy is more an exercise than a goal.

Moreover, objectives are difficult to define and even more difficult to pursue when more than one administrative agency is involved. For example, sharing of functions between the central and state government probably produces the problem of expenditure and control.

---

[27] Ibid., 10.
[28] C. Hay, 'Theory, Stylized Heuristic or Self-fulfilling Prophecy? The Status of Rational Choice Theory in Public Administration', *Public Administration* 82 (2004): 40.
[29] See Braybrooke and Lindblom, *A Strategy of Decision*; Dye, *Understanding Public Policy*.
[30] Simon, *Administrative Behaviour*, 79.

Difficulty in Securing Optimization

A rational policy is expected to produce optimal results. But in reality, it does not always do so. The public interest is taken to be more important than being merely the sum of individual interests in the polity. If air pollution control is a public interest because all share in its benefit, then the strategy might be to require every automobile sold to be fitted with an expensive set of anti-pollution emission control devices, making its cost more. Yet, few citizens are willing to pay more of their own money to reduce automobile emissions. If there are 'public goods', it stands to reason that there are 'public bads'.[31] If pollution control is a public good, then pollution is itself a public bad. A public bad, in fact, too often, results from the individual's rational perspective that 'everybody's doing it and my little bit won't really matter much'. Thus, the motivation for policymakers to try to maximize net goal–achievement is missing. They merely try to satisfy certain demands for progress. They do not strive to search until they find an alternative that will work. To even approach explanation requires some initial understanding.

Barrier to Rational Decision-making

Green and Shapiro condemn rational choice because in rational choice accounts, 'evidence is projected from theory rather than gathered independently from it'.[32] As already stated, policymakers are not motivated to make decision on the basis of societal goals, but try instead to maximize their own rewards, such as power, status and money. Second, the time for a thorough analysis of impending legislation may be short. In an emergency situation, action is sought immediately. But the time is too short for careful analysis. In routine policymaking also, the sheer number of potential issues limits the time available to analyse any one issue carefully.

It is also very difficult for the decision-maker to set out all policy choices and alternatives with the probabilities of their consequent outputs. Choices are also often arbitrary. This is because the decision-maker's information about his environment is at best on approximation to the real environment. A reason is that in large government departments, the search for solutions to problems is inevitably fragmented. In addition, individual values may not coincide with organizational values and goals. There is also no consensus on the societal values themselves. The many conflicting values prevailing among specific groups and individuals make it for the rational policymaker difficult to compare and weigh them.

Dilemma of Political Feasibility

Politicians usually are faced with the problem of searching a feasible policy. The dilemma of political feasibility concerns itself with what is possible. By political feasibility is meant 'the probability that, however rational and desirable, a policy option would actually be adopted and implemented by the political system'.[33] For example, Patton and Sawicki argue,

---

[31] James Buchanan, 'Public Goods and Public Bads', in *Financing the Metropolis*, ed. John P. Crecine (Beverly Hills, CA: SAGE Publications, 1970), chap. 1.
[32] Green and Shapiro, *Pathologies of Rational Choice Theory*, 42.
[33] See Ralph Huitt, 'Political Feasibility', in *Political Science and Public Policy*, ed. Austin Ranney (Chicago, IL: Markham, 1968), 263–75.

If the rational model were to be followed, many rational decisions would have to be compromised because they were not politically feasible. A rational logical, and technically desirable policy may not be adopted because the political system will not accept it. The figures don't always speak for themselves, and good ideas do not always win out. Analysts and decision-makers are constantly faced with the conflict between technically superior and politically feasible alternatives.[34]

Politicians too often resolve the dilemma of political feasibility by avoidance of conflict. Uncertainty about the consequences of different policy alternatives may force politicians to stick to previous policies. Elected officials do not want to sacrifice their chance of re-election at the cost of rationality, especially respecting the voice of the people. Moreover, the design of public policy is heavily influenced by the past decisions and policies. Postponement of the decision, appointment of the commissions and setting up of group studies are common means of reducing the likelihood of conflicts. For example, citing several representations against the measure from individuals and organizations, the GOI (Law Ministry) has put on back burner the Hindu Marriage Laws (Amendment) Bill to make marriage laws more women-friendly and allow both parties to file for divorce on the ground of 'irretrievable breakdown' of marriage.[35]

Securing the necessary cooperation in the setting of interrelated objectives and for monitoring of progress will be a difficult task.

Difficulty in Comparing Conflicting Benefits and Costs

It is difficult for the policymakers to calculate the cost–benefit ratios accurately when many diverse social, economic, political and cultural values are at stake. For example, it is not possible to determine how much of the expenditure incurred in restoring a person to health by hospital care contributes to the social objectives of minimizing pain and disability. Apart from these, policymakers have personal needs, inhibitions and inadequacies which render them incapable of making rational decisions.

Rational policymaking requires making hard choices among policy alternatives. But there are several constraints to gathering the amount of information required to be aware of all possible policy alternatives and the consequences of each alternative, including the time and cost involved in the information gathering. This point places limitations on rational choice theory and its responses to its internal and external challenges.

Bureaucratic Problems

Another important obstacle to rational policymaking is the environment of the bureaucracies. Dye observes, 'The segmentalized nature of policymaking in large bureaucracies makes it difficult to coordinate decision-making so that the input of all the various specialists is brought to bear at the point of decision'.[36] Fragmentation of authority, satisfying goals, conflicting values, limited technology, uncertainty about the possible

---

[34] Carl V. Patton and David S. Sawicki, *Basic Methods of Policy Analysis and Planning* (Englewood Cliffs, NJ: Prentice Hall, 1986), 25.

[35] See *The Tribune* (Chandigarh), 13 July 2015.

[36] Dye, *Understanding Public Policy*, 19.

policy alternatives, and consequences thereof, and other factors limit the capacity of bureaucracies and other public organizations to make rational policies.

Some policy analysts warn against placing too much reliance on the rational model. Following the rational model of analysis of facts, setting out alternatives, and choosing the alternative with the highest utility weight, would often be undemocratic. Denhardt argues that policy analysts typically apply technical solutions to the immediate problems and 'under such circumstances, technical concerns would displace political and ethical concerns as the basis for public decision-making, thereby transforming normative issues into technical problems'.[37]

For example, the National Green Tribunal (NGT) asked the Himachal government to explain within a week as to why the NGT should not order the arrest of top officers and attachment of treasury funds for ensuring compliance of its directions issued in its 6 February 2014 judgement. On 7 July 2015, the NGT banned all commercial activities, including horse riding, snow-biking and paragliding at Rohtang, Solang and Marhi.[38]

What does this mean for the limits of rational choice? 'The central problem of democratic administrative theory', Waldo argues, 'is how to reconcile the desire for democracy with the demands of authority'.[39]

Conclusion

Rational choice theory is best characterized as an approach to understanding the dynamics of public policy. However, observations of rational policymaking in government confirm that it is a very difficult exercise. Some decision-making theorists, and perhaps most decision-makers, believe that rational policymaking is impossible. Yet this model remains of critical importance for analytic purposes as it helps to identify the constraints to rationality. Indeed, rational choice theory has itself become at the very least the dominant yardstick against which to assess explanations of the policy process.

In his article, Simon argued that policymakers do not really 'optimize', but rather 'satisfy'. To him a 'good' decision will do even if it is not the best decision.[40] A rational decision depends on having clear and well-defined goals as well as sufficient authority to coordinate action. The more sharply goals can be defined and the more authority can be concentrated on achieving them, the more rational can the decision be made.

Private organizations are a profit-maximizing system compared with public organizations, that are never seen operating with a single-minded goal. Public organizations with scare resources should clarify goals, devise efficient means of reaching them, assess performance and discover the costs of different programmes. However, observations of policymaking in government confirm what has been experienced in all organizations:

---

[37] Robert Denhardt, 'Toward a Critical Theory of Public Organization', *Public Administration Review* 41(6) (1981): 631.

[38] See *The Tribune* (Chandigarh), 8 July 2015.

[39] D. Waldo, 'Development of Theory of Democratic Administration', *American Political Science Review* 46(4) (1952): 102.

[40] Herbert Simon, 'A Behavioral Model of Rational Choice', *Quarterly Journal of Economics* 69 (1955): 99–118.

that considerable modifications of the rationality model are called for while maintaining it as an ideal. Rationality has some positive purposes. It is somewhat like democracy. In this context, Lineberry says, 'But as democracy is the measuring rod of virtue in a political system, so, too, is rationality supposedly the yardstick of wisdom in policy-making'.[41] Therefore, it is important to keep rationality in mind as, at least, a goal, if not the realistic end.

PUBLIC CHOICE THEORY

Introduction

Public choice theory which evolved from the older normative theory of public finances is identical to the consumer theory of demand for a private good. Public choice theory has its base in the rational choice theory. It is oriented towards the understanding of the realm of public choice, that is, politics and bureaucracy. Most of the contributions under the rubric of public choice theory have the effect of making the science more effective in describing and prescribing changes in public decision-making in accord with individualistic, utilitarian form of rationality. D. Mueller defines the public choice approach in the following terms:

> Public choice can be defined as the economics of non-market decision-making, or simply the application of economics to political science. The subject-matter of public choice is the same as that of political science: the theory of the state, voting rules, voter behaviour, party politics, the bureaucracy, and so on. The methodology of public choice is that of economics, however.[42]

The origins of this approach may be found in the works of Gordon Tullock,[43] Anthony Downs[44] and William Niskanen.[45] The microeconomic approach attempts to show that our collective decision—making mechanisms are, in main, flawed, so that neither markets nor politics on their own serve us adequately. Markets are often imperfects and inequitable because they monopolize power, public goods and information. Government failures also do happen. Self-interested bureaucratic actors encourage agents within government to maximize their budgets and citizens form clubs to collectively provide some forms of public goods.[46] Also democratic decision-making, according to reasonable criteria, can become arbitrary and unstable.[47]

The intent of the public choice theory of policy formulation is to reject any such traditional idea of policy as the search for the public welfare. Like private entrepreneurs, politicians in their supply of public policy are guided by private concerns to the same extent as

---

[41] Lineberry, *American Public Policy*, 27.

[42] D. Mueller, *Public Choice* (Cambridge: Cambridge University Press, 1979), 1.

[43] G. Tullock, *The Politics of Bureaucracy* (Washington: Public Affairs Press, 1965).

[44] A. Downs, *Inside Bureaucracy* (Boston, MA: Little, Brown, 1967).

[45] William Niskanen, *Bureaucracy and Representative Government* (Chicago, IL: Aldine-Atherton, 1971).

[46] J. Buchanan, 'An Economic Theory of Clubs', *Econometrica* 32 (1965): 1–14.

[47] K.J. Arrow, *Social Choice and Individual Values* (New York, NY: John Wiley, 1951).

the private profits maximizer.[48] A maximization of politician's objectives results in the selection of those policies that minimize policy distance between citizen's expectations and those supplied by the government.[49] Thus, public choice theory assumes that all political actors—voters, candidates, legislators, bureaucrats, interest groups, parties and governments, seek to maximize their personal benefits in politics as well as in the marketplace.

CONTRIBUTIONS TO PUBLIC CHOICE THEORY

The microeconomic approach has led to a variety of contributions under the heading of public choice theory that show how individual interests influence both marketplace and public policy decisions.

Buchanan's Contribution to Public Choice Theory

James Buchanan, a Nobel Prize winning economist and a leading scholar in public choice theory, argues that individuals come together in politics for their own mutual benefit, just as they come together in the marketplace. And by mutual agreement among themselves, they can promote their own well-being, in the same way as by trading in the market-place.[50] Buchanan expresses his views:

> As the case with efficiency, persons are not likely to express interests in abstract distributional ideals for the society in general when in political decisions. They are likely, instead, to seek to further their own well-defined interests.[51]

In Buchanan's view, there are two normative rules which are constitutive of the public choice approach: (i) politics as exchange and (ii) economic constitutionalism or con-tractarianism as the basis of public policymaking. The first normative rule means that every public policy must be based on the consent of all citizens. To quote Buchanan, 'In the absence of individual interest, there is no interest'. The second normative principle means that 'existing constitutions or structures or rules are the subject of critical scrutiny'.

Buchanan also expresses the same views, 'As the case with efficiency, persons are not likely to express interests in abstract distributional ideals for the society in general when in political decisions. They are likely, instead, to seek to further their own well-defined interests'.[52] Thus, according to Buchanan, individuals come together in the politics for their own mutual benefit.

---

[48] A. Breton, *The Economic Theory of Representative Government* (London: Macmillan, 1974).
[49] A function consisting of the probability of re-election and private variables such as power, income, prestige and political ideals is maximized.
[50] Wayne James M. Buchanan and Gordon Tullock, *The Calculus of Consent* (Ann Arbor, MI: University of Michigan Press, 1962).
[51] James M. Buchanan, 'Market Failure and Political Failure', *Cato Journal* 8(1) (1988): 11.
[52] Ibid., 11.

Downs's Views on Public Choice Theory

Downs has also made an important contribution to the study of bureaucratic behaviour.[53] Downs provide a model which shows how bureaucratic growth takes place as a result of laws and how the motivations of officials and bureaux vary in the way in which they set about maximizing their interests. His model recognizes competition between government and opposition in which opposition reminds the citizens or voters about the size of the policy distance. Government itself arises from a social contract among people who agree for their mutual benefit to obey laws and support the government in return for protection of their own lives, liberty and property.

In common with Buchanan's views, Downs argues that the intent of the politicians is to maximize the likelihood of winning elections. In the political business cycle model, it predicts that the politicians in government will attempt to manipulate and stimulate the economy before an election and deflate the economy after the election. Often the government spending on programmes would be huge that are highly attractive and visible to the people before an election, only to impose more taxes or bring down deficits after the election. Such opportunistic behaviour, if effective, is favourable to a cycle in the economy running over election in contrast to true depressions. The political business cycle predicts that 'left-wing governments will especially try to reduce unemployment whereas right-wing governments will focus on reducing inflation'.

Downs in his book *Inside Bureaucracy* assumes that decision-making in bureaucracies is informed by the pursuit of self-interest. Downs argues that the motivations of individual officials are diverse such as power, money, income, prestige, personality, loyalty and security, and give rise to five kinds of bureaucrat:

> (i) Climbers: concerned with their power, income and prestige; (ii) Conservers: concerned with minimizing change; (iii) Zealots: highly motivated officials committed to push for a policy or programme; (iv) Advocates: who see their interests in terms of maximizing the role and resources for their bureau; (v) Statesmen: who have a sense of the public interest which may be advanced by increasing their power so as to realize their goals.

Downs claims, as there are different kinds of bureaucrat, there are also different kinds of bureaux whose aim is always to maximize self-interest by growing bigger. And this increase in bureaucracy size leads to a condition of bureaucratic life in which conflict is the norm.[54] Hence, bureaucracy requires strong supervision and control.

Niskanen's Prescriptions to Check Bureaucratic Evils

William Niskanen sets out to provide a model with the same assumption of self-interest maximization. Niskanen in his book *Bureaucracy and Representative Government* also argues that those who work in bureaucracies or bureaux seek to maximize their budgets

---

[53] Downs, *Inside Bureaucracy* 1.
[54] Ibid.

and the size of the bureau. He contends that it is only by increasing the budget that they can maximize their self-interest. Budgetary and bureau growth are in Niskanen's model regarded as the only ways in which bureaucrats can maximize their benefits. This is possible due to the way in which bureaux allocate resources and make decisions such as markets which make decisions by maximizing the difference between marginal utility and marginal cost. However, the bureau, unlike the firm, does not know what the benefits are, and thus can only increase the marginal utility by increasing the size of the bureau's budget. This can be done through politicians who are themselves pressured to make promises to enhance spending.

To limit the evils and discretion of bureaucrats, Niskanen prescribed certain checks which are as follows:

(i) Stricter control on the bureaucrats through legislature and executive interventions;
(ii) Increase in competition in the delivery of public services;
(iii) Privatization or contracting-out to reduce wastage; and
(iv) Dissemination of information about the availability of alternatives to public services.

Niskanen's critical remarks against bureaucratic monopoly have perhaps had more influence on public administration than any other idea drawn from the public choice literature.[55] Although economists and political scientists have recognized the decisive role played by individually motivated agents in the determination of bureaucratic outcomes, most, however, question Niskanen's assumption that bureaucrats are revenue maximizers.[56] It is now observed that newer models of bureaucratic behaviour have been developed that stress the informational endowments of bureaucrats, the implicit and explicit contracts that link their actions to rewards and their discretionary roles.[57]

Moe's Views on Public Choice Theory

Terry Moe also argues that political authorities, specially legislators, tend to favour administrative controls that are ineffective by design. Moe claims that legislators eschew serious policy control and instead seek particularized control because they 'want to be able to intervene quickly, inexpensively, and in *ad hoc* ways to protect or advance the interests of particular clients in particular matters'.[58]

Consequently, detailed rules that impose rigid limits on an agency's discretion and its procedures are needed.

---

[55] R. Miranda, 'Privatization and the Budget-maximizing Bureaucrat', *Public Product Management Review* 17 (1994): 17–34.
[56] A. Blais and S. Dion, eds., *The Budget-Maximizing Bureaucrat: The Empirical Evidence* (Pittsburgh, PA: University of Pittsburgh, 1991).
[57] J.J. Laffont and J. Tirole, *A Theory of Incentives in Procurement and Regulation* (Cambridge, MA: MIT Press, 1993).
[58] Terry M. Moe, 'The Politics of Structural Choice', in *Organization Theory*, ed. O.E. Williamson (New York, NY: Oxford University Press, 1990), 140.

Tullock's Approach to Public Choice Theory

Gordon Tullock's work is considered to be among the earliest contributions to the public choice approach. Tullock was perhaps also the first scholar to think about the consequences of rent-seeking. His stricture against self-serving nature of bureaucracy and his critique with Buchanan of party competition and its consequences may be said to have laid the basis for a debate on the dangers of the power of bureaucracy and the politicization of the public policy.[59] For him, the study of politics, policy planning and bureaucracy should be based on the same assumptions which might be used to explain the behaviour of firms, businesspeople and consumers. From this could emerge the following set of generalizations:

   (i) Political parties contesting elections make excessive promises to get votes.
   (ii) Politicians in power maximize the likelihood of winning elections through manipulating economy.
   (iii) The power of bureaucracy has increased by serving itself rather than the public interest.
   (iv) The political processes of liberal democracy are failing to supervise and control the growth of political and bureaucratic power.

Advocates of public choice model explain why political parties and candidates (seeking election) generally fail to offer clear policy alternatives in election campaigns. Parties and candidates are not interested in advancing policies but rather in winning elections. Thus, each party and candidate seek policy positions that will attract maximum votes.

These conclusions led to the introduction of market forces to control political and bureaucratic power. Tullock, in common with other advocates of public choice theories, recommended the introduction of competition into bureaucracy through contracting-out, privatization and increasing competition between government departments by rewarding performance.[60]

IMPLICATIONS AND CRITICISMS OF PUBLIC CHOICE THEORY

Public choice theory has changed the way people think about government and its bureaucracy. Its advocates are often cynical about politics and pessimistic about the workings of government. But the theory has influenced the design of a variety of institutional arrangements. The central issue in public choice is how to make the state more democratic and citizen-friendly. Public choice theory recognizes that government must do certain functions which the market cannot manage. In other words, the government must remedy certain market failures. First, the government must provide goods and services to the public which are of utmost importance. The most common example is the national defence, which is too expensive for a single person (or for that matter market) to buy.

---

[59] Wayne Parsons, *Public Policy* (Cheltenham, UK: Edward Elgar, 1995), 307.
[60] Tullock published his recommendations in the pamphlet for a think tank—*The Institute for Economic Affairs* (London: IEA, 1976).

Public choice theory recognizes justification of government intervention in 'externalities'. An externality or 'spillover effect' is the impact of a public policy in one sphere into other spheres. For example, the NGT on 7 July 2015 ordered the banning of all commercial activities, including horse bidding, snow-biking and paragliding at the Rohtang Pass in Himachal Pradesh to check environmental degradation and melting of the glaciers which were receding at the rate of 20 metres a year since 1986.[61]

Public choice theory also helps us to understand the behaviour of interest groups in dramatizing and publicizing their cause. Leaders of interest group must compete for members and money by exaggerating the dangers to society of overlooking their demands. Even if the government meets their old demands, leaders of the interest groups must generate new demands with new warnings of danger if they are to remain as leaders. In brief, interest groups, such as other political parties and candidates, seek to further their self-interest in the political marketplace.

Despite its popularity and recognition as an alternative to public services, the public choice theory is deficient in its conceptualization of human decision-making, as being essentially driven by individual as a self-interested maximizer.[62] The self-interest cannot be the major motivating factor in decision-making. Whereas the exponents of neoclassical economics hold that markets are the best decision-making mechanisms, Galbraith maintains that the real world of capitalism is shaped by the management decisions of big corporations and big producers, rather than by the interplay of producers and consumers. While producers manipulate demands of consumers, the large corporations manipulate the decisions of politicians and bureaucrats. For example, illegal allocation of a coal block to Kumar Mangalam Birla in 2005 by the former PM Manmohan Singh, as alleged by the Central Bureau of Investigation (CBI) on 12 March 2015, has, no doubt, damaged the credibility of the Congress government.[63]

The view that bureaucratic decision-making is prompted by the pursuit of self-interest which can only find expression in increased budgets and bigger bureaux needs empirical support. Moreover, we know little about the personnel's utility who work in bureaux in contrast to those who work in profit-maximizing firms. In Downs's model, the range of motivations is far more complex and diverse than self-interest of the kind which Niskanen advances that self-interest is a motivating factor towards budget-maximization and bigger bureaux, yet an explanation for this motivation is far from being adequate, as Lewin notes that the 'budget-maximization hypothesis is not sustained by empirical research'.[64]

It is pertinent to observe here that the models of Tullock, Downs and Niskanen were largely advanced in a period when the bureaucracy was on the march. However in the 1980s and 1990s, the experience in many developed and developing countries has been to question the idea that there is a realm of non-market decision-making. The empirical research which emerged in the 1980s pointed out that public choice models of bureaucracy are badly flawed. The experience of the 1990s and later years in many developed and developing countries was however that of a reduction in the number of civil servants

---

[61] See *The Tribune* (Chandigarh), 8 July 2015.

[62] J.K. Galbraith, *The New Industrial State* (Harmondsworth: Penguin, 1969).

[63] See *The Times of India* (New Delhi), 'Editorial', 12 March 2015.

[64] Ibid., 97.

and the introduction of markets to carry out those activities earlier assumed to be the domain of bureaucracy. In this context, Dunleavy, a leading critic of the school, argues

> Bureaucrats typically do not embark on collective action modes of improving their welfare unless they have exhausted individual welfare-boosting strategies.... Higher-ranking officials ... have much less to gain from increments and confront substantial advocacy costs in seeking to push through increases in the agency's base budget.... There are major differences between the agency types in the extent to which officials associate their welfare with the growth of the program budget.[65]

Dunleavy advances a bureau-shaping model (employing a public choice approach) which shows how self-interest works to very different outcomes than the bureaucratic decision-making models of Downs and Niskanen. Dunleavy's critique of the public choice model is based on the analysis of the privatization boom of the 1980s.[66] Dunleavy shows how privatization has served to promote the class interests of higher-ranking officials at the cost of job losses and bad conditions for the rank and file. Contracting-out and other forms of privatization, Dunleavy argues, are the continuation of the strategy of bureau-cratic elites to maximize their own interests by shaping their departments and budgets, rather than pursuing bigness. Thus, the bureau-shaping model advanced by Dunleavy appears to have a far better fit with the experience of bureaucracy in the contemporary society.

Jan-Erik Lane, an exponent of public sector approach, argues,

> It should be pointed out that there is one well-known public choice model that under-lines the preferences or interests of citizens: the vote popularity model. It predicts that the popularity of a government depends on how the voters perceive the economy, in particular their reaction to the rate of inflation and the level of unemployment.[67]

There is also a forceful argument that public choice model scores low on moral attrac-tiveness as public policy is modified as only rent-seeking behaviour from special interest groups.[68] The model has an orientation towards market values. It is also critical of the state and social welfare spending simply because it favours market forces for 'ideologically right-wing reasons'. This criticism is a serious one in the context of developing economies which adopted development planning as a policy instrument for the promotion of social and economic development. The role of public sector has not yet receded. Government itself arises from a social contract among individuals who agree for their mutual benefit to obey laws and support the government in exchange for protection of their lives.

---

[65] P. Dunleavy, *Democracy, Bureaucracy and Public Choice: Economic Explanations in Political Science* (Hemel Hempstead: Harvester Wheatsheaf, 1991), 208.

[66] P. Dunleavy, 'Explaining the Privatization Boom: Public Choice Versus Radical Approaches', *Public Administration* 64 (1986): 13–34.

[67] Jan-Erik Lane, *The Public Sector*, 75.

[68] J.M. Buchanan et al., *Toward a Theory of the Rent-Seeking Society* (College Station, TX: Texas University Press, 1980).

Downs himself explains why bureaucracy is 'here to stay' because there are a large number of social functions that 'must be performed by non-market-oriented organizations'.[69] This does not mean that they will be performed in an optimal fashion, but, Downs argues, that there will remain services and functions for which a hierarchy-type organization is necessary.[70]

CONCLUSION

Notions of public interest and the welfare state have been rejected by the public choice writers, yet it is not always true. The ideals of communitarianism and people's welfare have continued to gain acceptance in the society. The new economics of organization, Thompson writes,

> provides the new public management with the beginnings of the analytical foundation needed to understand how, when, and where to delegate authority, replace rules and regulations with incentives, develop budgets based upon results, expose operations to competition, search for market rather than administrative solutions, or use quasi-markets and contracting out to foster competition.[71]

In essence, application of rationality in public decision-making is a desire, but universally, it lacks acceptance. Rationality in policymaking will be of no importance to partisans and demagogues, and any effort to improve the basis of public decisions on scientific norms is unlikely to win their favour. But a procedural dimension, such as public participation, that improves the notion of rationality by bringing in communicative and legitimacy concerns, can be added to the basis of policy decision.

Review Questions

(i) What are the essential stages in rational policymaking?
(ii) Discuss how dilemma of political feasibility is a limitation of rational choice in policy formulation.
(iii) What are the principal postulations of public choice theory?
(iv) Briefly discuss James Buchanan's take on public choice theory.
(v) Elaborate on the major criticisms posed against public choice theory.

---

[69] Downs, *Inside Bureaucracy*, 32.
[70] Peter Self, *Political Theories of Modern Government* (London: George Allen & Unwin, 1985).
[71] Fred Thompson, 'The Political Economy of Public Administration', in *Handbook of Public Administration*, 3rd ed., eds. Jack Rabin, W.B. Hildreth and G.J. Miller (Boca Raton, FL: Taylor and Francis, 2007), 1073.

13

DECISION-MAKING
Styles, Process and Non-decision-making

INTRODUCTION

The importance of 'decision-making' in the policy cycle—formulation, implementation and evaluation—cannot be overstated. At each of these points of the policy cycle, decision-making is taking place. In fact, 'the task of 'deciding' pervades the entire administrative organisation'.[1] To Simon, 'decision-making processes hold the key to understanding organizations'. Some of these decisions involve the allocation of values (preferred choice) and the distribution of resources by the formulation of a policy, or through the ongoing conduct of a policy programme (say, Clean India Mission). Decision-making thus takes place in different arenas and at a variety of levels. Further, non-decision-making (to keep issues off the agenda) is no less important.[2]

In the complex field of service delivery and policy programmes, public administrators are often placed in the position of having to make a variety of decisions, ranging from routine situations to non-routine and unstructured situations. Making good decisions is something that every administrator endeavours, because the overall quality of administrative or managerial decisions goes a long way in determining the organization's success or failure. In this context, McCamy says, 'The reaching of a decision is the core of administration, all the other attributes of the administrative process being depending on, interwoven with and existent for the making of decisions'.[3]

Historically, as an analytical construct, decision-making emerged in the post–Second World War period as part of the policymaking and behavioural approaches to public administration. Its most influential proponents were Herbert Simon and Charles Lindblom, whose theoretical contributions to the field have been well recognized. They were concerned with the process of policy decision-making.

What Is Decision-making?

In simple words, decision-making is choosing one course of action among other competing courses of action. Decision-making is an analytical process (in a policy analysis context), and not just a simple exercise of choosing one alternative from two or more

---

[1] Simon, *Administrative Behaviour*, 1.
[2] P.S. Bachrach and M.S. Baratz, 'Decisions and Non-decisions: An Analytical Framework', *American Political Science Review* 57 (1963): 641–51.
[3] J. McCamy, 'Analysis of the Process of Decision Making', *Public Administration Review* 7 (1947): 41.

possible alternatives.[4] Decision is the outcome of judging any particular situation. Justice and Miller define 'decision' as 'a complex of some combination of one or more judgments and one or more choices'.[5] While judgement involves some understanding of situations, probabilities, causes and consequences, choice activity involves the selection of appropriate courses of action. Justice and Miller are of the view that decision-making can result in the most desired (best) ends with the use of instrumental logics. But it is significantly complicated by the twin challenges of 'uncertainty' about the probabilities of events and consequences and 'ambiguity' concerning causes, effects and preferences. While uncertainty can be reduced through the systematic collection of information about reality, ambiguity undermines the foundations of rational judgement and choice and points to the employment of practical reasoning and logics of appropriateness.[6]

Justice and Miller classify decision-making broadly into judgement and choice activities. For them, administrative and policy decisions by their nature involve all four elements (judgement, choice, uncertainty and ambiguity), because they involve evaluations of the desirability of actual and imagined states of the world as well as assessments of the actual characteristics of the world and the causes of alternative states. Thus, administrative and policy decisions are also subject elements of both uncertainty and ambiguity.

Here it would be useful to make a distinction between what constitutes policymaking and what decision-making is. Vickers makes a distinction between policymaking and executive decisions, 'the first being designed to give direction, coherence and continuity to the courses of action for which the decision-making body is responsible, the second designed to give effect to the policies thus laid down'.[7] Policymaking involves decision-making, but every decision is not a policy decision. Generally, administrators take decisions in their day-to-day work within the existing framework of policy. Policy decisions thus provide a sense of direction to the courses of administrative action.

DECISION TYPES

The fact that public administrators (public managers) are increasingly involved in decision-making does not mean that every decision is long, clearly evident or rational. Much of a public administrator's decision-making activity is routine. It offers few problems and can be managed quickly. But there are problems for which decisions are not available. In a decision-making situation, decision analysis is important.

'Decision analysis' is concerned with the use of information and knowledge of the decision process. It aims to provide explanations as to how a decision should be made. Decision analysis therefore requires that we understand the way in which facts and values interact, and the way in which ideas, interests (values) on the one hand interplay with

---

[4] George Terry, *Principles of Management* (Homewood, IL: Irwin, 1953), 52.
[5] Jonathan B. Justice and Gerald J. Miller, 'Decision Making, Institutions, Elite Control, and Responsiveness in Public Administration History', in *Handbook of Public Administration*, 3rd ed., eds. Jack Rabin et al. (Boca Raton, FL: Taylor & Francis, 2007), 253.
[6] W.R. Scott, *Institutions and Organizations* (Thousand Oaks, CA: SAGE Publications, 1995).
[7] Sir (Charles) Geoffrey Vickers, *The Art of Judgment: A Study of Policymaking*, 2nd ed. (London: Chapman and Hall, 1983).

information and reality (facts) on the other hand. Depending upon the type of problem a public manager faces in a decision-making situation, it is possible to categorize the type of decisions. Simon categorizes decision types into 'programmed' (routine decisions) and 'ill-structured' (non-routine decisions).[8]

Programmed Decisions

Programmed decision-making is relatively simple and tends to rely heavily on previous solutions. In the routine and repetitive decisions, definite approach has been worked out for handling them. Issuance of licences, award of contracts, distribution of uniforms to the scavengers or preparation of electricity bills are examples of programmed decisions. In programmed decisions, public managers have little discretion to exercise.

In repetitive cases, a manager can use a procedure that responds to a structured problem. Nowadays, some software programmes are being designed that automate routine and complex procedures. For example, in Chandigarh, the government administration has hurriedly adopted 'e-government technologies and ideas from simple, online communication of government information to real time, secure transactions for various processes and payments'.[9] The decision-making in such cases is merely executing a simple series of sequential steps. Invariably, public managers use rules frequently when they face a structured problem. In addition to use of systematic procedure and rule, the public manager falls back on a policy. A policy provides guidelines and parameters to the decision-making in a specific direction. Simon suggests that decision-making could be improved by increasing the scope of programmed decisions. In many cases, programmed decision-making becomes decision-making precedent.

Non-programmed Decisions

Non-programmed decisions are unique and non-repetitive. When problems are ill-structured, public managers must rely on non-programmed decision-making in order to develop unique solutions. Deciding whether or not to shut down a loss-making unit, or what type of strategy is needed for a terror strike, are examples of non-programmed decisions. In complex decision problems, only limited information is available. Further, disagreement may exist over the priority to be assigned to various objectives as well as over methods of evaluating progress.[10]

A few but important distinctions between programmed and non-programmed decision-making are shown in Table 13.1.

In the case of routine and repetitive administrative decisions, information is processed to the extent that it matches the required input format. At the other end, individuals in a public agency may be required to make decisions based on limited information. In a

[8] Herbert Simon, 'The Structure of Ill-structured Decision Processes', *Artificial Intelligence* 4 (1973): 181–201.
[9] R.K. Sapru and Yudhishthira Sapru, 'Good Governance Through e-Governance with Special Reference to India', *Indian Journal of Public Administration* 60(2) (2014): 314.
[10] K. Radford, *Complex Decision Problems: An Integrated Strategy for Resolution* (Reston, VA: Reston Publishing, 1977).

■ Table 13.1: Programmed and Non-programmed Decision-making

Programmed	Non-programmed
Routine and repetitive decisions	Non-routine and unique decisions
Standard procedures	No cut-and-dried solutions
Well-structured problems	Ill-structured problems
Use of information technology	Heuristic problem-solving methods
E-government communication	Computer-assisted decision-making
Programmed procedures	Operations research
Mathematical techniques	Systems analysis
	Monitoring of goal performance

Note: Aim to shift more decision-making into programmed zone.

terror strike on Air Force Base at Pathankot on 2 January 2016, for example, one could see so many problems for which no standard operating procedures or solutions exist. Subordinates or lower-level employees confronting familiar and repetitive problems typically depend on programmed decisions such as standard operating procedures, rules and organizational policies. They consult the higher-level employees only when they find their decisions to be non-repetitive and difficult to understand. Similarly, the higher-level employees pass along routine decisions to the subordinates so they can deal with ill-structured problems which require non-programmed decision-making. Programmed decisions minimize the need for public managers to act arbitrarily. To the other extreme, the more non-programmed decision-making a public manager is required to do, the greater the judgement needed.

DECISION-MAKING STYLES

According to Schermerhorn, there are three different ways managers approach problems in the context of decision-making: problems avoidance (problem avoider), problem-solving (problem solver), and problem seeking (problem seeker).[11]

(i) *Problem Avoidance*: In this approach to problems, the manager avoids or ignores information that points to a problem.
(ii) *Problem-solving:* In this approach, the manager tries to solve problems as and when they confront.
(iii) *Problem Seeking*: In this approach, the manager actively seeks out new opportunities to do things better. He takes a proactive approach to anticipating problems before they happen.

It may be added here that managers can use each approach depending upon the situation. For example, problem avoidance approach may be adopted when avoiding a problem is the best choice. At other times, being reactive is the only choice because the problem occurs so quickly. In the third situation, creative organizations need managers who actively seek opportunities to do things better.

[11] John R. Schermerhorn, *Management for Productivity*, 4th ed. (New York, NY: Wiley, 1993), 150.

Another perspective on decision-making styles proposes that managers differ along three dimensions in the way they approach decision-making: autocratic, democratic and laissez-faire.[12]

Autocratic Decision-making Style

Autocratic decision-making is an approach in which a public manager makes decisions with little or no consultation from others. Managers using the autocratic style make fast decisions and focus on the short run. Their efficiency and speed in making decisions with minimal information and with assessing few alternatives give the impression that they have low tolerance for ambiguity. Naturally, this approach makes implementation more difficult because those charged with implementation must be convinced of the relative worth of the decision itself. But in crisis situations, this form of approach is necessary as time becomes a critical factor. Some problems arise in using the autocratic approach when managers are not able to communicate the broader context of the situation.

Democratic Decision-making Style

In contrast to autocratic style, the democratic style emphasizes participative decision-making in which decision is sought to be made on support group among all those involved in the process. Implementation of the decision becomes easier under this form of approach because all concerned parties have provided some degree of input. Communication, which is the means of transfer of information, is greatly facilitated by this approach. However, democratic decision-making style may not be suitable in certain situations, particularly in which time factor is critical.

Laissez-faire Decision-making Style

A laissez-faire approach is one in which final decision outcomes come up with little or no direction from those in leadership positions. Examples of the laissez-faire approach are often found in matters that may be politically sensitive. This approach in decision-making may be damaging, either to the individual or to the organization overall. One way of addressing the issue is to postpone direct action, arguing instead for further analysis or some independent committee action. The use of this particular approach is not suggested because it tends to be highly risky and there appears to be no sound methods for gauging anticipated reactions from postponing action.

Although these three decision-making styles are distinct, most managers have characteristics of more than one style. Some public managers would think of exclusively on their dominant style, while others are more flexible and can shift their style depending upon the situation.

---

[12] Dennis P. Wittmer and Robert P. McGowan, 'Five Conceptual Tools for Decision-making', in *Handbook of Public Administration*, 3rd ed., eds. Jack Rabin, W.B. Hildreth and G.J. Miller (Boca Raton, FL: CRC Press, 2007), 317–18.

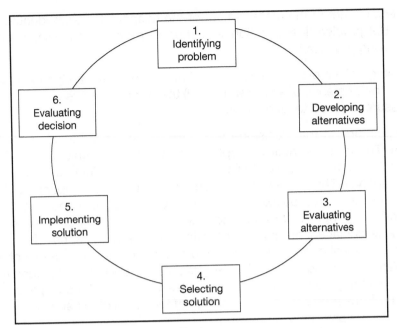

■ Figure 13.1: Decision-making Process (Steps)
Source: Adapted from Wittmer and Mcgowan (2007).

DECISION PROCESS

Decision-making entails choosing one course of action among other competing courses of action. It is a comprehensive process involving various steps (stages) from the issue or problem to final implementation and concludes with evaluating the decisions effectiveness (Figure 13.1).[13] In this context, Etzioni observes

> Decision Making falls between policy-formation and implementation ... however [they] are closely interwoven, with decisions affecting implementations and initial implementations affecting later stages of decision making which, in turn, affect later implementations.[14]

Problem Identification

The first stage of the decision process begins with the identification or existence of a problem. In identifying the problem, the decision-maker compares between what is happening and what should be happening. More specifically, the concern is on finding a discrepancy between an existing and a desired state of affairs.[15] To illustrate this point, we can relate to 'the decision to purchase a new luxury bus' for the public hospital. There is a discrepancy between the hospital need to have a luxury bus and the one that is old and functioning at capacity. The problem is obvious that the old bus in the hospital cannot

---

[13] W. Dunn, *Public Policy Analysis* (Englewood Cliffs, NJ: Prentice Hall, 1981).

[14] Etzioni, *The Active Society*, 203–04.

[15] William Pounds, 'The process of Problem Finding', *Industrial Management Review* Fall (1969): 1–19.

meet the requirement of the management of the hospital. Problem identification may be subjective. But problem identification is neither a simple nor an insignificant step of the decision-making process.[16]

At the first stage of the process, it is critical that the hospital management takes into consideration (i) the existence of a discrepancy, (ii) the resources necessary to take action and (iii) the pressure required to take action.

As already pointed out that decision-making is not just a simple act of choosing among alternatives. The process involves application of certain techniques. The use of brainstorming or Delphi method is particularly effective when defining the nature of the problem or discrepancy. The brainstorming technique requires participants to list their ideas in a free-form manner as quickly as possible. On the other hand, the Delphi method involves a different approach. Rather than have free-flowing input by all, a core group of experts on a particular set of issues is identified. This panel of experts then provides input as to the probability of certain events taking place, the nature of issues involved, solutions to the problem posed and the like. The results are then collected and transmitted back to the experts for their perusal. The critical variables in this process are (i) necessity of differentiating symptoms from causes, (ii) selection of the panel of experts and (iii) the rationale used to reduce the problems in question.

An example that illustrates this point is the setting up of a 10-member committee (chaired by former Delhi High Court Judge R.V. Easwar) on 27 October 2015 by the GOI to simplify provisions of the Income Tax Act and given it a mandate to identify clauses that lead to litigations and suggest modifications to bring predictability and certainty in tax laws.[17]

Developing Alternatives

The second stage of the process begins with the formulation of alternatives which is linked with the identification of the problem. This stage requires decision-maker to list the viable alternatives that could resolve the problem. The development of alternatives in the public sector surfaces the debate as to rationalism versus incrementalism.[18] The rationalist argument holds that all alternatives are considered, and it is the subsequent analysis which will determine the optimal approach. On the contrary, the incremental approach holds that, particularly in the public sector where many interests are involved, it is extremely difficult to both generate a list of alternatives and achieve consensus on them. However, there are ways to merge aspects of both rationalism and incrementalism. For example, James Brian Quinn puts forward an approach called 'logical incrementalism'.[19] Rather than concentrate on a few select alternatives, we tend to focus on a range—excluding, for the most part, the extremes. Quinn argues that we can avoid the expenditure of time in analysing all the alternatives, but at the same time, we have some degree of options.

---

[16] Roger Volkema, 'Problem Formulation: Its Portrayal in the Texts', *Organizational Behaviour Teaching Review* 11(3), 1986–87: 113–26.
[17] See *The Financial Express*, 28 October 2015.
[18] A. Wildavsky, *The Politics Budgetary Process* (Boston, MA: Little, Brown, 1964).
[19] J.B. Quinn, *Strategies for Change: Logical Incrementalism* (Homewood, IL: Irwin, 1980).

Evaluating Alternatives

Evaluating each alternative against the objectives allows the decision-maker to choose the best course of action. With identification of alternatives comes the role of analytical tools and techniques for appraising the worth of each alternative. These tools and techniques help public managers to make better decisions. The evaluation of alternatives with supportive methods involves two additional concerns. First, evaluation should take into account both the qualitative and quantitative aspects of programme or service delivery.[20] Second, evaluation should consider the use of standards or criteria (such as price, product and model) for judging performance or adherence to the overall goal. These may range from judging citizen satisfaction to programme cost maintenance. The strengths and weaknesses of each alternative become evident as they are compared with the criteria and weights evolved or developed previously.

Selecting Solution

The fourth stage in the decision process is the selection of the best alternative from among those assessed in the prior stage. It should be noted that the selection of solution, is largely dependent on the method of evaluation that has been utilized in the stage. For example, the nature of the critical path method (CPM) is to select the optimal path based on the allocation of resources as well as time. On the other hand, cost–benefit analysis (CBA) should similarly select the programme or service option that gives the greatest net benefit to net cost. The increasing introduction of computer-based techniques into the offices also greatly contributed to the choice of solutions. Further, administrators, those in upper levels of management, have a tendency to also rely on their own intuition and experience in selecting and backing a particular selection.[21] But they may have to face problems when public enquiries are held. Finally, choice of the solution, particularly in the public sector, involves the issue for a trade-off between efficiency and equity and public interest.

Implementing Solution

The fifth stage of the decision process involves the implementation process. Although the selection of decision is completed, the decision may still fail, if it is not implemented.[22] Implementation includes conveying the decision to the people who must support it and carry it out enthusiastically. For the implementation of a decision, the manager may adopt an autocratic or democratic style. If his priority is the relative quality of the decision, then an autocratic approach is called for, which means implementation of the decision is necessary. On the other hand, if the priority is acceptance of the decision as opposed to its quality, then a democratic approach is appropriate. In both cases, the individual may be trading off time at certain stages in the decision process.

---

[20] S.I. Haberman, *Analysis of Qualitative Data* (New York, IL: Academic Press, 1978).
[21] R.P. McGowan and S. Loveless, 'Strategies for Information: The Administrator's Perspective', *Public Administration Review*, 41 (1982): 331–39.
[22] W. Williams et al., *Studying Implementation: Methodological and Administrative Issues* (Chatham, NJ: Chatham House, 1982).

Evaluating Decision and Feedback

The final stage in the decision process, that is, evaluation and feedback, appears to be weakest point of the entire process. In the public sector, this is particularly crucial as the techniques of evaluation of formal programme and service delivery tend to be rudimentary under the control of Finance Ministry or Parliamentary Committees or some other decision-making units of the political executive of the government. Certain states and localities also have associated organizations, but in general, formal feedback and evaluative mechanisms for most public administrators are not widely in place, giving way in most instances to such evaluative means as legislative oversight, hearings and the like. In order to improve this stage of decision process, effort is required to tie such evaluation to the previously evolved standards for judging performance or adherence to the overall goal.

DYSFUNCTIONS IN DECISION-MAKING

Important decisions require input from everyone and not just from the 'boss'. Decisions that receive the 'yes-saying stamp' of subordinates may meet the immediate needs of top management (boss), and they often fail to meet goals of the organization or needs or its clients. Clearly, open and honest discussion of a possibility will result in a better choice of the decision. Listening to the paid employees and affected by the decision is more efficient and cost-effective than hiring well-paid consultants.

Second, bad decisions are made when members of the decision-making team are engaged in a power struggle. This leads to achieving nothing or reaching poorly contrived and compromised decisions that defeat the purpose of the organization or its clients. Over-conformity is yet another decision-making dysfunction. If, on the one hand, some members of the decision-making team are particularly assertive, and on the other, some members are passive to the point of failing to voice their opinions, there is a greater possibility that passive members will conform to the more assertive members. It is found that passive members typically censor their views, given the apprehension of being criticized by the more assertive members of the decision-making team. Also passive members do not succeed in resisting the conformity imposed by more assertive members in an effort to stay in the good graces of the group.

NON-DECISION-MAKING (POWER)

The idea of agenda being shaped by non-decisional power has also received wide recognition as a powerful model. Schattschneider argued, 'It is not necessarily true that people with the greatest needs participate in politics most actively—whosoever decides what the game is about will also decide who gets in the game'.[23] What the author has meant was that there was a bias which operated in favour of some and against others. The mobilization of bias theory was greatly expanded by the work of Bachrach and Baratz,

---

[23] Schattschneider, *The Semisovereign People*, 105.

whose approach addressed a different aspect of the pluralism.[24] In response to this view, Bachrach and Baratz argued that what the pluralist case had failed to appreciate was the extent to which those with power can actually exclude issues and problems from the policymaking agenda. Politics was not simply what Lasswell defined as the study of 'who gets what, when and how'[25] but also who gets left out—when and how.[26] To Bachrach and Baratz, non-decision-making will involve the constriction or containment of decision-making so as to be focused on 'safe issues by manipulating the dominant community values, myths, and political institutions and procedures'.[27] Bachrach and Baratz's empirical study was an examination of power and poverty in Baltimore and revealed how politicians and business leaders (elite class) sought to ensure that the demands of black people were kept out of the decision-making process by various means, including sanctions, force, manipulation of symbols such as the labelling of certain views as coming from communists or troublemakers and strengthening 'the mobilization of bias' by new barriers or symbols.[28]

Power is not simply the control of observable behaviour and decisions. Bachrach and Baratz argued that it also consisted in the non-observable realm of 'non-decisions':

> A non-decision, as we define it, is a decision that results in the suppression or thwarting of a latent or manifest challenge to the values and interests of the decision maker. To be more clearly explicit, non-decision-making is a means by which demands for change in the existing allocation of benefits and privileges in the community can be suffocated before they are even voiced; or kept covert; or killed to gain access to the relevant decision-making arena; or failing all these things, maimed or destroyed in the decision-implementing stage of the policy process.[29]

The point is that decision to not to do something is no less important than the decision to do something, and 'a non-decision is also a policy output'.[30] Non-decision-making suggests that policymakers wielding power can keep issues off the agenda which they control. Subsequently, Peter Saunders in his study of policymaking has sought to show how 'the powerful selectively interpret their perceived roles, and redefine the structure in which they are embedded...and how a largely unconscious routinization of bias, regularly favouring some interests while prejudicing others, may thereby be generated within political systems'.[31]

---

[24] P.S. Bachrach and M.S. Baratz, 'Decisions and Non-decisions: An Analytical Framework', *American Political Science Review* 57 (1963): 641–51. H.D. Lasswell, *Politics: Who Gets What, When, How* (Ohio: Meridian Books, 1936, 1958).

[25] H.D. Lasswell, *Politics: Who Gets What, When, How* (Ohio: Meridian Books, 1936, 1958).

[26] Bachrach and Baratz, 'Two Faces of Power', 105.

[27] Bachrach and Baratz (1963), 'Decisions and Non-decisions: An Analytical Framework', 632.

[28] P.S. Bachrach and M.S. Baratz, *Power and Poverty, Theory and Practices* (New York, NY: Oxford University Press, 1970).

[29] Ibid., 7.

[30] Birkland, *An Introduction to the Policy Process*, 253.

[31] Peter Saunders, 'They Make the Rules: Political Routines and the Generation of Political Bias', *Policy and Politics* 4(1) (1975): 31.

For examples, Article 44 of the Indian Constitution suggests the legislation of 'a uniform civil code throughout the territory of India'. But not to pursue this Article has as profound an effect on our national system as would a decision to legislate such a civil code. Non-decisional power is a powerful approach, in that it shapes the policy agenda and seeks to confine scope and extent of the conflict. Indeed, our constitutional framework is structured in a way that often restrict decisions or policies from being made.

CONCLUSION

Understanding decision-making and non-decision-making is certainly an important aspect of public administration. They are also part of the policy analysis. However, the field of decision-making in public administration or public management frequently defies clear-cut definition and categorization, yet it has particular bearing for public management today and in the future. But whether the sector is public or private, all human beings make decisions on the basis of their values and viewpoints they hold. But decision-making in public organizations is less autonomous (involving types, styles and processes) than in the private sector.

Review Questions

(i) What is the difference between policy decision and executive decision?
(ii) Enumerate the different decision-making styles as stated by Schermerhorn.
(iii) Discuss the major steps involved in the decision-making process.
(iv) Which typical aspects within an organization lead to bad decision-making?
(v) Explain the term 'non-decisional power' and elaborate on its significance in policymaking.

14
POLICY DECISION-MAKING
Tools and Techniques

INTRODUCTION

Policy decision-making is somewhat a difficult exercise. It does involve using quantitative and/or qualitative techniques. The use of such techniques is part of the scientific expertise. Techniques such as CBA, operations research, knowledge management (KM) and e-government are frequently used in policy decision-making. In this chapter, an effort is made to discuss old as well as emerging techniques that are rational for decision-making. Among the most notable tools and techniques of decision-making include

(i) Cost–benefit analysis
(ii) Strategic planning and management
(iii) Brainstorming approach
(iv) Simulation and gaming analysis
(v) Delphi technique
(vi) Supply chain management
(vii) Knowledge management
(viii) E-government

COST–BENEFIT ANALYSIS

Introduction

CBA or benefit–cost analysis is an older analytical technique used as an aid to decision-making in the public sector. Modern policy analysts still make a use of this technique as a guide to decisions. It is a means of budgetary analysis which measures relative gains and losses resulting from alternative policy or programmatic options.[1] Under the CBA, the costs of a service or programme can be calculated and set against benefits. The same procedure is carried out for all other options and the net benefits are compared.[2] In a choice between options the one with the maximum net benefit will be preferred. One reason for the application of this technique is that CBA forces managers to articulate the quantitative as well as qualitative aspects of a programme or service. It greatly increases an administrator's ability to make better decisions. This technique enables the

---

[1] Trevor Newton, *Cost-Benefit Analysis in Administration* (London: Allen & Unwin, 1972), 16–17.
[2] For a review of CBA as a technique of policy analysis, see Stokey and Zeckhauser, *A Primer for Policy Analysis* (New York, NY: W.W. Norton, 1978).

administrator to collect, organize and apply relevant information in the course of choosing desirable programme or a service.

The origin of the use of CBA can be traced to the Rivers and Harbors Act of 1902 in the USA which set out that the costs of projects had to be less than the benefits.[3] This technique remained fairly dormant until the post–Second World War emergence of operations research when quantitative techniques began to take hold and were applied to large-scale project and programme planning. The formal introduction of PPBS, first in the Defence Department under Robert McNamara and later expanding to other federal agencies, was CBA, frequently used to either justify the expansion/continuation of specific programmes or make trade-off decisions. Although the PPBS was abandoned by the Nixon administration in 1971, the use of CBA found again its importance with the passage of the Federal Paperwork Control Act, 1980[4] and the establishment of the Regulatory Analysis Review Group (RARG) in 1978.[5] The CBA was required in the federal government in the 1970s and 1980s for all proposed regulations to be issued by agencies, although the benefits of health, education and welfare programme are 'diverse and often intangible'. The Executive Order 12291 (1981), for example, specifies that 'administrative decisions shall be based on adequate information concerning the need for and consequences of proposed government action, and regulatory objectives shall be chosen to maximize the net benefits to society'.[6]

Applications of CBA

The application of CBA, on the face of it, is fairly straightforward. As Meier notes, the CBA involves approximately three steps.[7] First, the impacts (direct or indirect) of a programme or service are determined. These are generally classified along the lines of either benefits or costs and are subsequently defined as direct (first order) or indirect (second order).

In the reduction of air pollution in a city region, for example, the direct benefit is the reduction in the number of lung-related incidents. The improved health, as a result of the reduction in air pollution, would also translate to such indirect impacts as lower absenteeism and higher productivity. On the costs side, the installation of emission control equipment is regarded as direct costs. Indirect costs may include loss of employment opportunities as businesses are either forced to close or fail to locate in the area as a result of the enforcement programme or service delivery.

---

[3] K. Meier, 'The Limits of Cost-Benefit Analysis', in *Decision-making in the Public Sector*, ed. L. Nigro (New York: Marcel Dekker, 1984), 43–63.

[4] The Federal Paperwork Control Act, 1980 in the USA was intended to correct a number of deficiencies in information management. Specifically, it attempted to reduce the burden of information processing on the public and private industry by implementing standards for collecting information (e.g. prior approval by the Office of Management and Budget [OMB] of agency forms). In addition, it established an Office of Federal Information Policy in the OMB to monitor and direct, if necessary, information practices by government agencies.

[5] The RARG represented the effort on the part of the executive agency to exercise control over agency regulatory activities by requiring agencies to formally document and justify new regulations prior to implementation.

[6] Kaifeng Yang, 'Quantitative Methods for Policy Analysis', in *Handbook of Public Policy Analysis*, eds. Frank Fischer, Gerald Miller and Mara Sidney (Boca Raton, FL: CRC Press, 2007), 352.

[7] Meier, 'The Limits of Cost-Benefit Analysis'.

The second step which is involved in the CBA relates to money. Estimates in terms of rupees or dollar for each benefit or cost are made. For most costs and benefits, a market price is assigned. The purpose of this technique is to determine what today's rupees investment will yield in the future. For example, the Seventh Pay Commission (SPC) said the government's size vis-à-vis the GDP will 'stay roughly constant over the medium term', but an analysis by FE showed the pay, allowances and pension (PAP) of government staff (centre plus states) could rise to 10.3 per cent of GDP in FY17 from 7.88 per cent budgeted for FY16 if all states follow the award promptly.[8]

Third, it is often claimed that it is a difficult exercise to quantify certain benefits, yet it is an integral part of the analysis. In earlier example of the reduction of air or water pollution in a city region, a major benefit is improvement of the overall quality of life. Although this concept has many definitions and indicators, they must be considered. There are a number of unobtrusive ways of measuring this—ranging from selected neighbourhood surveys to determining willingness to pay on the part of the citizenry. For an example in the case of imposition of cess (tax on services from 16 November 2015) to implement a Clean India project, the editorial commented, 'Wasn't Swachh Bharat to be funded by corporates as part of their social responsibility?'[9]

Critical Observations

However, the practice of the CBA has met the resistance. Critics of the CBA model argue that there is disagreement about the values that are being applied to the project such as decisions which involve amenities or natural beauty. Further, it is easy to calculate the cost and benefit in a setting of a factory producing certain parts or products, compared with assessing value in terms of health or the environment in a different set of cost or benefit. Putting a price for each component of a programme or scheme is not as simple as the model suggests. Critics of the CBA model argue that this quantification is simply politics dressed up in techniques: 'nonsense on stilts'.[10]

Similarly, assumptions and values of welfare economics may not be applicable to some policy decisions: the prices and costs and utility of good health or 'noise' which may not be easily calculated and measured. Many problems arise from the equity and efficiency of the distributions of welfare that result from CBA. What constitutes 'equity' and what is 'efficient' are often subjects of values which are deeply problematic. Yet, as Colvin points out, most economists working in the public sector 'operate as if the theoretical problems were not there'.[11]

Despite its limitations, the CBA has proved a useful technique in decision-making. The attractiveness of CBA as a technique of decision-making is somewhat obvious: It provides an apparently neutral technique for identifying goals, their impacts and their costs

---

[8] See *The Financial Express* (Chandigarh), 21 November 2015.

[9] See *The Tribune* (Chandigarh), 17 November 2015.

[10] Peter Self, *Econocrats and the Policy Process: The Politics and Philosophy of Cost-benefit Analysis* (London: Macmillan, 1975).

[11] P. Colvin, *The Economic Ideal in British Government: Calculating Costs and Benefits in the 1970s* (Manchester: Manchester University Press, 1985), 189.

and benefits, and it creates a measurable 'objective' statement which can serve to aid the formulation and selection of options and alternatives.

With globalization and deregulation, the CBA has remained fairly dormant. Optimality, the public choice school argued, could best be attained when markets were allowed to allocate costs and benefits. However, it still remains the case that CBA provides the essential core of rational analysis in government decision-making and in the legitimation of decisions. Many of the criticisms which are levelled at the CBA model do indicate that in practice CBA encounters considerable methodological and political difficulties in being used in the real world. But, is there an alternative? In this context, David Pearce argues,

> CBA remains a controversial appraisal technique. As an aid to rational thinking its credentials are higher than any of the alternatives so far advanced. That it cannot substitute for political decisions is not in question, but social science has a duty to inform public choice, and it is in this respect that CBA has its role to play.[12]

There is little doubt that the contribution of cost–benefit has been dramatic.[13]

STRATEGIC PLANNING AND MANAGEMENT

Introduction

Strategic planning and management as a tool for decision-making gained recognition in the 1980s.[14] Strategic planning is involved in many of the decisions that public managers make. Strategic planning has been considered one of the hot innovations in public and nonprofit management.[15] While strategic planning and strategic management may be used interchangeably, one can distinguish strategic management as the implementation of strategic plans or the outcomes of strategic planning.

Prior to looking to its various applications, strategic management needs a clear definition. The term 'strategy' is often used in the army. What is conveyed by the term is the 'idea of critical goals achieved under battle conditions'.[16] Halachmi defines 'strategic management' as 'the process for implementing a strategic plan which integrates the organizations' goals, policies, and sequences into a cohesive whole'.[17]

---

[12] David Pearce, 'Cost-Benefit Analysis', in *The Social Science Encyclopedia*, eds. A. Kuper and J. Kuper (London: Routledge, 1989), 166.

[13] S. Tolchin and M. Tolchin, *Dismantling America: The Rush to Deregulate* (Boston: MA: Houghton Mifflin, 1983).

[14] Nandini Rajagopalan, Abdul Rasheed and Deepak Datta, 'Strategic Decision Processes: Critical Review and Future Directions', *Journal of Management* Summer (1993): 349–84.

[15] F.C. Berry and B. Wechsler, 'State Agencies' Experience with Strategic Planning: Findings from a National Survey', *Public Administration Review* 55(2) (1995): 159–168.

[16] D.F. Andersen, 'Strategic Information Management: Conceptual Frameworks for the Public Sector', *Public Productivity and Management Review* 17(4) (1994): 339.

[17] A. Halachmi, 'Strategic Management and Productivity', in *Public Productivity Handbook*, ed. M. Holzer (New York: Marcel, 1992).

Why is strategic management considered to be of critical importance in the public sector decision-making? As, in the case of business, government managers also function in increasingly turbulent environments. Given the turbulent conditions of most organizational environments, the strategic approach will systematically assess the conditions that prove new opportunities or pose new threats to the accomplishment of fundamental goals, if not basic survival, of the organization. This often involves examining the broad economic, political, social and technological trends influencing developments in today's environment. Compared with business, the ability to change mission in the public sector is more problematic in the public sector because managers are not in a position to make changes in fundamental goals.[18] On the contrary, managers in the private sector have generally much more freedom.

Characteristics and Strategic Planning Steps

Andersen identifies five features of a strategic orientation, suggesting that the government or business organization would be (i) concerned with mission-critical activities, (ii) long range in time orientation, (iii) looking outward from the organizational boundaries to stakeholders or customers, (iv) seeking maximum return on investment rather than minimum economic cost and (v) placing a high value on technological, human and information resources.[19] However, it is difficult to begin a strategic plan. Galloway, for instance, argues that a strategic plan should begin with a descriptive account of the mission, objectives and strategies that characterize the organization.[20]

Based on his review of private sector approaches to strategic planning, Bryson presents an approach that he believes is appropriate for public and nonprofit organizations. This approach includes the following eight steps:

(i) Initiating and agreeing on a strategic planning process;
(ii) Identifying organizational mandates;
(iii) Clarifying organizational mission and values;
(iv) Assessing the external environment: opportunities and threats;
(v) Assessing the internal environment: strengths and weaknesses;
(vi) Identifying the strategic issues facing an organization;
(vii) Formulating strategies to manage the issues; and
(viii) Establishing an effective organizational vision for the future.[21]

In one other approach, Halachmi identifies seven steps in a simple model of strategic planning: (i) developing the plan, (ii) taking stock, (iii) strategic analysis, (iv) alternative generation, (v) strategic choices, (vi) organization leadership and support and (vii) review and evaluation.[22]

---

[18] J.M. Stevens and R.P. McGowan, 'Managerial Strategies in Municipal Government Organizations', *Academy of Management Journal* 26(3) (1983): 527–34.

[19] Andersen, 'Strategic Information Management: Conceptual Frameworks for the Public Sector'.

[20] I. Galloway, 'Strategic Management in Public Sector Research Organizations: A Critical Review', *International Journal of Public Sector Management* 3(1) (1990): 5–24.

[21] J.M. Bryson, *Strategic Planning for Public and Nonprofit Organizations* (San Francisco, CA: Jossey-Bass, 1989).

[22] Halachmi, 'Strategic Management and Productivity'.

Since public sector organizations have distinct characteristics, they may have to tailor-make particular approach to strategic planning and management, especially because many of the strategic approaches were developed for business applications. For example, Andersen modifies Porter's competitive strategic analysis[23] by developing a collaborative model of analysis that includes providers, clients, entrants and substitutions in the service environment.[24] With a view to creating a strategic approach appropriate for public information management applications to public organizations, Anderson then combines this collaborative analysis with another business approach known as 'the strategic options generator' developed by Wiseman in 1985.[25]

Applications of Strategic Planning

Although there are a variety of approaches to strategic planning and management, and many Europeans states are now using strategic planning among local governments in their efforts to coordinate and democratize local government,[26] creating modifications may be necessary for their applications to public organizations depending on the level of government, the kind of service provided and other relevant factors.

There are a few examples of applications of strategic planning in the public and nonprofit sectors. Andersen cites an example of its application in the development of information technologies in the public sector. Similarly, Nutt and Backoff give an example of its applications of nonprofit or third sector organizations.[27] Kerr has also applied its applications in performance measurement and human resource management.[28] In their study of the use of strategic planning in municipal governments of over 25,000 people, Poister and Streib found some evidence of a growing sophistication with regard to using strategic planning.[29]

Critical Observations

A strong culture in the organization may act as a significant barrier to acceptance of a change in the organization's strategies. In a risk-aversive culture, for example, management is more likely to favour strategies that are defensive, that minimize financial exposure and that react to changes in the environment rather than try to anticipate those changes. Stewart also argues the strategic management remains under-theorized in the public sector owing to the issues raised relate to different fields of analysis, namely, the political, the policy-related and the administrative.[30]

---

[23] M. Porter, *Competitive Strategy: Techniques for Analyzing Industries and Competitors* (Lexington, MA: Lexington Books, 1983).

[24] Andersen, 'Strategic Information Management: Conceptual Frameworks for the Public Sector'.

[25] C. Wiseman, *Computers and Strategy: Information Systems as Competitive Weapons* (Homewood, IL: Dow Jones-Irwin, 1985).

[26] S. Abram and R. Cowell, 'Learning Policy: The Contextual Curtain and Conceptual Barriers', *European Planning Studies* 12(2) (2004): 209–29.

[27] P.C. Nutt and R.W. Backoff, *Strategic Management of Public and Third Sector Organizations* (San Francisco, CA: Jossey-Bass, 1992).

[28] D.L. Kerr, 'Managing Rosie the Riveter', *Public Productivity and Management Review* 17(3) (1994): 215–21.

[29] T.H. Poister and G. Streib, 'Elements of Strategic Planning and Management in Municipal Government: Status After Two Decades', *Public Administration Review* 65(1) (2005): 45–57.

[30] J. Stewart, 'The Meaning of Strategy in the Public Sector', *Australian Journal of Public Administration*, 63(4) (2004): 16–22.

Qualitative Techniques

In recent times, qualitative techniques have become quite important and contributed a great deal to the field of public sector policy decision-making. Certain problems faced by policy decision-makers are now approached by the application of qualitative techniques. Where problems involve strategic or policy decisions and raise conflicts of values, intuitions, judgements, opinions and so on, qualitative methods may be used. With the development of new public management and the growing influence of techniques from the private sector applied in the public sector, managerial approaches to decision-making are becoming more relevant to researchers and practitioners of public policy. Attempting to select certain techniques and tools that are current and useful for decision-making in public management is difficult at best. We intent to provide in this section a brief overview of important qualitative techniques.

BRAINSTORMING APPROACH

Among techniques that are useful for group decision-making, 'brainstorming' is relatively simple and has been extensively used. This technique is used for overcoming pressures for agreement that hinder the development of creative alternatives. It does so by using an 'idea-generating process' that encourages alternatives while withholding any criticism of those alternatives. The originator of 'Brainstorming' approach is Alex Osborn.[31] As an aid to decision-making, this method has been applied to the private as well as public sector.[32] Whereas other approaches are structured in the sense that analysis takes place within a procedure, brainstorming is based upon a deliberate break with judgements, criticism and censorship. Under this approach, the aim is to produce a quantity of ideas which can lead to the emergence of alternatives. As with other approaches, this approach is equally criticized. Research suggests strongly that brainstorming has a number of problems which need to be considered in appraising the value of such exercises. According to Huczynski and Buchanan, these are

(i) Does it inhibit creative thought?
(ii) Is there a danger of 'groupthink'?
(iii) Never mind the quantity, what about the quality of ideas?
(iv) Is creative thinking an undisciplined process?
(v) Do groups think more creatively than individuals?[33]

Brainstorming has mainly two variations. In one variation of brainstorming called 'storyboarding', participants identify major issues and brainstorm each of them in order to put together a complete story of the problem.[34] Another variation of brainstorming is 'lotus

---

[31] Alex Osborn, *Applied, Imagination: Principles and Procedures of Creative Thinking* (New York, NY: Charles Scribner's Sons, 1953).
[32] J. L. Adams, *Conceptual Blockbusting: A Guide to Better Ideas* (Harmondsworth: Penguin, 1987), 134–37.
[33] A. Huczynski and D. Buchanan, *Organizational Behaviour* (London: Prentice Hall, 1991), 245–51.
[34] L.F. Lottier, 'Storyboarding Your Way to Successful Training', *Public Personnel Management* Winter (1986): 421–27.

blossom technique' (a Japanese technique) in which a core thought is applied as the basis for expanding ideas into an ever-widening series of surrounding ideas (like the petals of a lotus blossom).[35] Brainstorming and its variations, however, are processes for generating, and not for evaluating ideas.

SIMULATION AND GAMING ANALYSIS

Simulation is a technique 'that constructs 'a framework of a real-world situation and then manipulates one or more variables in the framework in such a way as to derive some solutions and conclusions about the real situation. The general steps involved in the simulation are (i) define the system one intends to simulate, (ii) formulate the model one intends to use, (iii) identify and collect data necessary to test the model, (iv) test the model and compare its behaviour with the actual environment, (v) run the simulation, (vi) analyse the results and revise the solution if desired, (vii) rerun the simulation to test the new solution and (viii) validate the simulation.[36] Besides simulation, gaming as a technique is also used to deal with complex situations.

Simulation and gaming as techniques have been developed out of defence and foreign policy decision-making. Gaming may take the form of a computer simulated exercise or a manual game which involves role-playing. Gaming is designed to promote an exploration of a decision, which again may lead on to the application of more quantitative techniques. Lasswell holds that game-playing can 'shake-up' decision-making by challenging assumptions and predispositions, thereby revealing 'unrecognized expectations, demands and identifications'.[37] Lasswell argues that simulation exercises may be utilized in 'decision seminars' as they may succeed in 'conferring a vivid sense of reality' on the participants.[38] The application of games and simulations has been widely adopted in business and has found applications in decision-making in the public sector, especially in the context of urban planning. They are also used by engineers for creating thinking and open communication.

DELPHI TECHNIQUE

The Delphi approach 'as a technique is more complex' and time-consuming for improving group decision-making. As a technique, it was developed at RAND in the 1960s. The aim behind this approach was to reduce the influence in the decision analysis. It is observed that in many situations, face-to-face interaction may have a powerful influence on the analysis. In the Delphi approach, a group of anonymous experts is selected that communicates with the steering group and/or the computer, which then distributes their responses to other members. Out of this process of question, response and feedback, the steering group formulates a decision. The Delphi approach is, therefore, an aid to

---

[35] S.M. Tatsuno, 'Breakthrough: The Japanese Way', *R & D Magazine* (1990): 136–42.
[36] R.I. Levin et al., *Quantitative Approaches to Management* (New York, NY: McGraw-Hill, 1989).
[37] H.D. Lasswell, *A Preview of Policy Sciences* (New York: Elsevier, 1971), 154.
[38] Ibid., 153.

decision-making which is based on an exchange of information and expert analysis rather than on 'discussion' of a face-to-face contact. The Delphi method lays great emphasis on the capacity of the steering group and the technology to produce a consensus.

The following steps characterize the Delphi technique:

(i) The problem is identified, and members are asked to provide possible solutions through a series of carefully designed questionnaires.

(ii) Each member anonymously and independently completes the first questionnaire.

(iii) Results of the first questionnaire are compiled at a central location, transcribed and copied.

(iv) Each member receives a copy of the results.

(v) After viewing the results, members are again asked for their solutions. The initial results typically trigger new solutions or cause changes in the original position.

(vi) Steps iv and v are repeated as often as necessary until a consensus is reached.[39]

Critical Observations

As has been discussed, the Delphi technique insulates group members from the undue influence of others. Also, since it does not require the physical presence of members, a global company could use the technique with managers in Paris, New Delhi, New York or London.

Some policy analysts regard this as a method with considerable potential in those areas of decision-making in which there are conflicts which are not resolvable through the use of formal rational methods and models.[40] This Delphi technique is not without its criticisms. The method is extremely time-consuming. It is frequently not appropriate when a speedy decision is necessary. Further, the method might not develop the rich pool of alternatives that interacting groups manage.

Robson has suggested certain modifications in the Delphi approach. He suggests that a modified Delphi could use a process of individual judgements in a non-face-to-face way through asking a group to write down their ideas on cards.[41] A leader then arranges the ideas on a list, and members are asked to rank them in order of preference. This ranking then provides the basis of group discussion. Robson suggests that the modified procedure should be to '(i) review problem and data; (ii) generate ideas individually; (iii) combine ideas on to one list; (iv) individually rank ideas; and (v) discuss final ranking'.[42]

Although this Delphi approach is a more complex and time-consuming alternative and requires no physical presence of the group members, some managers at the global companies level are applying this technique with certain modifications.

---

[39] Quoted from S. Robbins and M. Coulter, *Management*, 5th ed. (New Delhi: Prentice Hall of India, 1998), 214.

[40] H. Linstone and M. Turoff, eds., *The Delphi Method: Techniques and Applications* (Massachusetts: Addison-Wesley, 1975).

[41] M. Robson, *Problem Solving in Groups* (Aldershot; Gower, 1993).

[42] Ibid.

SUPPLY CHAIN MANAGEMENT

SCM or 'value chain analysis' is an emerging tool which contributes a great deal to the field of decision-making in public sector. As a tool, the SCM is embedded in a number of critical activities: human resource management, finance, support service, research and development and the like. Although the SCM is a recently coined term, as a concept, its roots are found in systems logic and theory.[43] This would entail four concepts: holism, synergy, feedback and negative entropy.

The concept of 'holism' is basic to SCM. In a supply chain system, one needs to look at the organization (e.g. a forest region) as a whole as opposed to a singular aspect (a few tree in the forest) of the organization. Second, the concept of 'synergy' implies that one leverages resources in the most cost-effective manner. Given the pressure on the public sector to do more with less, this becomes more acute. For example, rather than going to a designated booth for voting, one can vote through e-mail. Third, 'feedback' concept implies that organization concerned receives information from its constituency and responds accordingly. Sampark services in many cities in India have made significant strides to be proactive. And finally, the concept of 'negative entropy' means that organization will do whatever it takes to survive and, hopefully, grow. This can be done through a variety of means: engaging in strategic alliances, finding a partner, merging resources with another enterprise and the like. An example is the PC, which was set up in 1950 under a Union Cabinet resolution was abolished on 13 August 2014. The Modi government chose to replace it with NITI Aayog to work towards cooperative federalism.

In brief, the concept of SCM is not something that is relatively new. Its roots are embedded in a number of long-established concepts.

Activity Areas of Supply Chain

According to Porter, every 'facet' of the organization provides value.[44] With reference to any governmental organization, value could be several things: having skilled personnel, delivering a service in a timely or cost-effective manner, reducing waste, budgetary savings and the like. A value system can also be fairly simple or complex, depending on the organization. Embedded in value systems are value chains. The value chain consists of three primary areas: primary activities, support activities and margin.

Primary Activities Area

A key sector in value chain management is primary activity. Primary activity refers to the core organizational activity. For example, in the Revenue Department, the primary activity is collecting taxes from individuals and corporations. Primary activities include inbound logistics, operations, outbound logistics, marketing and sales and service.

---

[43] Herbert Simon, 'The New Science of Management Decision', in *Management Decision Making*, eds. R Cyert and L. Welsch (New York, NY: Penguin, 1980), 13–16.
[44] Michael Porter, *Competitive Advantage* (New York, NY: Free Press, 1985).

(i) *Inbound logistics* refers to those value activities associated with getting and receiving raw goods and services. For example, Bharat Heavy Electrical in India has the objective of improving logistics operations and reducing costs.

(ii) *Operations*, the second sector in primary activities, is what Porter refers to as the transformation phase. In this area, raw goods are transformed into a product and service. For most service organizations, for example, public works, this is one of the more critical areas.

(iii) The third sector in primary activates is *outbound logistics* which involves the mechanics of delivering. For example, Postal Service in India emulates this—with different forms of express delivery (Speed Post), depending on the requirements of the customers, investors and clients.

(iv) *Marketing and sales* is the fourth sector in primary activities. Value activities here may entail several actions. For example, in several states, a portion of revenue from lotteries is allocated to a number of public organizations. Therefore, states will actively market their respective lotteries.

(v) *Service*, the final sector in the primary activities, includes service and support. What this means is that once a service is provided, the organization's involvement should not end. It may continue to provide follow-up, complaint resolution or further support. Many public sector organizations are beginning to realize that the support from their constituents can give them a competitive advantage in securing support as well as justifying future expenditures.

Support Activities Area

The final sector of the supply chain is support activities (other than primary and margin activities). This is typically referred to as overhead. While many look at this area as an added cost of doing business, a number of organizations have achieved value in this area as well. This area has a number of activities that are critical: human resources management, finance, accounting, procurement, research and development and the like.

The public organizations are required to identify and decide how they can give greater value to their primary activities. As, for example, the central government and state governments have decided to spend huge amount of money on outsourcing its IT services.

Margin Area

Margin area or sector is, in fact, the residual of both the support and primary activities. Margin refers to the fact that whatever savings in efficiencies occur in either primary or secondary sectors, the savings go straight to the bottom line. In other words, this margin of savings reduces the cost of operations. For private sector organizations, this margin in the form of profits can either be passed along to the customer, reinvested in the enterprise or paid as dividends to investors. For public organizations, the gain in margin presents a different scenario. This could mean that they will need to ask for fewer resources in the future, or the gains would revert back to the general revenue.

Critical Observations

In recent years, the field of SCM has attracted the attention of the public sector organizations in 'developed countries' (such as the USA and Great Britain). There are now professional groups, journals and academic centres promoting the practices and applications of the SCM. Professional groups include the Supply Chain Council and the Institute for Supply Chain Management. Professional journals include the *Journal of Supply Chain Management*, the *Supply Chain Management Review*, *Supply Chain Management: An International Journal*, *Supply Chain Forum: An International Journal* and *Supply Chain Systems Magazine*. Besides these, the Center for Public Policy and Private Enterprise at the University of Maryland includes as one of its programme areas the modernization of government SCM.

The adoption of SCM in the public organizations, however, has met with more resistance and has moved far more slowly than in the private sector.[45] To promote and enhance the adoption of supply chain systems in government, Korosec provides guidance in terms of identifying the components of SCM and suggests how it may be used to increase productivity in public procurement.[46]

The field of SCM is new and some countries are already making efforts to introduce it.[47] For its adoption, employees in the public organizations need skills training. Organizations in the public domain should witness use of Internet to replace the method of too many transactions. Finally, pubic managers need to view SCM as a continuous process in which activities are evaluated continually for further development.

KNOWLEDGE MANAGEMENT

Introduction

Of late, KM 'as a concept or tool' has acquired increasing importance for policy decision-making in the public sector. KM is not just an IT tool for enhancing the quality of decision-making process but the most valuable asset and intellectual capital in the organization. KM is associated with e-government and new digital technologies.[48] The core idea, like many other decision-making tools, is to recognize the importance and value of preserving and expanding the know-how of those in the organization. Recognizing this dimension of human knowledge, systematic efforts should be made to protect and enhance this knowledge asset. Therefore, managing knowledge is of critical importance in contemporary policy perspective.

Although KM concept has its root in systems logic, it must be defined. KM is defined as a business activity with two primary aspects:

(i) Treating the knowledge component of business activities as an explicit concern of business reflected in strategy, policy and practice at all levels of the organization.

---

[45] J. Gansler and R. Luby, *Transforming Government Supply Chain Management* (Lanham, MD: Rowman and Littlefield, 2003).

[46] R. Korosec, 'Assessing the Feasibility of Supply Chain Management within Purchasing and Procurement', *Public Performance and Management Review* 27(2) (2003): 92–110.

[47] G. Parker, 'A Purchase in Government', *Supply Management* 10(4) (2005): 17–20.

[48] Digital technologies that are changing the economics and practices of traditional business—cloud computing, mobile devices, data analysis and artificial intelligence—are better, cheaper and more widely available in India.

(ii) Making a direct connection between an organization's intellectual assets—both explicit (recorded) and tacit (personal know-how)—and positive business results.[49]

In simple words, KM can be defined as managing intellectual capital within the organization. In this context of KM, 'knowledge can generally be understood at the end of a continuum that begins with data, moves to information, and then to knowledge as the highest and most complex terminus of the continuum'.[50] In other words, KM involves the question of how major pieces of critical information are stored and indexed so that they can be retrieved easily when required.

Elements of KM

Since knowledge is an effective asset for decision-making, several elements are useful for understanding KM. In main, the following concepts and elements which are largely derived from Grover and Davenport's study[51] are briefly discussed here.

(i) *Knowledge*: Knowledge as refined information is understood to be an 'intellectual capital' which can be processed and used for decision-making in the organization.

(ii) *Explicit and Tacit Knowledge*: Knowledge can be both explicit and tacit. 'Explicit knowledge' is characterized by being able to be codified, documented, transferred and shared. Examples of explicit knowledge include business plans, patents, procedure manuals for employees or product manuals for customers. 'Tacit knowledge', on the other hand, is more difficult to articulate, formalize and codify. It is developed more from direct and interactive experience and shared more from interactive conversation. An example might be how to effectively navigate a desired change in the organization, knowing all the subtleties and key players in the organization. KM tries to leverage both explicit and tacit knowledge in organizations.

(iii) *Knowledge Processes*: Knowledge has to be created, processed and transferred for the achievement of organization's goals. According to Grover and Davenport, knowledge codification 'involves the conversion of knowledge into accessible and applicable formats'.[52] Knowledge transfer can be considered the process by which knowledge is shifted from one group to another or from generation to application or codification.

(iv) *Communities of Practice*: On generation of knowledge by individuals, communities can be formed with shared or common interests. Organizations are advanced by fostering such communities of practice, either formally or simply by creating environment where such creation and sharing can take place.

(v) *Knowledge Markets*: The knowledge as an asset or a good may be protected by its possessors in organization, and can be exchanged and shifted for other goods such as money, position or even other knowledge in a barter-like system.

---

[49] R. Barclay and P. Murray, 'What Is Knowledge Management?' www.mediaacess.com, accessed 22 June 2006.

[50] Dennis P. Wittmer and Robert P. McGowan, 'Five Conceptual Tools for Decision-making'. in *Handbook of Public Administration*, 3rd ed., eds. Jack Rabin, W.B. Hildreth and G.J. Miller (Boca Raton, FL: Taylor & Francis, 2007), 326.

[51] V. Grover and T. Davenport, 'Special Issue: Knowledge and Management', *Journal of Management Information Systems* 18(1) (2001): 7–8.

[52] Ibid., 7–8.

Applications of KM

KM is now being largely looked at as a business practice concept rather than as a technology-based concept.[53] Moreover, because '...all new knowledge stems from people',[54] it can be argued that KM must fundamentally be about managing people rather than technology tools.

Because managers rely on information to make decisions and because KM significantly alters the quantity and quality of knowledge, it can be concluded that an effective KM will improve management's decision-making capability. The effect will be seen in ascertaining the need for a decision, in the development and evaluation of alternatives and in the final selection of the best alternative. KM tools might include collaborative tools for identifying and sharing knowledge in organizations. Categories of such KM tools include 'knowledge repositories, expertise access tools, e-learning applications, discussion and chat technologies, synchronous interaction tools, and search and data mining tools'.[55]

But to reiterate, all the practices are directed towards identifying, codifying, sharing and utilizing knowledge in organizations. Organizations may adopt one or combination of approaches to KM. The idea here is the relative emphasis that organizations adopt in managing knowledge, that is, technology infrastructure, the culture and interactions of individuals or the knowledge in the system.

The GOI has established the National Knowledge Commission (an Indian think tank set up on 13 June 2005 with the objective of transforming India into a knowledge society), with the focus on developing and using information technologies that relate to acquiring, categorizing, storing and distributing knowledge in organizations. Besides other activities, the Commission conducts a survey of KM awareness and recommends for improving KM at the national level. It spends huge amount of money on KM products. The Department of IT is a natural fit for adopting KM strategies. Tools to share information and knowledge quickly become critical when responding quickly to terrorist threats. Besides the Commission, the National Informatics Centre in India is involved in steering information in over 675 districts. An intranet portal (Offerings) was created to facilitate a knowledge sharing culture. The portal includes a search engine, a document-sharing feature, mailing lists, yellow pages that identify personnel with expertise, online chats and other functions. Offerings is accessed by more than 10,000 employees from 1,500 locations.

Public agencies face different kinds of reasons for adopting KM strategies. For example, there is intellectual capital crisis in the central government due to retirements, early retirements, unfilled vacancies and hiring freezes. Hence, KM becomes an important tool for stemming the flow of valuable knowledge from organizations. Public organizations need to unearth the mountains of information by sharing experiences, participating in conferences and joining Internet-based networks such as the Public Performance Measurement.

In the USA, the Department of Homeland Security, the Department of State and the Department of Justice have adopted KM strategies. The UK has developed a

---

[53] M. Santosus and J. Surmacz, 'The ABCs of Knowledge Management', *Knowledge Management Research Centre*, www.cio.com, accessed 26 January 2004.
[54] Grover and Davenport, 'Special Issue: Knowledge and Management', 5–21.
[55] Santosus and Surmacz, 'The ABCs of Knowledge Management'.

knowledge-enhanced government strategy that involves the UK Knowledge Network. One purpose of this Network is to share learning, experiences and knowledge among 600 schools in the UK.[56] Similarly in many other developed and developing countries, KM strategies have been adopted for information and knowledge sharing. Governmental officials and public managers that are looking to improve public sector performance may use and share valid and reliable information.

Critical Observations

Advantages of successful KM are many and varied. Among others, advantages can include the following: fostering innovation through the free flow of ideas, improving customer service, enhancing employee retention and streamlining operations and reducing the associated costs.[57] As KM strategies are being adopted around the world, it is important to identify factors that are important for the success of KM. Han, for example, identifies following as those that are most important: (i) effective leadership, (ii) the commitment of resources, (iii) alignment of KM with the organizational strategy and (iv) a focus on people rather than technology. [58]

But it is noted that implementing KM is not without certain challenges. First to get tacit knowledge from the knowledgeable employees is a significant challenge because KM is driven by the people and strategy of the organization. Second, often new technologies are implemented without creating an effective KM system. This results in huge wastage of money and time. Third, challenge is to keep KM evolving and fluid. In a turbulent environment, knowledge is constantly changing and is affecting the organization. So it is very important to evolve a system that embraces change and new knowledge, including systems to facilitate and acquire knowledge. Web searches will yield a considerable body of sites and sources.

E-GOVERNMENT

'E-government', also known as e-gov, Internet government, digital government, online government or connected government (the terms are frequently interchanged), has acquired growing importance as a theory and practice since the mid-1990s in the field of public management. There is an overlap between e-government and e-governance as competing paradigms that intersect at times during their development.[59] Some suggest that government makes use of e-governance strategy to improve the quality of governance.[60] E-governance is the process of enabling governance experts using information and communication technology (ICT) to make governance effective for citizens in terms of efficiency,

---

[56] R.E. Neilson and J. McCrea, 'US and UK Governments Size Up Their KM Efforts', *KM Review* 5(5) (2002): 4.
[57] Santosus and Surmacz, 'The ABCs of Knowledge Management'.
[58] F. Han, 'Understanding Knowledge Management', *Public Manager* 30(2) (2001): 34–36.
[59] D. Calista and J. Melitski, 'E-government Reform: Negative Consequences of revisiting the politics–Administration Dichotomy' (paper presented at the International Association of Schools and Institutes of Administration Conference, Lake Como, Italy, 2005).
[60] R.K. Sapru and Y. Sapru, 'Good Governance Through E-governance with Special Reference to India', *Indian Journal of Public Administration*, 60(2) (2014): 313–14.

transparency and cost-effectiveness. E-government is defined as 'utilizing the internet and the world-wide-web for delivering government information and services to citizens'.[61]

The term 'e-Government' has been used too broadly to define initiatives and programmes that should rightly be deemed e-governance. Over the past few years, 'governments have hurriedly adopted e-government technologies and ideas from simple, online communication of government information to real time, secure transactions for various processes and payments. Demands generated from political leadership, other associated governments, capacity building needs and perceived citizens expectations all contribute' to adoption of e-government methods for good governance.[62] At a broader level, apart from delivering government services, e-governance includes integration of several stand-alone systems and services between government-to-citizens (G2C), government-to-business (G2B), government-to-government (G2G) as well as back-office processes and interactions within entire government framework. The overall objective of such a catalogue is to enable the administration to provide services with affordable cost and optimum time to the end user (citizen). In a broader sense, 'e-governance' is all about reform in governance facilitated by the creative use of ICT.

There is a growing wealth of information available related to 'e-government' that public managers may find useful. Since the mid-1990s, governments in many countries are providing efficient and cost-effective services, solutions and products to their respective customers.

In an increasingly connected virtual world of knowledge in cyberspace and with increasing spread of Internet and web-based information systems, time and distance have shrunk, and service delivery is now possible on 'anytime, anywhere' basis. Sequential steps in service delivery can in some cases be processes in parallel, making simultaneous delivery possible. Government interface with people can be re-engineered in a manner that human discretion is minimized. Like the personal computer, the Internet has become an indispensable tool in the day-to-day administration of government.

Applications of e-government

E-government is typically associated with ICT tools that increase the quality of decision-making process in public organizations. Its strategy includes the employment of Internet and the World Wide Web (WWW) for delivering government information and services to citizens. In the first decade of the 21st century, governments worldwide had made rapid progress in terms of embracing e-government technologies. The UN Global e-government Readiness Report of 2014 ranks UK at the top in list, based on the state of e-government readiness and the extent of e-government participation. Among countries, the South Korea has moved downward in constructing e-government organizations. India has been ranked 107 and has also made considerable progress in initiating e-government efforts. At the local level, there are initiatives to make digital cities.

---

[61] United Nations, 'Division for Public Economics and Public Administration and American Society for Public Administration', *Benchmarking E-Government: A Global Perspective* (New York: United Nations, 2002).

[62] David Coursey, 'Strategically Managing Information Technology', in *Handbook of Public Administration*, 3rd ed., eds. Jack Rabin, W.B. Hildreth, and G.J. Miller (Boca Raton: Taylor & Francis, 2007), 781–82.

To improve IT performance and productivity, the GOI approved the National e-Governance Plan (NeGP)[63] which seeks to improve delivery of government services to citizens and business establishments with the vision to 'make all government services accessible to the common man in his locality, through common service delivery outlets and ensure efficiency, transparency and reliability of such services at affordable costs to realize the basic needs of the common man'.[64]

India's e-governance transformation has been progressing rapidly. By 2016, over two billion e-government transactions have been logged and growth rate is rising exponentially. The government has taken several initiatives in the journey from e-governance vision to implementation. Some of the following purposeful steps and initiatives from vision to implementation include

(i) 44 mission mode projects (MMPs) across a wide range of public services such as passport seva, e-procurement digitization of land records and national citizen database.

(ii) The vision of e-Kranti with objectives of 'transforming e-governance for transforming governance', enhancing the portfolio of citizen centric services, and ensuring optimum usage of core ICT infrastructure.

(iii) E-government management structure comprising multiple committees to resolve bottlenecks and oversee programme execution.

Today, with the launch of State Electronic Mission and under the State Data Centre guidelines, inclusion of 'Citizen Services under Governance' has become a necessity in every state/UT. India's base of nearly 150 million Internet users is currently the third largest in the world. In the recent past, e-governance in India has successfully penetrated deeper and wider across various central and state government departments than ever before. The journey of e-governance is guided and empowered by the 44 MMPs under the NeGP which acts as a powerful driving force for today's presence of e-governance in all government ministries and departments.

Before the era of e-governance, government delivery of services was manual and opaque which caused great difficulties to the citizens. Scenes of overcrowded government offices, long queues, employees' absenteeism, arrogant and rent-seeking attitudes and inefficiencies were a common sight. It appeared that the focus of employees was more on corrupt practices than on citizen's service delivery. Government land and other registration records, birth and death registration, municipal permission and so on which were essential aids in getting benefits under welfare programmes remained buried in files. Citizens faced hardships in having access to government services because of the tedious office procedure and longer time lags.

---

[63] The NeGP, approved by the GOI on 18 May 2006, initially comprised 27 MMPs and 10 components. There are now over 7,000 websites related to the Indian government offering informational and transactional services.

[64] The NeGP has been formulated by the Ministry of Electronics and Information Technology (Meity) and Department of Administrative Reforms and Public Grievances (GOI).

Critical Observations

It is found that demand for IT usability and accessibility of e-government to different populations in India is increasing day by day. The impact of e-government on citizen trust and democratic institutions is a critical issue for the design and implementation of e-government strategies. Some associations like the International City Managers' Association (ICMA) have begun to examine the general benefits and advantages of e-government and the effect on democracy or the movement towards e-democracy.[65] In the USA, the Chief Information Officers Council (CIO Council) was established by Congress via the E-Government Act of 2002 for enhancing practices in the development, utilization, sharing and performance of federal information resources.

The UN e-Government Survey 2016 reported that many countries have put in place e-governance initiatives and ICT applications for the people to further improve efficiency and effectiveness and also further streamline governance systems to create synergy for inclusive sustainable development. But India does not show much progress on e-governance front compared with countries such as Republic of Korea, Australia, Singapore, Japan, Israel, Malaysia, the USA, the UK, France and Canada. These countries rank high at a global level and have robust e-governance delivery mechanisms.[66]

In developing countries, including India, there appears to be an insufficient number of qualified personnel at both the technical and management levels to accelerate the transition to e-government. This can be attributed to natural market forces, that is, such skilled personnel can receive higher compensation and benefits in the private sector. Further, most managers in the public sector have not been able to keep pace with the rapid pace of technology. Even in the USA, legislative actions such as the Government Performance and Results Act of 1993 and the Government Paperwork Reduction Act of 1980 have not had a significant impact on successful e-government implementations. In order to transform the organizational structure so that e-government implementation is more successful, the governments in India must institute a combination of employee and managerial rewards for those who encourage out-of-the-stovepipe e-government applications.

The main issues concerning e-government is the lack of equality in public access to the Internet, reliability of information on the web and hidden agendas of government groups that could influence and bias public opinions. There are many considerations and potential implications of implementing and designing e-government, including disintermediation of the government and its citizens, impacts on economic, social and political factors, vulnerability to cyberattacks and disturbances to peace-loving people.

Successful leveraging of e-government opportunity, therefore, involves concerted leadership building of institutional capabilities, increasing job exchange programmes with industry, adopting and implementing a sound e-governance policy and deepening the use of technology platforms.

---

[65] P. Foley, 'The Real Benefits, Beneficiaries and Value of e-Government', *Public Money and Management* 25(1) (2005): 4–7.
[66] See The UN e-Government Surveys 2014 and 2016.

CONCLUSION

The field of decision-making has particular bearing for public administration (or public management) today and in the future. In the complex field of government programmes and service delivery, public administrators are often put in the position of having to make a variety of decisions. Identification of tools and techniques that can be useful to public administrators in terms of effective decision-making is a challenging task. The key underlying feature of these tools and techniques is that they are created to aid the decision-making process to arrive at sound decisions for the organizations. In an environment of constant change and challenge, no single tool for decision-making will be adequate to achieve organizational goals. Managers and administrators in the government in particular will need to assess the strengths of various techniques and approaches before they are applied for organizational success.

Review Questions

(i) Discuss the application of CBA in policy decision-making.
(ii) Explain the major steps involved in strategic decision-making.
(iii) Discuss the main criticisms against the Delphi technique in decision-making process.
(iv) What is KM? How has the Indian administration approached KM in recent years?
(v) Critically analyse e-governance initiatives in India and their role in policymaking process.

CHAPTER 15

POLICY IMPLEMENTATION
Theory and Models

INTRODUCTION

In this chapter, an attempt is made to address the variety of contributions to the implementation theory and models.

Elinor Ostrom distinguishes between frameworks, models and theories.[1] Models 'make precise assumptions about a limited set of parameters and variables. Logic, mathematics, game theory, experimentation, and simulation, and other means are used to explore systematically the consequences of these assumptions in a limited set of outcomes'. Theories 'focus on a framework and make specific assumptions that are necessary for an analyst to diagnose a phenomenon, explain its processes, and predict outcomes'. A general framework 'helps to identify the elements and relationships among (these) elements that one needs to consider for institutional analysis. Frameworks organize diagnostic and prescriptive inquiry'.[2] A general framework (most comprehensive) is meant to enable theory formation and specified model building (limited).

For Lane, an implementation process is a combination of responsibility and trust. He argues, 'A reorientation to implementation theory would be to inquire into how accountability is to be upheld in the implementation of policies and how much trust is in agreement with the requirement of accountability'.[3] However, one is never sure how policy will actually be implemented once the policy interacts with the various aspects of the policy environment.[4] Theorists perceive the problem of implementation as simply about achieving compliance: the delivery of goods and services. But, implementation is fraught with challenges and obstacles.[5] There are three main approaches in which authors have sought to define and develop implementation research: top-down, bottom-up and a synthesis of top and bottom designs of approaches. The question is, in what ways the policy implementation is structured in order to enhance the likelihood of implementation success?

---

[1] Ostrom, 'Institutional Rational Choice', 26.
[2] Ibid., 25–26.
[3] J.-E. Lane, 'Implementation, Accountability and Trust', *European Journal of Political Research* 15(5) (1987): 543.
[4] Birkland, *An Introduction to the Policy Process*, 263–64.
[5] Larry N. Gerston, *Public Policymaking in a Democratic Society*, 2nd ed. (New Delhi: PHI Learning, Indian reprint 2009), 114.

■ Table 15.1: Contributors to Implementation Theories

Theories of Implementation	Principal Contributors
Top-down Theories	Pressman and Wildavsky (1973) Van Meter and Van Horn (1975) Bardach (1977) Sabatier and Mazmanian (1979, 1980) Mazmanian and Sabatier (1983)
Hybrid Theories	Majone and Wildavsky (1978) Scharpf (1978), Mayntz (1977) Windhoff-Heritier (1980) Ripley and Franklin (1982) Elmore (1985) Sabatier (1986) Goggin et al. (1990) Winter (1990)
Bottom-up Theories	Lipsky (1971, 1980) Elmore (1980) Hjern and Porter (1981) Hjern (1982) Hjern and Hull (1982)

Table 15.1 presents some of the principal contributors to the theories of implementation.

TOP-DOWN APPROACHES TO IMPLEMENTATION

Top-down theorists seek to simplify implementation in terms of control preoccupations. In other words, the focus then is on creating proper structures and controls to promote or compel compliance with the goals set at the top. DeLeon describes top-down approaches as a 'governing elite phenomenon'.

Pressman and Wildavsky's Approach to Implementation

Jeffrey Pressman and Aaron Wildavsky are celebrated as founding fathers of implementation studies.[6] Their original work followed a rational model approach. For them, implementation is clearly related to policy. They say, 'Policies normally contain both goals and the means for achieving them'. Much of the analysis in their book, *A Study of a Federally Mandated Programme of Economic Development in Oakland, California*, is concerned with the extent to which successful implementation depends upon linkages between different organizations and departments at the local level. They saw implementation as an 'interaction between the setting of goals and actions geared to achieve them'. Effective implementation requires, they argue, a top-down system of control and communications, and resources to do the job. Despite its limitations, Hogwood and Gunn defend their top-down approach on the ground that those who make policy are democratically elected.[7]

---

[6] J. Pressman and A. Wildavsky, *Implementation* (Berkeley, CA: University of California, 1984; 1st edition, 1973), xv.

[7] Brian Hogwood and Lewis Gunn, *Policy Analysis for the Real World* (Oxford: OUP, 1984).

Van Meter and Van Horn: Implementation Process Model

There are scholars who look at implementation as a process. For instance, Donald Van Meter and Carl Van Horn offer a model of systems building for the analysis of the implementation process. Their starting point is whether outcomes correspond to the objectives set out in initial policy decision. According to them, 'implementation will be most successful where only marginal change is required and goal consensus is high'. They suggest a model of six variables that shape the relationship between policy and 'performance'. The six variables are:

(i) policy standards and objectives, which 'elaborate on the overall goals of the policy decision...to provide concrete and more specific standards for assessing 'performance';

(ii) the resources and incentives made available;

(iii) the quality of interorganizational relationships (we find in their discussion of this, as in no much of the American literature on implementation, an extensive discussion of aspects of federalism);

(iv) the characteristics of the implementation agencies, including issues such as organizational control but also, going back surely to interorganizational issues, the agency's formal and informal linkages with the 'policymaking' or 'policy-enforcing' body;

(v) the economic, social and political environment; and

(vi) the 'disposition' or 'response' of the implementers, involving three elements their cognition (comprehension, understanding) of the policy, the direction of their response to it (acceptance, neutrality, rejection) and the intensity of that response.[8] They also highlighted two variables that slightly departed from the top-down mainstream. They argued that the extent of policy change has a critical impact on the likelihood of effective implementation.

It is clear that their model aims to encourage the compliance with the goals set at the top.

Sabatier and Mazmanian: Criteria for Implementation

Sabatier and Mazmanian, and Mazmanian and Sabatier, are classical scholars of top-down approaches.[9] Their starting point is the assumption of separation of policy formation from policy implementation. Their model lists six criteria for effectives implementation: (i) policy objectives are clear and consistent, (ii) the programme is based on a valid causal theory, (iii) the implementation process is structured adequately, (iv) implementing officials are committed to the programme's goals, (v) interest groups and (executive and legislative) sovereigns are supportive and (vi) there are no detrimental changes in the socio-economic framework conditions. They admit that the perfect hierarchical control over the implementation process is difficult to attain and can cause implementation deficit and

---

[8] Donald Van Meter and Carl Van Horn, 'The Policy Implementation Process: A Conceptual Framework', *Administration and Society* 6(4) (1975): 445–88.

[9] P.A. Sabatier and D. Mazmanian, 'The Conditions of Effective Implementation', *Policy Analysis* 5 (1979): 481–504; Sabatier and Mazmanian, 'A Framework of Analysis', *Policy Studies Journal* 8 (1980): 538–56; Mazmanian and Sabatier, *Implementation and Public Policy* (Glenview, IL: Scott, 1983).

failure. They therefore suggest that an adequate programme design can be crafted to ensure effective implementation.

Bardach's Political Game Model

Bardach acknowledges the political character of the implementation process and therefore regards implementation as a political game. According to Bardach, implementation is a game of 'bargaining, persuasion, and maneuvering under conditions of uncertainty'.[10] In this model, organization is seen as a structure composed of groups and individuals, all seeking to maximize their power and influence. Implementation from this angle is about self-interested people who are playing games. Implementers are playing to win as much control as possible and attempting to play so as to achieve their objectives. This model suggests that policies extend beyond the formal political institutions. Implementation is therefore seen as a political game which individuals play for the purpose of maximizing their power.

Bardach's work presents a view that implementation is a political process, and that successful implementation from a 'top-down' perspective must involve a very full 'follow-through'. This model urges us to redefine the boundaries between politics and bureaucracy, and between decision-making and decision delivery. Bardach thus provided ideas that also influenced bottom-up scholars.[11]

Important Assumptions and Problems of Top-down Approach

This top-down approach is seen as a prescriptive theory in the sense that implementation is about getting people do what they are told. Following are important assumptions on which the top-down approach is based:

(i) First, the policy contains a statement of objectives and goals. As Ryan notes, 'Top-down implementation strategies greatly depend on the capacity of policy objectives to be clearly and consistently defined'.[12]

(ii) Second, the policy contains clearly defined policy tools for the achievement of goals.

(iii) Third, the policy is reflected in a single statute or contained in an authoritative statement.

(iv) Fourth, in a top-down approach, there is an implementation chain starting from the highest-level policy designers through the lowest-level implementers.

(v) Fifth, policy designers have good knowledge of the strength and limitation of the implementing agency that will carry out the policy.

The focus in the top-down approach then is on creating adequate structures (accompanied with monetary and human resources) and controls to compel compliance with the goals set at the top. But this approach is not without its weaknesses. In the first place,

---

[10] Eugene Bardach, *The Implementation Game* (Cambridge, MA: MIT Press, 1977), 56.

[11] Helga Pulzl and Oliver Treib, 'Implementing Public Policy', in *Handbook of Public Policy Analysis*, eds. Frank Fischer, G.J. Miller and M.S. Sidney (Boca Raton, FL: CRC Press, 2007), 92.

[12] Neal Ryan, 'Unraveling Conceptual Developments in Implementation Analysis', *Australian Journal of Public Administration*, 54(1) (1995): 65–81.

it is difficult to reach a consensus on what programme goals are. Most national policies in India do not contain clearly defined goals. For example, electric crematorium was set up in Varanasi (UP) in 1989 as part of the Ganga Action Plan for cost-effective and river-friendly cremations. But the Minister for Water Resources (Uma Bharti) in a conference told environmentalists that 'religious leaders do not approve of electric cremations',[13] near riverbanks and that all bodies should instead be burnt in the traditional fashion with wood. When policymakers do not provide one goal or a coherent mutually compatible set of goals, implementation is hard as agencies and people charged with putting policies into effect pursue different goals.

Again in a top-down model of policy design, most policies made by the central government require considerable state and, in many cases, local governmental cooperation. Often they are reluctant to surrender their power and prerogatives to distant agencies headquartered in New Delhi. It is therefore very difficult for the central government to mandate any policy it sees fit, and if it attempts to do so, it can generate indifference or outright conflict with the states.

Again, there are strategic delays at the state level where states seek to slow implementation in order to develop ways to adapt the programme to local needs, or to induce the central government to provide more funding or other incentives. In the context of MPLAD scheme, for example, Datta notes, 'The overall picture that emerges is that a lion's share of the MPLAD funds is spent in a top-down manner without taking into consideration people's actual needs'.[14]

BOTTOM-UP APPROACHES TO IMPLEMENTATION

In the early 1980s, bottom-up approaches emerged as a critical response to the top-down schools. Exponents of the bottom-up model argue that top-down model lacks effective implementation in practice. They view implementation from the perspective of 'street-level bureaucrats'. This bottom-up model sees the implementation process as involving negotiation and consensus-building. Sabatier finds some of the methodological strengths of the bottom-up model: its effective incorporation of the study of networks, its strength in evaluating other influences on policy outcomes than government programmes and its value when a number of different policy programmes interact.[15]

Lipsky: Street-level Bureaucracy

Michael Lipsky is credited as the founding father of the bottom-up perspective. His work showed how the 'top-down' model lacked effective implementation in practice. His analysis of the behaviour of public service workers (e.g. teachers, social workers, police

---

[13] See *The Times of India* (Chandigarh), 9 October 2014. It is felt that religious objections should not become an impediment for scientific policy and its implementation.
[14] Prabhat Kumar Datta, 'Making Local Self-government in Rural India Work: Old Traditions and New Challenges', *Indian Journal of Public Administration*, LIX(1) (2013): 107.
[15] P.A. Sabatier, 'Top-down and Bottom-up Approaches to Implementation Research', *Journal of Public Policy* 6 (1986): 21–48.

officers), whom he calls 'street-level bureaucrats',[16] has an influential effect on implementation studies. The implication of this study was that control over people was not the mechanism to effective implementation. He argues that 'the decisions of street-level bureaucrats, the routines they establish, and the devices they invent to cope with uncertainties and work pressures, effectively become the public policies they carry out'. Lipsky argues that, therefore, to cope with the pressures upon them, street-level bureaucrats develop methods of processing people in a relatively routine and stereotyped way.

Lipsky, in brief, argues that students of public policy need to take account of the interaction of bureaucrats with their clients at a street level. He argues that where there is frequent interaction with the street-level bureaucrats, then there has to be decentralization of authority. The implication of this study was that control over people was inhibiting the process of implementation. So, instead of regarding human beings as cogs in a line of authority, policymakers must understand that policy is best implemented by the dedicated and committed people involved at the street level.

General Observations

The bottom-up model sees the implementation process as involving negotiation and consensus-building. These involve two environments: (i) the administrative capability and cultures of organizations involved in administering public policy and (ii) the political environment in which they have to carry out the policies. In the bottom-up model, great stress is laid on the fact that 'street-level' implementers have discretion in how they apply policy. Professionals—doctors, teachers, engineers, social workers—shape policy and have an important role in ensuring the performance by a policy. In other words, as Dunleavy notes, the policymaking process may be skewed by policy implementation which is largely dominated by the professionals.[17] Doctors, for instance, may develop ways of implementing health policies which actually result in outcomes which are quite different to the intentions of policymakers. This is possible because policy implementation involves a high margin of discretion. As Davis observes, 'A public officer has discretion wherever the effective limits on his power leave him free to make a choice among possible courses of action and inaction'.[18] In the discharge of policy delivery functions, implementers have varying bands of discretion over how they choose to exercise the rules which they are employed to apply. The importance of Lipsky's approach lies in the fact that it focuses on street-level actors on the one hand, and on the other, it shows that top-down approaches are not adequate to guarantee successful implementation.

Elmore: Backward Mapping Approach

In reaction to the flaws of top-down policy design, Richard Elmore, a key proponent of the bottom-up approach, comes out with an approach which he termed 'backward mapping' of problems and policy. His concept of 'backward mapping' suggests that analysis should start with a specific policy problem and then examine the actions of local agencies to

[16] Michael Lipsky, *Street-Level Bureaucracy: Dilemmas of the Individual in Public Services* (New York, NY: Russell SAGE, 1980).

[17] P. Dunleavy, 'Professions and Policy Change', *Public Administration Bulletin*, 36 (1981): 3–16.

[18] K.C. Davis, *Discretionary Justice* (Baton Rouge, LA: Louisiana State University Press, 1969), 4.

solve this problem. Elmore regards 'forward mapping' or the top-down approach as little more than a myth which was 'increasingly difficult to maintain in the face of accumulating evidence on the nature of the implementation process'.[19] In other words, analysis should begin at the stage when the policy reaches its endpoint, then analyse and organize policy from the patterns of behaviour and conflict which exist. The bottom-up model sees the process involving negotiation and consensus-building.

Hjern and Porter: Implementation Structures

Top-down frameworks do not satisfactorily explain implementation of programmes which requires a multiplicity of organizations causing complex pattern of interactions. Adopting a bottom-up approach, Hjern and Porter argue that implementation should be analysed in terms of institutional structures which comprise clusters of actors and organizations. A programme is not implemented by a single organization, but through a set of organizational pools. Hjern and Porter observe, 'Failure to identify implementation structures as administrative entities distinct from organizations has led to severe difficulties in administering the implementation of programmes'.[20] Therefore, they suggested that implementation analysis should start with the identification of networks of actors from all relevant agencies to solve their problems.

Barrett and Fudge: Policy–Action Continuum Model

Barrett and Fudge have developed a behavioural model which views implementation as action. They argue that implementation may be best understood in terms of a 'policy–action continuum'[21] in which an interactive and bargaining process is taking place over time between those who are responsible for enacting policy and those who have control of resources. In this model, more emphasis is placed on issues of power and dependence, interests, motivations and behaviour than in either the top-down or the bottom-up approaches. The focus in this model is on factors which affect the scope of action and behaviour of individuals and agencies. The policy–action model shows that policy is something which evolves. As Majone and Wildavsky note, 'implementation will always be evolutionary; it will reformulate as well as carry out policy'.[22]

Important Assumptions and Problems of Bottom-up Approach

Following are important assumptions on which the bottom-up approach is based.

First, the bottom-up approach recognizes that goals are ambiguous rather than clearly defined. While top-down approaches are concerned with compliance, the bottom-up approaches see the implementation process as involving negotiation and consensus-building. Second, in the bottom-up approach, policy can be characterized by a set of laws,

---

[19] Richard Elmore, 'Forward and Backward Mapping', in *Policy Implementation in Federal and Unitary Systems*, eds. K. Hanf and T. Toonen (Holland: Martinus Nijhoff, 1985), 20.
[20] B. Hjern and D.O. Porter, 'Implementation Structures: A New Unit of Administrative Analysis', *Organisation Studies* 2 (1981): 211–27.
[21] S. Barrett and C. Fudge, eds., *Policy and Action* (London: Methuen, 1981), 25.
[22] G. Majone and A. Wildavsky, 'Implementation as Evolution', in *Policy Studies Review Annual, 1978*, ed. H. Freeman (California: SAGE Publications, 1978), 116.

rules and norms that shape the ways in which government and interest groups address these problems. Thus, implementation can be viewed as a continuation of the conflicts and compromises in the policy process. Third, the bottom-up approach views implementation as working through a network of workers rather than through some rigidly specified process.

But there are some substantial weaknesses with the bottom-up approach. Sabatier argues that the bottom-up approach overemphasizes the ability of the street-level bureaucrats to frustrate the goals of the top policy designers. In the first place, street-level bureaucrats are constrained to act in a particular way based on their professional norms and obligations. Police officials, for example, who ignore procedural rules for handling suspects, can lose their jobs or face criminal charges.[23] States that fail to implement key features of federal policy put themselves at risk of losing substantial amounts of federal money, so states and local governments are under pressure to bring their agencies into compliance. Further, street-level bureaucrats do not have the necessary resources to thwart policy designers; they may delay but not entirely subvert implementation. In some cases, it is found that street-level bureaucrats may also want to follow the lead of top-level policy designers, supporting the implementation of national goals. It is also not true that groups in the bottom-up model are active participants in the implementation process. As Schneider and Ingram note that some target populations are going to be treated differently in implementation design than other groups.[24]

COMPARATIVE CHARACTERISTICS OF TOP-DOWN AND BOTTOM-UP APPROACHES

These two traditional approaches to implementation have their own weaknesses and strengths. But there are several characteristics that separate one school of thought from another in implementation theory. They are marked by such characteristics as research strategy goal of analysis model of policy process, character of implementation process and underlying model of democracy.[25]

(i) *Research Strategy:* In the first place, one can compare these two theories on the basis of research strategy. Top-down theories started from the assumption that policy implementation starts with a policy decision made at the top of the political system and works their way down to the implementers. In contrast, the bottom-up theories start out with the identification of actors who are involved in policy delivery at the bottom of the politico-administrative system.

(ii) *Goal of Analysis*: Second, the goal of analysis of top-downers is to predict whether the policy is likely to be implemented effectively. On the other hand, the goal of

---

[23] For example, an inquiry into the conduct of one SHO of Batala (Punjab) was held, when the police under his charge failed to recover the body of gruesome murder of a six-year-old body. See *The Tribune*, 11 October 2015.

[24] Anne Schneider and Helen Ingram 'The Social Construction of Target Population: Implications for Politics and Policy', *American Political Science Review* 87(2) (1993): 334–48.

[25] Pulzl and Treib, 'Implementing Public Policy', 93–95.

bottom-up studies in rather to give a description of the interactions and problem-solving strategies of employees involved in policy delivery.

(iii) *Model of Policy Process*: Third, it is found that top-down scholars are heavily influenced by the 'stagist model' which assumes that the policy cycle is divided into some clearly distinguishable stages. On the contrary, bottom-up scholars argue that policy implementation cannot be separated from policy formulation. The point is that bottom-up approaches pay attention to the whole policy process.

(iv) *Character of Implementation Process*: One can also compare these two schools of thought on the basis of character of the implementation process. In the top-down approach, persons who define policy objectives are capable of 'hierarchically guiding the process of, putting these objectives into practice'. In contrast, bottom-up scholars reject the idea of hierarchical guidance. Instead, they hold that the implementation process is greatly political in nature and the policies are even shaped by political decisions of the actors directly involved in policy delivery. In the bottom-up model, the focus is on the decentral problem-solving of local actors rather than on hierarchical guidance and control.

(v) *Underlying Model of Democracy*: Both approaches set upon contrasting models of democracy. Whereas top-down approaches are rooted in representative democracy, the bottom-up approaches follow participatory model of democracy (which includes those who are affected by a particular decision such as lower-level groups, private actors in policy formation).

Comments on Comparative Approaches

While top-down and bottom-up approaches to implementation have shortcomings, they certainly contribute to our knowledge of this essential elements of public policy. However, Sabatier argues that top-down approaches are much more useful when the researcher has limited resources to 'backward map' the implementation of a particular issue. In general, it is easier to look up statutes and policy statements issued by the high-level policy designers than it is to map all the various interests, agencies and street-level officials that will carry out a policy. By contrast, the bottom-up approach is best when there is no single, dominant programme (such as the Karnataka Guarantee of Services to Citizens Act, 2011 known as 'Sakala' is being implemented in 30 departments providing 265 services to the citizens of Karnataka)[26] and when one is more interested in the local dynamics of implementation than in the broad sweep of policy design.

Parsons observes that both top-down and bottom-up approaches exaggerated their respective positions and thereby over-simplified the complex implementation process.[27] As Sabatier rightly notes, top-downers overemphasized the ability of central policymakers to issue unequivocal policy objectives and to meticulously control the process of implementation.[28] Despite the debate as to the relevance of top-down and bottom-up

---

[26] S. Harsha. 'Decentralized Governance', *South Asian Journal of Socio-Political Studies* (Kerala) 14(2) (2014): 57–59.

[27] Parsons, *Public Policy*, 471.

[28] P.A. Sabatier, 'Top-down and Bottom-up Approaches to Implementation Research', *Journal of Public Policy* 6 (1986): 21–40.

approaches, it would be appropriate to agree on mutually acceptable theoretical models of implementations that pay attention to both central steering and local autonomy.[29]

HYBRID THEORIES AND SEARCH FOR SYNTHESIS

The implementation theory debate suggests that there are arguments between protagonists of the top-down and bottom-up perspectives. In the absence of a scholarly consensus, some authors have sought to define and develop implementation research through a synthesis of the original top-down and bottom-up types of approaches.

Elmore: Backward and Forward Mapping Approach

Elmore, previously a proponent of the bottom-up camp, revised his stand on 'backward mapping' concept and urged that programme success is dependent not only upon the element of backward mapping but also upon forward mapping.[30] Policymakers should therefore start with the consideration of policy tools and instruments and available resources for policy direction (forward mapping). Further, they should identify the incentive structure of implementers and target groups (backward mapping).

Sabatier: Advocacy Coalition Framework

Sabatier's work written with David Mazmanian on implementation in 1979 reflected the synthesis of the ideas of both top-down and bottom-up approaches into a set of six conditions for the effective implementation of policy objectives.[31] Backing away from his earlier work (1979), Sabatier, in his seminal article, proposes that a synthesis of two positions is possible: (i) drawing on the insights of Hjern et al. into the interorganizational dynamics of implementation and its network and (ii) the top-down approach (focuses on how institutions and social and economic conditions limit behaviour). Implementation takes place within the context of a policy subsystem, and is bound by 'relatively stable parameters' and 'events external to the subsystem'.

In the last part of the 1986 essay, Sabatier outlines what he sees as the way forward, involving the 'advocacy coalition framework', adopting

> the bottom-uppers' unit of analysis—a whole variety of public and private actors involved with a policy problem—as well as their concerns with understanding the perspectives and strategies of all major categories of actors (not simply program proponents). It then combines this starting point with the top-downers' concerns with the manner in which socio-economic conditions and legal instruments constrain

---

[29] L.J. O'Toole, 'Research on policy implementation: Assessment and Prospects', *Journal of Public Administration Research and Theory* 10(2000): 268.

[30] R. Elmore, 'Forward and Backward Mapping', in *Policy Implementation in Federal and Unitary Systems*, eds. K. Hanf and T. Toonen (Holland: Martinus Nijhoff, 1985).

[31] P.A. Sabatier and D. Mazmanian, 'The Conditions of Effective Implementation', *Policy Analysis* 5 (1979): 481–504.

behaviour. It applies this synthesized perspective to the analysis of policy change over periods of a decade or more.[32]

The 'advocacy coalition framework', which Sabatier developed further in his later work together with Jenkins-Smith in 1993, discarded the 'stage heuristic' of the policy process, aimed at empirically explaining policy change as a whole. This approach has some resemblance with the bottom-up theory as the analysis starts from a policy problem to the reconstruction of strategies for the target actors to solve the problem. Besides, it emphasizes the role of policy learning and recognizes the importance of social and economic conditions that may have effect on the policymaking process. However, the advocacy, coalition approach has failed to recognize the social and historical context in which change occurs.[33] The framework is designed to analyse institutional conditions and to produce a consensus which was not there in the original model. What Sabatier actually is struggling with is the difficulty of making a distinction between policy formation and policy implementation.

Goggin, Bowman, Lester and O'Toole: Negotiation and Communication Approach

Reconciling the top-down and bottom-up approaches, Goggin and his colleagues have developed a model of policy implementation that relies on the sending of messages between policymakers and policy implementers.[34] To them, implementation is as much a matter of negotiations and communication as it is a matter of command. They sum up their argument in two key propositions:

(i) Clear messages sent by credible officials and received by receptive implementers who have or are given sufficient resources and who implement policies supported by affected groups lead to implementation success.
(ii) Strategic delay on the part of states, while delaying the implementation of policies, can actually lead to improved implementation of policies through innovation, policy learning and the like.

Goggin and his colleagues found, in certain policy areas, that states that 'strategically delayed' implementation often had better success in implementing a policy than did states that immediately implemented a policy.

Winter: Integrating Implementation Research

Winter argues that 'looking for the overall and one for all implementation theory' is a 'utopian' objective which is not practical, and may even inhibit the creativity that comes from diversity.[35] He says therefore that we should look for partial rather than general implementation theories. From that point of view, Winter seeks implementation research as able to

[32] Sabatier, 'Top-down and Bottom-up approaches', 39.
[33] F. Fischer, *Reframing Public Policy* (Oxford: Oxford University Press, 2003), 99.
[34] Malcolm L. Goggin, Ann O.M. Bowman, James P. Lester and Laurence J. O'Toole, *Implementation Theory and Practice: Toward a Third Generation* (Glenview, IL: Little, Brown, 1990).
[35] S.C. Winter, 'Implementation', in *Handbook of Public Policy*, eds. B.G. Peters and J. Pierre (London: SAGE Publications, 2006), 151–66.

address concrete issues of a kind that an obsession with all-encompassing theories will tend to inhibit. He argues that there needs to be an emphasis on exploring the determinants of policy outputs, 'I suggest that we look for behavioural output variables to characterize the performance of implementers.... The first aim of implementation research then should be to explain variation in such performance'.

Wildavsky: Incremental Learning Approach

Wildavsky, previously a representative of the top-down camp, together with Majone, presented a model similar to the advocacy coalition framework.[36] Core argument is that implementation is an incremental learning process in which inputs are constantly changed and redefined in the course of the implementation of programmes.

Scharpf: Networks Approach

According to Scharpf, the transformation of policy goals into action depends upon the interaction of a multitude of actors with separate interests and strategies.[37] Introducing the concept of 'policy networks' to implementation research, he suggested paying more attention to processes of coordination and collaboration among separate but mutually dependent actors. The concept of policy networks later gained wide recognition as an approach to the study of policy change.[38]

Policy Network Approach

Implementation of policies in a federal context and IGR in general involves complex networks. Such networks may spread horizontally between organizations of equivalent power and stature as well as between organizations that are related vertically. The theoretical roots of the network approach lie in the interorganizational theory and the interactive perspective on public policy.[39]

Benson defines policy networks in terms of a 'complex of organizations connected to each other by resource dependencies'.[40] Similarly, Klijn and Koppenjan define policy networks as a (more or less) stable pattern of social relations between interdependent actors, which take shape around policy problems and/or policy programmes.[41] Their central assumption is 'that policy is made in complex interaction processes between a large number of actors which takes place within networks of interdependent actors'. The actors involved are

---

[36] G. Majone and A. Wildavsky, 'Implementation as Evolution', in *Public Studies Review Annual*, ed. H. Freeman (Beverly Hills, CA: SAGE Publications, 1978).

[37] F.W. Scharpf, 'Interorganizational Policy Studies', in *Interorganizational Policy Making: Limits to Coordination and Central Control*, eds. K.I. Hanf and F.W. Scharpf (London: SAGE Publications, 1978), 345–70.

[38] See B. Marin and R. Mayntz, eds., *Policy Networks: Empirical Evidence and Theoretical Considerations* (Frankfurt: Campus, 1991).

[39] W.J.M. Kickert et al. (eds.), *Managing Complex Networks: Strategies for the Public Sector* (London: SAGE Publications, 1997).

[40] J.K. Benson, 'A Framework for Policy Analysis', in *Interorganizational Coordination*, eds. D.L. Rogers and D. Whetten (Amsterdam: Iowa State University Press, 1982), 148.

[41] E.H. Klijn and J.F.M. Koppenjan, 'Public Management and Policy Networks', *Public Management* 2(2), (2000): 139.

mutually dependent because they need each other's resources to achieve goals. Policy networks thus form a context in which actors act strategically.

Indian networks literature recognizes that networks are crucial for the policy formation and its implementation.[42] On 1 July 2015, the central government (India) launched 'Digital India' campaign inviting domestic and foreign companies to make 'governance more technology-enabled and efficient. The aim is to improve systems, remove bureaucratic sloth and reduce red-tape that often delays processes and decision-making'. A study on digitization and mobility by the Associated Chambers of Commerce and Industry of India (ASSOCHAM) and Deloitte estimated app downloads in India to touch nine billion by 2015 with entertainment and social networking dominating use over utility, health or education apps.[43] The PMO App Contest and the eGovapp store also signal government intention to leverage technology to enhance efficiency, transparency and effectiveness of public services. For Smith, networks are particularly required to

(i) facilitate consultative style of government,
(ii) reduce policy conflict and make it possible to depoliticize issues,
(iii) make policymaking predictable and
(iv) relate well to the departmental organization of government.[44]

Thus, networks approach contributes both to a recognition of the need for new ways to formulate the issues about implementation and to highlighting the difficulties about the policymaking and policy implementation distinction. In this context, cooperation is a necessary condition in policy networks to achieve satisfying targets. But it does not mean that there would not be any conflict, since there is a tension between interdependency and the diversity of goals. This tension needs to be solved in any policy performance venture. Two types of steering strategies have been suggested: process management and network constitution. While process management has the aim of bringing about improvement of interaction between actors in policy performance venture, network constitution aims at changing the network. These strategies focusing on institutional changes are time-consuming.[45] Since cooperation between actors is a necessary condition in policy network approach, explanations for the success or failure of policy processes depend on the awareness of the actors of mutual dependencies, mutual interactions on the use of indispensable resources and development of reciprocal rules. Since actors are relatively autonomous in policy networks, there is the need of central coordinating actor for solving 'wicked' problems (e.g. flood control, pollution reduction) through flexibility 'upstreams' and for ensuring cooperating between involved actors.[46]

---

[42] Sapru and Sapru, 'Good Governance through e-Governance', 313–31.
[43] See *The Financial Express* (Chandigarh), 28 July 2015, 9.
[44] M.J. Smith, *Pressure, Power and Policy: State Autonomy and Policy Networks in Britain and the United States* (New York, NY: Harvester Wheatsheaf, 1993).
[45] Klijn and Koppenjan, 'Public Management and Policy Networks', 140.
[46] J.F.M. Koppenjan and E.H. Klijn, *Managing Uncertainties in Networks* (London: Routledge, 2004).

Comments on Hybrid Theories

Lane questions the search for an integrated theory of implementation. He suggests that implementation is seen as involving notions of both an 'end state or policy achievement' and 'a process or policy execution'.[47] He goes on to emphasize two alternative considerations in relation to top-down/bottom-up distinction: responsibility and trust. Lane further argues that top-down models are particularly concerned to emphasize 'responsibility' (policy accomplishment) side, while bottom-up models underline 'trust' (policy execution) side. Lane argues

> An implementation process is a combination of responsibility and trust.... Without the notion of implementation as policy accomplishment there is no basis for evaluating policies and holding politicians, administrators and professional accountable. On the other hand, implementation as policy execution rests upon trust or a certain amount of degrees of freedom for politicians and implementers to make choices about alternative means for the accomplishment of goals.[48]

A similar point is made by Winter who characterizes implementation as both a 'process' and an 'output' (sometimes 'outcome') of the implementation process, and urges us to concentrate on the output.[49]

Rothstein observes that the theme of trust has been neglected largely by implementation researchers. He goes on to point out, 'Without citizens' trust in the institutions responsible for implementing public policies, implementation is likely to fail'.[50] Rothstein stresses, 'Successful policy implementation is often a question of so organizing the implementation process so as to accommodate the need for flexibility and the uncertainty in the policy theory'.[51]

Palumbo and Calista's work aims to place implementation in the broader policymaking process. They argue, 'More recent research demonstrates that implementation is a legitimate part of the policy-making process—a part that can be neither diminished empirically nor de-legitimized normatively'.[52]

Hence, while it seems possible to combine some of the features of both the approaches, Parsons is also right in writing that some of the differences are so fundamental that the desire to construct a comprehensive model of both approaches is 'like trying to combine, in a Kuhnian sense, incommensurate paradigms'.[53]

---

[47] Lane, 'Implementation, Accountability and Trust', 528.
[48] Ibid., 542–43.
[49] Winter, 'Implementation', 159.
[50] B. Rothstein, *Just Institutions Matter* (Cambridge: Cambridge University Press, 1998), 100.
[51] Ibid., 113.
[52] Dennis Palumbo and Donald Calista, eds., *Implementation and the Policy Process* (New York, NY: Greenwood Press, 1990), 14.
[53] Parsons, *Public Policy*, 487.

LESSONS FROM IMPLEMENTATION RESEARCH AND CONCLUSION

Most relevant lessons learnt from implementation research since the publication of Pressman and Wildavsky's pioneering study (1973) are briefly highlighted here:

(i) Scholars of both top-down and bottom-up approaches seem to agree that implementation and policy formulation are highly interdependent processes.
(ii) Accepting the relevance of both approaches, scholars of both camps agree that implementation is a 'continuum' located between central guidance and local autonomy.
(iii) Representatives of bottom-up school have convinced the wider community of implementation scholars that implementation involves more than the carrying out of the political orders from above.
(iv) Further, the implementation process should not be viewed in isolation. Instead, extraneous factors such as social, economic and political developments or influences from other policy fields need to be taken into account as well.

Although theoretical models presented by implementation scholars have produced a number of important insights with regard to the field of implementation itself, the 'visibility of implementation analysis' is severely hampered by certain weaknesses (such as lack of cumulation, multitude of explanatory variables, shared positivist epistemology).[54] But this does not suggest that implementation research should be totally abandoned. Rather, it is very useful to invest time and financial resources into the study of how policies are translated into action.

Recognizing the problems of inconsistencies and incompleteness associated with models, Gareth Morgan maintains that if we are to understand complexity, it is important to adopt a critical and creative approach to thinking in terms of models or metaphors.[55] For him, there can be no single metaphor which leads to a general theory. Each approach has comparative advantages and provides some insight into a particular dimension of the reality of policy implementation. Mapping the context of problems offers the possibility of understanding the various dimensions of knowledge, beliefs, power and values which frame policymaking and policy implementation. As a student of public policy, the aim is to become capable in understanding the frameworks which are applied in the theory and practice of policy implementation in the contexts in which they take place.

Policy implementation indeed is one of the most difficult aspects of the policy process. It brings together many actors and forces that cooperate and clash with each other in order to achieve or thwart policy goals. In many cases, policies fail to achieve the desired outcomes, and in some cases, they succeed in the outcome of any public programme. The research in policy implementation contributes to theory-building in implementation

[54] See, for detail, Pulzl and Treib, 'Implementing Public Policy', 102–03.
[55] Gareth Morgan, *Imaginization: The Art of Creative Management* (Newbury Park, CA: SAGE Publications, 1986/1993), 362–65.

while providing useful information to policymakers and implementers on how to structure programmes for greater success.

Review Questions

(i) Briefly discuss the systems building model for analysis of policy implementation process.

(ii) What does the top-down approach to implementation of policies refer to?

(iii) What are the major limitations of the bottom-up approach to policy implementation?

(iv) Present a brief comparative analysis of the top-down and bottom-up approaches to implementation of policies.

(v) Policy implementation is one of the most difficult aspects of the policy process. Elaborate this statement with suitable reference to various hybrid theories.

CHAPTER 16

POLICY IMPLEMENTATION
Modes of Policy Delivery

INTRODUCTION

Pressman and Wildavsky's influential *Implementation* (1973)[1] and Hargrove's *The Missing Link* (1975)[2] highlight the concern that far too little attention has been paid to the question of policy implementation. In fact, implementation is viewed as an automatic extension of the policymaking process.[3] In the 1970s, there emerged a growing interest in the post-decisional phases of public policy. It became evident in the 1970s that many policies had not performed well. As it became apparent that policymaking in many areas such as population, health, education and agriculture in India had not achieved its desired goals, researchers in public administration and public policy began to focus on policy implementation. Policy implementation is of critical importance to the success of government. However good the political system, however noble the goals, however sound the organizational system, no policies can succeed if the implementation does not bear relationship to the intentions of the policy adopters.

In this chapter, an attempt is made to discuss important issues related to policy implementation.

Defining Policy Implementation

The starting point for a discussion on policy implementation must be to consider what we mean by the term 'implementation'. Implementation is what realizes decision, what generates outputs and what utilizes the scarce resources. It can be seen essentially in terms of the nature and degree of control exercised over the operations of a policy. Policymaking does not come to an end once a policy is approved or adopted. As Anderson points out, 'Policy is being made as it is being administered and administered as it is being made'.[4] Yet implementation is something separated from policymaking. Very few decisions are self-implementing, implying that there is no separate implementation stage. An influential definition of implementation has been formulated by Mazmanian and Sabatier:

---

[1] J.L. Pressman and A. Wildavsky, *Implementation* (Berkeley, CA: University of California Press, 1973).
[2] E.C. Hargrove, *The Missing Link: The Study of the Implementation of Social Policy* (Washington: Urban Institute, 1976).
[3] B. Guy Peters, American *Public Policy: Promise and Performance*, 6th ed. (Washington: CQ Press, 2004), 105.
[4] James Anderson, *Public Policy-making* (New York, NY: Holt Praeger, 1978), 98.

Implementation is the carrying out of a basic policy decision, usually incorporated in a statute but which can also take the form of important executive orders or court decisions. Ideally, that decision identifies the problems(s) to be addressed, stipulates the objective(s) to be pursued, and in a variety of ways, 'structures' the implementation process. The process normally runs through a number of stages beginning with passage of the basic statute, followed by the policy outputs (decisions) of the implementing agencies, the compliance of target groups with these decisions, the actual impacts—both intended and unintended—of these outputs, the perceived impacts of agency decisions and finally, important revisions (or attempted revisions) in the basic statute.[5]

Pressman and Wildavsky initially defined implementation as 'a process of interaction between the setting of goals and actions geared to achieving them'. They go on to say, 'Implementation, then, is the ability to forge subsequent links in the causal chain so as to obtain the desired results'.[6] Their definition embodies assumptions most commonly held about implementation.[7] First, they assume a series of logical steps—a progression from intention through decision to action—and clearly see implementation starting where policy stops. Second, they distinguish two definite steps in formulating intentions: policy-making—their 'initial conditions'—and the creation of programmes which form the 'inputs' to their implementation process. Third, they see implementation as a process of putting policy into effect, a process which is mainly concerned with coordinating and managing the various elements required to achieve the desired ends.

Van Meter and Van Horn attempt to provide a conceptual framework of the process of the implementation by observing, 'Policy implementation encompasses those actions by public and private individuals (or groups) that are directed at the achievement of objectives set forth in prior policy decisions'.[8] Barrett and Fudge take a view of the implementation process 'as a sequence of events 'triggered off' by a policy decision, involving the translation of policy into operational tasks to be carried out by a variety of actors and agencies, and substantial coordinating activity to ensure that resources are available and that things happen as intended'.[9]

John calls implementation 'the stage in the policy process concerned with turning policy intentions into action'.[10] DeLeon calls the study of implementation 'little more than a comparison of the expected versus the achieved'.[11] In a similar sense, Henry defines

---

[5] D.A. Mazmanian and P.A. Sabatier, *Implementation and Public Policy* (Glenview, IL: Scott Foresman, 1983), 20–21.

[6] J. Pressman and A. Wildavsky, *Implementation*, 2nd ed. (Berkeley, CA: University of California Press, 1973; 1984), XIV.

[7] It is pointed out here that these definitions are only the starting point of Pressman and Wildavsky's study.

[8] Donald Van Meter and Carl Van Horn, 'The Policy Implementation Process', *Administration and Society* 6 (1975): 445–88.

[9] Susan Barrett and Colin Fudge, 'Examining the Policy-Action Relationship', in *Policy and Action*, eds. Susan Barrett and Colin Fudge (London: Methuen, 1981), 13.

[10] P. John, *Analysing Public Policy* (London: Pinter, 1988), 204.

[11] P. DeLeon, 'The Missing Link Revisited: Contemporary Implementation Research', *Policy Studies Review* 16(3–4) (1999): 311–38.

implementation as 'the execution and delivery of public policies by organisations or arrangements among organisations'.[12]

One might say that implementation process includes what goes on between the pronouncement of a policy and its actual effect. It is important to look at implementation not only in terms of putting policy into effect, but also in terms of observing what actually happens (to the target group). Therein lies the process of implementation, the administrative task of transferring policy intentions into practice. 'As part of the public policymaking process', writes Gerston, 'implementation is the means by which decisions are converted into application'.[13]

Thus, public policy in the form of a statement of goals and objectives is put into action programmes that aim to realize the ends stated in the policy. More specifically the task of implementation is to form a bridge that allows the objectives of public policies to be achieved as outcomes of government activity. It involves the 'creation of a policy delivery system in which specific mechanisms are designed and pursued in the hope of reaching particular ends'.[14] According to Grindle, the general process of implementation can begin only when general goals have been designed, and when adequate funds have been allocated for the pursuit of goals.[15]

Dryzek defines policy design as 'process of inventing, developing and fine-tuning a course of action with the amelioration of some problem in mind'.[16] The design perspective calls attention to matching content of a given policy to the political context in which the policy is formulated and implemented. The crafting of policies typically entails a long process of analysis of problems and options, politically acceptable courses of action and an authoritative decision to enact a policy.

Barrett and Fudge say that policy implementation is dependent on

(i)   knowing what you want to do;
(ii) the availability of the required resources;
(iii) the ability to marshal and control these resources to achieve the desired end; and
(iv) if others are to carry out the tasks, communicating what is wanted and controlling their performance.[17]

INSTITUTIONAL ENVIRONMENT AND POLICY DESIGN

Characteristics of political, social, economic and administrative systems including rule of law, democratic structure and federalism of the country have their impacts and

---

[12] Nicholas Henry, *Public Administration and Public Affairs*, 12th ed. (New Delhi: PHI Learning, Indian reprint 2012), 341.

[13] Larry M. Gerston, *Public Policymaking in a Democratic Society*, 2nd ed. (New York, NY: M.E. Sharpe, 2008), 113.

[14] Van Meter and Van Horn, 'The Policy Implementation Process', 446.

[15] Merilee S. Grindle, 'Introduction', in *Politics and Policy Implementation in the Third World*, ed. M.S. Grindle (New Jersey: Princeton University Press, 1980), 3–19.

[16] John Dryzek, 'Don't Toss Coins in Garbage Cans: A Prologue to Policy Design', *Journal of Public Policy* 3(4) (1983): 346.

[17] Barrett and Fudge, 'Examining the Policy-Action Relationship', 13.

implications for the policy implementation. Some of the important concerns of the institutional environments have been already discussed in previous chapters. Here it should be understood that the political forces that shape policy design also greatly influence policy implementation. Further in implementing a policy design, a great deal of attention has to be given to such aspects as institutional arrangements, allocation of tasks to personnel, scheduling dependencies and making decisions which arise in the course of using resources and generating outputs.

Constitutional System

The country (India) stands out with its most dramatic manifestation of the federal system. Federalism requires accommodation to be reached in a context within which the constitutional division of power leaves matters for negotiation. A great deal here hinges upon the policy formation/policy implementation distinction explored earlier in this book. In that context, this is to suggest that high-level constitutional differences will have some effect on the policy implementation which could be ironed out through negotiations and in-built system of coordination and cooperation.

Policy Implementing Network

Implementation of policy is merely one more step in a logical sequence of policy management. It is the most important phase in the achievement of policy goals. It has the objective of anticipating deviations from planned performance and making proper adjustments. An important task of the policy implementing director/manager is to keep track of the range of implementing tasks, their functional relationship and their scheduling dependencies. The director has to be capable in resolving conflicts and making decisions which arise in the course of mobilizing resources and generating policy outputs.

For the implementation of a given policy, it is important for the policy implementation director to construct a policy implementation network which can help him ensure that policy tasks occur in proper sequence and on time. It should help him to identify which tasks in the policy are most critical to overall policy performance. The construction of the network requires to compose an activities duration list. This list should project activities for each activity and add the time required for each activity. For scheduling policy implementation activities, the network helps the public managers in depicting which activities are more important for economical and efficient management of the policy programme. Public managers need to go beyond merely accepting the existence of governance networks and become expert at using these structures to achieve specific policy goals.

Allocating Tasks to Personnel

Ultimately, implementation of policy programmes depends upon the personnel who are charged with the responsibility of policy execution. Implementation is seeing to it that the activities happen on time and within given budget. But, first, it requires implementing personnel. If policy is to be carried out, there has to be allocation of appropriate tasks to the personnel resources. Regardless of their status, specialized knowledge, experience and qualifications, all personnel need to work as a cohesive team for the purpose of achieving desired policy goals.

Public organizations are facing increasing pressures to perform at a high level, but several resources of tension may undermine efforts to improve implementation. Therefore, for an effective policy implementation, a manpower plan is needed. It helps the policy director assign staff to the policy implementation programme. Further, for the purpose of assigning role and responsibilities to a staff person, it is necessary to develop position classification like a job description. The position classification may include (i) status, role and duties of the staff; (ii) reporting relationships; and (iii) accountability criteria with a view to evaluate the incumbent's performance in the position. It is important to organize the staff for securing technical performance. This may involve such principles of organization as unity of command, span of control, division and integration of efforts and hierarchy of authority and accountability.

Also important are the degree and nature of constitutional checks and balances on the political and administrative exercise of power; the recruitment, selection and training of civil servants; and their professional identity. One of the findings is that the stronger the checks on the implementation activities of civil servants in a country, the greater is their inclination to execute rules 'according to the book', in order to protect themselves from possible liability claims or public accountability.

Decision-making Mechanisms

Government performance is an important concern to the public managers. This requires also a right decision. In the implementation of a policy programme, the manager has to be proficient at solving problems and making decisions which arise in the course of using resources and seeing what happens to the target group. Making decisions is the most difficult job for a policy implementing manager. Even with the best planning, there will always be a need to make good decisions in the face of unanticipated events in the policy management. For major decisions which impact resource requirements, technical outputs, this is a major activity because such a decision requires full support of several constituents (beneficiaries, sponsors, politicians, planning agencies, government). In this context of decision-making, three mechanisms have been suggested:

  (i) **Exception Principle:** The exception principle states that difficult decisions (other than routine decisions) involving unusual or unprecedented problems that have broader implications for the whole policy implementation should be reserved for senior staff at higher levels in the organization.
 (ii) **Delegation of Authority:** The above exception principle does not operate unless there exists some degree of delegation of authority. The authority is needed at each level for the implementing staff to perform their duties and tasks.
(iii) **Consensus-building:** Consensus in this context refers to an agreement to support a particular decision. Consensus-building in a participative management strategy ensures that no good ideas are ignored. It also builds a strong group among all those programme constituents involved in the implementation process.

For effective implementation of a policy programme, there is a need for forming a steering committee. The purpose of the committee is to ensure that a programme is being implemented within the budget and given time.

There are four dimensions that have been identified by Richardson in his work regarding differences in policy implementation:

(i) Anticipatory and consensus-seeking
(ii) Anticipatory and imposing decisions
(iii) Reactive and consensus-seeking
(iv) Reactive and imposing decisions

The study of policy indicates the complexity of the policy process. It involves an environment setting from which demands and needs are generated, a political system which first processes and then makes policy decisions and an administrative organization or system which implements policy decisions. In fact, the implementation of public policies is divided between these three settings.

A successful implementation is therefore dependent on inputs, outputs and outcomes. Inputs are the resources (personnel and finance) mobilized in producing outputs (decisions taken by the implementers) to achieve the outcomes (what happens to the target groups intended to be affected by the policy). Irrespective of the level of outputs of an implementing organization, if the intended effect in the target group is not found, something is wrong. Policy does not implement itself. Policy has to be translated into action programmes through various agencies.

MODES OF POLICY DELIVERY

Implementation of public policy is of utmost importance as it keeps institutions performing their functions, including maintenance of democratic values in the society. But policy does not implement itself. Implementation of public policy depends upon institutions tasked with the responsibility of putting policy into action.

The provision of public goods and services can be regarded as a complex mixture of contributions from government, market and voluntary organizations. Modes of delivery or systems of policy delivery have drawn the attention of the policy analysts. These delivery systems in terms of the way in which public goods and services are provided through a network of public and private institutions assume considerable importance. This fragmentation creates new problems for control and accountability in a democratic country such as India. People now face an often bewildering array of agencies responsible for the provision of public services. Simple tiers have given way to policy delivery systems which use a mix of partnerships between the public and private sectors (market mechanisms), and new roles are being defined for the voluntary sector and the community.

Thompson et al. distinguish between hierarchies, markets and networks as three general modes of social coordination.[18] Colebatch and Larmour focus on bureaucracy, market and community. For these scholars, people may organize by 'following rules defined by hierarchic authority' (bureaucracy); through 'individual exchanges which serve their interests' (market); or by 'acting in ways which are appropriate for some group of which they are

---

[18] G. Thompson et al., eds., *Markets, Hierarchies and Networks* (London: SAGE Publications, 1991).

a part' (community).[19] In the 'bureaucratic' model of organization, authority and rules are organizing principles; in the 'market' model, incentives and prices are central; and in the 'community' model, norms, values and networks are key factors.[20] Parsons observes that in the real world of public service delivery, there are almost always mixes. As Colebatch and Larmour state, 'The task is to identify the nature of the mix, not to place the organization into one box or another'. Parsons distinguishes four sorts of mixes: a governmental mix, regarding layers of government; a sectoral mix, concerning public–private relationships; and enforcement mix, regarding modes of enforcement; and a value mix, referring to underlying values.[21] For the enforcement or compliance mix, he makes a difference between two dimensions.

Parsons states that when the mode of organization is hierarchy, enforcement requires 'effective methods of command and the use of coercion or threat to ensure compliance with authoritative rules'. In the market mode of organization, the problem of gaining compliance will be perceived as one 'rooted in self-interested behaviour'. Network or 'community' organizational forms will rely on 'the operation of custom, tradition, common moral codes, values and beliefs, love a sense of belonging to a 'clan', reciprocity, solidarity and trust'.[22]

Here an attempt is made to discuss the mix of policy delivery: bureaucratic, market and community agencies.

BUREAUCRACY OR HIERARCHY

Bureaucracy or hierarchic authority is classified as the executive branch of government. It is an administrative organization consisting of a legal body of non-elected employed officials who are organized hierarchically into departments in accordance with the rules governing the conditions of their service. It is the bureaucracy which controls the personnel, money, materials and legal powers of government, and it is this institution that receives most of the implementation directives from the executive, legislature and judiciary. Public service is important because significant and sizeable activities of the society are carried out in the public domain.

Public servants are recruited in theory to serve the political masters by carrying out their decisions. Ministers decide on policies and civil servants take the necessary execution actions to implement them. The importance of the senior administrator's role in policy implementation arises because he is concerned with ends and not merely means. He is exclusively concerned with the implementation of policy decisions made by the politicians. More important is the work of the senior administrator on the development of major policies in line with government commitments. He has a constitutional responsibility to advise on the financial and administrative implications of different policy options, thus helping ministers to find ways of achieving their political objectives and societal goals.

---

[19] H.K. Colebatch and P. Larmour, *Market, Bureaucracy and Community: A Student's Guide to Organisation* (London: Pluto Press, 1993), 104.
[20] Ibid., 17.
[21] Parsons, *Public Policy*, 492.
[22] Ibid., 518–19.

Policy implementation by the administrator feeds back into policy formation so that he can advise authoritatively from experience on the practicability of different policy options. Much of the legislation and policy builds on the past administrative practice and accumulated experience. Further, the knowledge derived from direct experience of policy implementing gives the senior administrator a near monopoly of knowledge relevant to policymaking. New policy emerges as administrators bring their experience and ideas to bear on problems which political masters wish to solve. As repositories of knowledge and experience, senior administrators are able to give instructions and advice to the lower staff as to how to implement policy decisions. They can foresee the administrative and political difficulties likely to be encountered from the interests more affected. They are able to argue from positions of great strength about new methods of dealing with policy implementation problems for which no satisfactory solution has been found. In this way, the administrator's role in policy implementation is of considerable importance. Addressing bureaucrats on Civil Services Day (21 April 2016), PM Narendra Modi said, 'We get more results working in team than in isolation. We need to come out of silos and work together as a team for nation-building'.[23]

As a specific category of public servants, street-level bureaucracy (distinct from highly expert functionaries who are often described as professionals) has a relative autonomy. Street-level bureaucrats see themselves as decision-makers, whose decisions are based on normative choices, rather than as functionaries responding to rules, procedures or policies.[24] At the very end of the line, between policy goals and policy effects, street-level bureaucrats interact and interface with citizens. Facing all sorts of ordeals in those daily contracts, these servants practise coping strategies. Although the interface between public servants and citizens are certainly not symmetrical, there is a mutual dependency and even negotiations may take place. Much of what police officers, teachers, health workers and other public functionaries are doing has not been laid down in formal documents. In circumstances, these public servants are required to interpret the public policy involved in a creative but justifiable way. Being implementers, they may, in fact, sometimes practise 'formulation and decision-making' as additional functions related to the policy. Since these servants are familiar with the needs of citizens, they cope with shortcoming in as justifiable a way as possible. For them, almost by definition, resources are scarce, while nevertheless the conceptions of their occupation, practised in public service, urge them to make the best of it. Doing so, they see themselves as professionals.

It is to be noted that bureaucracy in most developing countries and India too has not been accepted as a mode of good governance. Bureaucracy is said to be afflicted with excesses of red tape, tedious rules and an attitude of unresponsiveness. Despite its maladies, it is important because implementation is the continuation of policymaking through other means. Legislation is never self-implementing but requires delegation to appropriate organizations and personnel. Placing a programme in perspective is the first task of implementation, and administering the day-to-day work of an established programme is the second. It is because delegation and discretion permeate bureaucratic implementation that it plays a crucial role in the power structure of policymaking and policy action.

---

[23] See *The Financial Express* (Chandigarh), 22 April 2016.
[24] S. Maynard-Moody and M. Musheno, 'State Agent or Citizen Agent: Two Narratives of Discretion', *Journal of Public Administration Research and Theory* 10(2) (2000): 329–58.

Technically, the task of all public organizations and personnel is to implement, execute and enforce law and policy. In doing so, most personnel do use bureaucratic discretion. It is pointed out that legislation does not minimize discretion and more details may even increase personnel discretion. According to Davis, 'A public officer has discretion wherever the effective limits on his power leave him free to make a choice among possible courses of action and inaction'.[25]

Requirements for Implementation Officials

For successful implementation of policies, bureaucracy must operate with following important elements at its disposal.

Translation Ability

In the first place, administrators must clearly understand the nature and significance of policies which the political masters have set. They are responsible for advising in the formulation of policies designed to achieve goals, and also mobilizing, organizing and managing the resources necessary to carry through these policies. There must be clear communication between the policymakers and the bureaucracy. They should be able to translate the general policy and its objectives into operational targets.[26] This function should also include analysis of probable costs and benefits of each way of achieving the operational targets. If bureaucrats are not sure of their job, they are entrusted to do, and they must get clarification from the public officials who developed it. Clarity about the policy and how it is to be carried out are important requirements for doing the task correctly.

As far as possible, they should adopt a rational approach and use management techniques to implement policies. Finally, they should be able to pay special attention to the question of coordination of policies and policy instruments. Civil servants should analyse the policy in question in relation to existing policies to see if any inconsistencies exist, and examine whether it complements or supplements existing policies to produce better results. Exhorting the civil servants to be 'agents of change' and work as a team aiming to 'reform, perform and transform', PM Narendra Modi on 21 April 2016 said that over the years, the scope of a civil servant's role had changed from a regulator to administrator to controller to one with keen managerial skills. 'Often, senior civil servants are too tired of work, leading to interruptions in implementation of government schemes they have to be cautious against this tired attitude'.[27]

Resources

A public policy or decision is not enough. It is sure to fail if it is not accompanied by adequate resources for its implementation. Resources (personnel, finance, equipment or enforcement assignments) must be given to the administrators to carry out their

---

[25] Kenneth Culp Davis, *Discretionary Justice* (Baton Rouge, LA: Louisiana State University Press, 1969), 4.
[26] Robert T. Nakamura and Frank Smallwood refer to this capability as a 'compliance mechanism'. See their book *The Politics of Implementation* (New York, NY: St. Martin's, 1980), 59–60.
[27] See *The Times of India* (Chandigarh), 22 April 2016.

implementation tasks. In fact, resources are critical links between public policymakers and administrators.[28]

Few Agencies for Implementation

Research has shown that too many agencies involved in implementation cause confusion and waste of resources. When a few or single agency is assigned implementation responsibility for a public policy, there is a greater likelihood of successful implementation. Sharing of responsibilities opens the opportunity for coordination problem.

Accountability

Like the elected public officials who are accountable to the public, bureaucrats are usually accountable to the political bodies that create, oversee and provide funds for this agency. The point is that a bureaucracy must complete its assignment on time, within budget and within rules governing its existence. As a general rule, administrators must file periodic reports or appear before public policymakers at special hearings or periodic meetings to show them that they have done their assigned tasks. In these instances, policymakers may respond in a variety of ways. Moving to a system of contractual appointments at all levels of government will enforce accountability.[29]

Since so much power and control over implementation is held by the administrative organizations and personnel, chief executives must put in efforts to control their discretion. Efforts to control bureaucratic discretion rest upon many strategies. First, if the public agencies do not implement a law to the satisfaction of the legislature, the policy can be legislatively changed. The executive may also overrule routine bureaucratic interpretation of legislation. Second, from time to time, most of the problems associated with administration could be solved either by transferring responsibility to a friendly agency or by replacing a recalcitrant agency head, or by paring the agency budget. Third, the legislature has an important role to play in curbing the bureaucratic discretion by making legislation more detailed. The bureaucracy can also be pressured through public hearings, the media and other forums. The point is that all senior government services, including IAS, require thorough overhauling.

Despite strong criticisms against the operational functions of the bureaucracy, it stays. It cannot be abolished; at rest, it can be improved. Without determined political support and without willing cooperation of many top administrators, little can be achieved.

LEGISLATIVE CONTROL

While bureaucracy is the primary organization for the implementation of policy programmes, the legislature's role is of nature of supervision and control and guidance. The legislature may affect the administrative organization in several ways. In law, the power of the legislature (Parliament in India) appears to be unlimited. It subjects administrative action to examination and criticism. It can lay down limits to administrative discretion and

---

[28] Gerston, *Public Policymaking in a Democratic Society*, 118.

[29] V. Ramani, 'IAS at the Crossroads', *The Financial Express*, 19 November 2015.

delegation. The more detailed the legislation passed, the less discretion does the bureaucracy have. It authorizes taxation and expenditure and holds the executive to account for its financial decisions. It may specify limits in the legislation over the use of budgetary funds. Further, it may issue statements or suggestions concerning how the legislation should be implemented. The Parliament, the Public Accounts Committee, the Committee on Public Undertakings, the Estimates Committee and the other standing committees of Parliament often attempt to influence the actions of administrative agencies that fall within their purview. Parliamentary approval is required for many top-level administrative appointments, and this may be used to influence the implementation process. Also, parliamentary approval is sought before some action is taken against them. Finally, it has been noted that much of the time of several legislators is devoted to casework which often involves problems that their constituents are having with administrative organizations. The constituents invariably depend on legislators for securing favourable actions for themselves. In India, the Parliament gets the opportunity of control over the political executive for its actions not only at the budget sessions but at other times as well. The control which Parliament exercises over executive is of three types: (i) control over policy (ii) control over implementation and the day-to-day working of the departments and (iii) control over public expenditure.

In addition, the members of the legislature can criticize the government for its alleged acts of omission as well as commission after the President's address to the new session. Further, during the general discussion on the Finance Bill and submission of Demands for Grants, members of both the houses of Parliament get ample opportunity to discuss the budget proposals and general policy of taxation. Members of the Lok Sabha can move three kinds of cut motions to assent, reject or reduce the amount of a demand. These are (i) Policy Cut Motion, indicating the disapproval of the policy underlying the demand; (ii) Economy Cut Motion, to project economy that can result from the suggestion of the member; and (iii) Token Cut, to ventilate a specific grievance. Issues of policy, economy, efficiency, grievances and so on may be raised and the minister concerned has to respond to the questions.

The first hour forms the most valuable part of the day's proceedings which is reserved for raising questions on executive's functioning. It serves the purpose of asserting the supremacy of the Parliament (e.g. denial of powers to the High Court to examine the constitutionality of central laws). Besides question hour, financial matters are also discussed during the zero-hour discussion, adjournment debates (discussion on matter of urgent public importance) and no-confidence motions (provide an occasion when the entire or part of the government policy is criticized).

However, it may be noted that any control which Parliament might be said to exercise over the executive is largely indirect, inducing self-control and responsibility under the threat of exposure, rather than control in the sense of actually implementing policies.

JUDICIAL ACTION

The rule of law guards against the tyranny of the parliamentary majority and executive decision by providing for an impartial judiciary. Judiciary plays a crucial role in enforcing decisions. In India and many other developing countries, most laws are enforced through judicial action. The Environment Protection Act, Income Tax Act, Urban Land Ceiling and Regulation Act, and the laws dealing with crimes are some examples. Many of the clauses stipulated in the Acts are subjected to judicial interpretation. Because of this and the power of review, the courts are both indirectly and directly involved in policy implementation. The Indian Constitution entitles the SC and High Courts to exercise judicial review of legislation. The implementation of policies in many fields has been influenced by judicial decisions. The judicial bodies can help, obstruct or nullify the implementation of particular policies through their interpretations of statutes and decisions. It is necessary to note that the role of the judiciary in responding to administrative action has usually been to protect the rights of the citizen faced with growing state power and is designed to defend the weak and the poor. Judges are more concerned with the procedural qualities of executive decision-making than with their substantive content. A classic example was the SC's ruling in September 2003 restraining the GOI from implementing disinvestment policy without seeking parliamentary approval regarding the disinvestment and privatization of Hindustan Petroleum Corporation Limited (HPCL) and Bharat Petroleum Corporation Limited (BPCL).

Another classic example of the SC's ruling on 16 October 2015 was the declaration of the 99th Amendment Act, 2014 and the NJAC Act, 2014 as 'unconstitutional'.

Similarly, the SC directed the companies manufacturing cigarettes and other tobacco products on 4 May 2016 to immediately comply with the new government rules mandating that the pictorial and text warnings such as 'tobacco kills' should cover 85 per cent of the surface area of each packet. It is emphasized here that the judicial control over administration is a direct outcome of the doctrine of rule of law and its scope is very wide. It can interfere with administrative orders whenever they interfere with the rights of citizens or violate any aspects of the Constitution while formulating or implementing public policies. The causes of judicial intervention can be (i) lack of jurisdiction (ii) errors of law; (iii) errors of fact-findings; (iv) abuse of authority and (v) errors of procedure.

In addition to the ordinary courts, there are a large number of administrative tribunals and agencies in India which are operating as courts for administrative adjudication. They operate to exercise checks on the functioning of implementing agencies and whosoever feels affected can approach these bodies. Though the verdict of these agencies and tribunals is final, the civil courts could interfere in case the agency or tribunal

(i) has acted on an issue outside its jurisdiction;
(ii) has overacted, which means acting in excess of its powers;
(iii) has acted against any rule of natural justice;
(iv) where the compliance of the provisions of Act has not been adhered to; and
(v) where its proceeding has been fraudulent and dishonest.

To check the functioning of Administrative Tribunals, some safeguards have been provided in the Constitution. As per Article 32(2) of the Indian Constitution, the SC is empowered to issue writs, namely habeas corpus, mandamus, prohibition, quo warranto and certiorari. Any individual feeling that his fundamental rights are being infringed through the implementation of a given policy, and has failed to get justice through the administrative adjudication agency or tribunal could move the court for protection and safeguarding of his rights.

Thus, the ordinary courts (especially the High Courts and the SC) and the Administrative Tribunals (created under the Indian Constitutional provisions) have a creative as well as a positive role in the implementation of social policies, especially relating to welfare of women and children and weaker sections of the community.[30]

INTEREST GROUPS AND VOLUNTARY SECTOR

Interest groups are generally nonprofit, non-violent associations of individuals or other groups that are independent of governments that aggregate interests and inject them into the policy process.[31] Politicians and bureaucrats generally welcome the inputs of interest groups because these provide information which helps to identify policy alternatives and choices.

It is also contended that group action is considered a more effective method than individual action for the implementation of public policies. NGOs and the pressure groups are important means of enhancing the effect of public opinion. They can communicate more effectively than individual citizens with public officials on implementation of public policies. They serve as links between individual citizens and policy implementers. They help the policy implementers by offering personnel and expertise in the policy implementation issues. For example, the Punjab government, succumbing to the pressure of private bus operators who had threatened to boycott Akali Dal's Sadbhavna rallies, accepted their demand to reduce motor (mini-buses) tax from ₹50,000 to ₹30,000 per annum.[32] CARE India (a known NGO) launched recently an ambitious project for promotion of some 2,500 self-help groups (SHGs) as a measure to empower women especially in the rural area which has improved a lot in many parts of Andaman and Nicobar Islands.[33]

In most situations, the government has to rely on the pressure groups for the implementation of its policies. Many government policy programmes would remain unimplemented without the cooperation of vested interests. Such interests can gain control in the formulation of policy as a price of its successful implementation. Protection of the human environment is an example. Hence, every policy programme has to be planned with the consent of those groups which they themselves have to implement. The cooperation within the implementation process is seen as a way of handling and channelling conflicts of interest. For example, the Chandigarh State AIDS Control Society often collaborates with Sustainable Education and Health Among Tribals (SEHAT), an NGO, for the implementation of programme against Drug Abuse and Illicit Trafficking.[34] More and more public agencies are becoming dependent on the voluntary sector and the interest groups to deliver services

---

[30] In a significance judgement, the Punjab and Haryana High Court said, 'Having failed to take care of physical needs and basic amenities of the parents in their old age, the appellant has made himself liable for avoidance of the transfer documents in terms of Section 22 of the Act'. See *The Tribune* (Chandigarh), 13 December 2015.

[31] R. Price, 'Transnational Civil Society and Advocacy in World Politics', *World Politics* 55(4) (2003): 579–606.

[32] See *The Tribune*, 13 December 2015.

[33] S.S. Sreekumar, 'Role of Gram Sabha in Human Development: The Case of Andaman and Nicobar Islands', *South Asian Journal of Socio-Political Studies* 16(2) (2016): 80–89.

[34] See *The Tribune*, 27 June 2014.

including the implementation of policies which they find either difficult to provide or have not the resources to provide or which have traditionally been provided by the voluntary sector.

A few NGOs are taking a lead in this regard and are working in the areas of social mobilization, awareness-raising, environmental protection and income generation. But the World Bank perspective of privatization of social welfare functions is playing havoc with the lives of vulnerable sections of society such as women, children, Dalits, tribals and the sick.[35]

COMMUNITY-BASED STRATEGIES

Community-based public policy strategies have been a significant development in new approaches to local policymaking and implementation since the 1980s. The Constitution (73rd and 74th Amendment) Acts, 1992 give a constitutional status to the panchayats and municipalities for formulation and implementation of policies and programmes for economic development and social justice for the local community.

The community is seen as an alternative to the markets and bureaucracies. At the forefront of advocating 'communitarianism' as an approach to public policy is Amitai Etzioni.[36] Community policy may, for instance, be directed at a neighbourhood or a part of a town, or it may be directed at a group of people who share a problem or an interest. The aim is to create a 'bottom-up' process in which people in the community participate in the making and implementation of policies. The community is seen as an agent of social change and reform. The strategy is to use the community as a channel of defending the interests and rights of individuals and groups who are threatened by the power of bureaucracy. In this connection, the SC dealt with the role of the Gram Sabha: The Gram Sabha had 'an obligation to safeguard and preserve the traditions and customs of the STs and other forest dwellers, their cultural identity, community resources etc'.

PUBLIC–PRIVATE PARTNERSHIP

Public–private partnership (PPP) is a contractual argument and arrangement between public and private agencies for the promotion of delivery of public goods and services efficiently, allowing the greater private sector participation than traditional involvement. The committee, headed by former finance secretary Vijay Kelkar, that reviewed the PPP model for infrastructure projects has recommended several measures for easy financing of these, including issuance of zero coupon bonds by banks to developers, equity divestment by the government from completed projects, reviewing model concession agreements (MCAs) to ensure equitable risk distribution, providing provision of renegotiation of MCAs in documents itself, setting up sector-specific regulators, PPP institute and tribunal and discouraging public sector undertakings (PSUs) from PPP projects unless strategically necessary.[37]

---

[35] Javeed Alam, 'A Look at Theory: Civil Society, Democracy and Public Sphere in India', *Journal of Social and Political Studies* 3(1) (2012): 35. See also Shantilin Lazarus, 'Promoting Women Empowerment and Protecting the Social Capital in the Era of Globalization', *South Asian Journal of Socio-Political Studies* 16(2) (2016): 44–49.

[36] A. Etzioni, *The Spirit of Community* (New York, NY: Crown Publishers, 1993).

[37] *The Financial Express,* 29 December 2015.

POLICY ENFORCEMENT

Implementation can have a tremendous impact on the target group. Such is the potential benefit of implementation and the potential harm from a policy's derailment in the case when implementation goes awry. But it must have enforcement or compliance capability; otherwise, it carries no meaning. Hood identifies four choices or modes of enforcement:

   (i) Set aside/modify rules: In order to bring about compliance, the government may choose either to set the rules aside or to modify the rules.

   (ii) Spread the word: The government may attempt to gain compliance by using publicity and persuasion.

   (iii) Pursue and punish rule violators: The government chooses to use legal and police action to deter non-compliance.

   (iv) Make it physically difficult, impossible, inconvenient to break rules: In this case, the enforcement method is not to use publicity to inform people about the 'grass', but involves making the grass physically difficult or inconvenient to get at in the first place.[38]

Enforcement Relationship to Policy Type and Regime

Burch and Wood set enforcement methods in terms of 'negative and positive consequences' and modes of 'formal and informal controls'.[39] The domain of positive sanctions and informal controls permits of a political regime in which enforcement takes place through bargaining. The domain of formal controls and positive sanctions is manipulated to induce compliance. The domain of formal controls and negative sanctions permits of a political regime in which the enforcement takes place in the use of law and threat, while the domain of negative sanctions and informal controls takes us into the areas of tyranny and autocracy.

Further, discretion is high in the domain of positive sanctions and informal controls, and low in the domain of negative sanctions and formal controls. Although Burch and Wood admit this classification is crude, it provides a way of understanding the mix of factors, which shape the delivery process.

Etzioni's Model of Enforcement

For Etzioni, there are three main reasons why people in organizations comply with laws and policies:

   (i) They may do so out of a sense of agreement, love or morality.

   (ii) They may comply because of fear.

   (iii) They do so because it is in their monetary interest.

For Etzioni, enforcement may therefore be the consequences of (i) normative (love), (ii) coercive (fear) or (iii) remunerative (money) power.

---

[38] C.C. Hood, *Administrative Analysis: An Introduction to Rules, Enforcement and Organisations* (Brighton: Wheatsheaf, 1986), 48–60.

[39] M. Burch and B. Wood, *Public Policy in Britain* (Oxford: Basil Blackwell, 1990).

In seeking to make sure a policy is carried out, implementation will require a mix of different enforcement modes. Etzioni argues that effective organizations are those which achieve a balanced mix between low levels of fear (coercion and alienation) and high levels of money (remuneration and calculation) and love (normative and moral) involvements. He posits that organizations with 'similar compliance structures tend to have similar goals, and organisations that have similar goals tend to share similar compliance structures'.[40] His appeal lies in pointing towards a middle way between the excesses of state regulation and reliance on pure market forces.

CONCLUSION

For policy designers and policy managers, policy implementation is a difficult aspect of the policy process. Policy is meaningful when it succeeds in the accomplishment of policy goals. Without its implementation and compliance, the delivery of public policy is unlikely and uncertain. It must be realized that a good policy, if it is to be implemented, must have effective means of enforcement. Bureaucracy, community, market and voluntary sector may be viewed in terms of different ways of enforcing policy decisions. Each implementer has its own role to play in the enforcement of public policies. Government increasingly resort to a variety of instruments for pursuing its policies. In short, while the bureaucracy, executive staff agencies and commission are the primary implementers of public policies, many other actors are involved, and they should not be neglected in our study of the policy implementation process. Hence, policy analysis should not exclude whoever has an influence on the implementation of a given policy. But the nature of what is at stake in processes of policy implementation may be 'subject to fundamentally different perspectives that are shaped by language, culture, and symbolic politics'.[41]

Review Questions

(i) Define the term 'policy implementation'.
(ii) Implementation of policy programmes depends upon the personnel who are charged with the responsibility of policy implementation. Describe the statement.
(iii) Critically discuss the role of pressure groups in implementation of public policies.
(iv) Briefly discuss Etzioni's model of enforcement and its applicability in real-life scenarios.
(v) Why has bureaucracy in India not generally accepted as a mode of good governance? Substantiate your argument with examples.

---

[40] Etzioni, *A Comparative Analysis*, 71.
[41] Helga Pulzl and Oliver Treib, 'Implementing Public Policy', in *Handbook of Public Policy Analysis*, eds. F. Fischer, G.J. Miller and M.S. Sidney (Boca Raton, FL: CRC Press, 2007), 103.

CHAPTER 17

POLICY MONITORING
Role, Approaches and Techniques

INTRODUCTION

Policy is meaningful, but without its implementation and adequate monitoring, the delivery of public goods and services is unlikely and uncertain. It must be realized that a policy, if it is to achieve its intended goals, its performance must be monitored and controlled. Monitoring is essentially a subset of the implementation process. It is an activity which occurs in the course of implementing a programme or policy. It is in the process of monitoring that the implementer actually gets to begin seeing the results of policy. The significance of the monitoring of public policy lies in seeing that intended results are achieved in time and through the efficient use of resources.

'Monitoring' is the process of observing what goes on. It is 'the process of inducing action for adherence to schedule'.[1] Policy monitoring has come to mean the process of observing policy implementation progress, resource utilization and anticipating deviations from policy expectations. Its implications are that management takes steps to ensure that all activities related to policy implementation are completed within time and budget.

For Mantel and his associates, 'monitoring is the collection, recording and reporting of project information that is of importance to the project manager and other relevant stakeholders.... Control uses the monitored data and information to bring actual performance into agreement with the plan'.[2]

But monitoring is not controlling. Controlling is the process of making adjustments which correct the deviations from planned progress. The purpose of control is (i) the stewardship of organizational assets and (ii) the regulation of results through the alteration of activities.[3] For example, if the factory management fails to install pollution control devices to prevent air pollution, we may simply decide to proceed against the factory management under the Air (Prevention and Control of Pollution) Act, 1981. On the other hand, if monitoring shows that a particular policy activity is deviating from planned parameters, then the management takes required measures to replan that particular activity. But if there is a significant variance from planned parameters, it is important to analyse the

---

[1] Sadhan Choudhury, *Project Scheduling and Monitoring in Practice* (New Delhi: South Asian Publishers, 1986), 20.
[2] Samuel J. Mantel et al., *Project Management,* 1st Indian edition (New Delhi: Wiley India, 2009), 286.
[3] Ibid., 303.

source of deviation before deciding what measure is needed.[4] Indeed, monitoring is of critical importance to the policy success.

OBJECTIVES AND ROLE OF POLICY MONITORING

The objective of policy monitoring is to ensure through the policy implementation process that resource inputs are used as efficiently as possible to yield intended results. The standards which are used for both efficiency of resource utilization and effectiveness of policy implementation are inherent in the policymaking process.[5] The monitor has to be able to appraise resource use, technical activities and policy implementation results with an amount of detail which permits him to make changes or corrections when necessary. On the contrary, if the monitor flies too high, as it were, then the details will be lost and the opportunity for effective policy control is lost. The monitor becomes, often, buried in the detail of policy programme and loses sight of overall policy performance standards and objectives. Policy monitoring helps in designing and implementing systems for the processes which provide just the right amount of detail for good control of the policy execution. Experience has shown that effective monitoring can ensure the proper execution of policy with good results in the shortest amount of time.

An effective monitoring of public policies aids in cost reduction, time saving and effective resource utilization. The key issue in monitoring is to create an information system that gives policymakers and policy implementers the information they need to make timely decisions and policies that will keep policy programme performance as close as possible to the objectives of the policy. Therefore, it is important that monitoring and control processes are given due importance and are designed properly. Further, monitoring also helps communicate the need for coordination among those working on the tasks and subtasks of the policy activity.[6]

STEPS IN MONITORING AND CONTROL

Monitoring requires proper planning and management. In all, six steps in monitoring and controlling are useful for policy achievement goals.

(i) **Planning:** Defining and scheduling technical activities and budgeting financial resources comprise what is meant by planning. Planning establishes expectations against which the implementer or policymaker monitors policy delivery process.

(ii) **Allocation:** Allocation simply refers to use of resources in activities of policy programme. In allocating them, we divide available resources among the policy programme activities.

(iii) **Implementation:** Implementation refers to doing the technical work planned in the policy delivery. It means to give practical effect to ensure of actual fulfilment by specific measures.

[4] Sunny and Kim Baker, *Project Management* (New Delhi: Prentice Hall of India, 1998), 223–27.
[5] James Anderson, *Public Policy-making* (Boston, MA: Houghton Mifflin, 2000), 98.
[6] Mantel et al., *Project Management* 292.

(iv) **Measurement:** Measurement means seeing performance indicators (PIs) on all parameters (technical, time and cost) in order to detect deviation from policy delivery activity.

(v) **Evaluation:** Evaluation is concerned with analysis of deviation from acceptable norms and its causes.

(vi) **Adjustment:** Adjustment means taking corrective measure against deviation from expected parameters. Usually, some adjustment can be made in resource availability or scheduling.

Monitoring and control are not possible to achieve the policy delivery targets in the absence of (i) performance measurement indicators, (ii) personnel accountability, (iii) finance and time availability and (d) corrective actions.

APPROACHES TO POLICY MONITORING

The renewed interest in policy monitoring has taken place within a variety of approaches. A few approaches in regard to monitoring of public policies are briefly discussed here.

Formative Approach

As already said, the monitoring starts with a schedule and works for the success of a policy programme when it is being implemented. The implementation stage therefore requires formative evaluation which monitors the way in which a programme is being administered or managed so as to provide feedback which may help to improve the implementation process.[7] Increasingly, this monitoring of the process of implementation provides policymakers and managers with techniques for evaluating the way in which a programme is being managed or delivered, so that this information is utilized to correct or improve the policy delivery process more effectively. This takes the form of management information system (MIS), including the use of computers to provide a centralized information system. KM helps an ongoing accumulation and organization of information which can feed into the managerial decision-making process. For example, PMKSY launched on 2 July 2015 mainly aims at increasing agricultural production would be monitored by an Inter-Ministerial National Steering Committee chaired by PM.

Performance Measurement Approach

For the promotion of successful implementation of public policies, monitoring is the best technique. It provides corrective measures. In this regard, performance measurement approach is applied to know about the effectiveness and efficiency of policy delivery. Measurement is akin to monitoring. It means watching PIs on all parameters with a view to detecting the earliest available signs of any deviations from desired results or performance. Once it is found that some aspects of the policy is deviating too far from expected parameters, then it is the job of a policy implementing manager to exert some influence on that aspect or change the parameters. Generally, some adjustment can be made in resource utilization or scheduling. Sometimes a new technical activity may be taken in hand.

---

[7] D.J. Palumbo, ed., *The Politics of Program Evaluation* (California: SAGE Publications, 1987), 40.

In this approach, PIs can be developed and used. Peter Jackson argues that measures of performance can provide an effective substitute for profits so as to improve the management of schools, hospitals, local government and other services.[8] Jackson identifies a range of roles to be performed by PIs. PIs can (i) increase accountability, (ii) provide a basis for policy planning and control, (iii) provide important information to monitor organizational activities and (iv) provide the basis of a staff appraisal system.

Monitoring of implementation aspects of the programmes can lead to significant savings. For example, the direct benefit transfer (DBT) schemes (launched on 1 January 2013), a major reform initiative to check leakages of welfare funds since then, has been universalized to cover all central sector and CSS, where cash benefits are transferred to individual beneficiaries. In order to give further fillip to it, DBT Mission was in 2015 shifted to Cabinet Secretariat and its implementation is being monitored by the PMO. DBT scheme for subsidies has resulted in significant savings across welfare schemes, including ₹21,000 crores in PDS, LPG distribution and MNREGS.[9]

The PMKSY scheme of the GOI has also got a National Executive Committee (NEC) constituted under the Chairmanship of the VC NITI Aayog for overseeing, such as the implementation, resource allocation, inter-ministerial coordination, monitoring and permanent assignment.

Despite the fact that the PIs have a number of advantages, including identifying problem areas and determining progress in moving towards goals, they, in practice, simply improve the capacity of the bureaucracy to control people, money and material resources.

Managerial Approach

Managerial approach to monitoring has more or less a businesslike style in order to generate the best policy outcomes. In this context, three approaches, namely (i) CPM, (ii) PERT and (iii) PPBS, have gained wide recognition not only in the private sector but also in the public sector.

CPM and PERT Approaches

CPM and PERT approaches are adopted as a means of addressing the issues of material and resource use in the most efficient manner. These refer to the planning of a particular programme, allocating people and other resources and monitoring progress. The aim of CPM and PERT is to control the execution of a policy programme by controlling the network of activities and events which compose the stages of policy implementation.[10]

CPM is a technique which aims to identify those activities which are critical to the successful implementation of policy programme on time. A network is drawn to show the starting period of the policy programme and the estimated time period involved in moving from one critical activity to another. The nature of CPM is to select the optimal path based on the allocation of the resources as well as time.

---

[8] Peter Jackson, 'The Management of Performance in the Public Sector', *Public Money and Management* 8(4) (1988): 11–16.
[9] See *The Financial Express* (Chandigarh), 11 May 2016; *The Indian Express* (Chandigarh), 9 May 2016.
[10] Robert P. McGowan and Dennis P. Wittmer, 'Five Great Issues in Decision-making', in *Handbook of Public Administration*, 2nd ed., eds. Jack Rabin et al. (New York: Marcel Dekker, 1998), 304–06.

On other hand, PERT is a technique which predicates that the duration of critical activities is uncertain. The PERT involves a graphic estimation of the time and resources necessary for policy execution. This can be applied to a number of efforts, ranging from a housing project to the scheduling and deployment of personnel. PERT systems are programmed on the basis of three types of calculation of this uncertainty: the most probable duration, the shortest forecast of duration and the longest forecast of duration. PERT analysis is often used in the implementation of large-scale policy programmes (such as rural development) where there is a high level of uncertainty surrounding the completion of a policy programme. Thus, CPM and PERT are seen to be good approaches for securing efficient use of material resources.

PPBS

PPBS is a system of resource allocation designed to improve government efficiency and effectiveness by establishing long-range planning goals. The PPBS approach seeks to set clear goals, outputs and values in the budgetary process and to create a system of analysis and review in which the costs and benefits of a policy programme could be calculated over several years. This approach is 'based on the ideas that an organization's activity can be viewed as the production of defined products or objectives. Costs and benefits can be determined'.[11] The PPBS aims at locating decisions about parts of the budget in the context of the whole of government spending strategy. The model is derived from a classically rational approach, beginning with the identification of goals, objectives, needs and problems and culminating in monitoring, review and feedback. It focuses, therefore, on objectives to be achieved and monitoring through an ongoing review of results.

As an approach, it aims at exercising monitoring on budget expenditures. However, it is argued that the PPBS proved ill-suited for monitoring. The PPBS simply failed to live up to its promise.[12] Although the PPBS was largely a failure, its introduction brought into policy management a more comprehensive approach to CBA. Moreover, the PPBS approach seeks to reduce the expenditure in aggregate at budget-making exercise.

Systems Approach

It is obvious that monitoring is an operational activity which occurs in the process of implementing a given policy programme. The main objective of monitoring is to ensure that resource inputs are used in such ways as to generate the high quality of policy outputs. An effective monitoring therefore requires proper structuring. Structuring in policy work can involve both the structuring of organization and structuring the policy programme itself and the combining of these two structures to provide a framework for integration. The structuring looks at implementation gaps as something that should be analysed in the context of 'system' which as a whole is involved in the delivery of policy programmes and services. The systems analyst is concerned in knowing how a total sequence of programme activities and inputs and outputs contributes to the success or failure of policy delivery programmes or services.

---

[11] Robert K. Whelan, 'A History of the Conduct of Inquiry in Public Administration', in *Handbook of Public Administration,* 3rd ed., eds. Jack Rabin et al. (Boca Raton: Taylor and Francis, 2007), 836.
[12] Self, *Econocrats and the Policy Process,* 178–203.

Increasingly, the monitoring of implementation also involves control. Carter and his associates suggest that a successful implementation system involves four types of control: (i) coordination over time, (ii) coordination at particular times, (iii) detailed logistics and scheduling and (iv) defending and maintaining structural boundaries.[13] It may be emphasized that systems approach lays stress on attaining good levels of cooperation and coordination within the policy programme by focusing on the importance of teamwork for effective monitoring. Effective implementation and its subset monitoring depend on such elements as formulating a strategy for the monitoring of the policy, analysing what has happened in terms of what should have happened according to the plan and implementing change so as to remedy the failure to realize an objective or goal.

Power and Compliance Approach

Policy carries no meaning unless it is accompanied by power of enforcement. Implementation, monitoring and control compliance of policy delivery in the form of goods and services fulfil finally the intentions of policymakers. In this context, Boulding distinguishes between three kinds of power: threat, exchange and love.[14] Enforcement through threats can have productive and integrative consequences (exercise of power by income tax authorities). The use of exchange power may involve bargaining to settle terms of trade. The power of love may involve an appeal to a moral sense or a sense of citizenship. It calls for compliance on the basis of social and personal responsibility. As a model for a delivery strategy, Boulding's classification points towards the mix of enforcements—threat, exchange and love.

In contrast to Boulding's classification of power, Hood examines and identifies four modes of administrative enforcement and their effectiveness:

(i) Set aside/modify rules (government may choose either to set the rules aside or to modify the rules);
(ii) Spread the word (government may choose to use publicity and persuasion);
(iii) Pursue and punish rule violators (government may choose to use legal and police action);
(iv) Make it physically difficult, impossible, inconvenient to break rules (in this case, the enforcement method involves making the grass physically difficult or inconvenient to get at in the first place).[15]

In seeking to make sure that a policy is implemented, Etzioni analyses also three kinds of power as providing a link between the enforcement of public policy and the problems of compliance within the organizations responsible for implementing it. He believes that there are three basic reasons which compel people in the organizations to comply with rules, orders, discipline or policies. First, people do so out of a sense of agreement, love or morality. Second, they do so because of fear. Third, they may do so because it is in their

---

[13] R.J. Carter et al., *Systems, Management and Change: A Graphic Guide* (London: Paul Chapman, 1984), 96.
[14] K. Boulding, *Three Faces of Power* (Los Angeles, CA: SAGE Publications, 1990), 25.
[15] C.C. Hood, *Administrative Analysis: An Introduction to Rules, Enforcement and Organizations* (Brighton, Sussex: Wheatsheaf Books, 1986), 48–60.

monetary or remunerative interests.[16] Enforcement may therefore be the consequence of (i) normative (moral), (ii) coercive (alienative) or (iii) remunerative (calculative) power. A policy may rely on coercion or monetary rewards/sanctions, or it may ask people to exercise a moral choice. Etzioni argues that effective organizations are those which achieve a balanced mix between low levels of (i) fear (coercion and alienation) and high levels of (ii) money (remuneration and calculation) and (iii) love (normative and moral) involvements. In seeking to make sure a policy is carried out, implementation will require a mix of different enforcement modes.

In addition to power approaches applied to monitoring and control compliance, individual responsibility is not less important. With the rise of mass communications and the use of information campaigns in several areas of social (health and education, women's empowerment and development) and environmental policies, an increasing emphasis is placed on individual's responsibility for problems. For example, campaigns on forest conservation, which is necessary for sustainable development, urge that we take the responsibility for forest protection and conservation.

TECHNIQUES OF POLICY MONITORING

Monitoring, like other activities in the policy cycle, requires a significant level of effort, including investment. Monitoring has several aspects in public policy delivery. It may involve physical progress of implementation of policies (water and forest policies), productivity and profitability performance for established public sector units in the core sector and maintenance of resource assets created to be monitored selectively so that expenditure is utilized purposefully.

From policy performance perspective, there are three areas in which policy monitoring has to play its role: (i) technical performance, (ii) time performance and (iii) cost performance. Monitoring of these three areas involves several techniques which are applied in the policy delivery.

Techniques for Monitoring Technical Performance

A number of technical activities which are involved in the policy delivery are required to be monitored and controlled through the application of certain techniques to achieve desired targets. Some important techniques are briefed here.

Activity Team as Monitor

In the first place, the activity team which is most directly responsible for conducting the work that leads to the deliverables should be assigned the task of monitoring.[17] To be effective, monitoring must be delegated to the operational levels of the policy delivery.

---

[16] Etzioni, *A Comparative Analysis of Complex Organizations.*
[17] Mantel et al., *Project Management*, 72–73.

Activity Bar Chart

For monitoring technical performance of the policy, an activity bar chart is a fundamental instrument.[18] The chart can provide information relating to (i) list of objectives to be achieved, (ii) calendar for the policy delivery, (iii) list of programmes/activities to be performed with starting and ending dates and (iv) list of people (personnel) with allocated functions and responsibilities. The activity bar chart plans each technical activity by time and deliverables. This is one place where deliverables become important instruments for policy management. They are tangible results which indicate performance. Sometimes, they are only written reports of tasks completed and results of those tasks. At other times, a planning document can be developed for showing staff allocation matrix which can be used to decide how we should assign available programme personnel.

Proportion-completed Measure

Some monitoring specialists think of other types of policy management in which a proportion-completed measure could be used to monitor technical performance.

For example, the National Health Policy (NHP), 2002 (replacing the NHP 1983) lays down certain targets to be achieved over a period of time. The NHP has come up with a comprehensive road map to a healthier India by ensuring better access to health care by the poor. Another example of this proportion-completed measure would be construction of a road. The new government under the prime ministership of Narendra Modi (w.e.f. 26 May 2014) announced policy measures in the 2014 budget to achieve 25 km/day of road construction in FY 2015—a big jump from 8 km/day in FY 2014.[19]

How then is technical performance monitoring done. As with all monitoring, it starts in the planning phase. At that time, the activity team predicts its rate of achievement on scale. It is, then, possible for the activity team to measure the actual proportion of road constructed at the end of, say, one month of this policy project. This is an example of rate of completion as one method for monitoring a policy programme/project. Tied to the policy deliverable approach, it becomes a very reliable tool for the government activity teams.

Peer Review

The term 'peer' simply refers to a group of technically qualified people (judges). Peers are used when more objective measures of technical performance are not available. The technique of measuring technical performance of a policy delivery depends on the ability of the group (peer review) to estimate the degree of technical completion at any point in time. The fact that they are peers suggests that they are colleagues with the programme implementing staff. It is useful especially to evaluate the quality of work done. The technical peers review the purpose and relevance of the policy programme, the technical problems faced and the path to policy programme completion. The peer review depends on its effectiveness, on the knowledge, capacity and attitude of the peers. Therefore, while selecting the peers, it is important that they possess these attributes and qualifications.

---

[18] Prasanna Chandra, *Projects: Preparation, Appraisal, Budgeting and Implementation* (New Delhi: Metropolitan, 1992), 477–78.
[19] See *Financial Express* (Chandigarh), 11 July 2014.

Third-party Technical Review

In the case of third-party technical review, the monitoring is done by a third party. The third-party technical review works like a peer review, but people in it are largely unknown by those most intimately involved in the policy programme. Sometimes, programme sponsors, funders or Steering Committee want to get technical performance monitored by parties which have no interest or stake in the policy programme. Sometimes, this approach is preferred for periods of crisis in the programme. But in large and complex policy programmes (forestry, health and education), they can be planned to occur at periods which help ensure adequate policy control. The main advantage is the objectivity and expertise which a third party can bring to the programme. It is especially effective if it is planned as part of the ongoing project management process. Further, it is added here that these five approaches to monitoring technical performance are more powerful when applied in combination. Success in monitoring of implementation is contingent upon time and cost performance.

Techniques for Monitoring Time Performance

The purpose of monitoring time is to ensure timely policy delivery. Time in the context of a policy delivery is planned in the form of schedules. If one indicates on the activity bar chart when programmes are expected to be completed or actually delivered, one then has a useful method of monitoring time in relation to technical performance of a given policy. For monitoring time performance, two techniques are found to be useful. These are resource bar chart and schedule of expenditure.

Resource Bar Chart

Mantel and his associates argue that 'the amount of resources that can be allocated, of course, depends on the timing of the allocation as well as on the total supply of resources available for allocation'.[20] Resource bar chart helps us to consider what the impact of schedule delays will be on all activities of the policy programme.[21] But this technique of monitoring time will have little meaning until the data is arrayed which helps in comparing actual performance against planned performance. For example, of the 500 cities to be rejuvenated over five years under the Atal Mission for Rejuvenation and Urban Transformation (AMRUT, launched on 25 June 2015) programme, 476 have been selected.

With the help of the resource bar chart, any kinds of resources can be arrayed against time in the chart and then one can find, for example, whether there has been some delay in mobilizing the consultants for policy manpower and management. Hence, this monitoring device helps us predict when logistics people have to make arrangement for consultants and so on. Matters relating to delay in the arrival of the specialists can be recorded in the resource bar chart. In a road construction project, the arrival of steel and other critical materials can be depicted in this way. For satisfactory result, the resource bar charts should be developed by the activity teams for their own use.

---

[20] Mantel et al., *Project Management*, 296–97.
[21] Mark Brown, *Successful Project Management* (Calcutta: Rupa, 1992), 70.

Schedule of Expenditure

Policy activities need to be carried out on schedule. It is also possible to array costs against the time dimension. Much as with technical performance of the policy programme, it is possible to plan the schedule of expenditure for the programme. For instance, once one has budgeted the individual activities, the budgets can be aggregated by output. Then the division heads can calculate the monthly expenditures expected throughout the programme. Thus, on the basis of activity-level monitoring data, the format permits the policy management team to monitor the rate of expenditure for the policy delivery.[22] The graph or chart can be developed for the purpose of knowing rate of expenditure across all activities of the policy programme.

Techniques for Monitoring Cost Performance

Budget generally reflects the policies the government pursues. Since the 1980s, with the advance of computer-aided technology and better standardization, budgeting has made significant advances in terms of both techniques and methodology (PPBS, ZBB, POB, etc.).[23]

Performance Budget as a Tool for Monitoring

The overall policy programme budget can be a tool for monitoring if it is compared to actual costs as they are incurred.[24] Its primary shortcoming, however, is that notice of a financial deviation may come too late to do anything about it. This is because the programme budget comprises of aggregated cost category totals. But if we have cost category budgets at that level, then we can begin to find financial deviations earlier in the process. For this purpose, the financial expert can help the activity team set up a simple monthly statement which compares actual to planned expenditures per category. The point is that against the backdrop of the total budgeted amount for each cost category, this periodic statement reflects financial activity during the current period, for the entire programme up to this point in time, how much is committed, what is expected to be spent and an anticipated variance.[25]

Performance to Budget as a Tool for Monitoring

Performance to budget as a tool for monitoring has the objective of monitoring productivity of those operations with specific budget amounts. Performance to budget statement with time component has been also developed as a tool to monitor cost performance. Before it computes a subtotal of actual expenditure to date, it adds an expected expenditure to date, and adds an expected expenditure to completion of the policy programme which is calculated on the basis of an average expenditure per unit of time. It is based on an assumption that the programme will continue spending, on average, at the same rate it has over the first, say, six months. As long as that assumption is more or less correct, this appears to be a good way to monitor cost performance.

---

[22] A.T. Peart, *Design of Project Management Systems and Records* (London: Lower Press, 1971), 141.

[23] A. Schick, *The Federal Budget, Politics, Policy, Process* (Washington: Brookings Institution, 1995).

[24] Charles C. Martin, *Project Management* (New York: AMACOM, 1978), 186.

[25] Mantel et al., *Project Management*, 296–97.

Cash Flow Projection

Cash flow is another useful tool for monitoring policy programme finances.[26] Cash flow projection combines the parameters of cash (budget) and time. It is useful in situations in which the authorities wish to monitor expenditures in comparison to income from donors[27] (such as World Bank for funding primary school education in select districts in Haryana). It may be stated that the cash flow projection is often used because programmes generally are funded on a schedule of payments which is designed to match the plan of expenditures. This helps in estimating the costs and actual incomes of the policy programme. The cash flow projection, in a way, permits the monitoring staff to not only assess the costs and incomes but also anticipate cash shortages, pertaining to the whole programme.

Monitoring All Three Elements Together

It is essential to remain sensitive to deviation in all the three elements, that is, technical, time and cost performance. Policy results can be best realized when monitoring is done simultaneously of all the performance criteria. As already emphasized in the preceding pages, it is not sufficient to monitor cost or time performance alone. It is possible, for example, for a programme to be on schedule and within cost and still in problem. The graph, properly developed, can show what has been achieved and what remains to be achieved. The plan can call for about 15 per cent of the technical work to be completed by the end of March, 30 per cent by 30 September, 45 per cent by 31 December and so on. The chart is a very useful tool for monitoring a policy programme. It should present three dimensions: technical, time and cost performance. The difficulty in maintaining such a chart is in determining the percentage completed in a valid manner.

The graph can be used to assist considerations of when a noted deviation is requiring correction or change and when it is not. The policy monitoring and control system, through its reports and meetings, assist in deciding what corrective action is feasible and effective.

CONSTRAINTS IN POLICY MONITORING

Policy programmes or activities have to be properly monitored in order to produce the greatest efficiency in resource utilization. But quite often, monitoring is constrained by many factors and forces operating at the internal and external levels.

In the first place, the problem relates to poor design of the policy monitoring and control system.[28] Poorly designed monitoring framework affects the efficiency in resource utilization while ensuring the probability of quality policy results. Second, time is a constraint for policy monitoring. Too often the implementing staff feel so pressed to achieve results that they take shortcuts and avoid management steps such as monitoring and control. Experience has shown that monitoring and control, when adequately designed and executed, are processes which can generate the highest-quality results in the shortest amount of time. Third, a common constraint for the policy implementation manager is

[26] Stephen Robbins and Mary Coulter, *Management*, 5th ed. (New Delhi: Prentice Hall of India, 1998), 304.
[27] Peart, *Design of Project Management Systems and Records*, 150–52.
[28] Mantel et al., *Project Management*, 304–05.

the shortage of corrective actions which could be applied when the programme is shown to be deviating in some respect from projected performance. For example, cost overruns owing to fluctuations in financial markets often leave managers with the feeling that their implementation task is becoming difficult.

Fourth, pervasive obstacle to policy monitoring is ignorance about its role and methods. It is often observed that the monitoring staff and key personnel associated with implementing policies are not well prepared to monitor and control policy programme performance. Fifth, there is no in-built mechanism introduced in the policy programme for making an analysis of the monitored information. The Union Transport Minister Nitin Gadkari, for instance, pointed out projects should never have been awarded to developers without all clearances in place.[29]

REMEDIAL MEASURES FOR EFFECTIVE MONITORING

As already mentioned in the beginning of this chapter, monitoring is an activity which occurs in the process of implementing a policy programme. To generate the highest-quality policy output, monitoring requires a significant level of effort. Investing in monitoring is a direct investment in policy management. Following are some ways and means of enhancing the capacity of policy monitoring.

Designing the Monitoring System

One of the most important roles of the policy management director in monitoring is to design and implement systems for the processes which provide just the right amount of good control of detail for good control of the policy delivery programme. In this connection, Mantel and his associates observe, 'The key to setting up a monitoring system is to identify the special characteristics of performance, cost, and time that need to be controlled in order to achieve the project goals as stated in the action plan'.[30]

With a view to monitoring property, it is equally important to define precisely which specific characteristics of technical, cost and time performance should be controlled. It is important to remain sensitive to deviations in all three elements: technical, time and cost performance. It is not enough to watch cost performance or scheduling alone. It is possible for a policy delivery to be on schedule and within budget and still in deep trouble. Activity bar chart, resource bar chart, cash flow projection tools can be properly designed and developed for monitoring policy performance. These charts and tools can be used to assist considerations of when a noted deviation is worthy of correction and when it is not.

Communicating About Performance

A good monitoring and control system requires a monitoring communications system which works efficiently from the activity level of the programme to planning/policy market level. Monitoring system ought to be constructed with the use of electronic mechanisms

---

[29] See *Financial Express* (Chandigarh), 1 June 2015.
[30] Mantel et al., *Project Management*, 288.

so that it addresses every level of policy management. The role of routine communications during a policy performance is invaluable.

Policy progression, deviations from planned progress, corrections and plans to completion are key components of policy communications. Every person involved in the policy programme requires ongoing communication at various levels of detail. Higher-level management (secretary, director of the department concerned or local agencies) requires summary reports on the policy status. Operational members for the programme require more detailed information. The objective of communication is to keep people informed, on track and involved in tile policy. Further, regular meetings to review policy progression must be held at all levels in the organization.

Monitoring Progress

The objective of monitoring and control is to ensure, through the policy implementation process, that resource inputs are used as efficiently as possible to produce the high quality of policy outputs. Policy managers must compare the time, cost and technical performance of the policy to the budget, schedule and tasks defined in the policy programme. This should be done in a systematic manner at regular intervals and not in a haphazard way. Any significant deviations from the planned performance (technical, cost and time) must be reported immediately, as these anomalies affect the viability and success of the whole policy programme. In a report tabled in Parliament on 18 July 2014, the CAG said, 'Railways needs to strengthen its mechanism for effective monitoring of all projects'. It asked the national transporter to adopt a uniform approach to all PPP projects and frame a 'model concession agreement' for executing its projects within the stipulated time frame.[31]

Further, it is important that the policy plan is updated regularly to be useful. It must also reflect the current status of the policy and any changes that become necessary because of new information, budget constraints or schedule. To ensure effective monitoring, it is important to hold regular meetings to review programme progress. Regardless of their frequency, monitoring meetings should be regular and anticipated.

Improving Capacity of Monitoring Staff

Effective monitoring largely depends upon the ability, commitment and attitude of the monitoring staff. The process of monitoring requires some level of effort on the part of the people who are particularly skilled in the process. It requires skills in planning and accounting as well as general management. The monitoring staff need to be delegated adequate powers authorities to monitor and control. Key individuals should be made responsible for meaningful contributions and for presenting monitoring data.

For monitoring the quality of expenditure in key result areas, it is suggested that a committee with representatives of both the centre and states be set up to formulate a plan action for the monitoring staff.

---

[31] See *Financial Express* (Chandigarh), 19 July 2014.

Control Alternatives

The policy monitoring through its regular reports and meetings should also decide as to what corrective action to take or recommend to secure effective monitoring. Three general types of actions are suggested to be taken.

(i) **Correction:** Correction means reallocation of resources which also include time. With a corrective action, it is presumed that the policy programme will be completed in time.

(ii) **Replanning:** Replanning is another control mechanism. It means changing people's expectations of the results of the policy programme. Here the same technical outputs may be changed but at greater cost and more time. But the replanning should not be undertaken without the concurrence of the Steering Committee. Replanning may include (a) increase in person hours, or (b) increase in the staff, or (c) increase in budget, or (d) changing the staff, or combination of (a), (b) and (c) actions.

(iii) **Cancellation:** Cancellation is the most drastic action. In the worst possible case, the manager may desire to recommend to the Steering Committee the cancellation of the whole policy programme where it appears that the increase in cost, or technology, or the expected decrease in benefits no longer make the programme worthwhile.[32] In order to do this, the manager should carefully review the policy design and proposal documents. Sometimes, this is needed, particularly in situations in which the policy was poorly conceived or when the policy is doomed to failure.

CONCLUSION

Monitoring is the heart of policy management. Its objective is to ensure, through the policy programme implementation, that resource inputs (such as people and money) are used as efficiently as possible to generate the highest-quality policy outputs. In setting up any monitoring system, it is important to identify the key factors in the programme/policy action plan to be monitored and controlled. These are performance (specifications), cost (budget) and time (schedule). These, after all, encompass the fundamental objectives of any policy. There is no doubt that organizations, specially public, do not spend sufficient time and effort on monitoring policy. Monitoring should concentrate primarily on measuring various facets of policy output/outcome rather than data collection. But monitoring, like all other aspects of the policy management, requires a significant level of effort, including investment. And investment in monitoring policy programme is a direct investment in public policy management. For the policies to succeed, it is imperative that focus should shift to creating an inclusive and engaging working environment that empowers employees to contribute and help the organization achieve the policy objectives.

---

[32] Mantel et al., *Project Management*, 335.

Review Questions

(i) Briefly discuss the significance and importance of policy monitoring.

(ii) What are the six major steps in monitoring of policy goals?

(iii) Explain CPM of monitoring policy outcomes.

(iv) What are the main techniques of monitoring technical performance?

(v) What do you think are the principal constraints which affect effective policy monitoring?

18

POLICY FAILURE, LEARNING AND CONDITIONS FOR IMPLEMENTATION

INTRODUCTION

In the context of public policy implementation is the carrying out of a policy decision. Implementation is a process by which a policy enacted by the government is put into effect by the implementation actors or agencies (in a government department, they are referred to as 'bureaucracies'). The widely accepted view, which emerges from numerous international, regional and national studies and evaluations, is that 'implementing machinery' is a critical factor in achieving policy goals.

But because there have been so many purported policy failures, there is an awakening to the crucial need for analysing factors or variables which hamper the policy implementation process. One may say that the policy has failed to meet its goals or that the policy was doomed to fail because the goals of the policy were just too difficult to achieve. Sometimes we say that the policy is unsuccessful, if not completely failure, because the policy does not serve the people 'targeted' or because of resource shortfalls. The key problem then is the identification of factors or variables which impede the policy implementation process.

EXPLANATIONS FOR POLICY FAILURE

Ingram and Mann argue that 'Success and failure are slippery concepts, often highly subjective and reflective of an individual's goals, perception of need, and perhaps even psychological disposition toward life'.[1] For example, one person may argue that education policy has failed, while another person might look at it as a first step towards a larger goal of some education programmes for the poor children (say of SC/ ST parents). A summary of reasons for policy failure as argued by Ingram and Mann is listed in Table 18.1.

A few but important possible reasons and problems that cause or contribute to policy failures are detailed here.

Poor Policy Design

Successful policy implementation depends largely upon the formulation of a sound policy design. In fact, it is not possible to separate the process of designing a policy from its implementation aspects. A policy design is a process by which policies are 'designed

---

[1] Helen Ingram and Dean Mann, 'Policy Failure: An Issue Deserving Attention', in *Why Policies Succeed or Fail*, eds. Ingram and Mann (Beverly Hills, CA: SAGE Publications, 1980), 12.

■ Table 18.1: Reasons for Policy Failure

Alternatives to policies tried	Failure needs to be assessed in terms of the option to let present trends continue, and in terms of the likelihood that other options would have been more or less successful
The impact of changing circumstances	Changing circumstances can render policies less successful, such as energy policies that provided price relief they created dependency on oil and natural gas
Relationships of one policy to another	Policies are interrelated, and these relationships must be taken into account. For example, a stricter policy against illegal immigrants may endanger broader policy goals surrounding our relations with Mexico, such as oil supplies or drug interdiction
The boundary question	Political boundaries (e.g. between states) will influence policy success
Excessive policy demand	We may expect too much from policies
Realizable policy expectations	Policies sometimes fail when they go beyond what we know we can achieve now. But ambitious policymaking can be the result of 'speculative argumentation' that seeks to induce innovation. The stated purpose of a policy may not be the actual purpose; there may be more symbolic goals than substances
Accurate theory of causation	Policy will fail if it is not based on sound causal theory
Choice of effective policy tools	The choice of ineffective tools will likely yield failure. But the choice of tools is often a function of compromise or ideological predisposition
The vagaries of implementation	The problems inherent in policy implementation can contribute to policy failure
Failure of political institutions	'Policy failure is simply a symptom of more profound ailments within our political institutions', such as the breakdown of political party power, devolution of power from congressional leaders to the committees and subcommittees

Source: Ingram and Mann (1980).

both through technical analysis and through political process' to attain a desired goal. After the policy is designed, it requires enactment and implementation.

Hogwood and Gunn see policy failure or problems of implementation from the conceptual standpoint. They argue that the chances of a successful outcome will be increased if at the stage of policy design, attention is given to potential problems of implementation.[2] In order to avoid considerable degree of failure in the implementation, they offer 10 propositions that policymakers should ensure:

(i) Circumstances external to the implementing agency do not impose crippling constraints;

(ii) Adequate time and sufficient resources are made available to the programme;

(iii) Not only are there no constraints in terms of overcall resources but also that, at each stage in the implementation process, the required combination of resources is actually available;

(iv) The policy to be implemented is based upon a valid theory of cause and effect;

(v) The relationship between cause and effect is direct and that there are few, if any, intervening links;

(vi) There is a single implementing agency that need not depend upon other agencies for success, or if other agencies must be involved, that the dependency relationships are minimal in number and importance;

---

[2] Hogwood and Gunn, *Policy Analysis for the Real World*, 199–206.

(vii) There is a complete understanding of, and agreement upon, the objective to be achieved, and that these conditions persist throughout the implementation process;

(viii) In moving towards agreed objectives, it is possible to specify, in complete detail and perfect sequence, the tasks to be performed by each participant;

(ix) There is perfect communication among, and coordination of, the various elements or agencies involved in the programme and

(x) Those in authority can demand and obtain perfect obedience.

Thus, Hogwood and Gunn draw attention to the general neglect of the issues of policy implementation. For example, National Food Security Act (2013) lacks an adequate policy design. Problems of policy design in this policy include ambiguous and ill-defined objectives, inappropriate measures to achieve the stated goals, lack of political will and social support.[3] These problems in policy design result from the nature of federalism and from symbolic politics that emphasizes policy as an instrument to appease certain interest groups rather than policy which is designed to achieve intended outcomes.

Birkland also draws attention to the neglect of issues of the policy design process. He points out that decision-makers must consider five elements of policy design: policy goals, cause and effect theory, policy tools, policy targets (target groups) and policy implementation aspects (implementing agencies).[4]

Most public policies in India are formulated with no policy design, or these lack sound policy designs. For example, the 14th Finance Commission has suggested necessary institutional changes to minimize discretion and improve the design of fiscal transfers, especially with regard to CSS from the centre to states with a view to ensuring cooperative federalism.[5]

In their book *Policy Design for Democracy*, Schneider and Ingram present a framework that brings the discrete stages of the policy process into a single model and emphasizes the connections between problems definition, agenda setting and policy design on the one hand, and policy design, implementation and impact on society on the other.[6]

Sudden Focusing Events

Some public problems become evident through changes in the indicators of a problem, such as swine flu (H1N1 pandemic), dengue or Ebola virus. For example, in 2015, swine flu gained attention as a public policy problem when the general public became aware of it.[7] Swine flu is now a worldwide problem. Ebola virus is highly contagious, but it is not airborne.[8]

---

[3] See also Bala Ramulu, 'Governance of Food Security Policies in India: The Need for Democratic Governance', *Indian Journal of Public Administration* (New Delhi) 59(1) (2013): 50–68.

[4] Birkland, *An Introduction to the Policy Process*, 230–52.

[5] See *Financial Express* (Chandigarh), 25 February 2015.

[6] A.L. Schneider and H. Ingram, *Policy Design for Democracy* (Lawrence, KS: University Press of Kansas, 1997).

[7] In 2015, swine flu caused nearly 100 deaths in India.

[8] According to the WHO, Ebola virus disease claimed 1,069 deaths between August 10 and 11 (2014) in Guinea, Liberia, Nigeria and Sierra Leone.

Other problems gain attention as a public policy problem which are sudden events such as earthquakes,[9] unprecedented floods[10] or terrorist attacks.[11]

Another class of focusing event is when an influential member of a policy community (e.g. an MP) contracts disease or dies. In such a case, more attention is paid to the problem than would ordinarily be paid. Nearly, all the aspects of policy design will flow from this definition of the problem.

Goal Conflict

Policy design can also reveal conflict over policy goals. Because policies and their goals are often vague when they are originally set, it is sometimes difficult for the agencies charged with implementation to satisfy the demands of everyone involved in formulating and approving the broad policy. Lindblom argued that the governmental decision process often is one of 'muddling through' or 'partisan adjustment'. Decisions are not necessarily made only on the grounds of rationality or on attempting to achieve effectiveness or efficiency. Instead, policymakers place premium upon agreement among participants in the policymaking process.[12] Compromise and accommodation then become the central concern. Following compromise and accommodation emerges a policy with which stakeholders involved (such as political leaders, planners, implementers and target groups) are willing to live. Failure, on the other hand, occurs when a policy generates excessive conflict opposition and perhaps violence.[13]

Another conceptual problem in policy design relates to lack of key regulatory principles in most public policies in India. It has been observed, for example, that most industries in states have not come out strongly to comply with provisions of the EPA, 1986 and the Water (Prevention and Control of Pollution) Act, 1974. Industry management hesitates to comply with conditions imposed by the State Pollution Control Boards, such as treating the effluents and discharging them in an appropriate manner. Further, even when an industry installs a treatment plant, management may evade its operation in order to save

---

[9] The death toll from 25 April 2015 quake in Nepal topped 8,500, making the temblor the deadliest of all times for the Himalayan nation, triggering as many as 240 aftershocks and injuring around 20,000 people. The monster temblor last month and its aftershocks killed as many as 8,567 people till today. See *The Tribune*, 18 May 2015.

[10] Unprecedented floods in Srinagar in August 2014 caused death to more than 2,500 people.

[11] A terrorist attack in Mumbai on 26 November 2008 claimed 166 lives.

[12] For example, (i) Shibu Soren, an MP, in August 2008 threatened to withdraw support from the UPA government at the centre on the Indo-US nuclear energy deal if he is not made the CM of Jharkhand. See *The Tribune* (Chandigarh), 24 August 2008. (ii) The Right to Fair Compensation and Transparency in Land Acquisition, Rehabilitation and Resettlement (Second Amendment Act, 2015) was passed by the Parliament (earlier the Land Bill was referred to the Joint Parliamentary Committee of the Lok Sabha and Rajya Sabha in May 2015) after compromise and accommodation among participants in the policymaking process.

[13] Child activists slammed the amendments to the Child Labour (Prohibition and Regulation) Amendment Bill 2012 saying a majority of the children were working in home-based occupations in India and the government by making exceptions had excluded a vast section (some 12.6 million working children) of child labour from protection. However, the Amendment allows banning employment of adolescents (14- to 18-year-olds) in hazardous occupations. See *The Tribune* (Chandigarh), 14 May 2015.

the unproductive expenses of running the plant. Industries often use various means to circumvent the provisions of law.

Similarly, the revised National Water Policy (NWP), 2002 (NWP was first adopted by the National Water Resources Council in 1987) lacks a blueprint of action. The PCPNDT Act, 2002 was passed in September 1994 to ban the sex determination which leads to the elimination of female foetus due to several sociocultural factors. However, absolute and unguided powers under the Act and its regulations are likely to be misused, especially in the circumstances where senior authorities and even states are fighting among themselves to meet targets of actions against the scan centres instead of focusing on ways to save the girl child.[14]

Policy Analysis

Policy analysis has permeated into policy formulation and evaluation, especially in regard to the physical projects (dams, roads, power plants, etc.). However, application of policy analysis has its own limitations. Implementation of public policies in India has been also hampered by conceptual weakness in policy capability. For example, India's Population Policy (2000) lacks an adequate policy analysis. It was adopted without examining alternative policy options. Similarly, most of the State Pollution Control Boards in India suffer from lack of professional staff, sufficient time and data. In addition, major policies have been adopted without much discussion over the policy alternatives, reflecting a strong adherence to secrecy within the bureaucracy. A survey conducted by the Central Pollution Control Board (CPCB) in the 60 cities of India showed that Delhi alone accounted for nearly 20 per cent (689.52 tonnes) of the total plastic waste (nearly 3,501 tonnes a day of 60 cities). A report by a leading channel claimed a high concentration of particulate matters (PM) 2.5 level (recorded on 8 December 2015), which is four times polluted than the safe level of air.[15]

Policy Statement

It is observed that in many cases, policy statements announced by the government contain ambiguous and contradictory terms, posing problems in implementation. The implementers at the field level often face a variety of problems because they do not find the policy statements made in clear words and terms. For example, the Punjab government policy notification in May 2015, permitting regularization of illegal colonies constructed outside the municipal limits, albeit after getting a CLU (change in land use), is full of

---

[14] A doctor in Safidon, Haryana, was shot dead for asking identity proof of the pregnant woman before conducting the scan. He was trying to comply with the mandate of the Act, which irritated the family members of the woman, who thought the doctor was prying on her privacy. In another case, a victim of PCPNDT Act, a female doctor consumed poison in the courtroom in Rampura, Punjab. Last month in Haryana, all the ultrasound centres shut down their labs for a day, in protest against the high-handedness of the Appropriate Authority (often, the chief medical officer) and other enforcing agencies imposing the Act. Their common grouse is, doctors are arrested and made out to be the culprits for the clerical errors committed in filling up the 'Form F', either by the semi-literate clients or the assisting staff at the ultrasound clinics. See *The Tribune* (Chandigarh), 25 May 2015.
[15] See *The Tribune* (Chandigarh), 4 April 2013; See *The Tribune*, 11 December 2015.

contradictions.[16] Consequently, implementers use their own discretion while implementing them or they refer the statements back to the higher rungs of administration for clarification. In both the cases, the policy implementation is adversely affected. A contradictory policy statement is often subject to different interpretations by the courts in India amounting to a new policy.

Time Targets

The pressure of time creates often the implementation gap. The time period fixed for according benefits as per the policy is not pragmatic. Normally, while fixing the time frame, the policy formulators do not take into consideration the conditions prevailing. They become idealistic while setting the time targets and forget the workload at hand with the respective implementing agencies. Consequently, the head offices press the agencies for speedy implementation. The implementers under such conditions are unable to perform their duties properly with regard to the said policy as well as other works at hand.

POLITICAL AND ADMINISTRATIVE PROBLEMS

Political problems arising from the policy process are serious and complex. These not only stand in the way of securing effective implementation but also derail the political process. Some common political problems are discussed in the following sections.

Centralized Policy Process

The central government is dependent on the states to implement its policies and programmes. But frictions between the central and state government relations have affected the policy implementation process adversely. In the area of environmental protection, for example, the policy process is heavily centralized. Policy decisions taken at the central level, including setting goals and procedure, ignore the local culture. It has been also observed that the central government was more than willing to adopt population, health, education and environmental policies and programmes, but when the time came for their implementation, state governments often lacked political will to proceed. It is still questionable whether health or environmental quality has improved at all in terms of safe water, clean air and healthy living conditions.

For example, rural India is witnessing massive gaps in health infrastructure, with the availability for health sub-centres (1,53,655), primary health centres (25,308) and community health centres (5,396) as of 31 March 2015 being far less than the requirement for a rural population of 83.3 crores. Of 5,396 community health centres, only 751 have four specialists—surgeons, obstetricians and gynaecologists, physicians and paediatricians. Again, India's rural infant mortality rate (IMR per 1,000 live births) is 51 as against the urban IMR of around 31 and the country's average IMR of 47.[17]

---

[16] This policy of the Punjab government is applicable only to those buildings that were constructed after 21 January 2015. See *The Tribune* (Chandigarh), 9 May 2015.
[17] See *The Tribune* (Chandigarh), 24 August 2015.

Policymakers at the central level increasingly realize that wide implementation gaps exist in several social policies. As a whole, the organizational structure for implementation of social policies is in better shape at the central level than at the state level, especially in terms of finances, technical expertise and the linkage between various ministries. On the contrary, serious financial problems exist at the state level because of budgetary deficits. The financial problems increase the reluctance of states to allocate resources for the implementation of public policies, especially in the area of education health, environment and population which are perceived as a non-productive investment.

Political Interference

There is no guarantee that the public policy after its approval will be implemented, and often it is the case that it may not be implemented at all. This leads to what can be called an implementation failure. Implementation failure can be the cause of political interference and lack of political will. National Population Policy (2000) has not been able to achieve its objectives owing to poor political commitment.

It has been said that good governance has become a casualty of political interference and bureaucratic pliability.[18] In another case of non-implementation of the SC's revocation of then Bahujan Samaj Party (BSP) government's 2007 notification on reservation in promotion in 2012, the Apex Court on 20 August 2015 expressed dissatisfaction at the UP government's action taken report regarding reverting of personnel promoted.[19] The issue of demoting nearly 20,000 Class-I employees who had been promoted under the reservation for promotion had huge political implications ahead of the 2017 Assembly elections in UP.

Organized Interests Politics

Another glaring implementation gap is the organized interests politics. In many cases, for example, industry influences the environmental policy implementation process through the business lobby and representatives of business interests. Pressure by industries associations during consideration of EPA in Parliament resulted in a weakening of the penalties for non-compliance and also forced the government to delay enforcement of the passed legislation. At the same time, it is important to note that the labour unions have not taken any major initiatives for the control of pollution problems inside or outside the factory or for the safe operation of hazardous facilities. Most industrialists in India are politically powerful. They have links with the ruling parties in both the central and the state governments. Also it is observed that the policy implementers face many problems and challenges from the vested interest groups. Every subsection of the society clamours for the protection of its interests. For doing so, the mobilized people go to any extent to safeguard their interests. The implementers are influenced, the official working is obstructed and efforts are made to get the policies implemented in a way which suits the specific interests. Because of political influence, the implementation of policies in land acquisition, environment protection, population control and the like remains weak and tardy.

---

[18] B.G. Deshmukh, 'What Does Public Service Really Mean?', *g-files* 3 (2009): 6.
[19] See *The Tribune* (Chandigarh), 24 August 2015.

Besides political problems, obstacles to implementation of policies are administrative. Hood analyses implementation problems in terms of 'limits of administration'. He uses the term 'perfect administration' in comparison to economist's use of 'perfect competition'. He defines 'perfect administration' as a condition in which 'external' elements of resource availability and political acceptability combine with 'administration to produce perfect policy implementation'.[20] Implementation of development programmes and policies in a developing country such as India is greatly affected by varying capacities of the governmental institutional machinery and personnel policies. Major problems facing administration in the policy implementation are briefly discussed here.

Insufficiency in Personnel and Financial Resources

In India, a large number of social policies (education, health, poverty alleviation, women and child welfare) remain on papers or fail because of lack of certain resources. Thoroughly planned-out policies fail to attain the proper goals without competent personnel. Implementation implies allocating personnel resources to the appropriate tasks and activities, motivating them to do well and rewarding them for their action. Regardless of their status, specialized knowledge, experience and qualifications, all policy programme personnel need to work as a cohesive team for the purpose of achieving policy results. But often, there is no allocation of tasks to the personnel resource. Further, the facilitative aspect of the leadership variable could have important consequences on the inputs critical to the policy and programme implementation.

Invariably, and often, policymakers do make provisions for the money for carrying out the policy goals, but provision of funds in the budget does not mean much because the sanctioned amount does not reach the implementing agency on time. Furthermore, often the amount sanctioned is not enough to meet the requirements. At the state level, serious financial problems exist of budgetary deficits. Most states have deficit budgets, needing central government support to balance the budget. These budgetary problems increase the reluctance of states to allocate resources for the social sector policies, which are perceived as non-productive investment areas.

Even with the availability of funds for a particular cause, money is misutilized. For example, the SC on 23 August 2015 slammed the centre and state governments for virtual non-utilization of a whopping ₹27,000 crores collected in form of 1 per cent cess on the construction industry for providing health care to the workers' families and education to their children. It directed the Delhi government to return to the welfare fund of about ₹2.7 crores utilized for publicity over the years.[21]

Deficiency in Administrative Apparatus

Politicians and people perceive bureaucracy as 'inflexible, inward-looking, and insensitive to outcomes'.[22] A leading newspaper reports and reveals, three senior bureaucrats are embroiled in CBI probes years after they retired:

---

[20] Christopher Hood, *The Limits of Administration* (London: John Wiley, 1976), 6.
[21] See *The Tribune* (Chandigarh), 23 August 2015.
[22] Abhishek Jain, 'Issues and Challenges Before the District Collector in the Present Era of Governance', *Indian Journal of Public Administration* 56(1) (2010): 8.

Pradip Baijal for irregularities in the allotment of telecom spectrum in 2007–08, Shyamal Ghosh for an earlier allocation of spectrum and PC Parakh for Coalgate. Durga Shakti Nagpal, a young Indian Administrative Service, or IAS, officer in Uttar Pradesh, was suspended for taking on the coal mafia (the official reason given was that she was disturbing communal peace), though she was recently reinstated after public outcry. Ashok Khemka, the Haryana whistle-blower, finds himself mired in investigations. If the Right to Information Act of 2005 had made the bureaucrat cautious, CBI's new-found investigative zeal has stopped him dead in his track. The fear of regime change in states as well as centre has made matters worse: everybody fears that decisions might be reopened and looked at in a different light.[23]

As a result, most bureaucrats across states are dithering from taking decisions and sticking to only routine matters. It is seen that the officials involved in the process of implementation do not find enough scope for calling motivation. In the present environment, officials are not likely to feel enthusiastic about implementing policies, especially enforcing environmental laws. Even in cases where public officials are inclined to implement the environmental laws, their authority and positions are undermined by the alliance of industrial magnets and local politicians. They fall to the captivity of economic interests and monetary incentives and find their escape in formalistic enforcement.

It is worthwhile here to quote a civil servant in connection with the role of AIS: 'The AIS which were visualized by Sardar Patel to be kept above party, and free from political considerations are increasingly getting politicized'.[24]

The unionization of bureaucracy, especially the lower one, has not only destroyed the work culture and discipline but also demoralized the supervisory levels into withdrawal and the line of least resistance. The higher and the middle levels of bureaucracy are too powerless and marginalized to give any relief to citizens in cases of corruption and unresponsiveness by lower-level staff at the cutting edge of administration. Further, endemic political interference by the political executive has compounded the marginalization of the higher bureaucracy, thereby undermining its capacity to implementing public policies.

Lack of Capacity and Coordination in Governing Institutions

Institutional structure and administrative capabilities are determinants to the implementation of laws and policies. But they are by no means adequate in the face of complexities of political, social and economic problems. Here the institutional structure refers to the whole system of rules and regulations by which administrative capabilities, tasks and responsibilities are clearly defined among the administrators. In the wake of terror attacks on Mumbai on 26 November 2008, first woman IPS officer Kiran Bedi said,

---

[23] See *Business Standard* (Chandigarh), 9 November 2013.
[24] U.C. Agarwal, 'Role of All-India Services in Centre-State Relations', *Indian Journal of Public Administration* 49(1) (2003): 12.

Our system is old and medieval and the neighbours know this. We have not let the police system become professional and fully accountable because politicians and bureaucrats want to retain control. Professionalizing the police means true rule of law. The police is fully accountable to law and no one else.[25]

Similarly, giving an example of poor regulation of mining in India, Sunita Narain writes that the key problem is 'the utter lack of capacity of mining regulators to oversee the industry and to push for resolution of problems'.[26]

Besides lack of institutional capacity, poor coordination and missing links among the administrative institutions have stood in the way of implementing policy actions. For example, at the administrative level, different departments are concerned with implementation of policies relating to poverty alleviation programmes (Ministry/Department of Urban Employment and Poverty Alleviation, Ministry/Department of Social Justice and Empowerment, Ministry/Department of Rural Department, Ministry/Department of Tribal Affairs, etc.).

In the case of implementation of NREGS, it was pointed out by the CJI, Justice K.G. Balakrishnan, that the scheme was one of the most progressive welfare measures, but it was hindered by factors such as corruption, lack of transparency and nexus between contractors and officials.[27] Describing the menace of corruption as a 'social calamity', a SC Bench on 10 December 2015 said, 'This warrants a different control and hence the legislature comes up with special legislation with stringent provisions'. Consequently, the implementation process remains weak and tardy.

Lack of People Support

In a developing economy such as India, most social policies remain neglect for want of people mobilization and support. Public involvement in policy implementation programmes, such as education, health, population control, control of pollution and forest conservation, is important to produce results. By staging demonstration, protests and mass movements, the public has largely offset the power base of vested interest groups and built a power structure of its own to implement policies. The Chipko movement in the UP hills and the Appiko movement in Western Ghats of Karnataka were launched against tree-felling for commercial purposes. However, the people in India have not been enthusiastic in creating people movements for implementing and enforcing public policies.

POLICY LEARNING

No doubt, policies fail because of this or that reason. But there is always the scope to learn more from failures. Policy failure provides an opportunity to learn from the mistakes. This is a major concern of most organizations. The evaluation and feedback process provide learning opportunities for the organization to change its behaviour.

---

[25] See *The Tribune*, 8 December 2008.
[26] Sunita Narain, 'The Mining Mess', *Business Standard* (Chandigarh), 9 September 2013.
[27] See *The Tribune*, 23 November 2008 and 11 December 2015.

Policy Learning Defined

As defined by Sabatier, 'policy learning' or 'policy-oriented learning' is 'relatively enduring alterations of thought or behavioural intentions which result from experience and which are concerned with the attainment (or revision) of policy objectives'.[28] Sabatier's definition, by concentrating on individual actors as members of advocacy coalitions, avoids attributing cognitive processes to organizations, while broadening policymaking to include influential actors, such as academics and journalists, that institutionally focused analyses tend to overlook. This focus on the individual as policy actor also overcomes the tendency to think of agencies or institutions as the agents of learning.

As the unit of analysis, we can think of learning at the individual (agency head, interest group leader, academic, etc.) and organization levels. While individuals learn by retaining information and experience, organizations depend on information storage and retrieval (institutional memory), Bennett and Howlett note that learning can be a more active and 'deliberate attempt to adjust the goals and techniques of policy in the light of the consequences of past policy and new information so as to better attain' the policy goals.[29] Indeed, organizations make concerted efforts to improve their learning capacity by creating systems to store and disseminate information.[30]

Types of Learning

Here it may be pointed out that organizations engage in two types of learning. First, single-loop learning: In single-loop learning, organizations learn about techniques (tools) that fail and make adjustment to improve them or replace them with techniques that work better. Second, double-loop learning: In double-loop learning, organizations learn about values that support the whole range of actions around a goal. In fact, double-loop learning is learning about single-loop learning.[31]

Peter May divides learning into three categories: instrumental policy learning, social policy learning and political learning. In all three types of learning, policy failure provides feedback for learning about how to make and implement policy for better results.

(i) **Instrumental Policy Learning:** Instrumental policy learning focuses on techniques and tools for policy implementation. It concerns learning about 'viability of policy intervention or implementation designs'. Evidence of instrumental policy learning involves changes in the implementation design that improve its performance.

(ii) **Social Policy Learning:** Social policy learning involves learning about the 'social construction of a policy or programme'. This type of learning involves learning the causes of problems and making of effective interventions to address those problems. May argues that prima facie indicators of social learning involve 'policy redefinition entailing changes in policy goals or scope—e.g., policy direction,

---

[28] Paul Sabatier, 'An Advocacy Coalition Framework of Policy Change and the Role of Policy-oriented Learning Therein', *Policy Sciences* 21 (1988): 133.
[29] Colin Bennett and Michael Howlett, 'The Lessons of Learning', *Policy Sciences* 25(3) (1992): 276.
[30] Chris Argyris, *On Organisational Learning*, 2nd ed. (Malden, MA: Blackwell Business, 1999).
[31] Birkland, *An Introduction to the Policy Process*, 275.

target groups, rights bestowed by the policy'.[32] One example of this type of learning concerns the way communities address rape of young girls.

(iii) **Political Learning:** This type of political learning is quite different from instrumental and social learning. Peter May defines political learning as focusing on 'strategy for advocating a given policy idea or problem', leading potentially to 'more sophisticated advocacy of a policy idea or problem' and effective political advocacy. Political learning happens when advocates change their strategy for policy change in the light of new information or facts related to the political system. For example, in this case of Land Acquisition Bill, PM Narendra Modi said on 30 August 2015 that 'the government was willing to make changes to the Bill and accept suggestions that were in the interests of farmers'.[33]

CONDITIONS FOR EFFECTIVE IMPLEMENTATION

Success and failure in public administration are subjective and often reflective concepts of an individual's perception. One may say that policy has achieved success, while another may argue that policy has failed on many areas. In other words, failure of a social policy or programme is perhaps reflective of a beholder's vision. Thus, policy implementation is seen varying along a continuum ranging from successful to aborted. Successful implementation involves many operations and conditions as well as time and resources. However, successful implementation should not be equated with impact measures as implementation is not the same thing as impact.

David Mazmanian and P. Sabatier formulate a set of six sufficient and necessary conditions for the effective implementation of legally stated policy objectives.[34] These comprised

(i) The enabling legislation or other legal directive mandates policy objectives which are clear and consistent or at least provides substantive criteria for resolving goal conflicts.

(ii) The enabling legislation incorporates a sound theory identifying the principal factors and causal linkages affecting policy objectives and gives implementing officials sufficient jurisdiction over target groups and other points of leverage to attain, at least potentially, the desired goals.

(iii) The enabling legislation structures the implementation process so as to maximize the probability that implementing officials and target groups will perform as desired. This involves assignment to sympathetic agencies with adequate hierarchical integration, supportive decision rules, sufficient financial rules and adequate access to supporters.

(iv) The leaders of the implementing agency possess substantial managerial and political skill and are committed to statutory goals.

---

[32] Peter J. May, 'Policy Learning and Failure', *Journal of Public Policy* 12(4) (1992): 336.
[33] See *The Tribune* (Chandigarh), 31 August 2015.
[34] D.A. Mazmanian and P.A. Sabatier, *Implementation and Public Policy* (Glenview, IL: Scott Foresman, 1983), 41–42.

(v) The programme is actively supported by organized constituency groups and by a few key legislators (or a chief executive) throughout the implementation process, with the courts being neutral or supportive.

(vi) The relative priority of statutory objectives is not undermined overtime by the emergence of conflicting public policies or by changes in relevant socio-economic conditions which weaken the statute's causal theory or political support.

Effective implementation requires a good chain of command and a capacity to coordinate and control. On these lines, Christopher Hood proposed a model of perfect implementation in common with Weber's ideal type of bureaucracy.[35] Hood sets out five such conditions for perfect implementation:

(i) that ideal implementation is a product of a unitary 'army'—such as organization, with clear lines of authority;

(ii) that norms would be enforced and objectives given;

(iii) that people would do that they are told and asked;

(iv) that there should be perfect communication in and between units of organization;

(v) that there would be no pressure of time.

Above scholars and policy analysts in their studies argue that implementation problems can be avoided by anticipating complications and difficulties in advance. But a policy to be implemented must be given a concrete shape. In particular, the presumptions glide over the whole issue of consensus, either in a party-political or ideological sense, or in terms of organizational interests affected by policy.

Chase says in an article that it is difficult to obtain compliance where policy or a programme is to be implemented by agencies whose intentions do not necessarily coincide with those of the policy formulators.[36] Solutions to this difficulty are, therefore, seen in terms of (i) gaining credibility, (ii) reference to higher authority and (iii) financial incentives. It seems that Chase has ignored the relationship between interests, politics and the balance of power among those making, implementing and affected by policy. Any policy in order to be implemented needs translation, clarity and concreteness. Thus, the appropriateness of policy implementation depends on degree to which the preconditions are met as expressed in the combination of political will and administrative capability. It assumes a great deal about goal definition and human interaction and behaviour, or involves the relationship between policy as the input and implementation as the administrative output.

In addition to conditions as analysed by policy analysts, effective implementation involves many operations as well as time, manpower, financial and technological resources. These requirements allow bureaucrats and their workforce to carry out their tasks.

---

[35] Christopher Hood, *The Limits of Administration* (London: John Wiley, 1976), 6–7.

[36] G. Chase, 'A Framework for Implementing Human Service Program: How Hard Will It Be?' *Public Policy* 27(4) (1979): 387–435.

Emphasis on Institutional Capacity and Administrative Capability

Successful implementation requires institutional capacity and sufficient administrative capabilities. Administrative capability is a key factor in determining the achievement of policy goals. Stated in systems terms, we may assume that implementing capability could be a measure in converting or processing inputs of the programme into certain outputs in the form of policy delivery. In this implementation process, critical inputs include

(i) Resources: These include personnel, financial and material and so on.
(ii) Structure: This refers to certain stable organizational roles and relationships which are policy-relevant.
(iii) Technology: This refers broadly to knowledge, techniques and practices essential to the operation of organization (coordinating planning and allocating resources, etc.).
(iv) Support: This refers to political, legal and managerial support which tend to promote the attainment of certain organizational roles.
(v) Translation Ability: This means that there must be clear communication between the public policymaking authority and the bureaucracy.

Being clear about the policy and how it is to be done are key administrative capabilities for carrying out the job correctly. It must be assumed that these inputs are not only essential and critical to the implementation of policies but that they also vary in terms of their magnitude and quality. Ample resources increase the likelihood that the job will be carried out as per the instructions of the public policymakers.

Accountability

Policymakers (politicians in offices) as well as bureaucrats (implementers) are accountable to the legislators or others who put them in their positions of authority. In the case of a bureaucrat, he must perform his functions on time, on budget and within all of the rules governing his position. As a general rule, a bureaucrat must file periodic papers or appear before public policymakers at hearing or special meetings to demonstrate that he has performed his assigned tasks. When policymakers decide that bureaucrats have not carried out their responsibilities as originally defined, they (policymakers) may take actions against them (bureaucrats).

Leadership and Motivation Capabilities

Leadership and motivational capabilities are the dominant factors in policy implementation, particularly in terms of their ability to alter the critical inputs in the implementation. Leadership refers broadly to three qualities of the behaviour and activities of key policy managers:

(i) those concerned with facilitating the implementation process (facilitative role);
(ii) those concerned with solving problems arising in the course of implementation (problem-solving role); and
(iii) those concerned with motivational and behavioural aspects to ensure a commitment to achieve desired policy goals (motivational role).

It may be pointed out that while the leadership determinant directly affects the critical inputs, it is also constrained in certain characteristics of these inputs. A weak organizational structure, inadequate and uncertain resources, weak support and poor technological capability could impose a heavy strain on the facilitative, problem-solving and motivational capabilities of principal policy managers.

CONCLUSION

Policy implementation is one of the most difficult aspects of the policy process. It is a continuing process and brings together many actors and forces that cooperate and clash with each other in order to achieve or thwart policy objectives. No policy formulator can assume that decisions will automatically be implemented as foresighted.

The theoretical models presented by implementation scholars typically comprise a variety of explanatory factors. Yet it is difficult to know which of these factors are more or less important. But this does not mean we should stop doing research in policy implementation sphere. But with a view to advancing our understanding of implementation beyond the level that has already achieved, implementation research needs to take new directions. It is emphasized in the policy literature that 'processes of cross-fertilization' could improve our understanding of implementation processes. In addition, there is much to be learnt from constructivist approaches, which argue that policy objectives and implementation problems often cannot be visualized on an objective basis. It is again emphasized that policy implementation is a continuing process with no discernible beginning and no clear end but with learning opportunities, one may make better policies for their successful implementation.

Review Questions

(i) According to you, what are the key factors that impede the successful implementation of a policy?

(ii) What role does political interference play in success/failure of a policy? Explain with examples taken from recent times.

(iii) How has bureaucracy turned out to be one of the major impediments to successful policy implementation?

(iv) Briefly discuss the concepts and practices of policy learning.

(v) What are the six major conditions for effective implementation of legally stated policy objectives?

19

POLICY EVALUATION
Approaches, Techniques and Impact

INTRODUCTION

Public policy evaluation is of great importance as it tells us much about the performance of the public policy. Specifically, it shows whether goals have been met. By reviewing the outcome in terms of the success of the goals, we judge the merit or utility of the public policy. The national experience with many public programmes reveals the need for careful evaluation to know their worth.

Thomas Dye defines 'systematic evaluation' to mean 'careful, objective, scientific assessment of the current and long-term effects of policies on both target and non-target situations or groups, as well as an assessment of the ratio of current and long-term costs to whatever benefits are identified'.[1]

Policy evaluation has two aspects: (i) the evaluation of the policy and its effects on the target population (evaluating policy programme) and (ii) the evaluation of the personnel charged with implementation of the policy programme (evaluating personnel). In this process, it is important to look at not only the different approaches and techniques adopted by policy analysts and policy evaluators but also the impact evaluation.

APPROACHES FOR EVALUATION

Policy evaluation gets us into the question of whether the policy is worth or whether it stands the test of objectives set out by the public policymakers. To find the answer to this question, policy analysts and administrators tend to adopt varied approaches. Each evaluation approach is important in its own right, although sometimes one is more useful than the other.

Quantitative Measurement Approach

Gerston advanced two approaches, namely, quantitative measurement and qualitative measurement (judgement), for comparing outcomes with intentions.[2] For Gerston, each approach contributes to the answer of a simple question: 'Has the policy succeeded?'

---

[1] Dye, *Understanding Public Policy*, (2004), 54.
[2] Larry N. Gerston, *Public Policymaking in a Democratic Society*, 2nd ed. (New York, NY: M.E. Sharpe, 2008), 143–50.

'Quantitative measurement' has a 'bean counting' focus that ex⌐
rather than the value of the outcome.[3] The evaluator using this
to 'the facts' in terms of measuring the extent to which a pub⌐
mented. Here there is no question of judgement. With quan⌐
evaluator will (i) match the policy objectives with policy outcon⌐
to which the policy has been put into place, (iii) attempt to
failure and (iv) make recommendations for corrective action.

An easy way to answer the question—'Has the policy perf⌐
to perform?'—is by measuring the extent to which the impl⌐
job in accordance with the directions. However, if the policy
its objectives, then the implementing agency would need to report impi⌐
and recommend ways to respond to that failure.

However, this approach to evaluation is not so simple. Even with such specificity, there can
be times when quantitative evaluation gets mushy or imprecise.[4] As one notes, capturing
all of the variables and sorting out causal relationships from the merely coincidental may
not be easy. For example, if a large number of teachers do not come to teach because
of the flu, is it possible that there will be causes other than student's behaviour for the
results? Further, if implementation is subjected to interpretation because of ambiguous
objectives or poorly defined measurement, then it will be difficult to evaluate the success
of the policy programme.

Qualitative Measurement Approach

'Qualitative measurement or judgement approach' has been also advocated by Larry
Gerston. Whereas quantitative measurement tells us much about whether the policy has
succeeded according to the policy design, 'the qualitative judgement responds to the
wisdom of the policy itself'. In this form of evaluation, the question centres on the 'worth'
of the policy that has been put into place. In other words, 'Does it make sense, and if so,
to whom?'

Indeed, it is not an easy job for an evaluator to measure, say, 'social justice', or determine
whether a particular policy has been successful in attaining it. Such subjective ideals or
criteria must be translated into clear goals so as to enable the policy evaluator to do his
job impartially. For example, does the public policy have unintended consequences? Or,
does the policy create new problems? Or, is the evaluator impartial in his assessment of
the policy? These are some of the major concerns related to qualitative measurement.

First, under ideal conditions, a public policy is formulated to respond to the issue that has
been defined by or for the policymakers. Still, even a carefully designed and executed
policy may have unintended effects that create another issue as serious than the original

---

[3] For a discussion of quantitative methodologies, see Lawrence B. Mohr, *Impact Analysis for Program Evaluation* (Pacific Grove, CA: Brooks, 1988).

[4] Walter A. Rosenbaum, *Environmental Politics and Policy*, 6th ed. (Washington: C.Q. Press, 2005), 79–80.

Second, a public policy may be carefully designed and implemented in the [...] of the issue that policymakers intend to address. But in solving one problem, the [...] may expose another issue because of the lack of information prior to formulation of [...] policy that has been put into place. Third, an evaluator who works for a public agency [...] erally keeps his subjective feelings far from the policy that he is asked to assess. And [...] et, it is sometimes very difficult for the policy evaluator to be impartial, and has a bias regarding one issue or another because of certain human weaknesses.

And fourth, because of changing values and societal changes, many controversial public policies have been re-evaluated. For example, the 'Right to Property' as a Fundamental Right originally guaranteed to every citizen in 1950 was omitted by the Constitution's 44th Amendment Act, 1978, with effect from 20 June 1979.[6] This was done because of change in our society's values as a result of the belief in socialistic pattern of society. Changing values can sometimes prompt dramatic reversals in public policy. And more recently in July 2014, the SC of India ruled that sharia courts had no legal or constitutional sanction.[7] Such a decision is likely to have a profound impact upon the members of the Muslim society. Thus, a policymaker cannot fully anticipate the consequences or effects of a policy initiative, or what a court of law might say about it.

Multiplist Approach

'Multiplist approach', which has been advocated by Cook, typifies the disillusionment with the methods and politics of evaluation as a form of rational analysis. Cook maintains that as there can be no correct policy option or evaluation, a multiplist approach should be used which aims to use a wide variety of options and data.[8] Cook holds that social science is 'concerned not with guaranteeing truth or utility, but with offering defensible interpretations of what is in the outside world'.[9] Evaluation in this sense involves testing arguments and claims to knowledge rather than advancing 'the correct solution'. As there is no way of proving what is correct, the evaluation process, and the policy process in general, should be predicated on the importance of securing a multidisciplinary knowledge and techniques. In this approach, options are not proved but pitted against one another so as to 'see which one is superior' or most useful.

Design Approach

Usually, a public policy is launched with a design, which is simply a schematic framework for seeing it through. The design guides the implementing agency on such elements as budget, timeline, procedures and anything else necessary for the success of the public policy.

---

[5] For example, National Skill Development and Entrepreneurship Policy (2015) holds the promise of vocational skills to some 40.2 crore people by 2022, and yet some professionals have concluded that this policy has serious implications about its viability.

[6] The provision in Article 31 'Right to Property' has been transferred as Article 300 A to Part XII of the Constitution. Now it is no more a Fundamental Right.

[7] See *The Tribune* (Chandigarh), 8 July 2014.

[8] T.D. Cook, 'Postpositivist Critical Multiplism', in *Social Science and Social Policy*, eds. R.L. Shotland and M.M. Mark (California: SAGE Publications, 1985).

[9] Ibid., 45.

'Design approach' has been advocated by Trudi Miller[10] and Bobrow and Dryzek.[11] Miller has argued that we should seek to design the goals for performance improvement in a way which involves the articulation of values which can be achieved in different circumstances. In other words, we should define values we want to achieve. For Bobrow and Dryzek, policy design is 'like any kind of design, which involves the pursuit of valued outcomes through activities sensitive to the context of time and place. These activities revolve around factors that can be affected by the volitions of human beings'.[12] However, the policy analyst and policymaker face a complex world wherein there are many values and interests and little control. They propose a scheme or procedure for policy analysis by design. They do not present this design as a mechanical linear set of stages, but as a 'recursive process, in which the latter stages can both advance upon and reopen earlier phases':

(i) Address values: Clarify the values being sought: their complexity, timing, quantity, priority and so on.

(ii) Capture context: That is, the milieu external to the policy process, within which policy will take effect: complexity, uncertainty, feedback potential, control, stability and audience (who will hinder/advance a policy).

(iii) Select appropriate approaches: What frameworks may be used to analyse a problem/policy programme?

(iv) Apply the appropriate approaches: Interpretation of problem and performance goals from the perspective of different frameworks:
   (a) identification and collection of needed information
   (b) invention and stipulation of policy alternatives
   (c) assessment and comparison of policy alternatives.

In the design approach, the aim is not to evaluate but to examine different ways of looking at problems from the perspective of different frameworks of values and methodology. Thus, this approach is all the more important as it serves as a road map for implementers.

Naturalistic Approach

'Naturalistic approach' or 'Negotiation approach' which has been developed by Guba and Lincoln is based upon a dialogue.[13] Advocates of this approach share a belief in value-pluralism and hold evaluation as a form of negotiation rather than a search for objective truth. Guba and Lincoln set out what they regard as the four 'generations' of evaluation:

(i) *Technical:* After the First World War, evaluation was seen as a technical exercise of measurement. The role of the evaluator was seen as that of a 'technician'.

---

[10] T.C. Miller, 'Conclusion: A Design Science Perspective', in *Public Sector Performance*, ed. T.C. Miller (Baltimore, MD: Johns Hopkins Press, 1984).

[11] D.B. Bobrow and J.S. Dryzek, *Policy Analysis by Design* (Pittsburgh, PA: Pittsburgh University Press, 1987).

[12] Ibid., 9; 211.

[13] E.G. Guba and Y.S. Lincoln, 'The Countenance of Fourth-generation Evaluation', in *The Politics of Program Evaluation*, ed. D.J. Palumbo (Los Angeles, CA: SAGE Publications, 1987).

(ii) *Descriptive:* During the 1940s, a second generation emerged which was focused on describing 'patterns, strengths and weaknesses' of stated objectives. The evaluator's role was, in addition to a technician, a 'describer'.

(iii) *Judgement:* In the 1960s and 1970s, evaluation developed into a judgemental science in which objective research and standards were used to measure the efficiency and effectiveness of programmes. The role of the evaluator was seen as that of a judge.

(iv) *Responsive:* Advocates of this approach argue that we are now in the midst of a 'fourth generation' of 'responsive' models of evaluation.

These models take as their point of focus not objectives, decisions, effects or similar organizers, but the claims, concerns and issues put forth by members of a variety of stakeholding audiences, that is, audiences who are in some sense involved with the evaluation.[14]

Evaluation in the fourth-generation sense views the constructions of stakeholders as being a primary focus of inquiry, and they include agents (financiers, implementers); beneficiaries (target groups); and those who are excluded victims; and that there should be an opportunity for all stakeholders to contribute their input to all stages of evaluation, from defining the terms of investigation, its goals and design to data collection, analysis and interpretation. In this way, evaluation is a learning process, and the evaluator's role is to mediate and facilitate learning and change. The aim in this evaluation is to provide a dialectical discussion between all concerned parties, so that a consensus emerges which can form the basis of policy decisions.

But, the fourth-generation approach cannot be readily co-opted into existing legitimate approaches.[15] The implications of this approach are that social inquiry involves power relations, which are not so easily changed. To them, 'fourth-generation evaluations end when time and money run out, and not when some full complement of questions have been asked'.[16] Thus, this fourth-generation of evaluation research appears to be a critique of liberal democracy and suggests that new forms of social inquiry can form the basis of a new kind of politics.

It can be briefly concluded that however systematically we may have defined policy objectives, framed policy design and selected policy criteria, often we cannot account for all of the variables that come into play in explaining why policy succeeds and why policy fails.

Framework of Evaluation

As already mentioned in the introduction, policy evaluation is mainly concerned with evaluating policy programme and evaluating people who are implementing the policy. In other words, the dominant framework of evaluation consists of

(i) a form of rational analysis (Evaluating Policy Programmes) and
(ii) a tool for the management of human resources (Performance Appraisal of Personnel).

---

[14] Ibid., 208.
[15] Ibid., 255–57.
[16] Ibid., 277.

EVALUATING POLICY PROGRAMMES (TECHNIQUES)

When evaluating a policy programme, two questions are to be addressed: (i) how a policy can be measured against the goals it sets out for achievement (this may be called 'formative evaluation') and the actual impact of the policy (this may be called 'summative evaluation').

Formative or implementation evaluation is that evaluation which is done when a policy is being implemented. On the other hand, summative evaluation seeks to measure how the policy/programme has actually impacted upon the problems to which it was addressed.

Here an attempt is made to discuss the analysis of evaluation as an activity involved in the measurement of goal performance. Mainly, there are four techniques for evaluation analysis, namely:

(i) CBA
(ii) Performance measure technique
(iii) Experimental evaluation
(iv) Quantitative and qualitative techniques

Cost–Benefit Analysis

CBA or benefit–cost analysis (terms are interchanged) is an analytical technique that has had a significant effect on policymaking in the public sector. The use of techniques and methods to measure the relationship of costs to benefits and the efficiency and effectiveness of policies and programmes has an obvious application to the evaluation phase in the policy process. This CBA technique suggests that all factors in a decision/policy should be quantified so as to provide a more rational basis for policymaking. The attractiveness of CBA as a tool of evaluation is obvious in the sense that it provides an apparent neutral technique for identifying costs and benefits of the policy programmes.

However, CBA is not without its critics. Some critics of CBA approach argue that this quantification is simply politics dressed up in techniques: 'nonsense on stilts'.[17] At the same time, there is little doubt that the contribution of cost–benefit has been profound. It has challenged policy evaluators to look at the long-term effects and to articulate its impact on quantitative as well as qualitative aspects of a programme or service.

Performance Measure Technique

'Implementation' phase of the policy cycle as suggested by Palumbo requires formative evaluation which monitors the way in which a policy/programme is being implemented so as to provide feedback which may improve or promote successful implementation.[18] Rossi and Freeman describe this mode of evaluation as being directed at three questions:

(i) the extent to which a programme is reaching the appropriate target population,
(ii) whether or not its delivery of services is consistent with programme design specification, and

---

[17] Self, *Econocrats and the Policy Process*.
[18] Palumbo, *The Politics of Program Evaluation*, 40.

(iii) what resources are being or have been expended in the conduct of the programme.[19]

Information gathered at the phase of implementation may be used to correct or control the policy delivery process more effectively. This may take the form of MIS which facilitates the collection and organization of information that can feed into the managerial policy-/decision-making process. In the MIS (now KM) approach to evaluation, the performance measurement as a technique figures imminent.

Among other features, performance measure aims at arriving at a ratio of inputs to service outputs. Where this is not apt, a performance measure may be expressed as how efficient the use of given resources has been: how much should have been achieved, and how much was actually achieved. Measures of performance can provide an effective substitute for profits so as to improve, for example, the functioning of schools, hospitals, local government and other services.

Jackson uses the term 'performance indicators' which, he says, can provide (i) a basis for accountability, (ii) a basis for policy planning and control, (iii) important information to monitor organizational activities, (iv) information for ex-post-strategic management post mortems and (v) the basis of a staff appraisal system.[20] Jackson further opines, 'Performance indicators are a means of assisting responsible management to make efficient decisions. They are not, however, a mechanical substitute for good judgement, political wisdom or leadership'.

Here, it is pertinent to mention that development of performance evaluation is generally understood in the context of the need to control public finances and attain higher levels of value for money, efficiency and effectiveness. As such, the control is not neutral or purely loaded with values, politics and power. Some questions raised are Who sets up the criteria for measurement? How is it calculated and what counts as efficient and effective? Or what the value for money is? Is it possible to compare one public hospital or school to another on the basis of a selected performance measurement? Advocates of this technique, however, contend that it improves personnel management, indicates progress towards goals and identifies problem areas.

Experimental Evaluation

It is argued that policy experimentation offers the best opportunity to gaze the impact of public policies. The term is taken from early experiments at the Hawthorne plant of Western Electric Company in Chicago in 1927 where it was found that worker output increased with any change in routine. In undertaking impact evaluation at the post-implementation phase, evaluation seeks to arrive at an estimate of the net and gross effects of intervention. It is a comparative mode of inquiry, that is, comparing before and after intervention. In this method, one could compare the impact of intervention on one group and another (who were not the subject of intervention) and also this method makes

---

[19] P.H. Rossi and H. Freeman, *Evaluation: A Systematic Approach*, 2nd ed. (California: SAGE Publications, 1993), 163.

[20] Peter Jackson, 'The Management of Performance in the Public Sector', *Public Money and Management* 8(4) (1988): 11–16.

proving that a particular policy has had this or that impact. Palumbo's policy cycle refers to summative evaluation as an impact evaluation which is done at the post-implementation stage of the policy cycle.[21]

Experiments are used to test the impact of a programme. An experiment seeks to study a problem before and after intervention. Here one may use a control group (before intervention) and an experimental group (after intervention) which may then be compared with another so as to measure the effectiveness of the intervention. Dye, in this context, suggests that experimental approach has a number of problems as a mode of evaluation:

(i) Society is a complex thing. How can an experiment be conducted which excludes so many factors? What judgements are involved in setting the parameters of which factors will be examined?

(ii) Given the above, how can research be designed to obtain 'good' results when experiments have cash limits and time constraints?

(iii) Not only are there cost and time constraints, the experiment also depends on management and implementation problems.

(iv) Can social experiments be conducted which involve comparing groups which may, in all probability, be very difficult to one another?

(v) In social experiments, people may be/will be conscious of being experimented upon (the so-called Hawthorne effect).

(vi) What of moral issues? Is it right that one group will be deprived of resources or another may be a guinea pig? People may not like the idea of being experimented upon.

(vii) From a political point of view, experiments take time. Policymakers may not have the time, and when at last an experiment is completed, the situation may have changed.[22]

Critics of experimental evaluation would add more to this list.[23] However, experimentation may be good and appropriate in some circumstances. Campbell makes a strong case for use of experimentation as a means of improving evaluation and advances the idea of an 'experimenting society'.[24] In the experimenting society, the focus would be on problems rather than the advocacy of solutions. He maintains that the experimenting society is a response to the limited resources facing policymakers and public, and a way of addressing the problem of inequity in access to power. Dye also makes a strong case for experimentation when he comments, 'It is exceedingly costly for society to commit itself to large-scale programs and policies in education and welfare, housing, health and so on, without any real idea about what works'.[25] Recently, the Indian PM said to a gathering of civil servants, 'People who do work differently and experiment, they get a different satisfaction'.[26]

---

[21] Palumbo, *The Politics of Program Evaluation*.
[22] Dye, *Understanding Public Policy*, 2nd ed. (New Jersey: Prentice Hall, 1987), 368–69.
[23] See F.P. Scioli and T.J. Cook, 'Experimental Design in Policy Impact Analysis', *Social Science Quarterly* 54 (1973): 271–91.
[24] D.T. Campbell, 'Experiments as Arguments', *Knowledge* 3 (1982): 331.
[25] Dye, *Understanding Public Policy*, 372.
[26] See *The Financial Express* (Chandigarh), 22 April 2016.

Quantitative and Qualitative Techniques

Policy analysis mainly concerned with evaluation involves using quantitative and qualitative techniques to define a policy problem, demonstrate its impact and present potential solutions. Evaluation tells us much about the performance of the public policy. It shows whether goals have been met or not. For good results, evaluation should involve a variety of techniques and approaches. Quantitative as well as qualitative techniques are used for evaluating policy performance also. Quantitative measurement 'involves evaluation measures which generate data in a standardized framework of predetermined responses or analysis categories'. On the other hand, 'qualitative measures are designed to avoid limiting the observations which can be made about policy performance'. Qualitative measures permit the management team to record and understand peoples' reactions to the programme in their own terms in contrast to terms of quantitative research methodologies. There are three types of data in a qualitative measurement: (i) detailed descriptions of observed situations; (ii) direct quotations from people explaining their own experiences with programme outcomes; and (iii) excerpts from documents, records or case histories.

Quantitative evaluation measures outcomes in terms of the intentions set out in the policy design. Quantitative measures are systematic, standardized and easily presented in a short space. On the other hand, qualitative measures are longer, more detailed and variable in content. Analysis is difficult because responses are not systematic. The key to data collection in qualitative measurement is direct participation in the activities of the beneficiaries of the programme. By contrast, quantitative measurement injects an element of artificiality into the evaluation situation. The qualitative techniques are valid and feasible alternatives to more quantitative techniques. Further, many problems of artificiality of programme evaluation can be circumvented through the use of qualitative techniques. On the other hand, quantitative methods evaluate magnitudes of the effects of the policies on social, economic and political factors, and find better policy alternatives.

It may be added that no policy, however well crafted, can be made immune to such evaluation. The policymaker cannot fully anticipate the consequences of a policy initiative.

PERFORMANCE APPRAISAL OF PERSONNEL

Evaluation in public policy also involves performance of the people who work in the public sector at both street and managerial levels. At the core of evaluation of people is the belief that more control through the performance evaluation of personnel can ensure better outcomes of the policy programmes. Thomason, a leading scholar of personnel management, defines performance evaluation in human resource management (HRM) as involving

   (i) the identification of tasks to be performed, together with the criteria to be used to measure successful performance.

  (ii) the evaluation of the performance given, by assessment either of the results where these are measurable, or of input of relevant effort or behaviour where they are not.

(iii) the determination of the amount of reward, remuneration or 'reinforcement' to be given to improve, maintain or advance the current level of performance.[27]

In addition to the development of MIS (or KM) techniques for evaluating policies, there has also been an emphasis on adoption of 'HRM' and 'organizational development' (OD) techniques in the public sector. These techniques of people evaluation largely drawn from HRM and OD comprise (a) performance-related pay schemes, (b) personnel assessment and appraisal and (c) OD strategies. For Thompson, the aim of an HRM strategy is to change people so as to become more

(i) committed (commitment can be improved);
(ii) competent (competencies can be developed and can bring improved product quality and productivity);
(iii) cost-effective (ideally costs should be low and performance high and so on); and
(iv) in sympathy with the aims of the organization (are the values and expectations of all parties in agreement?).[28]

The focus in HRM approach is on to improve the performance by developing a sense of commitment in each employee, rather than just compliance to hierarchical command or instruction.[29] This increase in commitment is to be achieved through recruiting the right kind of people, training, regular staff appraisal and rewarding them for their performance. The idea of rewarding performance in practice has meant the attempt to link between pay and performance.

Performance-related pay system is a technique to evaluate individuals and groups in terms of the performance of output and profits. Here, money is the best kind of motivator. In practice, rewarding by performance is not without difficulties. It involves several issues such as: Is money the best motivator in the government service? What are the measures to evaluate performance? How can the increased performance of doctors, engineers or police be measured? Performance evaluation (and reward) is a political minefield as well as problematic at a level of personnel management.[30] Nevertheless, the performance-based pay systems have been in operation in both public and private sectors around the world. In the USA, an Act was passed which includes, among its major features, a requirement to develop and institute systems that strengthen the link between pay and performance.[31]

In the appraisal of people, it is argued that more control is needed over bureaucrats and professionals to ensure that objectives set out by the policymakers are implemented efficiently and effectively. This kind of managerialism is seen as the extension and continuation of Taylorist 'madness' to those 'white-collar' and professional domains which were

[27] G. Thomason, *A Textbook of Human Resource Management* (London: Institute of Personnel Management, 1988), 328.
[28] J.L. Thompson, *Strategic Management: Awareness and Change* (London: Chapman, 1990), 307.
[29] J. Storey, 'Human Resource Management in the Public Sector', *Public Money and Management* 9(3) (Autumn 1989): 19–24.
[30] Thomason, *A Textbook of Human Resource Management*, 328–29.
[31] OECD, *Public Management Development: Survey*, 1992 (Paris: OECD, 1992), 11.

for so long regarded as different to the factory or the profit-driven office.[32] The Taylorist methods used in private sector are now challenged as they erode the professional autonomy and bureaucratic rationality in the government organizations.

In context of it, the Second Administrative Reforms Commission (GOI) in its 10th Report (November 2008) recommended, 'A good employee performance appraisal system is a prerequisite for an effective performance management system'. The trend in evaluation has been to move increasingly towards modifying the behaviour of people in organizations, rather than organizations as systems.[33] HRM is now concerned with improving rationality in terms of performance by changing the attitudes, motivation and culture of the people who work in policy delivery areas.

EVALUATING IMPACT AND APPROACHES

Evaluating impact, impact evaluation or IA, as commonly used in the literature of public policy, is an integral and important component of the policy cycle. No policy is worth its effort if it does not make a difference. It is therefore, as far as the citizen is concerned, the criterion of policy programme performance. How has the National Environment Policy (2006) made a difference to the environment? How has National Youth Policy (2014) impacted on the development of the Youth of India? Has the law on 'Protection of Children from Sexual Offences' (2012) made the children safe from sexual assault? In other words, has the policy solved problems or made matters worse? The question is what impact has the policy actually had. Although evaluating impact of social, economic or some other aspect of the public policy is a difficult exercise, it cannot be overlooked. By examining the effects of the public policy, we get a handle on whether to continue, amend or terminate the policy altogether.

Meaning and Purpose of Impact Evaluation

As defined by Rossi and Freeman, 'Impact assessments are undertaken to estimate whether or not interventions produce their intended effects. Such estimates cannot be made with certainty but only with varying degrees of plausibility'.[34] In a wider context, Dye notes that policy impact enables to know the consequences of policy on

- (i) some specific target situation or group;
- (ii) 'spillover effects' on situations or groups other than the target;
- (iii) future as well as immediate conditions;
- (iv) direct costs, in terms of resources devoted to the programme; and
- (v) indirect costs, including loss of opportunities to do other things.[35]

The main objective of an IA is to produce an estimate of the 'net effects' of an intervention. Since evaluation tests whether public policy has worked as intended, the policy impact

---

[32] B. Doray, *From Taylorism to Fordism: A Rational Madness* (London: Free Association Books, 1988).
[33] India, Administrative Reforms Commission (Second), *Refurbishing of Personnel Administration* (New Delhi: ARC, November 2008), 10th Report, 218–42.
[34] P.H. Rossi and H. Freeman, *Evaluation: A Systematic Approach* (California: SAGE Publications, 1993), 215.
[35] Thomas Dye, *Understanding Public Policy* (Singapore: Pearson Education, Indian reprint 2004), 313.

seeks to measure how the public policy programme has actually impacted upon the problems to which it was addressed. For example, has the family planning methods including the use of contraceptive improved the health situation of a village (the indicator could be the number of children born to a couple in a family).

It involves the role of the IA. In undertaking IA at the post-implementation phase, evaluation seeks to arrive at an estimate of the net and gross effects of the government's intervention through a policy. It is a comparative mode of enquiry that is comparing before and after intervention. The aim of assessment is to show how a given policy or a programme has worked or not worked, met the policy or programme goals or not met the goals, so as to sustain the construction of the problem.

Again, it is through the IA that the utility of a policy could be ascertained. If the policy fails to deliver the intended services, it could be terminated. Policy impact, thus, contributes to the process of a policy change. Where the policy is found to be worth, policy succession is likely to take place. Impact evaluation provides the inputs for future policy refinement.

Prerequisites for IA

Public policymakers and government agencies are presumed to be keen in seeking favourable outcomes and impact from their policies. The question requiring answer is, Does a specific policy generate what is intended and with what unexpected effects? Answer to this question is complex as it involves notions of reliability and quality of IA. For adequate IA of a policy programme, it has to, at minimum,

(i) provide an adequate description of the programme or techniques whose impact is being tested;

(ii) provide clear assurance that the programme or techniques can be learned and applied by others also;

(iii) divide the study population into groups on a random basis, so as to wash out as many confounding variables as possible;

(iv) provide 'before' and 'after' measures of the behaviour, which were targeted for change; and

(v) establish definitions of 'success' or 'failure' that provide valid standards for assessing the outcomes of the study group under impact assessment.

IA TECHNIQUES AND APPROACHES

Impact evaluation or IA has a number of approaches or techniques. A few notable methods and approaches are briefly discussed here.

Measuring Costs Against Benefits

CBA was framed to make calculations as to the optimal distribution of costs and benefits. This approach focuses on measuring costs against the benefits which have taken place as a result of intervention. The quantitative outcomes of cost–benefit calculations show whether the gains exceed the total costs or not. This method is also useful in estimating the impact of existing programmes and comparing them with that of the proposed programmes and ranking their effectiveness. Results are typically expressed in terms of a benefit–cost ratio which is equal to the benefits of policy programme divided by its costs.

In this context, Dror opines that optimal public policy must specify and evaluate its resources (financial, human and infrastructural resources) not only in terms of their consumption but also in terms of their potential uses for making and implementing policies. In other words, the resources used for any policy programme should be quantified in monetary terms. The benefit out of the resources utilized should, in any case, be not less than the resources put to use. If it is not so, then the policy does not have a positive impact. While attempting to know the impact of the policy vis-à-vis the resources used, efforts ought to be made to find out which, where and how a particular given resource used has not provided the desired result or was used more than required.

Comparing Outcomes with Objectives

A simple method to ascertain policy impact is through comparing what has happened with the specified goals or targets of a policy or programme. In other words, it means comparing a problem or situation with what it was like before the intervention. For example, following the National Civil Aviation Policy, 2016, the union government scrapped the decade-long controversial 5/20 rule for new airlines to fly abroad provided they deployed 20 planes or 20 per cent of their total capacity for domestic operations.[36]

Measuring Impact by Experimentation

The evaluation of the actual impact of policy on social or economic problems can be assessed by experimentation. Experimental approach attempts to quantify success in achieving initial policy objectives, based on some form of 'before' and 'after' study of those involved in the experiment in comparison with a control group. In this approach, experiments are conducted to test the impact of a programme on a group or an area against what has happened to a group or an area which has not been the target of intervention. An experiment may seek to study a problem before and after intervention. The evaluator can be reasonably sure that the policy programme has had some measure of impact.

Using Performance Measurements

Another method to ascertain policy impact is through using performance measures and indicators. This method is applied to assess if goals or targets have been met or otherwise.

According to Jackson, measures of performance can also provide an effective substitute for profit so as to improve the management, for example, of schools, hospitals and other services.[37] Under this approach, the implementing agency may be assigned the task of assessing the impact of services.

---

[36] See *The Tribune* (Chandigarh), 16 June 2016.
[37] Peter Jackson, 'The Management of Performance in the Public Sector', *Public Money and Management*, 8(4) (1988): 11–16.

Using Qualitative Judgement Approaches

Whereas quantitative measurement deals with determining the impact of a policy in terms of certain PIs, qualitative judgement responds to the wisdom of the policy itself. Here we move to the concerns of social justice, values, principles and ideals. With this form of IA, the fundamental question centres upon the worth of the policy that has been put into place.

For example, under social policy pronouncements and legislation, there is some progress in improving the position of SCs, STs and OBCs in school enrolment, and in parameters such as literacy and the percentage of people below the poverty line (BPL). And yet gaps still persist and a large number of people of these classes continue to be discriminated in education and employment opportunities. To quote from an article, 'The problems of dalits keep on increasing day by day, even though there are many government programmes available exclusively for dalits, they are still oppressed, exploited and their living condition in the rural area is pathetic'.[38]

Under this approach, IA is undertaken by a number of professional and non-professional persons. Broader judgements and conclusions are then arrived at through communication between team members. The techniques associated with this method are interactional, such as direct observation, informal communication with key informants and group discussions. These judgemental approaches help evaluate success/failure of policy and programmes.

Using Beneficiary's Feedback

An old and popular method to assess policy impact is through beneficiary's response to provision of social and economic services. It is seen that a large number of social programmes concerning health, education and social security are given a wide publicity to the weaker sections of the community in developing countries. The implementing agencies are expected to follow the procedures and rules as given or required by the authorities. In case of any kind of diversions by the administrative agencies, the prospective beneficiaries may complain to the appropriate authorities or they may air their grievances through the media. Though somewhat crude, this method is simple for getting some kind of feedback. If the number of complaints or grievances are few and negligible, it would indicate the positive impact or good work of the implementing agencies. However, the method is not without its shortcomings. Not all citizens voluntarily submit complaints against policy programmes of the government.

POLITICS, POLICY ANALYSIS AND POLICY OUTCOMES

Policy analysis is primarily concerned with the front end of the policy process. It is a rational process which involves a set of sequences including problem identification, formulation, implementation, evaluation and impact of the policy. It involves measurement of

---

[38] Emmanuel Johnson, 'Participatory Action Research on the Economic Status of Suppressed Community (Dalits) in India', *South Asian Journal of Socio-Political Studies*, 14(2) (2014): 14–19.

benefits and costs and the interpretation of the results. Value conflicts intrude at almost every point in the evaluation process, but policy analysis cannot resolve value conflicts.

Politics is the management of conflicts. Policymakers rely so little on the policy analysis. To them, a political approach is better than a rational approach. Compromise and conciliation and a willingness to accept the modest net gains form the basis for conflict resolution. The search for mutually beneficial outcomes ('I will support your proposal if you support mine') and bargaining among diverse groups take the front end of the political approach.

In the political approach, politics becomes a substitute for policy analysis. At best, policy analysis plays only a secondary role in the policymaking process. But it is a significant role. In this context, Lindblom explains,

> Strategic analysis and mutual adjustments among political participants, then, are the underling processes by which democratic systems achieve the level of intelligent action that they do. Since time and energy and brainpower are limited, strategic analysis must focus on those aspects of an issue that participating partisans consider to be most important for persuading each other.[39]

Politics may well have a significant impact on policy, but to what extent does it make much of an impact on policy outcomes? Does it really matter from the point of view of solving or ameliorating problems? Recent research in policy outcomes in India indicates that the impact of government policies on various aspects of economic and industrial outcomes (GNP, employment, inflation, etc.) is at best marginal, compared with wider factors, such as the impact of the international economy. Furthermore, the fact is that policymaking and implementation take place in the context of past policies and earlier decisions, which severely limit choices and innovation.[40]

Similarly, although the party in power has an important impact on a policy, it cannot bring about more policy change because of severe limitations such as commitments of the past, public opinion, bureaucracy and international constraints on the national policies. In short, 'liberal democratic governments operate at the margin, seeking to react to developments they do not control and which often they cannot foresee'.[41] de Bono also advances the argument that policymaking is all too frequently driven less by moving towards objectives than by reacting to what he terms the 'rear-end' objectives.[42] Of course, policy may be the result of what Lindblom terms 'muddling through'.[43] But this does not mean that policymaking is of no value. Public managers identify weak areas within an organization and make corrective changes.

[39] Lindblom and Woodhouse, *The Policy-making Process*, 31–32.
[40] R. Rose and P.L. Davies, *Inheritance in Public Policy: Change Without Choice in Britain* (New Haven, CT: Yale University Press, 1994).
[41] Martin Harrop, ed., *Power and Policy in Liberal Democracies* (Cambridge: Cambridge University Press, 1992), 277.
[42] E. de Bono, *Atlas of Management Thinking* (London: Temple Smith, 1981), 89.
[43] C.E. Lindblom, 'Still Muddling Through', *Public Administration Review* 39(6) (1979): 517–25.

Determinants of Policy Outcomes

The term 'policy outcomes' has come to mean the substantive results of the implementation of a policy. To argue that policy 'outcomes' are the results of social and economic forces is to underestimate the importance of politics. As Sharpe and Newton comment in their defence of politics, 'Viewed as the whole process of policymaking, the political factor embraces not just the determination of public policy outputs, but also the selection and processing of the inputs of the political system'.[44]

As such, the shape of the path of policy outcomes must be set in the context of a multiplicity of factors: political leadership, economic and social conditions, technology, international economic forces, political parties and interest groups, present and past politics, institutional arrangements (executive, legislature, judiciary, bureaucracy, and so on) and distribution of power. One or more of these forces as having a determining or dominate role would contribute to outcomes of public policy. The outcomes in education, health, reduction in poverty and so on may be viewed as formed by an array of inputs and forces, of which 'policy' is but one and possibly not one of the most influential of forces at work on the 'real-world' problems. In this context, Hancock et al. argue that many aspects of system performance 'are influenced by external economic and other factors beyond the control of national policy actors. None the less, national policymaking structures and processes mediate the domestic economic and social consequences of exogenous trends and events'.[45] These outcomes are often hard to measure.

PROBLEMS FACING EVALUATION IMPACT

Problems of evaluating impact of policy programmes of the government are diverse and vary from country to country. Some notable problems are discussed here in brief.

Variations in Analysis of Policy Impact

Both outputs and outcomes are important to measure, but for different reasons. To answer what effects policy has had is difficult. Evaluating the impact of a policy programme on the 'quality of life', for example, turns on what the idea of 'quality of life' means. James Wilson argues that analysis of the effects of public policies is contingent on 'where you sit'.[46] According to him, if the research is carried out by those implementing the policy, then the research will show that it has delivered the right results. On the other hand, if the research is carried out by independent analysts, it will show negative effects. In other words, the evaluation of the actual impact of policy on problems is a matter of wisdom or values rather than facts. Impact evaluators in the government generally lack research capabilities. Ambiguity, lack of appropriate bases for comparison and lack of concrete evidence increase the administrator's control over assessments, or at least to minimize the criticism in case of failure.

---

[44] L.J. Sharpe and K. Newton, *Does Politics Matter? The Determinants of Public Policy* (Oxford: Oxford University Press, 1984), 206–08.

[45] M.D. Hancock et al., *Politics in Western Europe* (London: Macmillan, 1993), xix.

[46] James Wilson, *Political Organizations* (California: SAGE Publications, 1973), 132–34.

Political Influence in Policy Impact Evaluation

Often, it is argued that policy outcomes are the result of political influence. When policy-makers constitute enquiries or research as to the impact of their policies on health, education, unemployment and so on, they are engaged in shaping the context and agenda within which problems are being defined and constructed. In this sense, therefore, impact evaluation takes us back to the start of the policy process. It means impact claims and constructions have to face the assessments which are deployed by other political parties, interest groups, think tanks, researchers and so on, who seek to show how a policy is not working in order to make the case for their claims and constructions. For Lincoln and Guba who are critics of the quantitative approach to IA, the political nature of evaluating the impact of a policy/programme means that more 'qualitative' forms of evaluation are necessary in order to counteract the distorting effects of apparently objective facts.[47]

Complexity in Comparison of Policy Outcomes

Different nations produce and use different data, and those data have specific contexts. But comparing sets of statistics is a very difficult exercise. However, even though there are such clear methodological problems with the idea of comparing policy outcomes, it is the case that in the modern world, outcomes are compared by the use of data produced by international organizations such as the WB and Organisation for Economic Co-operation and Development (OECD). Policy analysts and politicians seek to know why different political systems differ in terms of the actual outcomes: Why do countries spend certain proportions of their GDP on health, rural development, education and so on? Why do the performance and effective implementation of policies differ from country to country? Explanations to such questions are, however, different and complex.

Moreover, the study of impact and evaluation in public administration has been seriously neglected. It suffers not only from the lack of interest and initiative, but also from deficiencies on the methodological front. While doing impact analysis and fixing of standards, policymakers tend to rely on comparisons with the past. Dror notes that comparison with the past, in many respects, is misleading because it does not provide any 'zero point' for reliable conclusion.[48] The experience of India, in particular, has amply demonstrated that borrowing successful models from countries very different to India has confirmed the fact that several economic policies have failed to make their impact on the social improvement.

CONCLUSION

It may well be that policy outcomes are best understood as involving 'symbolic' rather than purely 'substantive' outcomes. As Dye upholds, 'Policies do more than effect change in societal conditions; they also help hold people together and maintain an orderly state'.[49] With a focus on the right kind of attitude, adequate resources, appropriate skill and techniques,

---

[47] Y.S. Lincoln and E.G. Guba, *Naturalistic Inquiry* (California: SAGE Publications, 1985).
[48] Y. Dror, Public *Policymaking Re-examined* (New Jersey: Transaction Publisher, 1989).
[49] Dye, *Understanding Public Policy*, (2004), 315.

the implementing agencies can bring out a realistic position of policy impact. Policy evaluation helps in knowing what the government is doing. It is the mechanism which enables us to compare promise with performance. But the process of evaluation is often influenced by values of those individuals and agencies entrusted with the evaluation work.

Review Questions

(i) Briefly discuss the multiplist approach to policy evaluation.
(ii) What are the four 'generations' of policy evaluation?
(iii) Why is performance appraisal of the people working in the public sector vital as a part of policy evaluation?
(iv) What do you mean by IA in public policy evaluation?
(v) Qualitative judgement responds to the wisdom of the policy itself. Explain the statement.

CHAPTER 20

POLICY EVALUATION
Purpose, Criteria and Evaluators

INTRODUCTION

Evaluation is essentially an important component of the policy process. Yet it has drawn little attention from the policymakers.[1] Much of the interest in the policy process centres on the dynamic energy that goes into decisions. In fact, it is only during the implementation–evaluation phase that we learn whether the policy was carried out as the policymakers designed and intended. By comparing intended goals with performance, we are able to determine the extent to which a public policy has matched expectations. Wholey, Abramson and Bellavita note that evaluation is critical to determining whether programmes live up to their expectations.[2] And by reviewing the outcome of the objectives, we judge the merit of public policy. Viewed as a follow-up experience, evaluation helps us understand the impact of the policy on the target group (people) that it has been designed to address. In a sense, 'evaluation provides the ammunition for future change and policy refinement'.[3]

What Is Policy Evaluation?

Policy evaluation appears to be the final stage of the policy process in the sequential pattern of activities. Evaluation is concerned with what happens once a policy has been put into effect. In the words of Wholey, 'Policy evaluation is the assessment of the overall effectiveness of a national programme in meeting its objectives, or assessment of the relative effectiveness of two or more programmes in meeting common objectives'.[4]

Wollmann defines policy evaluation as:

> [A]n analytical tool and procedure meant to do two things. First, evaluation research, as an analytical tool, involves investigating a policy program to obtain all information pertinent to the assessment of its performance, both process and result; second, evaluation as a phase of the policy cycle more generally refers to the reporting of such information back to the policy-making process.[5]

---

[1] It was during the 1960s and 1970s and also with the setting up of the journal *Evaluation Review* in 1976 that the subject of policy evaluation gained wide recognition.
[2] Joseph S. Wholey, Mark A. Abramson and Christopher Bellavita, eds., 'Managing for High Performance: Roles for Evaluation', *Performance and Credibility* (Lexington, MA: Lexington, 1986), 2.
[3] Gerston, *Public Policymaking*, 137.
[4] Joseph S. Wholey et al., *Federal Evaluation Policy* (Washington: Urban Institute, 1970), 25.
[5] Hellmut Wollmann, 'Policy Evaluation and Evaluation Research', in *Handbook of Public Policy Analysis*, eds. F. Fischer, G.J. Miller and M.S. Sidney (Boca Raton, FL: CRC Press, 2007), 393.

Rossi, Lipsey and Freeman specify evaluation as a systematic application of social research procedures for assessing the conceptualization, design, implementation and utility of social intervention programmes.[6] According to them, it is also necessary to take into account the individual needs of the clients while undertaking programme evaluation.

Difference Between Evaluation, Monitoring and Implementation

A distinction is required to understand the terms 'evaluation' and 'monitoring'. Evaluation is not monitoring. Monitoring, however, is a prerequisite for evaluation. Monitoring is concerned with establishing factual premises about public policies. It is fundamentally about control and the exercise of power. Monitoring answers the question, 'What happened, how, and why?' On the contrary, evaluation answers the question, 'What difference does it make?' Evaluation is retrospective and occurs after actions have been taken. It is concerned with trying to determine the impact of policy on real-life conditions. It is through experimentation that we are able to better determine the impact of a policy.

It is also difficult to grasp the line between implementation and evaluation. Evaluation follows implementation. The difference is that, in implementation, the focus is on putting the policy into action; in evaluation, the focus is on determining the extent to which public policy has matched expectation.

Purpose of Policy Evaluation

In a sense, evaluation helps us understand the impact of a policy on the politico-socio-economic system of the country. By examining the consequences of the public policy on the target people or the system in place, we get a handle on whether to continue, amend or possibly scrap the policy altogether.

The main objective of policy evaluation is to reduce the problem in the face of policy delivery. Policy evaluation is generally used for one or more of three purposes:

(i) to assess whether public policy has worked as intended (efficiency assessment);
(ii) to assess the consequences of the public policy (impact assessment);
(iii) to assess whether to continue, amend or scrap the public policy (future action assessment).

Evaluation performs several functions in policy analysis. In the first place, it provides reliable information about policy performance. The prime purpose of the evaluation is to measure the impact of policies on society. It reveals the extent to which particular goals have been achieved (e.g. increase in the life expectancy at birth). It helps us understand the degree to which policy issues have been addressed.

Second, it is a tool whose main purpose is to appraise the operation of a policy programme and provide feedback to those involved in the earlier stages of the policy cycle. Evaluation helps clarify the values that underline the selection of goals and objectives. Values are clarified by properly defining goals and objectives. Since the appropriateness of

---

[6] P.H. Rossi, M.W. Lipsey and H. Freeman, *Evaluation: A Systematic Approach*, 7th ed. (California: SAGE Publications, 2004).

policy goals and objectives can be questioned in relation to the problem being addressed, evaluation provides procedures for evaluating goals and objectives themselves.

Third, evaluation may result in efforts to restructure policy problems. It may also contribute to the emergence of new objectives and potential solutions. For example, by showing whether a previously adopted policy alternative should be replaced with another one or abandoned. In the course of policy implementation, the policy actions may be either restructured to the new conditions or terminated altogether, either because the needs have been met or because policy actions have created more problems than they have resolved. Thus, evaluation is primarily an effort to analyse policy outcomes in terms of some set objectives. It determines the social utility and worth of public policies.

Fourth, at times, programme evaluation is undertaken to appease policymakers or advocacy groups that are pressuring a government agency or department for some accountability.

POLICY EVALUATION TYPES

To Thomas Dye, evaluation is 'learning about the consequences of public policy'.[7] In the context of evaluation of policy, two questions are: how a policy may be measured against the goals it sets out for achievement (this may be called 'formative evaluation') and the actual impact of the policy (this may be called 'summative evaluation'). A few important evaluation types are discussed in this chapter.

Implementation (Formative) Evaluation

Formative or implementation evaluation is that evaluation which is done when a policy is being implemented. The implementation requires formative evaluation to monitor a policy/programme in such a way as to provide feedback which may improve or promote successful implementation. The mode of evaluation is directed at three questions: '(1) the extent to which a program is reaching the appropriate target population, (2) whether or not its delivery of services is consistent with program design specifications, and (3) what resources are being or have been expended in the conduct of the programme.'[8]

Implementation evaluation is conducted with a view to ascertaining the worth of a policy programme. Through this activity policymakers determine future plans and directions. An important function of 'ongoing' evaluation is to feed relevant information back into the implementation process at a point and stage when pertinent information can be used in order to adjust, correct or redirect the implementation process.

Impact (Summative) Evaluation

Impact evaluation is an effort to ascertain whether the policy programme actually had the impact the policymakers intended. Dye looks at evaluation in terms of the consequences of public policy, that is, with 'policy impact'.

---

[7] Dye, *Understanding Public Policy*, 312.

[8] P.H. Rossi and H. Freeman, *Evaluation: A Systematic Approach*, 2nd ed. (California: SAGE Publications, 1993), 163.

The impact of a policy is all its effects on real-world conditions, including

   (i) Impact on the target situation or group
  (ii) Impact on situations or groups other than the target (spillover effects)
 (iii) Impact on future as well as immediate conditions
 (iv) Direct costs, in terms of resources devoted to the program
  (v) Indirect costs, including loss of opportunities to do other things.

All the benefits and costs, both immediate and future, must be measured in both symbolic and tangible effects.[9]

Impact evaluation is done at the post-implementation phase of the policy cycle. It is to measure the impact of policy on the target group. It seeks to measure how the policy/ programme has actually impacted upon the problems to which it was addressed. It involves the role of IA. In undertaking IA at the post-implementation phase, evaluation seeks to arrive at an estimate of the net and gross effects of intervention. It is a comparative mode of inquiry that is comparing before and after intervention. In this method, one could compare the impact of intervention on one group and another (who were not the subject of intervention). It makes proving that this policy has had this or that impact.

Conducting impact studies on social and economic policies and programmes is all the more a difficult exercise. It may take much time for a noticeable improvement of a programme. For example, in the NDA government's budget 2014–15, wide-ranging announcements were made on infrastructure, particularly in transportation and distribution, with massive allocations made for roads, water, gas distribution and for making the Ganga navigable.[10] The impact of their implementation would be analysed through studies after four to five years. In impact evaluation, an experimental approach may be used. An experiment seeks to study a problem before and after intervention. Summative evaluation seeks to measure how the policy has actually impacted upon the problems to which it was addressed.[11] Characteristically, policy (or programme) evaluation has been given primarily two tasks. First, it was meant to produce an assessment about the degree to which the intended policy goals have achieved (goal attainment). Following from this task, there is the conceptual problem of identifying measurable indicators in order to make such assessments of goal attainment. Second, the evaluation of policies and programmes was also expected to answer the question as to whether the observed effects and changes have been related to policy in question. From this is the methodological issue of use of tools and skills capable of solving the problem.

Meta-evaluation

Meta-evaluation is another type of evaluation which is meant to analyse an already completed (primary) evaluation using a kind of second analysis. Two variants of this type are methodology reviewing and synthesizing. In the case of first variant, the meta-evaluation may review the already completed piece of (primary) evaluation as to whether it is up to

---

[9] Dye, *Understanding Public* Policy, 313.
[10] The budget was presented by the Union Finance Minister on 10 July 2014 in the Lok Sabha.
[11] Parsons, *Public Policy* (Cheltenham: Edward Elgar 1995), 550.

methodological standards. In the case of second variant, the meta-evaluation may have to accumulate the substantive findings of the primary completed evaluation and synthesize the results.

Comprehensive Evaluation

The exercise of evaluation process can be an eye-opening experience for policymaking agencies as well as individuals. A comprehensive evaluation is the combination of process and impact evaluation as explained earlier. Properly conducted, comprehensive evaluation closes the loop on the policymaking process, confirming a successful response to perceived needs and suggesting new needs that require further action.

Performance Appraisal

Appraisal of employee's performance is of critical value to the organization. Performance appraisal is used to provide information relating to appraisal of people who are implementing policies. Usually, evaluators focus on technical performance of individuals as set against the objectives of organization. Such an appraisal may be done by the manager or a steering committee appointed by the policy management. At the international level, donors or sponsoring agencies such as WHO, WB, ILO and UNESCO have also been keen to require a performance appraisal. Appraisal may also be in the context of the development of the potential of the individual.

Audit

The notion of evaluation in public policy has widened to encompass audit as an important instrument for financial performance of the policy programme. More than that, it is designed to assess the efficiency in the use of other resources in the policy management. Power argues that we are in the midst of an 'audit explosion'.[12] The system of audit has improved the policing and control capabilities of the management.

FRAMEWORK FOR EVALUATING POLICY

Sometimes, we do not evaluate carefully public policies because evaluation involves much time and huge resources in terms of finance and personnel. But, all the more, policy evaluation is very important. It reveals the extent of achievement of goals of a specific policy.

Policy evaluation requires a framework. Hypothetically, it involves several steps. Usually for conducting an evaluation, five steps are the most significant:

    (i) Identifying purposes of evaluation
    (ii) Identifying areas for evaluation
    (iii) Choosing evaluation methodology
    (iv) Analysing the results
    (v) Reporting evaluation results.

---

[12] Michael Power, *The Audit Explosion* (London: Demos, 1994).

Identifying Purposes of Evaluation

As mentioned earlier, implementation precedes evaluation. So the first step in conducting policy programme evaluation relates to identifying the purposes of evaluation. The public institutions or policy planners who seek evaluation should articulate questions as to why they want to evaluate this policy. The evaluators then should identify the management concerns, questions and issues on which the evaluation should focus. Government servants are asked by the Chief Executive or legislators to give testimony of their programmes.

Identifying Areas for Evaluation

Through evaluation activity, it is possible to determine future plans and directions. Once the evaluation questions have been articulated, it becomes possible to identify areas of focus for the programme. For example, if the question relates to unanticipated environmental impact of the forest policy, then the evaluation had better focus on technical aspects of the policy. The management team can identify those areas of the programme which will yield the most helpful information. The focus has been primarily on the activity of government.

Choosing Evaluation Methodology

Since evaluation tests whether public policies have worked as intended, we need to select appropriate evaluation methodology. It involves collection of reliable data from different sources. Here it also involves developing the equipment for recording information and pilot-testing them. The pilot test is helpful especially if data collection is going to be entrusted to other people who may not have background in policy management. When the methodology is developed, the next step is the processing of orchestrating data collection and organization. The whole process of data evaluation involves collection, cleaning, tabulation and analysis of data. Methodological issues of evaluation need to be given such attention.

Analysing the Results

Evaluation is concerned with knowing what happens after a law is passed. Data collection and cleaning, being a step in the data analysis, means culling data which is incomplete, and combing data sets according to the questions which they are designed to answer. Data tabulation means codifying the data into an analysable form. After the tabulation, the data is ready for report writing. In many respects, the systematic collection of data and information helps make reasonable judgements, about the disposition of policy programme inputs and outputs (evaluation). We must acknowledge that the political milieu often shapes policy research.

Reporting Evaluation Results

Evaluation reporting entails summarizing all the indicators and comparing data to the targets. The evaluation report requires the maximum attention. It should be well written and should cover all the major points of the evaluation. It should be a summary of the recommendations of the management issues that launched the evaluation. Besides this, the evaluation report should be accompanied with technical appendices. The entire document should be comprehensive and should enable other analysts in knowing the methodologies and analytical tables at some later point of time.

General Observation

It is pertinent to mention here that policy evaluation is a rational exercise involving CBA. The outcome of the policy evaluation will be quite different from the intended expectations. Further, its results may not be politically feasible.

EVALUATION CRITERIA

Whether conducted by a public or private agency, evaluation tells us much about the performance of the policy implementers. Specially it shows whether desired objectives have been achieved or not. The criteria for policy evaluation are many, but in main they focus on the policy objectives.

Frohock has suggested four concepts—equity, efficiency, Pareto optimality and public interest—as helpful in evaluating policy.[13] On the other hand, Poister argues that the criteria '…to evaluate policies and programmes all relate to goals and objectives, either focusing on the objectives themselves or on the means/ends relationships between strategies and objectives'.[14] He then outlines the performance variables as effectiveness, adequacy and appropriateness.

Suchman proposes a five-dimensional scheme for evaluating success or failure[15]:

  (i) *Effort* refers to 'the quantity or quality of activity that takes place';
 (ii) *Performance* 'measures the results of efforts rather than the effort itself';
(iii) *Adequacy of performance* measures 'the degree to which effective performance is adequate to the total amount of need';
(iv) *Efficiency* concerns the question, 'is there a better way to attain the same results?';
 (v) *Process* deals with the complex problem of 'how and why a programme works or does not work'.

We may consider the following eight major categories for policy programme evaluation:

Efficiency

By 'efficiency' is meant the amount of effort required to produce a given level of effectiveness. Efficiency is thought of 'gaining the most output for a given level of input, or getting more bang for the buck'.[16] In other words, it refers to the capacity of a policy programme unit to utilize inputs such as time and resources to produce results with the least amount

---

[13] Fred M. Frohock, *Public Policy: Scope and Logic* (Englewood Cliffs, NJ: Prentice Hall, 1979).
[14] Theodore H. Poister, *Public Program Analysis: Applied Research Methods* (Baltimore, MD: University Park Press, 1978), 9.
[15] Edward A. Suchman, *Evaluation Research* (New York, NY: Russell Sage Foundation, 1967), 61–66.
[16] Birkland, *An Introduction to the Policy Process*, 233.

of wastage. It is a sort of allocative efficiency in the sense that inputs or resources are allocated in such a way that no shift will bring about an increase in outputs. Efficiency in equated with economic rationality. When efficiency is expressed in monetary terms, it refers to the ratio of monetary income from the outputs to the monetary costs of inputs. This ratio means profitability which is generally used as an indicator of the policy performance. Efficiency is often measured by calculating the costs per unit of a product or service. The efficiency criterion tells how much time and costs is involved on providing services. Policies that achieve the greatest effectiveness at the minimum costs and time are said to be efficient. But efficiency measurement in terms of costs and incomes of a public service is not so easy.

Effectiveness

Effectiveness indicators deal with results or quality of services being measured. The criterion of 'effectiveness' is the most common method of policy evaluation. How effective is the policy? Is it achieving the goals it set out to achieve? The policy is deemed to be a failure if it has not achieved its objectives. Effectiveness is a measure of the policy programme's productivity in yielding the desired technical results. By effectiveness is meant the degree of objective achievement. It refers to whether a given course of action results in the attainment of an objective. It is often measured in terms of units of products produced or services rendered or their monetary costs. If the objective of a public organizational unit is to render n unit of service a year, then effectiveness may be measured by the percentage of n rendered in the year (account should normally be taken of the costs of producing n). For example, if thermal plants produce more energy than solar collection devices, the former are regarded as more effective, since power plants produce more of a valued outcome (objective). Similarly, an effective environment policy is one which provides more qualitative environment to more people, assuming that qualitative environment is an objective.

However, it is difficult to judge the extent of the success or failure of a particular policy meant to raise living standards, reduce poverty, provide health and educational services and so forth. Further, goals and objectives change as policy is being implemented.

Adequacy

The criterion of 'adequacy' is also gaining importance in policy evaluation. Adequacy refers to whether a given level of effectiveness results in the satisfaction of needs or values. While the policy effectiveness criterion deals with the relationship between policy goals and their achievement, the adequacy of a policy refers to the relationship between the policy and the problem to which it is addressed.[17] A clear distinction exists between effectiveness and adequacy in the sense that a policy may be judged to be a success in achieving its listed objectives, but it has little impact upon the problem being addressed by the policy. For example, sustained efforts are made to deal with the homeless problem in Delhi, but the problem persists. Thus, the criterion of effectiveness is related to sufficiency for a specific requirement of the policy programme.

---

[17] Poister, *Public Program Analysis: Applied Research Methods,* 10–15.

Many studies indicate that the beneficiaries and other target groups often view government action as not adequate, while the political executive is prone to argue that enough is being done. For example, the central government claims that socio-economic conditions of the rural people have improved substantially by the MGNREGS; on the contrary, it is argued that there has not been any substantial improvement in rural life.[18]

Equity

Equity is defined as equal pay for equal work. 'Equity' refers to fairness and relates to principle of justice in law. For example, the criterion of equity raises the question, 'Are costs and benefits distributed equitably among the different groups?' The criterion of equity is closely related to fair or just distribution of effects (monetary benefits) and effort (monetary costs). Policies designed to redistribute income, employment opportunities or access to public services are often recommended on the basis of the criterion of equity. A given programme might be effective, efficient and adequate, yet it might be rejected on the ground that it would result in the inequitable distribution of benefits. However, the criterion of equity is not totally satisfactory. The reason is that conflicting views about the rationality of society as a whole cannot be resolved simply by adopting formal economic rules. Such concepts as equity, fairness and justice are related to political power. What satisfies one person or group may not satisfy another. However, public policies which are discriminatory in purpose generate conflicts from those who feel they are ill-treated in various sectors. Such policies, as are of partisan political purposes, are also deemed to be failures. For example, expressing concern over the grave consequences of caste consideration, Rajesh Shukla writes, 'The way forward then is to focus on segments that continue to be disadvantaged and impoverished in terms of access to resources, infrastructure and the economic well-being rather than on the basis of their caste'.[19]

Responsiveness

By 'responsiveness' is meant that a policy satisfies the needs or values of particular groups. Policies designed to promote educational opportunity or health status of the people are sometimes recommended on the basis of the criterion of responsiveness. For example, a family planning programme might be very good from the standpoint of population control, but if it is unresponsive from a particular class of society, the population policy will fail in the achievement of its goals. Consensus and consultation, therefore, become the central concerns, as the determination of objectives becomes entangled with the search for suitable means and alternatives to achieve those objectives. In this context, Nakamura and Smallwood opine that constituency satisfaction and clientele responsiveness are important determinants in policy evaluation.[20] In fact, the criterion of responsiveness is important because it helps the analyst assess critically whether the competing criteria of effectiveness, efficiency, adequacy and equity reflect the needs and values of target people or not.

[18] See Vinod Kumar, 'Socio-economic Impact of MGNREGS on Rural People: A Study in Mandi District of Himachal Pradesh', *Indian Journal of Public Administration* 59(2) (2013): 373–90.
[19] See *The Financial Express* (Chandigarh), 21 August 2015.
[20] Robert Nakamura and Frank Smallwood, *The Politics of Policy Implementation* (New York, NY: St. Martin's Press, 1980).

Appropriateness

The criterion of 'appropriateness' raises the questions, 'Are the desired outcomes (objectives) actually valuable?' The criterion of appropriateness is closely related to rationality. Appropriateness refers to the worth of the objectives of a policy programme. Is the policy based upon appropriate values and ideologies? Will the policy lead to disruption and violence or be greeted with agreement? This dimension is concerned with judgements about a policy's fitness and suitability.

Judging policy failure and success by appropriateness is to see where conflicts are likely to be more intense. Public policies which are based upon unacceptable values and ideologies are deemed to be failures. Some policies are deemed to be unpopular decisions. For example, policies regulating people's behaviour in traffic laws and taxes are seldom popular with the general masses.

Pareto Optimality

According to economist Pareto, an optimal distribution of welfare is when everyone is better off: costs – benefits/benefits exceed costs. After his name, 'Pareto optimality' is used as a criterion of evaluation. According to 'Pareto optimality' criterion, a policy that makes one or several persons better off without hurting anyone else is desirable.

A policy that helps some at the expense of others is, therefore, undesirable. However, Pareto optimality is not without shortcomings. Some policies, such as those related to welfare, do not fare well under Pareto optimality. Welfare is, in essence, social transfers: some are made better through the distribution of social resources, and distribution requires making some poorer by taking their wealth to make others better off. Does this mean that welfare always, by definition, fails to Pareto optimal test? Because optimality is difficult to achieve in any context, rational choice concerns a Pareto improvement 'that makes one or more members of society better off without making anyone worse off'.[21]

Public Interest

For Frohock, 'public interest' is quite helpful in evaluating public policy. At the time of considering the policy demands, the policymakers and planners ought to take into account what the people actually want. The government should come out with policies that serve the needs of the people. After the policies have been implemented, the policy monitors and evaluators should focus on policy objectives. And the heart of the evaluation lies not in the technologies, but in the intent and focus of evaluation in terms of criterion of public interests. 'The human development cannot be achieved if the policy implementation is not in favour of the socially, politically and economically (weaker) castes, even the dominating OBCs'.[22]

General Observations

Evaluation offers the opportunity to assess outcomes of the policymaking process. But to reach the policy outcomes, a checklist for evaluating policy programme is required to be

---

[21] E.J. Mishan, *Economics for Social Decisions* (New York, NY: Praeger, 1972), 14.
[22] Santosh Kumar, 'Modernization, Social Exclusion and Empowerment of Other Backward Classes in India', *South Asian Journal of Socio-Political Studies* 15(2) (2015): 33.

designed. However, it may be added here that description of these eight-dimensional criteria for policy evaluation does not always apply. It is often found that policy and programme evaluators make use of the dimensions of effectiveness and efficiency or a combination of both. There is a tendency to apply the criterion of efficiency in evaluating development programmes and projects. In health and welfare, effectiveness appears to dominate. Implementation failure is linked with the failure of goal achievement and efficiency. This is certainly a narrow perspective. This myopic view can conceal from analysis the broader concerns of problem definition, the causes of the failure of policy as well as the overall social, economic and political context in which the problem or the policy occurs. The emphasis upon policy effectiveness and efficiency as the central criteria to be applied should not be accepted to the point where they dominate the policy evaluation. What is needed is to make use of multiple criteria for making judgements about a policy's outcome.

POLICY EVALUATORS

To ascertain the worth of a public policy, it requires to be evaluated properly. By comparing promises with policy outcomes, we are able to determine the extent to which a public policy has matched expectations. Evaluation is carried out in a variety of ways by a variety of evaluators. Sometimes, it is highly systematic, while at other times rather casual. In some cases, policy evaluation is formal, while in others, it is quite informal. It may be carried out by those delivering the programme (the concerned government department or ministry), or by private agencies outside the government. The communication media, researchers in private and public institutions, organized interests, commissions and public interest organizations, all make evaluations of programmes and policies that have greater or lesser effects on the public officials. A few forms of policy evaluation are briefed here.

Evaluation by Special Agencies

To get the evaluating job done professionally, decision-makers often call upon special agencies or individuals with experience in the policy area under review. Often these people are professionals such as economists, statisticians or accountants who have particular skills to evaluate policy programmes. A big advantage of evaluation by specialized staff is that they do not have any vested interest in the continuation of any given programme. However, some tension is bound to take place between the operating staff and the evaluators owing to the unpredictability of the evaluation and its results.

A question may arise whether it is proper for an organization to be wholly responsible for its own evaluation. As Wildavsky puts it, 'No matter how good its internal analysis, or how persuasively an organization justifies its programmes to itself, there is something unsatisfactory about allowing it to judge its own case'.[23] Periodically, therefore, even a self-evaluating organization should be subjected to independently conducted evaluation inquiries or to an audit of the methods used in its evaluation. The goal of independent evaluation studies would be to find out whether the impacts of various programmes are significantly different from one another, and if so, what particular actions or unforeseen events might explain the difference. Further, the more neutral the evaluator, the more likely that his assessments will carry weight with those who have called for the review.

---

[23] A. Wildavsky, 'The Self-evaluating Organization', *Public Administration Review* 32 (1972): 518.

Evaluation by Operating Staff

Evaluation may be conducted as an internal evaluation. Most government agencies make some efforts to review the policy programme by their own staff. Evaluation by those delivering the programme has important implications. A big advantage is that an insider will have little problems regarding access to information. He has detailed knowledge of just what is involved. Second, the possible clashes of interest between operating staff and policymakers would be minimal. In this form, evaluation requires a well-established internal reporting system which permits the continuous generation of programme-related information. However, those who are insiders may lack the requisite skills to carry out evaluation in their areas of work. Another disadvantage of evaluation by the operating staff is that it may fail to obtain a fully rounded evaluation of results of the activity of the organization engaged in service delivery.

Often in the government departments, policy programme evaluation is done by the administrative agencies, either on their own or at the direction of the government. These administrative agencies generally lack the specialized skills for good evaluation. Sometimes, they fail to develop measures of the costs and benefits of many programmes. To give some notion of this source of evaluation, one can take the example of the intro-duction of zero-base budgeting in 1988 at the central level. It was feared that zero-base budgeting would cause administrative agencies to achieve or provide a means for evalu-ating the worth of existing programmes and show the government where to spend money so as to achieve the best results. It has now become more common for administrative agencies to be specifically directed by the government departments to determine the worth or success of a policy programme.

The evaluation studies undertaken by the state or central government agencies are designed to assess the performance, process of implementation, effectiveness of the delivery systems and impact of programmes. These studies also aim at identifying the factors contributing to success and failure of various programmes and deriving lessons for improving the performance of existing programmes and better designing future pro-grammes. For their part, evaluators need to put their own biases aside as much as possi-ble when they review a policy programme (such as National Youth Policy, 2014 or National Environment Policy). This gives credibility to the evaluation findings and recommenda-tions of evaluators.

Evaluation by Legislative Committees

Although evaluation takes place at every level of government, much of the evaluation lacks objectivity. To seek better information, the Parliament which gives authority to policy appoints its own committees to assess the worth or success of a policy. Parliamentary evaluation may be exercised through a number of techniques, including committee hearing and investigations and casework. In India, the Public Accounts Committee, the Estimates Committee, the Committee on Public Undertakings and the Select Committee attached to Parliament also conduct evaluation functions. The reports of the Public Accounts Committee, for example, have made perceptible impact on the Union execu-tive by making the latter agree to conduct performance reviews, institute enquiries in the cases of frauds and financial irregularities, investigate leakages of revenue, streamline the functioning of autonomous bodies and generally to improve procedures and tighten financial control. For example, the PAC took up the Augusta Westland Chopper scam as the CAG of India made some adverse comments against it in its report alleging bribery charges in the Rs. 3600 crore deal to buy 12 helicopters for use of VVIPs.[24]

In the course of investigations, members of the parliamentary committees reach certain conclusions regarding the efficiency, effectiveness and impact of particular policies and programmes. Parliament is a natural candidate for initiating and conducting evaluation of policies inaugurated by them. However, MPs are also more likely to be concerned with policy initiation and adoption rather than with the evaluation of policy programmes.

Evaluation by Office of the CAG

The office of the CAG of India which is regarded as an arm of the Parliament/state legislatures has broad statutory authority to ensure the accountability of the executive to Parliament or the state legislature. It assists the legislatures in the effective exercise of their financial control. In recent years, the office of the CAG has become increasingly concerned with comprehensive reviews and appraisals of schemes and with systems audits to ensure value for money. The Parliament by passing the CAG's (Duties, Powers and Conditions of Service) Act, 1971 has also increased its authority and responsibilities.

In the 2G spectrum allocation, the CAG of India in its report to the SC (November 2010) pegged a national loss of ₹1.76 trillion to the Indian exchequer. In the performance audit report on the PPP projects in the Indian Railways, which was laid in both Houses of Parliament on 18 July 2014, the CAG reported that 'the execution of the projects is marred by arbitrary concession periods, weak project monitoring, lack of a model concession agreement that lead to delays in project execution and additional financial burden of ₹128 crore'. The report says the Indian Railways executed eight PPP projects since 2000 through Special Purpose Vehicle out of which CAG sampled six projects for clarity, transparency and completeness of concession agreement and financial prudence. These six projects which cost about ₹2,167 crore include four gauge conversion projects and two ongoing new line projects. The report says the Railways faltered in assessing the economic viability of Hasan–Mangalore gauge conversion and Obulavaripalle–Krishnapatnam new line project. The internal rate of return in both these projects was less than the benchmark provided by the Ministry of Finance.[25]

A decision to evaluation studies may be taken up by the office of the CAG on its own initiative, on the basis of directives in legislation, at the request of financial committees, or sometimes at the request of individual MPs. Such reviews conducted by the CAG through a process of dispassionate and searching analysis based on records make a significant contribution in reviewing public policies and in bringing about the improved performance of the administrative system.

Evaluation by Statutory Commissions

In addition to the CAG's evaluation studies, Inquiry Commissions constituted under the Commissions of Inquiry Act (1952), the Central Vigilance Commission (1964), National

---

[24] See *The Indian Express* (Chandigarh), 28 May 2016; *The Tribune*, 29 December 2016.
[25] See *The Tribune* (Chandigarh), 19 July 2014.

Commission for Scheduled Castes and Scheduled Tribes (1992), National Commission for Backward Classes (1993) National Commission for Minorities (1993), National Commission for Women (1992), National Police Commission (1977–80), the First (1985) and the Second (2010) Commissions on Centre–State Relations, Commission on the Review of Administrative Laws (1998), the National Commission on Urbanization (1989), the First (1966–70) and the Second (2005–09) Administrative Reforms Commissions and many more have been set up and can also be used as a means of policy evaluation. Whether set up specifically for evaluation in some areas or for other purposes, such as fact-finding, making policy recommendations or simply creating the appearance of concern, most commissions do involve themselves in policy evaluation. They are commissioned to ensure greater public confidence in the evaluation results, either for reasons of expertise or because a report from the Commissions might appear to be objective. However, it appears that the policy evaluations made by commissions do not have much immediate effect on policymaking. An evaluation commission is likely to have the largest effect when its findings are in accord with the ruling party's policy preferences or when some members can influence the acceptance of its recommendations. The SC as well as High Courts often ask governments to review certain laws and policies in the context of changed situations. For example, the SC of India on a PIL by Punjab-based NGO, Youth Kamal Organization, on 21 August 2015 asked the central government to deal with the problem of farmers' suicide in the country seriously and to ascertain as to whether the suicides were linked to possible shortcomings in the National Policy for Farmers 2007 and review it if necessary.[26]

DILEMMA OF ACCEPTABILITY OF EVALUATION FINDINGS

Evaluation is a tool for assessing the policy performance. It can show that the policy is a poor fit for the objectives. It may also test that public policy has worked as intended. The point is policy evaluation provides the data for future change and policy refinement. The policy evaluator has done his job depending upon his calibre and wisdom. The policy evaluator assumes that it will immediately be taken up by the policymakers, especially if the evaluation had been commissioned by the government. Later, he finds that the evaluation results have not been utilized in most cases. In certain cases, if the policy implications of evaluation are not clear, 'the programme manager winds up complaining about the irrelevance of the evaluation for his programmatic concerns'.

If evaluation results are to be utilized, they have to be in a communicable language comprehensible to decision-makers. Such communication should include an indication of the limitations of the research, measurement problems and the quality of information collected or the method of analysis. Evaluation findings may also not be utilized because they do not fit in the framework of decision-making. The results of formal evaluation require the exercise of political judgements regarding their acceptability. There may be also an organizational resistance to the implications of evaluation findings. Members of the organization may express reluctance to tolerate disruption of existing working practices and career structures and are likely to point out the time and costs involved in bringing about policy changes. Particularly where the programme involves delivering a new service, there may be resistance from the employees' unions.

---

[26] See *The Tribune* (Chandigarh), 22 August 2015.

Further, an evaluation of a programme may be ignored, or attacked on the ground that the evaluation was poorly designed, the data used was inadequate, or the findings are inconclusive. This may lead to a great deal of pessimism as to the utility of evaluation findings. However, it will be wrong to assume that there is no potential for their utilization. The study of the reports of various commissions in India indicates that while only a small minority of evaluation reports have a direct effect on specific decisions, the findings may in the long run affect how policymakers and planners perceive issues in their policy area. Policy analysis devotes less attention to what governments look for.

POLICY EVALUATION PROBLEMS AND REMEDIAL MEASURES

At one level, policy evaluation appears to be simple. But the job really is not as easy as it looks. Guy Peters observes that the evaluation process, right from the initial stage of goal specification to that of measurement of performance, may appear to be simple policy, but in the public arena, it is quite arduous.[27] Evaluating a policy programme is a difficult exercise. It involves specifying the goals of the programme, measuring the degree to which these goals have been achieved and perhaps suggesting changes that might improve the performance of the organization. The evaluation of public programmes under different policy measures and plans is confounded by many factors. Some of these are explained in the later sections.

Confounded Policy Goals

Evaluation, in main, is a matter of comparing outcomes with desired policy goals and objectives. But invariably, policy goals are drawn from the Constitution, the UN aims and principles and policy agenda of the political party in power. Theoretically, these goals look fine and attractive, but when they are translated to form a policy statement, a lot of confusion creeps in. The policymaker cannot fully anticipate the effects and consequences of a policy initiative or what a court of law might say about it.[28]

On the other hand, if policy goals are unclear or are not specified in any measurable form, determining the extent to which they have been achieved becomes a complex and cumbersome task. Officials such as legislators and administrators who are in different positions in the policy system may define goals of a programme differently and reach differing conclusions about the accomplishment of the policy programme.

Despite the fact that goals are clear, they may not be practical. The Preamble to the Indian Constitution, for example, expresses a number of goals for the government, but few, if any, are expressed in concrete language that would enable an evaluator to verify whether the goals are being achieved or not. Specifying such goals and putting them into effect would require further political action within the organization. The specification of goals may also lead to the division of responsibilities among those who implement the policies.

---

[27] B. Guy Peters, *Public Policy in America: Process and Performance*, 2nd ed. (London: Macmillan, 1986).
[28] The SC on 16 October 2015 struck down as unconstitutional the NJAC Act, 2014 and restored the over two-decade-old collegium system for appointment of judges to the higher judiciary. An agitated government said the verdict, 'ignored the unanimous will of Parliament' and called it a 'flawed' one, setting the stage for an unusual fight for balance of power between the legislature and the judiciary. See *The Tribune*, 17 October 2015.

Therefore, there is an important role for the policymakers to specify goals to be achieved in a particular policy area. Once it is done, the evaluator's job becomes easy.

Unreliable Criteria for Measurement

However, systematically, we may have defined our goals and objectives and selection criteria, often we cannot account for all of them. It is observed that our criteria are not always reliable. There is the difficulty of measuring the extent to which these goals have been achieved. In the public sector, measuring results is still more difficult. It is difficult to measure the performance of the public sector programmes in the absence of any ready means of judging the performance. For example, although the short-term goal of education is to improve reading, writing and learning, in the long run, the goal of education is to improve the quality of life for those who receive it. This seems to be an elusive quality to measure when an evaluation must be made quickly. In the absence of measurement's rod, side effects are hard to trace.

Problems of Methodology and Statistics

It is argued that statistics are not relevant and valid. The facts are often distorted in the study of public organizations. For example, the Rangarajan Panel puts the number of poor at 363 million in 2011–12 compared with the 270 million in 2011–12, as per the formula of the Tendulkar Committee—a rise of 35 per cent. According to the Report, the number of poor in India was much higher in 2011–12 at 29.5 per cent of the population which means that 3 out of 10 persons are poor. As per Rangarajan panel estimates, a person spending less than ₹1,407 a month (₹47/day) would be considered poor in cities. In villages, those spending less than ₹972 a month (₹32/day) would be considered poor.[29] This is at variance with the Tendulkar methodology under which poverty was estimated at 29.8 per cent in 2009–10 and declined to 21.9 per cent in 2011–12.

Even when the facts are neatly organized for evaluation, the evaluator must be careful in the conclusions, he draws from them. A minister, for example, may claim that crime rate in his constituency has declined because of a particular policy he was responsible for formulating. But this may not be necessarily the result of a particular policy. It may have been the result of other factors unrelated to the policy. For example, if we are to evaluate the effectiveness of a health programme on a poorer section of the community, we may find it difficult to isolate the effects of that health programme from those of a nutrition programme or those of an education programme. In fact, all these programmes may have the effect of improving the health of the population, and we may find it difficult to determine which programme is the effective means of improving the health of that community. All these problems indicate the measurement in policy analysis is a cumbersome exercise.

Little Effect on Target Population

The data necessary to evaluate the policy programme may not be true or misleading. The information gathered in the course of delivery of policy may highlight much about the

---

[29] The Rangarajan Report submitted to the Union Planning Minister in the first week of July 2014 pointed out that those spending over ₹32 a day in rural areas and ₹47 in towns and cities should not be considered poor.

characteristics of the people actually receiving the benefit but little regarding the target population. Programmes that have significant effects on the population as a whole may not have the desired effects on the target population. In a number of cases, it is observed, that the advantaged sections of the society grab the programme benefits, though the benefits are, in fact, meant for the disadvantaged strata.[30]

The rural development programmes directed at the poor and the less educated frequently face difficulties in making the availability of the programme widely known among the target population. Again, administrative procedures and the real difficulties in utilizing the benefits produced may make the programme less effective than desired. The Social Justice Bench of the SC, for example, on 22 August 2015 slammed the centre and state governments for virtual non-utilization of a whopping ₹27,000 crore collected in the form of 1 per cent cess on the construction industry. It noted that instead of spending the money for providing health care to the workers' families and education to their children, some of the states had misused the funds.[31] It directed the Delhi government to return to the welfare fund of about ₹2.7 crores utilized for publicity over the years.

Political Interference Biasness

Elected officials and ministers sometimes express themselves about their favourite public policies and want them to be evaluated in their language. It has been pointed out in a study that 'extremist forces have accrued so much political and economic capital that states ignore women's rights violations in order to appease these forces'.[32] Faced with the same set of circumstances, those in office point with pride while their opponents seeking office 'view with alarm'. It is ironical how political leaders in competition emphasize different facts within the same data set.

To this extent, the evaluator will need to be careful in evaluating his predetermined favourites. It is because their conclusions are very important to policymakers, administrators and, sometimes, segments of the public. The expectation is that evaluator will do everything possible to keep his own subjective feelings far from the policy that he is asked to evaluate. Nevertheless, it is sometimes very difficult for the public policy evaluator to step outside of his own values. If there is self-awareness of prejudice, the evaluator may ask to be removed from the assignment. Alternatively, if policymakers perceive a bias on the part of evaluator, they may request another evaluation as a form of insurance. Professionalism of a high order can enable objective evaluation.

With the renewed importance given to evaluation, there is the felt need of strengthening evaluation capacity in public organizations and also network with evaluation capacity that exists outside the government.

---

[30] Alok Tiwari, 'Rethinking the Microfinance Recovery Framework', *Indian Journal of Public Administration* 59(2) (2013): 370–72.
[31] See *The Tribune* (Chandigarh), 23 August 2015.
[32] Rajesh Kumar Singh and Aparna Mishra, 'Religion, Politics and Women in South Asia', *South Asian Journal of Socio-Political Studies* 15(2) (2015): 59.

CONCLUSION

Evaluation examines whether public policies have brought about changes as predicted. It offers an opportunity to assess outcomes to the public policymaking process and reshape the direction of that process. It is a technique that compares objectives with performance, as well as the linkage between the present and the future. Evaluating public policies has an important role to play in achieving the policy objectives. Quality evaluation of scores of policy programmes would not only ensure good performance in the functioning of public institutions, but also address a broad range of issues relating to economy, efficiency and relevance of public investment in many a critical policy area. Evaluation of public policies, therefore, helps policymakers understand the extent to which their policies have succeeded or failed, as well as the emergence of issues and policies they never predicted.

Review Questions

(i) What is the difference between policy evaluation and policy monitoring?
(ii) What are the main objectives of policy evaluation?
(iii) Briefly explain the most significant steps in the framework for policy evaluation.
(iv) Discuss the role of statutory commissions in evaluation of public policies.
(v) What are the most common factors that make it difficult to effectively evaluate policies?

CHAPTER 21

POLICY SCIENCES
Crises and Perspectives

INTRODUCTION

As a discipline, the 'policy sciences' have a brief history. Its intellectual seeds were probably sown in the 1940s. It is claimed that aspirations among a small core of American social scientists, such as John Dewey (1927), Charles Merriam (1926), Merton (1936) and Harold Lasswell (1951), for producing societally relevant knowledge led to what is known as 'policy sciences'. Thus, the contemporary policy sciences have a particularly American and 20th-century flavour.[1] Lasswell, like all other social scientists of the 1940s through the 1960s, felt that the increasingly sophisticated research techniques would allow the social scientists to study social problems and generate knowledge to solve them. Lasswell argued that quantitative analysis and the scientific method were important elements of any policy science.

Although policy sciences as a discipline or an area of study achieved marvellous success in altering the landscape of academic and public organizations, their credibility has been challenged for failure to produce societally relevant knowledge. Some scholars saw policy sciences analysis as a substitute for politics. Brooks maintains, 'While not anti-democratic, the analytical approach to public policy-making aspires to the de-politicisation of the policy process'.[2] Although the term 'policy sciences' is mostly associated with works of Lasswell and Dror, a policy orientation was evident in work of America's first social scientists.[3] Highlighting the value of 'policy sciences', Brooks writes, 'These visions of a new politics share a conviction that the institutionalization of scientific analysis into the policy-making process is a necessary condition for the attainment of democratic government in a modern society'.[4]

---

[1] The term 'policy sciences' can be treated back to year 1943 when Harold Lasswell crystallized the concept. See Harold D. Lasswell and Myres S. McDougal, 'Legal Education and Public Policy Professional Training in the Public Interest', *Yale Law Journal* 52 (1943): 203–95.
[2] Stephen Brooks, 'The Paradox of Policy Science', *Indian Journal of Public Administration* 29(2) (1983): 222.
[3] R. Scott and A. Shore, *Why Sociology Does Not Apply: A Study of the Use of Sociology in Public Policy* (New York, NY: Elsevier, 1979), 7.
[4] Brooks, 'The Paradox of Policy Science', p. 223.

HAROLD LASSWELL AND ARTICULATION OF POLICY SCIENCES

The Deweyism which pervades policy sciences has been acknowledged by Lasswell when he wrote, 'Policy sciences are a contemporary adaptation of the general approach to public policy that was recommended by John Dewey (1927) and his colleagues in the development of American pragmatism'.[5] Harold Lasswell, perhaps, stands out as the pre-eminent moving spirit behind the movement of the policy sciences. Since Lasswell's famous *The Policy Orientation* in 1951, the field of the policy sciences expanded in theoretical scope and applicability throughout the 1970s and 1980s. However, the period of 1990s saw a partial reformation in its approach. Some scholars such as Peter DeLeon and Danielle Vogenbeck propose ways in which the policy sciences might be amended.

The concept of 'policy sciences' was first articulated by Harold Lasswell in 1951 in his co-edited work *The Policy Sciences*.[6] This work is regarded as the first systematic efforts towards building a new field of enquiry to deal with social problems. Lasswell's call for a science of public policy was driven by a desire not only to generate sound social science but also to solve social problems. He, being regarded as the founder of the policy sciences, described policy sciences as the culmination of efforts to define a discipline for producing and applying 'societally relevant knowledge'.

Parsons defines policy sciences as 'the disciplines concerned with explaining the policy-making and policy-executing process, and with locating data and providing interpretations which are relevant to the policy problems of a given period'. According to Lasswell, the policy sciences include (i) the methods by which the policy process is investigated, (ii) the results of the study of policy and (iii) the findings of the disciplines making the most important contribution to the intelligence needs of our time.

Lasswell's vision of the policy sciences was subsequently developed by the policy sciences community and can be traced to three principal defining characteristics as set forth by Lasswell:

(i) Multidisciplinary perspective,
(ii) Problem-oriented perspective and
(iii) Explicitly normative perspective.

Multidisciplinary Perspective

Lasswell's article which appeared in the first number of the journal *Policy Sciences* in 1970 set out the state of policy sciences. His idea of policy orientation is multidisciplinary in nature. Lasswell writes,

> A policy orientation has been developing that cuts across the existing specialization. The orientation is two-fold. In part, it is directed towards the policy process (disciplines concerned with explaining the policy-making and policy-executing process), and in part, towards the intelligence needs of policy (concerned with knowledge in and for the policy process).

---

[5] H. Lasswell, *A Preview of Policy Sciences* (New York, NY: American Elsevier, 1971), xiv.
[6] Lasswell, 'The Policy Orientation', 3–15.

According to Lasswell, the 'policy sciences' were not to be equated with 'applied social science' or 'applied social and psychological science'. 'Nor', he admonished, 'are the policy sciences to be thought of as largely identical with what is studied by the political scientists'. To Lasswell, every social and political problems has multiple components closely linked to the various disciplines without falling clearly into one discipline's exclusive domain.

Problem-oriented Perspective

Lasswell introduced the idea of knowledge of the policy process in 1970 and argues that the distinctive outlook of the policy sciences is that it is problem-oriented. The policy sciences were framed as being problem-oriented, addressing public policy issues and posing prescription of recommendations for their relief. Regarding problem-oriented and contextual policy orientation, Lasswell in 1971 identified two separate approaches to the policy sciences: one emphasizing knowledge of the policy process and another emphasizing knowledge for use in the policy process. Lasswell's chosen phrase to define these was 'the policy sciences of democracy'.

Explicitly Normative Perspective

The third vision of policy sciences is characterized by normative as value-oriented perspective. The emphasis on values has remained a basic characteristics of the policy sciences from their very conception. In Lasswell's words, 'The policy sciences approach...calls forth a very considerable clarification of the value goals involved in policy'.[7] This value orientation was largely in reaction to behaviouralism in social sciences, and in recognition that no social problem nor methodological approach is value-free. As such, to understand a problem, one must acknowledge its value components. It is important that idea of values should be recognized and made an explicit part of the analysis of social sciences.

However, it is often said that the normative aspects of the policy sciences were neglected for three reasons. One, some claimed that in government's programmes, an incremental approach to policy would incorporate normative postures. Two, others argued that the application of quantitative methodologies to operations research and economics was essentially value-free and therefore did not have concern with ethics or values. And three, some analysts argued that ethics and values were the discretion of the policymakers and that for analysts to interject their values would be wrong and professionally unethical.

Some policies with quantitative indicators such as weapons of mass destruction, building of houses for the poor or illiteracy rates are directly derived from one's moral and ideological precepts. This is objectively the domain of policy sciences, a problem-oriented process of choice among competing alternatives for policy action. The point is that normative overtones cannot be avoided, and the emphasis on values remains the beacon of the policy sciences approach. However, this narrative pays little attention to three perspectives of the policy sciences approach: 'there is little direct attention to the problem orientation of the activity, the multidisciplinary are largely neglected, and the normative groundings of policy issues (and recommendations) are often overlooked'.[8]

---

[7] Lerner and Lasswell, *The Policy Sciences*, 16.

[8] Peter deLeon and D.M. Vogenbeck, 'The Policy Sciences at the Cross Roads', in *Handbook of the Public Policy Analysis*, eds. Frank Fischer, C.J. Miller and Mara S. Sidney (Boca Raton, FL: CRC Press, 2007), 5.

Thus, the stress on 'sciences' was in envisioning a rational analysis of a social problem, while the stress on 'democracy' led to a vision of politicized governmental processes. While distinguishing between 'analysis of policy' and 'analysis for policy', Ham and Hill observed

> The distinction is important in drawing attention to policy analysis as an academic activity concerned primarily with advancing understanding; and policy analysis as an applied activity concerned mainly with contributing to the solution of social problems.[9]

This vision of scientific method and democratic humanism, however, proved operationally difficult as the policy sciences moved to realize status and recognition during the 1960s and 1970s. Policy sciences were divided into two approaches—process and content—that strengthened their respective identities, each claiming some sort of conceptual superiority. Operationally, the two approaches are policy analysis and policy process.

Realization of these ambitious goals became the concern of policy sciences community in the second half of 20th century. Each represents different emphases and has an explicit impact on the evolution and acceptance of the policy sciences.

NATURE OF POLICY SCIENCES

The term 'policy sciences' is seen as a rational approach to the processes of policymaking. V. Subramaniam characterizes policy sciences as 'the practical application of all relevant knowledge in the social, physical and natural sciences to specific policy problems identified well ahead of time'.[10] The rationalist model involves a 'commitment to scientific planning'. This means an overhaul of the traditional approaches to making of decisions.

Besides Lasswell, the writings of Horowitz[11] and Tribe[12] provide a more detailed picture of the emergence of policy sciences. A group of converging factors, such as war, poverty, crime, race relations and pollution are seen to be responsible for producing a great interest in policy sciences in the late 1960s.[13] Brooks adds, 'Policy science is the most recent, and certainly the most explicit manifestation of this quest for an independent vantage point, above the political fray, affording objective criteria upon which policy decisions can be made'.[14]

From Lasswell to Dror, the central idea of policy sciences is that it entails a 'theory of choice', an approach to the determination of policy choice.[15] As Nagel expresses, 'As

---

[9] Christopher Ham and Michael Hill, *The Policy Process in the Modern Capitalist State* (Brighton: Harvester Wheatsheaf, 1984), 4.

[10] V. Subramaniam, *The Science of Public Policy Making: Towards a New Discipline* (The University of New South Wales: Division of Postgraduate Extension Studies, 1980).

[11] I. Horowitz, 'Social Science Mandarins: Policy-making as a Political Formula', *Policy Sciences* I(3) (1970): 339–60.

[12] L. Tribe, 'Policy Science: Analysis or ideology?', *Philosophy and Public Affairs* Fall 2 (1972): 66–110.

[13] E.S. Quade, 'Why Policy Sciences?', *Policy Sciences* I (1970): 1.

[14] Brooks, 'The Paradox of Policy Science', 225.

[15] Y. Dror, *Design for the Policy Sciences, and Ventures in Policy Sciences* (New York, NY: American Elsevier, 1971).

social science does more analysis of hypotheses, predictions, causation, and optimizing, there develops a body of potential premises that can be used in deducing conclusions, just as chemistry was able to deduce the existence of new elements before they were empirically discovered'.[16]

Contributions in the form of articles and books devoted to the teaching of policy studies and the training of policy analysis reveal the fact that policy science is a scientific approach centring around the development of professional analysts who are expert in rational decision-making. Nagel advocates the development of a code of ethics, professionalism and institutionalized checks.[17] Most writers on the subject seem to agree on the fact that policy science constitutes an interdisciplinary approach which is concerned mainly with improving the policy process through the use of systematic knowledge, structural relationship and organized activity. What Dror emphasizes is that the policy science 'is not directly concerned with the substantive contents of discrete policy problems but rather with improved methods of knowledge, and systems for better policy making'.[18] In a similar way, Lasswell also stresses, 'Knowledge of the decision process implies systematic and empirical studies of how policies are made and put into effect'.[19] While most authors on the subject seem to agree on the basic aims of policy sciences, they generally do not provide an operational definition of the concept due to the cross-disciplinary nature of knowledge involved in the formulation, implementation and evaluation of policy issues.

Lasswell who is a great proponent of the policy sciences argues that policy science like physics and chemistry is a science. The empirical aspect of policy science is stressed by Lasswell thus '...to insist on the empirical criterion is to specify that general assertions area subject to the discipline of careful observation. This is a fundamental distinction between science and non-science'.[20] On the contrary, there are social scientists who argue that policy science like other social sciences is not an exact science because substantive science is concerned with the pursuit of truth which it seeks to understand and predict. The writer is of the view that policy science is merely an approach which is concerned with improved methods of knowledge and systems for better policymaking. It is a technique which helps the decision-maker to take decisions with improved methods of knowledge. Carol Weiss describes policy science as a decision-driven model of research use. This sequential model has the following stages: (i) definition of the social problems, (ii) identification of missing knowledge, (iii) acquisition of the relevant data using social research techniques, (iv) interpretation for problem solution and (v) policy choice.[21]

Policy science may contribute to the selection of policy options. As conceptualization, it has two thrusts: (i) it contributes to the way in which policymaking is done and (ii) its policy options may percolate into society, influencing 'the way that a society thinks about issues, the facets of the issues that are viewed as susceptible to alteration, and the alternative measures that it considers'.[22]

---

[16] S.S. Nagel, *The Policy Studies Handbook* (Toronto: D.C. Heath & Co., 1980), 204.
[17] Ibid., chap. 9.
[18] Y. Dror, *Design for the Policy Sciences, and Ventures in Policy Sciences,* 52.
[19] Lasswell, *A Preview of Policy Sciences,* 1.
[20] Ibid.
[21] Carol Weiss (ed.), *Using Social Science Research in Public Policy-Making* (Lexington, KY: D.C. Heath, 1977).
[22] Ibid., 16.

Briefly, policy sciences can have an influence upon the political agenda through sensitizing both policymakers and the mass of people. Nagel also argues that policy analysis provides 'new insights' and enables policymakers to make better-informed choices and, by implication, a better policy.[23] Stokey and Zeckhauser also declare that 'no sensible policy choice can be made without careful analysis of the advantages and disadvantages of each course of action'.[24] These statements echo Dror's belief that institutionalized policy science would result in improved policy options.

Thus, it is argued that the subject of policy sciences is an approach which is directed to improving the knowledge needed to enhancing the policymaking process.

BASIC ASSUMPTIONS IN POLICY SCIENCES

Policy sciences are laden with certain assumptions. Some of them are briefed here.

Unity of Knowledge

Power flows from the knowledge, and policy is the use of knowledge for the purpose of governance. Unity of knowledge is the prominent theme in policy sciences. Dror, the most forceful advocate of policy sciences, argues that the maturation of policy science would affect the state of knowledge in three ways: (i) it would lead to bridging the gap between basic and applied research through a 'synergic relationship' between moral science and policy science[25]; (ii) with the emergence of policy scientist, a 'specialist in general approach and method', the dichotomy between specialist and generalist would be irrelevant; and (iii) interdisciplinary in policy research would finally give way to supra-disciplinary, in consequence of (a) 'continuous exchange between social, natural, and administrative scientists working on common policy problems, and (b) deliberate development of professionals trained in the policy orientation'. Any good organization has always recognized the importance and value of knowledge for policymaking.

Use of Research Techniques

Lasswell, like many social scientists, felt that the increasingly sophisticated research techniques available to social scientists would help them to study public problems. Improved methods and techniques occupy the central position in analytical approach to policymaking. What Dror emphasizes is that policy science 'is not directly concerned with the substantive contents of discrete policy problems but rather with improved methods of knowledge and system for better policy-making'.[26]

Principle of Rationality

A number of contributors have been pre-eminent in the study of rationality in public policy. They include Lindblom, Simon, March and Cohen. In their writings, the concept

---

[23] Nagel, *The Policy Studies Handbook.*
[24] E. Stokey and R. Zeckhauser, *A Primer for Policy Analysis* (New York, NY: W.W. Norton, 1978), ix.
[25] Dror, *Design for the Policy Sciences, and Ventures in Policy Sciences.*
[26] Ibid., 52.

of rationality figured in the analysis of decision-making. Policy sciences are concerned with better achievements of goals through the use of structural rationality. The rationalist model involves a 'commitment to scientific planning'.[27] This implies an overhaul of the traditional patterns of policymaking. MacRae advocates greater rationality in policymaking which can be achieved through the deliberate creation of a policy analysis culture.[28]

Centrality of Utilitarianism

It is argued that policy sciences are laden with utilitarian assumptions. Tribe argues that policy sciences aim at exaltation of utilitarian and self-interested individualism, efficiency and maximized production.[29] Notwithstanding these characterizations, the idea of the use of policy sciences as an approach to the selection of policy choice remains vigorous. Policy sciences involve primarily the development of professional analysts who are expert in rational decision-making.

SCOPE EXPANSION OF POLICY SCIENCES

Behind the idea of policy sciences, Lasswell felt that basic democratic values of the polity were at stake and threatened. Lasswell expressed,

> Today we are living in a world of ever-deepening shadow, in which basic democratic values are challenged as never before and in which even the survival of the human species is at stake. Under these circumstances, it makes sense to develop a strategy of using our limited intellectual resources for the defense and extension of our values.

To Lasswell, policy sciences clarify the process of policymaking in society, or supply data needed for the rational judgements on policy questions.

Since 1951, Lasswell and his intellectual heirs had been clarifying and expanding the scope of policy sciences. Through the 1970s and 1980s, the direction of the march of policy sciences was influenced by (i) policy scientists who struggled to expand the scope of policy sciences and by (ii) the social and political events of the period.

The community of policy scientists formed in the late 1960s recognized both the limitations of and the opportunities for their knowledge and skills. Lasswell setting out the perspectives on policy sciences in 1951 writes that the policy sciences include '(i) the methods by which the policy process in investigated; (ii) the results of the study of policy, and; (iii) the findings of the disciplines making the most important contribution to intelligence needs of our time'.[30]

DeLeon links analytic activities related to specific political events (1960–70) with an evolving requirements for policy analysis within government offices. In particular, he suggested

---

[27] Scott and Shore, *Why Sociology Does Not Apply*, 71.
[28] Duncan MacRae, *The Social Function of Social Science* (New Haven, CT: Yale University Press, 1976).
[29] Tribe, 'Policy Science: Analysis or ideology?', 105.
[30] Lasswell, *The Policy Sciences*, 4.

five political events—Second World War, war on poverty, Vietnam War, Watergate scandal and energy crisis of the 1970s—as having been pivotal in the development of the policy sciences. As a function of these and other events, the policy sciences grew in both theoretical scope and applicability throughout the 1970s and 1980s. The community of policy scientists in its pursuit of policy sciences studies addressed topics of evaluation, utilization, implementation and termination in a more or less orderly manner, though lacking any strategic coordination. Thus, expansion of the theoretic constructs of the policy sciences is tied to interactions with the world of political reality.

Evaluation

An important area of the policy sciences was the evaluation of social programmes so that their results and findings could be used for more effective programmes. Evaluation helped in learning from public policies and taking necessary steps for better results. In the early 1970s, the policy analysis community focused on policy evaluation in areas as varied as education, health, crime rates and public welfare. New methodologies, often from social and clinical psychology, were brought to bear while others were modified to match special needs.

However, most of the evaluators working within academic circles failed to appreciate the policy sensitivities of working with public officials or making sure that their findings matched the client's needs. Consequently, policy evaluation failed to achieve the desired objectives.

Utilization

The perceived shortcomings of social sciences as they applied to public policy issues led to a general identity crisis and widespread pessimism. Weiss asked whether the social sciences could do little more for public policymakers than fulfil an ambiguous, 'enlightenment function'.[31] Lindblom and Cohen claimed that the likelihood of success for policy analysis alleviating policy problems was little better than random occurrence.[32] These assessments offered a thoughtful cause to pause. However, there was a demand from every government agency to establish its own policy bureau. The policy sciences, without ever reaching closure on the question of utilization, would move on to more pressing matters.

Implementation

Implementation is an important area of the policy sciences. Given the evaluation and utilization concerns, the focus of policy analysts shifted to the policy failure in the mid-1970s. It was felt that the real culprit of policy failure was the administrative delivery system. Pressman and Wildavsky in their landmark study found virtually no constructive research on implementation.[33] There had been numerous problems in the implementation of policies because of federal structure of a country such as India. And again, like the

---

[31] Weiss, *Using Social Science Research in Public Policy-Making.*
[32] C.E. Lindblom and D.K. Cohen, *Usable Knowledge* (New Haven, CT: Yale University Press, 1979).
[33] Pressman and Wildavsky, *Implementation.*

earlier problems with utilization and evaluation, this focus on implementation produced more confusion than clarification. Implementation turned out to be far more complex and difficult than the implementation analysis proponents had recommended. Like the earlier emphases on programme evaluation, the focus on implementation was seen to be salutary.

Termination

Towards the end of the 1970s and beginning of the 1980s, government on all levels was besieged with demands for greater economy. Consequently, the policy research focused on programme termination under such labels as 'cutback management', 'sunset legislation' and 'fiscal retrenchment'. This was in response to demands for greater economy and reduction in government expenditures. At present, the trend in India is towards disinvestment in public enterprises, downsizing of the government and decontrol. With sufficient reports and data, policy scientists turned their attention to describing and prescribing termination strategies. But like the earlier emphasis on programme implementation, evaluation and utilization, termination studies also largely failed to provide solid programme advice.

General Observations

A careful analysis of the policy sciences would show that two items have remained on the agenda for the policy sciences since the 1990s. First, the policy sciences were to become normative; and second, policy sciences were to be related to public management.

In the 1990s and the first few years of the 21st century, the policy sciences revisited old themes in an effort to reconcile long-existing conflicts. The policy appears to be moving from a simple theory of rational choice to a theory of reason in society from policy sciences to policy inquiry.

The expanding scope of policy sciences remains the issue of intellectual pursuit. Moreover, it is clear that the policy sciences are intimately affected by exogenous events. They are, by definition, problem-oriented, so they cannot remain absent themselves from the political and social environments.

FOCUS ON POLICY NETWORKS

One of the premises of the policy sciences is the role of knowledge in society which can also be enhanced through the use of social networks analysis. Nearly four decades ago, Hugh Heclo introduced the concept of 'issue networks', in which he noted '...it is through "networks of people" who regard each other as knowledgeable...that public policy issues tend to be refined, evidence debated, and alternative options worked out—though rarely in any controlled, well-organized way'.[34] These horizontal relationships can include individuals, organizations, lobbyists, legislators or whoever plays a role in policy advocacy.

---

[34] Hugh Heclo, 'Issue Networks and the Executive Establishment', in *The New American Political System*, ed. Anthony King (Washington: American Enterprise Institute, 1978).

Heclo's work evolved into the concept of *social network analysis*.[35] The role of networks in policymaking gained recognition on the research agenda in the late 1980s. Policy researchers began to both theoretically and empirically focus on how networks between public, private and nonprofit actors shape processes of policymaking and governance.

As a concept, the policy networks have been extensively used in the 1990s to analyse policymaking within the EU, which is now frequently characterized as a new system of governance based on negotiations between (i) national governments, (ii) the European commission, (iii) the European parliament, (iv) large companies and (v) national or European associations.[36]

Carlsson defines policy networks as 'clusters or complexes of organizations connected to each other by resource dependencies and distinguished from other clusters or complexes by breaks in the structure of resource dependencies'.[37]

To Hanf and Scharpf, the policy network approach is a tool to evaluate the 'large number of public and private actors from different levels and functional areas of government and society'.[38]

The term 'policy network' is used with different meanings and different purposes. Three dimensions of the concept has been identified: network as an empirically tool, network as a social structure and network as a form of governance. Network analysis, according to Kenis and Schneider, is not a neutral statistical method, nor is it a theory. It is an empirical tool to describe social structure on the basis of relations between social entities.[39]

Network is also seen as a social structure with very specific features. In policymaking, Kenis and Schneider suggest, network is regarded as an arrangement characterized by a predominance of informal communicative relations, a horizontal as opposed to a hierarchical pattern of relations and a decentralized pattern of actors' positions.

Third, the state as a central actor has lost much of its ruling position. On the other, the network approach is conceived and interpreted as a discrete form of governance and, together with market and hierarchy, as an ideal type of coordination.

Under the social networks approach, the structure of the network is the central focus. Schneider et al. note that network-based structures are characterized by 'high levels of interdependence involving multiple organizations, where formal lines of authority are blurred and where diverse policy actors are knitted together to focus on common

---

[35] Stanley Wasserman and K. Faust, *Social Network Analysis* (Cambridge: Cambridge University Press, 1994).

[36] T.A. Borzel, 'What's So Special About Policy Networks', *European Integration Online Papers* (EIOP), I, (1977), accessed 22 November 2016, http://eiop.or.at/eiop/pdf/1997-016.pdf

[37] L. Carlsson, 'Policy Networks as Collective Action', *Policy Studies Journal* 28 (2000): 502–27.

[38] Kenneth Hanf and Fritz Scharpf, 'Introduction.' in *Interorganizational Policy-making*, eds. K. Hanf and F. Scharpf (London: SAGE Publications, 1978), 12.

[39] P. Kenis and V. Schneider, 'Policy Networks and Policy Analysis: Scrutinizing a New Analytical Toolbox', in *Policy Networks: Empirical Evidence and Theoretical Considerations*, eds. B. Martin and R. Mayntz (Frankfurt, KY: Westview Press, 1998), 25–62.

problems'.[40] They further argue that 'the resulting formal and informal interactions have the potential to increase policy effectiveness at less cost than authority-based structural changes arrived at through formal reorganization'. They argue that policy networks have the ability to increase the likelihood and scope of policy agreements 'by increasing available information about potential agreements and enhancing the credibility of commitments to fulfill the agreements'. The likelihood of successful policymaking can be increased by spanning organizational boundaries, exploring the details of organizational decision-making and discovering barriers to implementation.

On the contrary, Dowding argues that while policy network approach 'has proven useful for cataloguing policy procedures into different types of networks, it cannot be used to provide a fundamental reassessment of the policy process'.[41] However, others state that a network approach can influence the policy process. Carlsson suggests that a network approach is useful, but claims that, as of now, it is not a viable policy analysis approach because it lacks 'a theoretical scaffold', and must find theoretical support from well-defined theories such as a collective action theory.[42] However, it may be added that Carlsson has failed to appreciate the explanatory power of network analysis. The key to this approach is understanding how certain relationships are formed and which parts of the network are the strongest and most knowledgeable, that is, the most related to others. Ample empirical research has now shown good effects of networks on the advancement of policy analysis. Proponents of this approach claim that it is possible not only to achieve more conceptual clarity but also to develop a refined analytical instrument with which actor coordination in concrete policy can be modelled as a specific mixture of these ideal types.[43]

CRITICAL PERSPECTIVE AND APPRECIATION

Dewey's pragmatic approach to the policy sciences continues to be echoed even today in every major policy text. Today, the policy sciences have gone far beyond naïve aspirations for 'societally relevant knowledge'. However, the credibility of policy sciences has been increasingly questioned for its failure to produce empirical and normative truths. Scientific rationality which was once its base is being replaced by a broader theory of reason in society. Some scholars such as Ingram and Schneider acknowledge that there is a shift from the policy sciences through policy inquiry to policy design.[44]

The field of policy sciences since its emergence (roughly in the late 1940s) has been faced with a number of challenges, though expected owing to its nature and three central conceptual touchstones. The first dilemma is reflected in what Douglas Torgerson has shown as

---

[40] M. Schneider et al., 'Building Consensual Institutions: Networks and the National Estuary Programme', *American Journal of Political Science* 47 (2003): 143–44.

[41] K. Dowding, 'Model or Metaphor? A Critical Review of the Policy Network Approach', *Political Studies* 43(1) (1995): 136.

[42] Carlsson, 'Policy Networks as Collective Action', 502–27.

[43] P. Kenis and V. Schneider, eds., *Organization and Networks* (Frankfurt: Campus Verlag, 1977), 20.

[44] H. Ingram and A. Schneider, 'Constructing Citizenship: The Subtle Messages of Public Policy Design', in *Public Policies for Democracy*, eds. H. Ingram et al. (Washington: Brookings, 1993).

The dynamic nature of the (policy sciences) phenomenon is rooted in an internal tension, a *dialectic opposition between knowledge and politics*. Through the interplay of knowledge and politics, different aspects of the phenomenon become salient at different moment ... the presence of dialectical tension means that the phenomenon has the potential to develop, to change its form. However, no particular pattern of development is inevitable.[45]

As the recurring theme of the policy sciences deals with the democratic ethos and human dignity, there is a conflict in terms of two cultures that is politics and science.

Second, some scholars such as John Dryzek and Fischer suggest that the policy sciences suffer from the methodological problems. It is contended that there has been a transition from an empirical (positivist) methodology to a more context-oriented (postpositivist) methodology, and with it a return to the democratic orientation that Lasswell had earlier championed. They argue that since positivist methodologies (based on tenets of social welfare economies, e.g. CBA) were fundamentally flawed, as such, it should not be astonishing that the resulting analysis were also flawed. Referring to positivism as 'instrumental rationality' which, Dryzek claims, 'makes effective and appropriate policy analysis impossible...(and, most critically) is antidemocratic'.[46]

Third, Lasswell argued for greater citizen participation in the policy process under the phrase of 'participatory policy analysis'[47] or 'deliberative democracy'[48] to realize democratic values. This realization is critical because the human condition is often temperamentally beyond the ability of the quantitative approaches to capture. Like the other orientation reviewed earlier, this approach too his its shortcomings. However, this participatory policy analysis has also been severely criticized by some theorists as being 'too cumbersome' or demanding too much or including too many participants to move towards policy closure, especially today's megapolicies.[49] Some have characterized it as little more than a publicity exercise.

Fourth, policy theorists began to realize that the sociopolitical problems are quite complex and often required very different perspectives and newer methodologies to solve them. With their short history, policy sciences appear to hold an implicit assumption about the benefits of government intervention. The conservative political movements in the 1990s challenged this by questioning whether government intervention is required *in* social change. Increasingly, policy analyses could be found to support the wide spectrum of political ideologies. Savas, for example, talked of privatization as the strategy for better management.[50]

[45] Douglas Torgerson, 'Between Knowledge and Politics: Three Faces of Policy Analysis', *Policy Sciences* 19 (1986): 52–53.
[46] John S. Dryzek, *Discursive Democracy: Politics, Policy and Political Science* (Cambridge, UK: Cambridge University Press, 1990), 4–6.
[47] Peter deLeon, *Democracy and the Policy Sciences* (Albany, NY: SUNY Press, 1997).
[48] John Dryzek, *Deliberative Democracy and Beyond* (New York, NY: Oxford University Press, 2000).
[49] P. deLeon, *Democracy and the Policy Sciences*.
[50] E.S. Savas, *Privatization: The Key to Better Management* (Chatham, NJ: Chatham House, 1987).

Moreover, if the socio-politico context and the individuals within it were a function of social construction, as scholars such as Fischer[51] and Schneider and Ingram[52] have contended, then a deliberative democracy model becomes more useful as affected parties try to reach an agreement, and a CBA becomes less useful.

CONCLUSION

The foregoing discussion on the policy sciences points to four major themes that mark its progression. First, policy sciences as an academic field have just a half century of activity with some success. A conceptual trend emerging over the years has been acceptance of the policy approach and its three central conceptual touchstones:

(i)   The policy sciences were framed as being 'problem-oriented' addressing public policy issues and posing prescription of solutions;

(ii) The policy sciences are characterized as being 'multidisciplinary' in their academic and practical approaches; and

(iii) The policy sciences approach is deliberately 'normative' or 'value-oriented'.

Second, the pre–Second World War aspirations among a small core of social scientists for producing societal relevant knowledge provided greatest impetus to the policy sciences. But to reinvigorate the policy approach, the traditional analytic toolkit is, at worst, 'ineffective...and anti-democratic'.[53] One obvious requirement is that 'policy researchers will need to acquire a new set of analytic skills dealing with public education and negotiation and mediation, that is, helping to foster new policy design models that are less hierarchical than has been the case, rather than simply advising policy-makers'.[54] DeLeon and Vogenbeck suggest that 'the policy scientist should become more fluent and practiced in addressing the potential effects of decentralized authority', for it is observed that most governments are 'moving at the moment toward a more localized, state-centred form of government'.[55]

Third, in the 1970s and 1980s, much efforts were devoted to expand the relevance while adhering to the scientific rigours of the policy sciences. Finally, the future of the policy sciences will depend less on its adherence to scientific rationality and more on its ability to serve the knowledge needs of the administrative and political community in the form of directed policy inquiry and social network analysis. The final progression presents a vision of future where policy sciences work towards their goal of providing societally relevant knowledge to create successful public policy development.

---

[51] Frank Fischer, *Reframing Public Policy* (Oxford, UK: Oxford University Press, 2003).

[52] Anne L. Schneider and Helen Ingram, eds., *Deserving and Entitled: Social Construction and Public Policy* (Albany, NY: SUNY Press, 2005).

[53] John S. Dryzek, 'Policy Analysis and Planning: From Science to Argument', in *The Argumentative Turn in Policy Analysis and Planning*, eds. Frank Fischer and John Forester (Durham, NC: Duke University Press, 1993), 21–42.

[54] Peter deLeon and Danielle M. Vogenbeck, 'The Policy Sciences at the Crossroads', in *Handbook of Public Policy Analysis*, eds. F. Fischer, G.J. Miller and Mara Sidney (Boca Raton, FL: CRC Press, 2007), 12.

[55] Ibid., 12.

Review Questions

(i)   Trace the evolution of the term 'policy sciences'.

(ii) Argue in favour or against the following statement: 'Policy science like physics and chemistry is a science.'

(iii) What are the core assumptions behind the pursuit of policy sciences?

(iv) Discuss the relationship between policy sciences and social network analysis.

(v)   Do you think policy science has developed enough to be treated as an independent area of study and research? Support your view with relevant illustrations.

INDEX

CPSIA information can be obtained
at www.ICGtesting.com
Printed in the USA
FSHW021009110419
57141FS